The Founding of the Socialist Workers Party

The Founding of the Socialist Workers Party

Minutes and resolutions 1938–39

PATHFINDER
New York   London   Montreal   Sydney

Edited by George Breitman

Copyright © 1982 by Pathfinder Press
All rights reserved

ISBN 978-0-87348-837-2
Library of Congress Catalog Card Number 82-82052
Manufactured in the United States of America

First edition, 1982
Ninth printing, 2022

PATHFINDER
www.pathfinderpress.com
E-mail: pathfinder@pathfinderpress.com

Contents

Preface   15

PART 1: INTRODUCTIONS, NOW AND THEN

Answers to questions   25
by George Breitman
Reminiscences and impressions by a then young delegate to the first and second conventions of the SWP.

The convention of the new party   55
by the editors of the New International
A preconvention appraisal of the road to the SWP founding convention by leaders of the expelled Socialist Party left wing.

The new party is founded   67
by James P. Cannon
A public postconvention report of the founding convention by the SWP's newly elected national secretary.

A letter to the International Secretariat   79
by James P. Cannon
A confidential report of the founding convention written for leaders of the Movement for the Fourth International.

PART 2: MINUTES, FIRST NATIONAL CONVENTION OF THE SOCIALIST WORKERS PARTY (CHICAGO, DECEMBER 31, 1937–JANUARY 3, 1938)

Minutes   91

Attachments:

Delegate list 133
Used by Credentials Committee.

Report of Trade Union Commission 139
Reporter Farrell Dobbs.

Report of Unemployment Commission 143
Reporter Art Preis.

Statements 151
by Carl Pemble, St. Paul; Melos Most, Chicago; Emil Revyuk, Chicago and Paul Zimmerman, Louisville.

PART 3: CHICAGO CONVENTION RESOLUTIONS

The political situation and the tasks of the party 157
The crisis of world capitalism; the drive toward World War II; the role of U.S. imperialism at home and abroad; SWP perspectives in the coming war; political possibilities in the U.S.; the labor party question; opponent political tendencies; the pressures of petty-bourgeois ideology; proletarianizing the party.

The trade union movement and the Socialist Workers Party 181
The enormous growth of unionism; industrial unionism and the CIO; craft unionism and the AFL; new forms and channels of struggle; trade union unification; class collaboration and bureaucratism; the possibility of blocs with other tendencies; reorienting our party and the bulk of its work; a responsible approach to strikes; for a nationally connected left-wing movement based on the class struggle; a general left-wing platform.

Resolution on the Soviet Union 209
Twenty years after the Russian revolution; the cycle of bureaucratic degeneration; Leninism vs. Stalinism; a historical summary; the international character

of the revolution; the present class character and contradictions of the Soviet state; political change and economic structure; the need to defend the USSR against imperialist attack; the need for political revolution to oust Stalinism and establish proletarian democracy.

Amendment to resolution on the Soviet Union   229

An amendment by James Burnham and Joseph Carter holding that the Soviet Union cannot be considered a workers' state in any sense but advocating its defense against any and all imperialist powers as long as its nationalized economic structure remained unchanged.

Resolution on the Russian question   237

A document by Martin Glee and twenty-one other members presenting the view that no state, including the Russian, can be called a workers' state in the absence of workers' democratic control of the means of production.

Resolution on Spain   239

A crucial phase in the civil war; the Barcelona events, May 1937; a decisive test for every tendency—Stalinists, right-wing Socialists, left-wing Socialists, anarchists and anarcho-syndicalists, the POUM, the Bolshevik-Leninists, and the Friends of Durruti; the fall of the Caballero government; the rightward course of the Negrín government; growing influence of interimperialist rivalry; the progressive nature of the military struggle against Franco; for technical and military aid to the Loyalist government without the slightest political confidence or support; the difference between material support and political support.

The internal situation and the character of the party   259

The need for party democracy and party discipline; the Leninist principle of democratic centralism; rights and duties of members and of leaders; continuity of leadership and renewal of leadership; the criteria for membership; the rights of minorities and the rule of the majority.

The internal situation and the task of the party   265

A minority resolution by James Burnham, Joseph Carter, and Hal Draper. The strengths and weaknesses of the new party; proletarianization and recruitment; greater attention to concrete and specific issues; systematic departmentalization of activities; the Joerger and Glee groups; democratic centralism; potential sources of bureaucratism; mere advocacy of Soviet defeatism is not incompatible with membership.

**The present war in the Far East
and the tasks of the party**   275

Japan's war against China is an imperialist war, China's against Japan is a war for national liberation; the role of the Chinese bourgeoisie and the Kuomintang; Stalinist and Bolshevik-Leninist policies in China; U.S. imperialism seeks domination of the Pacific; the campaign for a consumers' boycott of Japanese goods; how American workers and revolutionists can aid China.

Constitution of the Socialist Workers Party   283

Thirteen articles defining and guiding rules, relations, and functioning of the new party.

Declaration of principles   291

Part I: The decline of capitalism; wars and revolutions; fascism; the position of the United States; the only road; the role of the working class; the capitalist state; the conquest of power; the workers' state; the socialist society. Part II: The revolutionary party; the Second International; the Third International; centrist parties and groupings; the new International; parties in the United States: 1) the Socialist Party, 2) the Communist Party, 3) labor and farmer-labor parties; the SWP. Part III: The aim of the SWP; the trade unions; the middle classes; Negroes and other oppressed racial groups; the unemployed; the youth; the struggle against imperialist war; colonial peoples; the defense of the Soviet Union; coalition governments; democracy and fascism; the People's Front; the united front.

PART 4: MINUTES, SWP NATIONAL
COMMITTEE PLENUM
(NEW YORK, APRIL 22-25, 1938)

Minutes 341

Documents:

On the Ludlow Amendment 367
by the SWP National Committee
Why the SWP is changing its position to favor a national referendum on war and to participate in the movement supporting this.

The decline of American capitalism and the revolutionary transitional program for the next period 369
by the SWP Political Committee
An American adaptation of the international Transitional Program approved by the April 1938 plenum.

The problem of the labor party 381
by the SWP National Committee majority
Reasons why the SWP should now advocate the formation of an independent labor party in this country.

Minority resolution on the labor party 389
by Hal Draper for the SWP National Committee minority
Reasons why the SWP should continue to oppose the formation of labor parties, as it did at its founding convention.

Theses on the Jewish question 403
adopted by the SWP Political Committee
A class-struggle approach; democracy and assimilation; a bridge from Jewish nationalism to class struggle; for unrestricted immigration; the Jewish bourgeoisie; Stalinism; other minorities and the workers; the Transitional Program; the Jewish youth; a program of action.

Open the doors to victims of Hitler's Nazi terror! 415
by the SWP National Committee
A call for action against the mass pogroms unleashed in Germany on 'Kristallnacht' (November 10, 1938).

PART 5: MINUTES, SWP NATIONAL
COMMITTEE PLENUM
(NEW YORK, NOVEMBER 19–20, 1938)

Minutes 421

Documents:

Trade union resolution 443
A trend to labor unity; we remain pro-CIO; labor party and transitional demands in the unions; the Lewis-Stalinist bloc; blocs with non-Stalinist elements; syndicalist and anti-'politics' tendencies; modest progress since our convention; national fractions being formed; trade union department needs strengthening.

Report on amendments to resolutions acted upon by party referendum 451
How to dispose of amendments that were not clearly provided for or given a clear structure.

Resolution on twice-weekly *Socialist Appeal* 455
A decision to expand the SWP newspaper's publication from once to twice per week.

Resolution on organization of party work 459
Toward systematic and planned activity organized on the Bolshevik campaign principle: popularizing the Transitional Program, exposing the role of Stalinism, increasing and strengthening the SWP's professional staff, more and better direction of work in the unions; financial stabilization of the party press.

Resolution on world conference of Fourth International 463
Endorsing the founding conference of the Fourth International and its resolutions and pledging continued support to its work.

Resolution on the youth 467
Why a separate youth organization is needed; it must be an auxiliary of the party, politically subordinated while retaining organizational autonomy within its sphere of work; in the past year some non-Bolshevik habits and methods have appeared in the YPSL: a budding youth 'vanguardism,' an unhealthy atmosphere around the labor party discussion, notions of the YPSL as a 'youth party' for younger workers alongside the SWP as a party for adult workers, cynicism and pseudo-intellectualism; YPSL morale has been affected by lack of progress in last year; on uniforms, salutes, banners, emblems, etc.; educational functions; twenty-one should be the upper age of membership.

Resolution on the SWP and the youth 477
A minority resolution by Joseph Carter presenting a more favorable balance sheet of YPSL activities in the last year; the cause of 'vanguardism' and 'youth party' conceptions; a better division of labor is needed between the SWP and the YPSL; the YPSL should work among youth fourteen to eighteen years old and the SWP should work among the more mature youth.

Resolution on defense work 481
A decision to broaden the American Fund for Political Prisoners and Refugees and turn it into a mass membership organization with local branches to handle labor defense and relief cases supported by the SWP.

Unemployed resolution 483
A decision to support progressive elements expelled or breaking away from the Workers Alliance of America and establishing independent unemployed organizations.

Yankee imperialism at Lima 487
A manifesto of the Socialist Workers Party. The Lima conference as the first act of the U.S. imperialist counteroffensive against Germany and Japan; what Wall Street means by 'defense of the Western Hemisphere'; totalitarian objectives in Latin America; what they mean by 'democracy'; reactionary dictators backed by Washington; how to fight fascism in Latin America; tasks of the Bolshevik-Leninists.

PART 6: SECOND NATIONAL CONVENTION
OF THE SOCIALIST WORKERS PARTY
(NEW YORK, JULY 1–5, 1939)

Minutes 505

Attachments:

Information about the delegates 547

A partial list of delegates' names 549

PART 7: NEW YORK CONVENTION RESOLUTIONS

Political resolution 553
The U.S. course toward war; from New Deal to War Deal; U.S. capitalists aim at world hegemony; attacks

on labor and the unemployed; the party's main
task; parts of the war machine; slogans we advance;
Latin American tasks; social convulsions ahead; if
war is delayed; the fight for jobs; boldness with the
Transitional Program, a method to link the party with
mass struggles; more attention to the CP; growth of
fascist groups; workers' defense guards more urgent;
labor party relevance; possibilities of party growth;
recruiting; the campaign principle.

Resolution on workers' defense guard 569

Changes in the fascist movements; we must start
building the guard now; comparison with picket
squads; wherever possible, through the unions;
antifascist labor squads: skeletons or embryos;
broadest possible united fronts; a political weapon too.

**The right of self-determination and the Negro
in the United States of North America** 577

Ten percent of the population; discrimination and
exploitation; a lack of historical imagination; why
the demand for a Black state is possible; the Garvey
movement; what can happen in a revolutionary crisis;
practice will solve the national minority question;
if the masses favor a separate state, the SWP will
support it fully; a Black state as a stage toward unity;
the right of self-determination and the slogan of self-
determination; Blacks have not decided yet; the duty
of Black SWP members.

The SWP and Negro work 583

Potentially the most revolutionary element; crucial
for the party's development; a national department
to initiate and coordinate; obstacles to winning the
masses; the capitalist parties; degeneration of the
CP; a desire for action not controlled by whites;
Black chauvinism and white chauvinism; nationalist
tendencies fortified; for an independent Black mass
organization.

Resolution on organization of the unemployed   589
by E.R. McKinney
SWP should modify its orientation toward a new national unemployed movement; Roosevelt's offensive against relief standards and WPA projects; Workers Alliance on the government's side; union attention to the jobless weak and sporadic.

Resolution on unemployed work   593
by Art Preis
Mass unemployment is a permanent feature of American capitalism; appropriations for war up, for jobs and relief down; jobless resistance not organized; unemployed groups atomized; unions should organize jobless; we must work in union-led formations or independent groups, or help organize local groups; it is unrealistic for us to adopt the perspective of a new national organization.

Resolution on work in trade unions   597
We must be in the mass industrial unions; concentration on a few basic industries; fight for the shorter workweek; unions must organize unemployed; for mass resistance to antilabor laws; union defense guards; Stalinism in the unions.

Glossary of people, groups, and periodicals   599

Index   625

Preface

Political resolutions are not usually the most popular or most enjoyable type of literature, and they rarely become more readable with the passage of time. So why publish political resolutions written more than forty years ago, or the minutes of conventions and committee meetings of that same pre–World War II period, when conditions were quite different from those of today? Not because we think that masses of readers are panting to get their hands on this book. Not because we think that reading Socialist Workers Party documents of 1938 and 1939 can provide a short-cut to answers for the political problems facing us in the 1980s and 1990s.

Then why publish this book? Because if properly used it can be an educational tool in the study of Marxism, Marxist political parties in general, and the Socialist Workers Party in particular. After nine years of clarification, experiment, unifications and splits, stagnation and growth, and the consolidation of cadres continuing the most advanced practice, theory, and traditions of previous revolutionary generations, the SWP was founded at a national convention in Chicago (December 31, 1937–January 3, 1938). It is possible to be interested in the SWP and its many campaigns, and even to be active in it, without knowing much about its origins and evolution. But no one can fully understand the SWP's history without studying the documents in this book.

Political movements, like other organizations and institutions in class society, are shaped by the environments in which they exist and the struggles of their time.

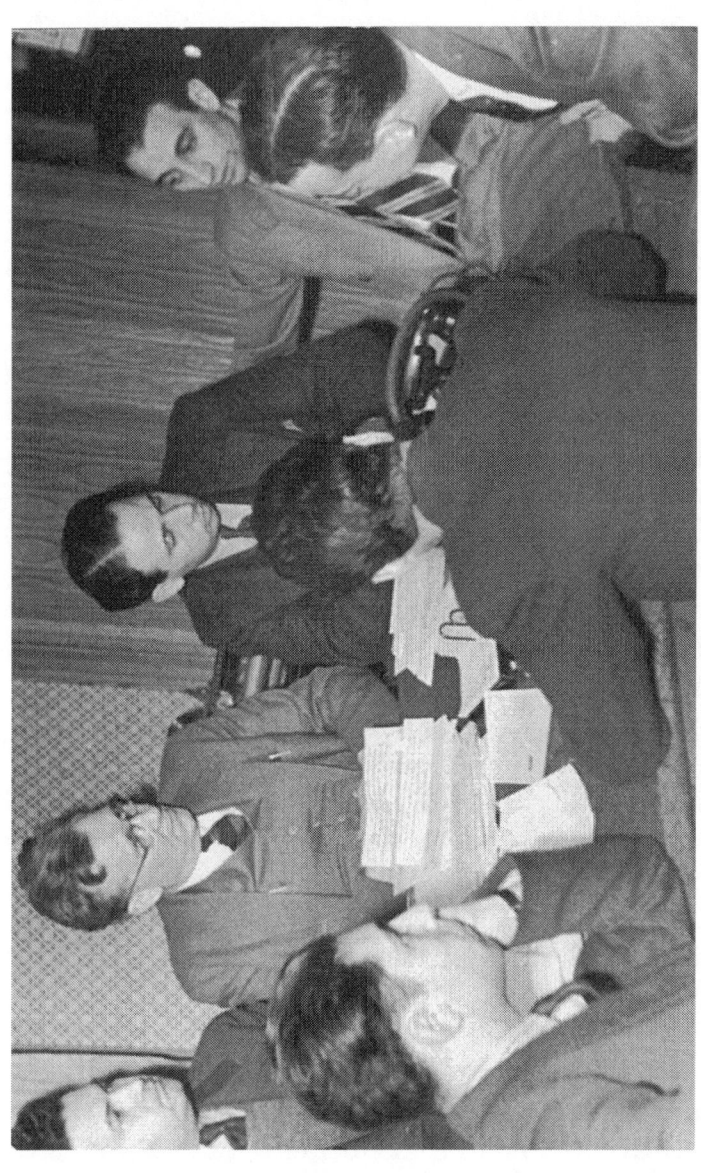

SWP Political Committee meeting, December 1938. Clockwise from top left: Felix Morrow, James P. Cannon, Max Shachtman, George Clarke, James Burnham, Nathan Gould, Martin Abern.

This also applies to Marxist political parties, which are, or should be, more conscious than others of the influences bearing down upon them. Like other living things they go through phases of development—growing up, maturing, growing old; becoming stronger, weaker, or stagnating. They do not forever remain the same, do the same things, or say the same things. This is true not only of Marxist political parties but also of their theories, their ideologies, their programs, and their methods. These *develop* too, and even when Marxists remain true to their original aims and goals, they change how they say things in the light of new conditions and/or an improved grasp of reality. It would therefore be naive to expect that the SWP documents of the 1930s said exactly the same things that SWP documents do today. They are animated by the same principles and the same historic goals, yes, but in certain respects they are different. If they weren't, it would mean that the SWP was incapable of learning from the history of the intervening years; that it was incapable of improving its theory and practice; that it was, in short, a hopeless sect which used Marxism as a dogma rather than a guide to revolutionary action. That, fortunately, is not the case, as is shown by comparing the SWP's positions before World War II with its positions of today. But readers who want such comparisons had better be familiar with the SWP's current positions and prepared to make such comparisons themselves, because that is not done in this book. It only provides the raw material for making them, or rather one part of the raw material.

Part One of this book consists of several introductory articles, three written in the 1938 period and one prepared recently. The only thing that needs to be added to them in this preface is an explanation of what the word *founding* means in the title and scope of this book. The

Chicago convention that established the SWP at the beginning of 1938 is frequently called the party's founding convention—correctly, since it brought a new entity onto the political scene. This new party had its roots in previous organizations and never would have been formed without the experience gained from them. In spite of that, it represented something distinct and different from its predecessors, and the term *founding convention* is entirely justifiable.

But the concept of founding used in the title of this book refers to more than the Chicago convention and its documents. It also includes documents of a four-day meeting of the SWP National Committee in New York in April 1938; the text of resolutions voted on by the SWP membership in a national referendum vote in the summer of 1938; documents of a two-day meeting of the SWP National Committee in New York in November 1938; and the documents of the SWP's Second National Convention, in New York, in July 1939. The reason why all these documents belong together is that the Chicago convention, although it accomplished a great deal of work, was not able or prepared to complete the programmatic foundations of the new revolutionary party. It completed the major part of the foundations but it left some parts unfinished or in a condition that required correction or change shortly after the convention.

An example of unfinished work was the Black struggle in the United States. The Chicago convention resolutions barely mentioned the issue and its Declaration of Principles contained only a routine section on the subject. It was not until the second SWP convention a year and a half later—following an important preconvention discussion that involved two leaders of the Fourth International from abroad (Leon Trotsky and C.L.R. James)—that this deficiency was corrected through the elaboration of a Marxist program for Black liberation. With this addition, the SWP was able to play an active and prominent role fighting racism in World War II. Without it, the SWP certainly would not have been completely armed programmatically for the war that began a few weeks after the second convention.

There was another reason why the Chicago convention has to be seen as a part of the founding rather than as its beginning and ending. It was held only a few months before Trotsky raised programmatic questions that compelled the SWP leadership to reconsider certain policies and premises that had been affirmed at the Chicago convention. Trotsky, then in Mexico, was preparing the major programmatic document to be presented to the founding conference of the Fourth International, which took place in France in September 1938; this document later was known by the name of the Transitional Program. Trotsky wanted the SWP to sponsor this program in the international discussion that preceded the founding conference. Before he could get their sponsorship he had to convince the SWP leaders of the correctness of this program. That did not happen automatically or instantly. Some of Trotsky's ideas and arguments seemed novel to them. Some of the party leaders were uncomfortable with the method Trotsky was using in the Transitional Program, fearing that it might be opportunist in some respects and adventurist in others.

In the end they were persuaded by Trotsky, accepted not only the Transitional Program but also the transitional method lodged in it. This led them to change their positions on two important issues of the day where Trotsky thought they were making an error. One of these concerned a movement around an amendment to the U.S. Constitution that would prohibit Congress from declaring war unless it had first been approved in a national referendum; the change consisted of a decision to become participants in this movement instead of merely standing off on the sidelines criticizing and exposing its shortcomings. The other change involved the SWP's attitude toward the formation of an independent labor party based on the unions in the United States. At the Chicago convention the SWP had reaffirmed the position its predecessors had espoused for several years—that revolutionists could not advocate the formation of a labor party even though they should work in it after it was formed. At Trotsky's initiative the SWP discussed this anew in the spring and summer of 1938 and decided that it could and should advocate the formation of a labor party.

These changes did not come easily for some of the SWP leaders and members. At a meeting of the SWP National Committee in April 1938 there was still considerable uneasiness and confusion. So the labor party question and the Transitional Program were submitted to a national SWP discussion, concluding in a membership referendum vote on these questions. A majority of the members voting favored the new labor party position and an overwhelming majority supported the Transitional Program, but these issues continued to stimulate questions and discussion up to the second convention in July 1939. The Transitional Program and the transitional method have been hallmarks of the SWP ever since that time, so closely associated with it that the concept of an SWP without them seems anomalous. Until they were adopted, the founding of the SWP had certainly not been completed.

Shortly after the second convention, World War II began and the SWP was plunged into a bitter factional crisis and conflict that threatened to destroy it as a revolutionary force. This struggle, which preoccupied the SWP from September 1939 until April 1940, when almost half the members split away, was as decisive for the future of the SWP as the founding period had been. But since the 1939–40 fight is already documented in two books—Trotsky's *In Defense of Marxism* (Pathfinder Press, 1973) and Cannon's *The Struggle for a Proletarian Party* (Pathfinder, 1972)—this book should and does end with the documents of the second convention.

Most of this book is reprinted from the SWP press in 1938 and 1939 (the weekly paper *Socialist Appeal* and the monthly magazine *New International*) or from the SWP's discussion bulletin and other internal documents. Minor changes have been made for stylistic consistency and to correct obvious typographical errors.

The footnotes are by the editor. Names of individuals, organizations, and periodicals mentioned in the texts are briefly identified in the glossary that begins on page 599. Whenever the 1938–39 documents refer to a particular page and paragraph number in the original convention or plenum resolutions, we have added, inside brackets, the place where these citations can be found in this book.

We would like to publicly thank Mike Taber, Rob Cahalane, James Kutcher, and Dorothea Breitman for their help in preparing this book for publication.

George Breitman
JANUARY 1981

PART 1

Introductions, now and then

Answers to questions[1]

by George Breitman

INTERNATIONAL SOCIALIST REVIEW: A while ago we asked if we could interview you about the founding convention of the Socialist Workers Party, whose fortieth anniversary we are commemorating in our January 1978 issue. You said we could after you refreshed your memory by looking over documents of that period. Can we proceed with the interview now?

BREITMAN: Yes, so long as it is clear that the SWP does not have an "official" position which members have to accept on this or most other historical questions, and so I speak only for myself when I express opinions on them.

---

1. An earlier version of this article, entitled "How the Socialist Workers Party Began," was published as an interview in *International Socialist Review*, a supplement of *The Militant*, January 13, 1978. That version, which dealt mainly with the first SWP convention, has been revised and expanded for this book to cover subsequent developments in 1938 and 1939, through the SWP's second convention shortly before the start of World War II in Europe.

ISR: According to the minutes, you were a regular delegate to the convention from Newark, New Jersey, and a member of the convention's Credentials Committee and Unemployed Commission. Can you remember your impressions at the time?

BREITMAN: Very vividly, some of them. But you must bear in mind that I had belonged to the movement for only a couple of years. I joined the Workers Party in Newark in 1935 when I was nineteen, my first political affiliation. So I was relatively uneducated and inexperienced, and there were many nuances I did not grasp and strengths and weaknesses I was not aware of. It was only the second convention of the revolutionary movement I had attended, and it was difficult for me to make useful comparisons with other conventions or other movements.

But that didn't prevent me from feeling that the convention represented a milestone in the history of the American revolutionary movement. I am sure most of the delegates shared my conviction that we had participated in something truly significant: the launching—at last!—of the party that would lead the American workers in their coming socialist revolution.

The whole process has proved to be slower and more complicated than it seemed to me in Chicago forty years ago. Hindsight, further experience, study, and a better grasp of theory enable me to see the process more fully and clearly now. But none of these have altered that initial belief. The SWP founding convention did represent something unique in American Marxist history.

I lacked the knowledge to serve as the basis for such an assessment in 1938, but since then I have studied the lives and careers of Debs, DeLeon, Haywood, and other American radical leaders before the Russian revolution of 1917, and of the founders and leaders of the early Communist

Party, and I have no hesitation in saying that the revolutionary cadre assembled at the SWP founding convention was superior in understanding, talent, dedication, and all-round ability to anything the working-class movement in this country had ever known.

Mind, I am making a comparative judgment; superior, not perfect or without defects.

ISR: Doesn't the story of the SWP convention really begin before 1938—as far back as 1928, when James P. Cannon, Max Shachtman, and Martin Abern were expelled from the Communist Party because they said they agreed with Trotsky's criticisms of the Soviet bureaucrats who were running the Communist International? And weren't these three, who then founded the first Trotskyist organization in this country, also the central cadre of the new SWP in 1938?

BREITMAN: The SWP certainly was rooted in the events you refer to and in others; the delegates did not go to Chicago by accident. The connection between the CP expulsions in 1928 and the SWP convention in 1938 was vital.

But you are barely touching on the links of causality and continuity out of which the SWP evolved.

Before the CP could expel Cannon for holding a minority viewpoint, the Communist International initiated by Lenin and Trotsky in 1919 had to be bureaucratized and the minority represented by Trotsky and the Left Opposition had to come into existence. Before the CP could expel Cannon, one of its founders, it first had to be founded in 1919 as a revolutionary party. But before the CP could be founded, there had to be the prewar radicalization that is sometimes called "Debsian," the treachery of the Second International in World War I, the development of a revolutionary wing in the American Socialist Party and the IWW, the Russian revolution of 1917, and so on.

I am not disputing your point at all, only saying that it can be extended profitably. One of the greatest strengths of the SWP cadre lay in its continuity with the struggles from the start of the century—the IWW and revolutionary syndicalism,[2] Debs's fighting election campaigns, opposition to U.S. entry into World War I, efforts to absorb the meaning of the Russian revolution and Leninism, the development of a left wing in the SP, the birth of the new CP and its early attempts to adapt to American realities.[3]

Cannon and his comrades, especially the older ones like Carl Skoglund, V.R. Dunne, and Arne Swabeck, had not merely read or heard about these events; they grew up in them and were shaped by them. Their experience provided the basic political capital of their movement and explains its ability to avoid many of the costly mistakes beginners are prone to make.

I think you are right to mention that Cannon, Shachtman, and Abern were the central figures in the movement in both 1928 and 1938, but I think it would be wrong to imply that little or nothing had changed, except that they were nine or ten years older. In my opinion, a great deal changed in that time, quantitatively and qualitatively. In 1928 the Stalinists used to deride them as "three generals without an army." In 1929 they did not have more than 100 followers, but in 1938 they claimed fifteen times that number, and the leadership was broader and included a

---

2. Revolutionary syndicalism advocated the conversion of the unions into revolutionary bodies that would lead the struggle for the abolition of capitalism; in distinction from Marxism, there was no room in this theory for a revolutionary workers' party.

3. Cannon's appraisals of these events are in his books, *The First Ten Years of American Communism* (Pathfinder, 1973) and *The History of American Trotskyism* (Pathfinder, 1972).

new generation of rebels against capitalism.

Cannon, Shachtman, and Abern themselves were different in 1938—they had grown and matured. It is a mistake to think of them as "Trotskyists" in 1928 merely because they decided that year that Trotsky was right and Stalin and Bukharin were wrong. Calling yourself something doesn't automatically make you that, even if you think you are.

The leaders expelled in 1928 had been miseducated by Stalinist bureaucratism parading as democratic centralism[4] and had acquired some bad habits in the factional jungle that the American CP had become by the mid-twenties. It took work and time to shed all this. Fortunately, they had a good teacher, Trotsky; they learned a lot about principled politics; and they became effective Marxist politicians. It was not an easy thing to do, and they deserve a lot of credit for doing it under circumstances that were often discouraging.

ISR: What was the political climate in this country at the time of the founding convention?

BREITMAN: Before answering that, we'd better complete the historical background, which I'll condense as much as possible.

The founding of the SWP marked the third phase of our movement's development. The first phase lasted from 1928 to 1933, and during those five years the overriding aim of the Left Oppositionists in this country (who named themselves the Communist League of America in 1929)

---

4. Democratic centralism is the central organizational principle of Marxism, initiated and developed by Lenin's Bolshevik Party. See the SWP resolution on the character of the revolutionary party, page 259, and its Declaration of Principles, page 291. Stalin retained the name but drained it of all democratic content.

was to reform the CP and the Communist International, to regenerate them along Leninist lines, and thus to make them capable of leading successful revolutions here and abroad. All the other sections of the International Left Opposition, which was founded in 1930 after Trotsky's deportation from the Soviet Union, followed this same "reform" policy.

The CLA educated a cadre of serious revolutionaries, but it did not win many people from the CP and it did not stem the degeneration of the CP and the Comintern. After five years of propaganda work, the CLA had only around 200 members and little influence.

This was during the "third period" of Stalinism, when the CPs said the revolution was just around the corner and then embarked on the most sectarian and ultraleft adventures in the history of the working-class movement, effectively isolating themselves.[5]

It was easy for the Left Oppositionists to show that third-period Stalinism was a perversion of Leninist strategy and tactics, but doing so did not change the relationship of forces. Most radicals, even when they rejected the third-period line, continued to believe that it was "to the left" of, and therefore "more revolutionary" than the Left Opposition's line.

ISR: Cannon's book, *The History of American Trotskyism,* is entirely devoted to the pre-SWP decade, isn't it?

BREITMAN: Yes, it is the fullest written account of the events leading up to the 1938 convention, a series of

---

5. The "third period" was supposedly the last phase of capitalist rule, to be quickly replaced by successful proletarian revolutions. While it was in effect, 1928–34, the Comintern's tactics were marked by opposition to united fronts with other workers' organizations, the building of small "red" unions, and other stupidities of the kind that helped Hitler come to power so easily in Germany.

popular talks given in 1942, and is easy to read and follow.

The first phase ended in 1933 when Stalin's pseudoleftism prevented a united front of the German workers against the Nazis and enabled Hitler to take power without a real battle and to crush all the workers' organizations and all democratic rights. When the Comintern defended the policy that had produced this defeat, the Left Oppositionists decided that the Stalinist parties no longer could be reformed and that it was necessary to build a new International and revolutionary parties in all countries.

To accomplish this in the United States, the CLA had to adopt a new orientation. It stopped concentrating almost exclusively on the CP and began to approach other tendencies moving toward the left under the impact of the radicalization stimulated by the depression and of the lessons being drawn all over the world from Hitler's victory.[6] The most promising of these tendencies was the American Workers Party, a left-centrist group led by A.J. Muste.[7]

Simultaneously, the CLA began its turn "from the propaganda circle into the mass work" in the union and unemployed movements, as Cannon phrased it in a letter a few weeks after the SWP convention.[8] Revolutionary propaganda work was now combined with other kinds

---

6. The Great Depression, extending from the stock market crash in 1929 until after the start of World War II in Europe in 1939, resulted in many important economic, political, and social changes in American society and its institutions, including radicalization of the working class. The Nazi triumph in 1933 stimulated antifascist moods and movements in many countries, including the U.S.

7. Centrists, in Marxist terminology, are forces vacillating between the poles of revolution and reformism. Left centrists are those moving toward the revolutionary pole, etc. For an SWP summary, see the Declaration of Principles, page 291.

8. For Cannon's letter in February 1938, see p. 79

of work where CLA members were working with larger groups of people.

The first big break in the CLA's mass work came in 1934 in Minneapolis, where its members led the Teamsters' strikes that set a model for militant unionists throughout the country.[9] Even before these strikes the CLA took the initiative in approaching the AWP for a fusion of the two organizations. The fusion was consummated at the end of 1934 in the form of the new Workers Party of the United States.

The Fourth Internationalists in Europe followed a similar course. In France their approach to leftward-moving forces led them to join the Socialist Party, where they operated as a left wing working for the Fourth International. This was called the "French turn," later followed in other countries including the United States.[10] It led to splits from the movement by sectarian and dogmatic elements who condemned the new tactic as a betrayal of Marxism.

A left wing had begun to develop in the Socialist Party and Young People's Socialist League in this country. At the end of 1935 the most right-wing elements split from the American SP, and Cannon and Shachtman proposed that the members dissolve the Workers Party and join the SP.

After an intense discussion, this proposal was approved by a national convention at the end of February 1936. In the spring of 1936 we joined the SP, where we constituted a left wing called the Appeal caucus, after our

---

9. A report and analysis of the Minneapolis strikes and their aftermath will be found in Farrell Dobbs's books, *Teamster Rebellion* (1972), *Teamster Power* (1973), *Teamster Politics* (1975), and *Teamster Bureaucracy* (1977), published by Monad Press and distributed by Pathfinder Press.

10. For the results of the "French turn" in France, see *The Crisis of the French Section, 1935–36* by Trotsky (Pathfinder, 1977).

journal, the *Socialist Appeal.*

ISR: Now you're getting to the immediate background of the founding convention.

BREITMAN: That's right. We remained in the SP until the summer of 1937, when our differences with the coalition of centrists and right-wingers in the leadership of the party came to a head. At bottom were two irreconcilable conceptions of a party, but the disputes centered on the issue of People's Frontism in various forms and places.

People's Frontism, or class collaboration between working-class and capitalist parties, was the predominant tendency of the radical and labor movements of that period.[11] Under our pressure the SP had adopted an abstract criticism of People's Frontism at a national convention in March 1937, but then its leaders embraced the policies of the Spanish People's Front government that was repressing revolutionaries and leading the struggle against Franco to defeat. They ordered us to cease all political criticism of that government, even inside the SP. Here at home they decided to withdraw Norman Thomas, the SP's candidate for mayor of New York in 1937, in favor of the People's Front candidate LaGuardia (running on the Republican Party and American Labor Party tickets).

Unable to contain our growing influence by other means,

---

11. People's Front–type coalition governments including Socialist parties had existed for decades, but the Communist parties did not advocate or join such governments until 1935. From then until the Stalin-Hitler pact in 1939, promoting People's Frontism was the main function of the CP in all capitalist and colonial countries. See the Declaration of Principles, pages 315 and 334. People's Front governments came to power in three countries in the mid-1930s: Spain and France in 1936, Chile in 1938. No People's Front was established in the U.S. at that time. Deciding that the Democratic Party was a People's Front all by itself, the Communist Party supported it and sent many CP members into it.

the SP leaders tried to gag us and expelled us wholesale when we refused to accept the gag.

The same thing had happened in France in 1935, but our gains here were bigger, partly because our leaders learned from the mistakes of our French comrades, partly because they were able to benefit more from Trotsky's advice than the French leaders had, and partly because they were more competent politicians than their French counterparts.

The SP leaders saved the party from "Trotskyism," but in the process they virtually destroyed it by expelling the best and most active members. We emerged with more than twice the numbers we had on joining and won a decisive majority of the YPSL too. Morale was high, because our self-confidence had also grown as we met the various challenges posed to us by the SP environment and acquired new know-how from its easier access to the mass movements of the time.

ISR: What was the internal life of the movement like while you were in the SP? How were differences resolved?

BREITMAN: It was not a normal situation in that respect. Trying to establish ourselves as good party builders, we were discreet at the beginning in order to overcome our reputation as perpetual hairsplitters and in order not to give unnecessary weapons to opponents who were eager to find reasons for expelling us.

Once the Appeal caucus was firmly established and recognized, our policies were arrived at through the mechanism of that caucus. But even then the accent was always on the centralist side of democratic centralism. People who had differences or grievances usually and voluntarily postponed them until a time when raising them would not benefit our common opponents.

It was an abnormal situation in many ways. We had

not had a real national convention for almost two years, and all of us, members and leaders alike, did not have a very good idea of what our movement was like, how it had changed, what its caliber was, and so on, until we met at the founding convention. That was one of the reasons for the unusual excitement we felt there—we were about to get answers to questions that had accumulated for two years.

ISR: Why was there such a long interval between the expulsions and the convention?

BREITMAN: Expulsions began in July 1937 with a few people in New York. Most former Workers Party members knew that this meant the whole Appeal caucus would be expelled, but we had to take into account those who still had illusions about the SP leadership. So we appealed the expulsions, demanded a referendum, the calling of a special SP convention, and so on. On Labor Day the SP leaders expelled everyone who wouldn't repudiate the Appeal caucus.

Some of our people thought we should hold our convention as soon as possible, afraid that delays would seem like indecision and produce demoralization. At first, Thanksgiving weekend was chosen as the date for a convention of the suspended or expelled branches and members. But our leaders soon decided to postpone it until New Year's in order to facilitate the broadest possible preconvention discussion.

This was a wise decision and led to a truly democratic discussion and convention. Differences long bottled up were ventilated. New ideas were openly presented and considered on their merits. The emphasis now was on the democratic side of democratic centralism. It made a very attractive contrast to the bureaucratic suppression decreed by the SP leadership.

ISR: What were the main differences at the convention?

BREITMAN: If you don't mind, I'd first like to make a few comments on your previous question about the political atmosphere of the country.

A powerful wave of radicalization had swept the country, generating bitter strike struggles and the formation of the CIO and the first strong unions in many basic industries. The Roosevelt administration offered limited concessions and reforms which the labor leaders, CIO as well as AFL, pointed to as justification for labor support to the Democrats.

Economic conditions improved slowly and gradually after Roosevelt came to office, but then, suddenly, in 1937 came a new economic downturn, which shot the unemployment rate up from about 15 percent to about 20 percent in less than a year. It seemed to us that this would surely sharpen the class struggle and boost the radicalization, which had temporarily been marking time, onto a higher and more political plane.

The ruling class's answer to the 1937 recession was a decision to rearm and prepare for the coming of World War II. This was the meaning of Roosevelt's renunciation of "isolationism" in his famous quarantine-the-aggressor speech in Chicago in October 1937.[12]

From then on, one's attitude toward the coming war became the first touchstone for every working-class tendency. Our convention was, in a real sense, our answer and our alternative to the new policy expressed in

---

12. "Isolationism" was a label applied to different tendencies. These included many Americans, disillusioned by the results of World War I, who simply did not want the U.S. to go to war again, and a smaller group that wanted the U.S. to "mind its own business" in the Western Hemisphere and build up such a fortress there that it would be invincible even if attacked.

Roosevelt's speech.

The CP had grown into a sizable force, becoming the most abject apologist and supporter of Roosevelt and People's Front class collaboration. In 1938 its membership was between 50,000, the lowest figure I've seen, and 75,000, the figure of a congressional committee. It had strong positions in several CIO unions, controlled the unemployed and student movements, and had a near-monopoly of the American left, which it used to expel and isolate left-wing opponents wherever it could.

By comparison, the delegates to our convention reported a membership of 1,500 plus. This turned out to be an exaggeration because it included people who had sided with us against the SP leadership but who did not actually join the SWP once it was set up and they saw what it demanded of them. A figure of around 1,000 would be more accurate. That means the ratio of the CP's membership to ours was at least fifty to one and maybe seventy-five to one. Since the ratio today is roughly an equal one, you may have some trouble appreciating what a disadvantage we had. Perhaps you can do it by imagining what American radical politics would be like today if the CP were fifty times its present strength.

Besides the CP and the SWP, there were only two other radical groups at the time worth mentioning. One was the Socialist Party. Shachtman dubbed the SP "a head without a body" in 1938, but it wasn't much of a head either.

The other was the Lovestoneites, the American contingent of the Right Oppositionists who had been purged from the Comintern for allegedly sympathizing with Bukharin after Stalin broke with him. In 1938 they called themselves the Independent Labor League. At this time they were engaged in reexamining and then repudiating the Leninism they had avowed since their expulsion from the CP in 1929. Three years later they voted to dissolve and thereafter devoted themselves individually to the defense of capitalism and its labor agencies.

The Lovestoneites were an early example of the ideological retrogression then besetting the radical movement. Two of the big Moscow "confession" trials had occurred in 1936 and 1937 while we were in the SP, where we did important work helping Trotsky prove that they were frame-ups engineered by Stalin; the third took place two months after our convention.[13] It is hard to exaggerate the devastating effect these trials had on most radicals of the time.

Many who knew or sensed that the trials were frame-ups were terribly demoralized by them and by the mistaken belief, which now began to gain currency among radicals, that Stalinism with its bloody purges and repression—in the Spanish civil war[14] as well as in the Soviet Union—was only the logical continuation rather than the opposite of

---

13. Stalin staged the Moscow trials as part of his drive to destroy the generation that had led the Russian revolution in Lenin's time and to discredit the forces that were trying to build a new, Leninist, International. Most of the defendants in these proceedings were compelled to "confess" that they had plotted with the imperialists to overthrow the Soviet Union, assassinate Stalin, etc. Trotsky's analysis of the trials is in *The Case of Leon Trotsky* (Merit Publishers, 1968); *Writings of Leon Trotsky (1936-37)* (Pathfinder, 1978); and *Writings of Leon Trotsky (1937-38)* (Pathfinder, 1976). For the 1937 report of the Commission of Inquiry into the Charges Made Against Leon Trotsky in the Moscow Trials (the Dewey Commission), see *Not Guilty* (Monad, 1972).

14. The Spanish civil war began in July 1936 when the fascists set out to overthrow the People's Front government that had been legally elected in February. In the course of the war the Spanish Stalinists, acting under the orders of Stalin's secret police in the Kremlin, arrested and murdered many of their political opponents on the Spanish left, including anarchists, Socialists, and Fourth Internationalists. The war ended in March 1939 with the victory of the Spanish fascists.

Leninism. A.J. Muste, for example, quit our movement a week after the first trial in Moscow. So did Peter Schmidt, chairman of our Dutch sister organization.

So we were in the midst of a deep radicalization, which had been stymied temporarily but was far from having exhausted its potential. Such radicalizations are, of course, the best soil for the growth of a revolutionary party. On the other hand, Leninism was under severe attack from all sides—from the social-patriotic Stalinist agents of Roosevelt, who were trying to drive us out of the labor movement, and from other renegades and backsliders, who not only equated Leninism and Stalinism, but sought to cover the tracks of their capitulation by equating Stalinism and Trotskyism.

So it was a very contradictory situation. Of course, you can also say that about the situation we face today and about most of the situations between then and now.

ISR: The convention agenda, according to the minutes, was quite long for a four-day convention. Were all the points really taken up and discussed adequately?

BREITMAN: Almost all were taken up, and most were discussed to the satisfaction of most of the delegates, I think. You must remember that there had been a very thorough preconvention discussion, and often there was not much new to be said. Of course that doesn't stop some people.

On the last day we had an international report given by Maurice Spector and adopted a resolution to affiliate the new party to the Movement for the Fourth International (the International itself was not founded until later in 1938).[15] I remember that clearly, but I can't remember a

---

15. All the resolutions adopted by the first SWP convention are reprinted in this book, with one exception: no copy of the international resolution could be located.

single other thing about the report or the discussion. That was because the real decision on this point had been made many months before in the minds of the membership.

ISR: Cannon says in a postconvention article[16] that a trade union resolution and plans to make the party membership more proletarian were a major topic of discussion. What kind of union activity was the party engaged in?

BREITMAN: I can't add anything to what Cannon said on the convention discussion, except that I can personally confirm that many of the branches had been doing good work despite the lack of attention from the leadership center in New York.

Our chief union stronghold was Minneapolis, where our comrades in the Teamsters union led by Dunne, Skoglund, and Farrell Dobbs, were showing the whole country what a union led by revolutionaries could do. It was our aspiration in Newark, and I am sure elsewhere, to meet the high standards they were setting. The story of their activity can now be read in Dobbs's books about the Teamsters.

Another gain of that time was the organization of our fraction in the maritime industry, starting on the West Coast. Although he was not at the founding convention, Tom Kerry was elected to the National Committee at this convention, partly in recognition of his work in this fraction, which also served as a model for the party.

Most of our other activity was centered in the new CIO unions that were being born at the time—steel, auto, electrical, and so on. We helped to sign up workers to join the unions, both in the plants and in their homes; we participated in strikes to win recognition and bargaining rights; we joined forces with others to gain, extend, or preserve

---

16. For Cannon's article, "The New Party Is Founded," reprinted from the *New International*, February 1938, see page 67.

democracy inside the unions.

The main difference was that the unions then were less bureaucratized and the workers had a greater interest in their unions than they do today. That made it easier for militants to get a hearing from the members in those days.

ISR: The top leaders agreed on most of the issues debated at the convention, but weren't there some where they were divided? For example, in the discussion on the class nature of the Soviet state?

BREITMAN: Yes. The majority's resolution, supported by Cannon, Shachtman, and Abern, reaffirmed our previous analysis of the Soviet Union as a degenerated workers' state, which we defend against imperialist attack and seek to regenerate through a political revolution against the Soviet bureaucracy.[17]

An amendment was introduced by James Burnham and

---

17. The creation of a workers' state is a principal objective of the socialist revolution, according to revolutionary Marxists. Representing the rule of the working class to the same degree that a capitalist state represents the rule of the capitalist class, the workers' state makes it possible to reorganize society on socialist foundations and to prepare the conditions under which the state can wither away. From their inception, all sections of the Left Opposition—the Russian in 1923, the American in 1928—regarded the Soviet Union as a workers' state which had to be defended against imperialism despite its bureaucratic deformations. At first it was thought possible to regenerate the Soviet state through reform, but beginning in 1933 this approach was replaced by advocacy of a political revolution against the Stalinist bureaucracy. Trotsky coined the term "political revolution" to designate a working-class uprising that would oust the Stalinist bureaucracy from political power and restore proletarian democracy on the basis of the same social system that had been created by the revolution of 1917 (nationalized and collectivized property, state monopoly of foreign trade, etc.) Those who favored defense of the Soviet Union against imperialism even though the Stalinists remained in power were called "Soviet defensists" and those who opposed such defense were called "Soviet defeatists."

Joseph Carter denying that the Soviet Union could any longer be considered a workers' state but pledging to defend it against imperialist attack as long as its economy remained nationalized. Despite some heat, the differences were seen as largely terminological rather than politically substantive, pending further developments. Shachtman spoke for the majority, supported by Cannon and Abern, and Burnham for the minority.

Two other minority positions were given time during this discussion at the convention. One, presented by Martin Glee, represented a small group in New York that was against defense of the Soviet Union under any circumstances, and its members quit the SWP before its second convention. It got even fewer votes than the Burnham-Carter amendment.

A couple of years later, in World War II, the Soviet issue led to a serious split in the SWP. This caused some members to conclude that we had done something wrong at the founding convention, that we neglected our duty to "smoke out" the defeatists there or to take a strong enough position against them politically.

On the contrary, I think the leadership's attitude on this question was exemplary. They took a strong and clear stand in favor of Soviet defensism, but they did not try to put words into the mouths of the Burnham group or to denounce them for implications that the minority denied holding. As long as the Burnham group said they were defensists too, they were taken at their word, pending further developments. Any other course would have meant forcing a struggle prematurely, before the issues were clear, a sure way to miseducate and disorient a party.

A similar approach prevailed on another important point that Cannon did not directly refer to in his letter or article. This was called the "internal situation" point, where Cannon was slated to speak for the majority of the leadership and Burnham for a minority including himself, Carter, and Hal Draper.

This concerned the party's organizational principles. Cannon's resolution defended the Leninist approach without reservation. The minority resolution was less clear and more diffuse, putting a greater emphasis on dangers of bureaucratism and arguing explicitly that no reprisals against members who held a defeatist position on the Soviet Union should be taken on the basis of their opinions or arguments in the discussion but only on the basis of violation of discipline.

Again it was possible for the more experienced members to foresee all kinds of grave deviations, but at most they were potential rather than present dangers. And when in the course of the convention the minority decided to withdraw its resolution in return for some minor concessions, the majority agreed to the concessions and to postponement of debate over the differences.

One of the concessions reworded the majority resolution's assertion that the party had the right to discipline "dilettantes, do-nothings, phrasemongers, triflers, and windbags" (Cannon's language), replacing these terms with "irresponsible elements." A more serious change stipulated that no positions taken in the preconvention discussion that were not specifically prohibited by the convention could be prohibited after the convention without specific decisions through a party referendum at another convention. The Burnhamites here were trying to protect Glee and the other defeatists.

Cannon thought that such people did not belong in the SWP, but his resolution had not called for ousting them on the basis of their ideas, and he did not find the concession difficult to make. In his postconvention letter to the International Secretariat he still maintained his belief that "advocacy of defeatism with respect to the Soviet Union is incompatible with adherence to our movement for the Fourth International."

But he did not propose any disciplinary measures on this point in 1938. During the 1939–40 fight he agreed with Trotsky that defeatists could remain SWP members if they abided by its discipline. And in 1947 he took the initiative in recruiting into the SWP a group led by C.L.R. James that held a defeatist ("state capitalist") position.[18]

I think this episode reflected a maturity, sense of realism, and patience on the part of the central SWP leadership that would not have been possible when they first started the Left Opposition and still had too great a tendency to shoot from the hip.

ISR: Cannon didn't mention it, and neither have you, but wasn't there also sharp struggle over the Spanish civil war at the convention?

BREITMAN: You're right, there was. It was one of the disputes that got deferred while we were in the SP. I've said that we were lucky to lose some of our most hidebound sectarians before we entered the SP. I should have added that we were not so lucky in picking up more of the same kind while we were in the SP.

---

18. According to the theory of "state capitalism," ownership and control of the economy are transferred out of the hands of private capitalists or corporations and into the hands of the state, which runs the economy in the interests of the capitalist class as a whole. The idea that the Soviet Union is a variety of state capitalism rather than a postcapitalist state was first advanced by Social Democrats shortly after the revolution of 1917 ended the rule of capitalism in Russia. Advocates of this theory hold that the Soviet Union is ruled by a new capitalist class; most of them regard the Soviet state as retrogressive in comparison with "democratic" capitalist states; and virtually all of them are "Soviet defeatists."

Their happiest moments came from denouncing us as betrayers of the Spanish revolution, because, among other things, we advocated military (but not political) support to the Loyalist government in the war against Franco. Essentially, they were abstentionists in that war and in colonial China's war against Japanese imperialism,[19] crying a plague on both their houses and trying to dress up their miserable defaults in the class struggle with all kinds of fancy words like "revolutionary defeatism."[20]

Albert Goldman spoke for the leadership's resolution on Spain, and Glee for one of the minorities. The vote was fifty-six for the resolution, with four abstentions.[21] I

---

19. Japanese imperialism invaded China in 1931, and after seizing Manchuria, expanded its invasion in 1937. China was then a semicolonial country under the military dictator Chiang Kai-shek. The Fourth Internationalists defended China unconditionally in this war despite their irreconcilable political opposition to Chiang; for the resolution authorized by the first SWP convention, "The Present War in the Far East and the Tasks of the Party," see page 275 of this book.

20. Revolutionary defeatism was the name applied to the antiwar position taken by Lenin during World War I and continued by Leninists since then in all analogous situations. The policy advocated by Lenin in Russia from 1914 until the revolution in October 1917 was based on the fact that the Russian government and its German opponent were both conducting an imperialist war. For this reason the Bolshevik Party called on the Russian workers to not support the government and to continue the struggle for a socialist revolution regardless of the effects this struggle might have on the military front. Since China was not conducting an imperialist war against Japan in 1937, those who put the label of "revolutionary defeatism" on their refusal to defend China were making a caricature of Lenin's policy.

21. The leadership's resolution on Spain was the only one voted on by the convention because it was the only one presented there for a vote. Other resolutions and articles on Spain were put forward in the preconvention discussion (a majority of those in the internal bulletin were hostile to the leadership's resolution), but no delegates were

think every one of these ultraleft abstentionists quit the SWP before the next convention, in 1939. The best thing about them was watching them go. But even this experience was not altogether wasted because it further inoculated the party against dogmatism and schematism.

Some minor points got disproportionate time and attention. One was mentioned in Cannon's letter, the disciplinary action that had been taken by the Chicago leadership against two members: one an agent of a sect that had split away in 1935, the Oehler group; the other a wild man who had joined us by mistake. Under a report by the Committee on Grievances and Conflicts, the convention censured the Chicago Executive Committee for not following the procedures formally required for bringing charges against members. In the midst of the Moscow trials and on the heels of our own unceremonious ejection from the SP, we were supersensitive to the rights of anybody accused of anything.

Besides the points cited by Cannon, there was also a political resolution, reported on by Shachtman; an Unemployed Commission report by Art Preis; disputes over seating of certain delegations; a report on party organization and the party by Abern; a report on the party press by Abern; the reports of the Resolutions Committee, some of whose proposals were adopted like the Declaration of Principles, and some of which were referred to the new National Committee; and a youth report that got squeezed

---

elected to the convention on the basis of the minority resolutions on Spain. Glee did not offer his own minority resolution on Spain and he did not support any of the ultraleft minority resolutions in the bulletin, but he was given time to present the position that he had expressed in an internal bulletin article defending the Spanish POUM (Workers Party of Marxist Unification) against allegedly slanderous criticisms by the Appeal group's leadership.

out for lack of time. And, oh yes, a welcoming speech by Goldman and a closing speech by Farrell Dobbs, who also headed the Trade Union Commission and served as reporter for an unstructured kind of nominating commission.

ISR: What kinds of things did the report on unemployed work take up?

BREITMAN: It noted that many of the "new unemployed" resulting from the 1937 recession were CIO members who were putting pressure on their unions to fight for the jobless, and it urged efforts to get the unions involved in this fight along the lines of the Teamster-sponsored Federal Workers Section in Minneapolis.

It called attention to the good work that some of the branches were doing in the Workers Alliance of America, the only national unemployed group, which had suffered a serious decline after being taken over by the Stalinists in 1936; urged that all unemployed members be assigned to the Workers Alliance; and criticized the national leadership for neglecting this area.

It also recommended against attempts to create "our own" national unemployed movement, while sanctioning independent groups locally where the unions could not be involved and no Workers Alliance existed.

ISR: Under what point was the party's name selected?

BREITMAN: Under the point on the party constitution, and only after a debate, as usual. The Convention Arrangements Committee favored the name International Socialist Party and all the draft resolutions we got when we arrived referred in their texts to the ISP; but it was explained that we would settle the question on the last day when we took up the constitution and that the name chosen then would be inserted in all the convention resolutions.

Five names were proposed, and there was a speaker for each: Shachtman for International Socialist Party; Glen

Trimble of California for Socialist Workers Party; Bill Sherman, the convention secretary, for Workers Party; Glee for Independent Socialist Party; and Abern for International Workers Party. A ballot reduced the choices to two, and the second gave a decisive majority to SWP.

Cannon supported SWP as the name, like most of us, as a way of symbolizing the fusion of the forces that had come together from the Socialist and Workers parties. Abern, who had opposed entering the SP, asked to be recorded against SWP as the name.

ISR: Would you say that that fusion was the major accomplishment of the convention?

BREITMAN: I would say that it completed a fusion already achieved before the convention on the basis of a program derived from the theoretical and political conquests of the revolutionary movements here and abroad since the start of the century. It fused the revolutionary survivors of the Debsian radicalization and the founding of the CP with the best young workers and students produced by the radicalization of the thirties.

I find it hard to single out "the" major accomplishment. None was more important, in my opinion, than the way the convention armed us politically to meet the test of war, to which we were soon submitted. It was a harsh test. The first blast cost us almost half our members in the 1940 split led by Shachtman, Abern, and Burnham.[22]

---

22. The Workers Party was organized by most of those who split from the SWP in April 1940 because of differences that began over defense of the Soviet Union in World War II but spread to include a long list of political, theoretical, and organizational issues. In 1958, the survivors of this group, who were called the Shachtmanites, dissolved it and joined the Socialist Party, where most of them, as part of a right wing, supported the U.S. government's war in Vietnam. Trotsky's articles about "the petty-bourgeois opposition" in the SWP, as he called

Then came government persecution that imprisoned most of our top leaders, attempts to suppress *The Militant,* and other moves to silence and isolate us. But we survived and even grew during the war.

We have every reason to be proud of the party's long antiwar and anti-imperialist tradition. There is a striking consistency in the positions we took on all the major wars of U.S. imperialism in the past forty years—World War II, the Korean War, and the Vietnam War. We not only opposed them but we fought against them to the best of our revolutionary ability.

Can any other tendency in this country make a similar claim? It can't be done by any of the varieties and offshoots of Stalinism, including the Maoists, because they or their political ancestors supported the government in World War II, broke wartime strikes, and called for the imprisonment of Blacks who dared to fight for their democratic rights during the war. And they *still* think it was correct to support that imperialist war.

ISR: The convention evidently put a lot of emphasis on the need to improve the party's composition with the stress on class composition, recruiting workers, getting the members into industry and the unions, and so on. Was there also attention given to increasing the number of women, Blacks, and other minorities in the party and its leadership?

BREITMAN: No, not much and not enough. It was not until the second convention, in 1939, where we adopted our first resolution on self-determination, that we began to understand the centrality of the Black struggle. This led

---

the Shachtman group, are collected in his *In Defense of Marxism* (Pathfinder, 1973). Cannon's writings on the same group are in his book *The Struggle for a Proletarian Party* (Pathfinder, 1972).

us to greatly expand our activity in the Black community during World War II, where we did some valuable work. But even then our improved understanding didn't sink in all the way until the rise of Black nationalism in the early 1960s. And it wasn't until later in the 1960s with the second wave of feminism that we perceived the combined character of the struggles for women's liberation and workers' power.

In most areas the SWP in 1938 was far ahead of both American society and the American radical movement, but in others it was not. The fact that we have made considerable progress in some of these areas since 1938 is not a cause for complacency but it is evidence that the party we launched then must have had foundations solid enough to enable us to correct shortcomings. No party is perfect, all parties make errors; the question is whether they can recognize their errors and correct them.

The SWP's ability to do this was put to a test on several occasions in the following year and a half up to its second convention in July 1939. In preparation for the founding conference of the Fourth International, which was held in France in September 1938, Trotsky, then living in Mexico, had been working out and applying to the conditions and tasks of the 1930s a programmatic synthesis of ideas, practices, and traditions developed by the revolutionary movement internationally since the days of Marx and Engels. This came to be known in our movement as the Transitional Program, after being adopted at the founding conference of the Fourth International.[23]

---

23. The Transitional Program was designed to help the sections of the Fourth International complete their turn from propaganda circles to parties of action. The first series of classes on the Transitional Program in New York, for which Cannon, Burnham, and Shachtman were an-

In the autumn of 1937, Trotsky tried to exchange ideas about his work on this program with the leaders of the movement in New York, but they were too preoccupied with preparations for the founding convention of the SWP to pay much attention to his brief remarks. After the convention, however, in March 1938, they sent a delegation—consisting of Cannon, Shachtman, Vincent R. Dunne, and Rose Karsner—to Mexico, where Trotsky had an ample opportunity to discuss with them his ideas about the Transitional Program and how it would affect the work of the SWP, among other things.

As you can see from reading the transcripts of these discussions,[24] some of Trotsky's ideas and formulations came as a surprise to the SWP leaders since they required rethinking answers to questions already settled in the past and now taken for granted. That's not an easy thing to do and it took even the top leaders of the SWP a little time before they could absorb the meaning and logic of the method in the Transitional Program. Considerable confusion and uneasiness were still manifested a month later at a meeting of the SWP's National Committee in New

nounced as the teachers, was entitled "The Bridge to Revolutionary Action." The advertisement said, in part: "The crying contradiction of our epoch: a world economically ripe for Socialism—the masses disoriented by illusions, false leadership and false politics. The problem of the practical revolutionist is how to bridge the gap [with] a program of action for mobilizing the masses."

24. There were six transcripts of the discussions in Mexico, which lasted over a week. Three of these are in the Trotsky collection *The Transitional Program for Socialist Revolution* (Pathfinder, 1973) and the other three are in *Writings of Leon Trotsky (1937–38)*. The former book also includes the final text of the Transitional Program itself, entitled "The Death Agony of Capitalism and the Tasks of the Fourth International," and transcripts of other discussions Trotsky had with SWP members after he wrote the Transitional Program.

York, and it was some time after that before most members of the NC realized that they agreed on the essential elements of the Transitional Program and its application to the United States.

Among other specific questions that the SWP had to reconsider at this time were its positions on the Ludlow amendment and the labor party question. Ludlow, a Democratic member of Congress, had proposed an amendment to the U.S. Constitution to require a national referendum before the U.S. government could enter the war, and a movement in its favor had sprung up with strong support in the labor movement. The SWP's original attitude to this movement was negative, but under prodding from Trotsky the National Committee reversed its position in April 1938 and decided to support and participate in the anti-war movement around the Ludlow amendment.[25]

The labor party question proved to be even harder to rethink. For several years our movement had been opposed

---

25. Early in January 1938 a Gallup poll showed that 72 percent of the American people favored the amendment that Rep. Louis Ludlow (D-Ind.) had introduced in the U.S. House of Representatives. But a few days later the Roosevelt administration, supported by the Communist Party, succeeded in voting down the amendment in the House by a small margin. On the same day the new Political Committee elected after the SWP founding convention voted to oppose the amendment on the ground that it generated and sustained pacifist illusions. When Trotsky read their decision in Mexico, he wrote letters explaining why he disagreed and why he thought the SWP should support the referendum and participate in the movement behind it at the same time that it disassociated itself from harmful illusions. The Political Committee then changed its position from opposition to abstention. The text of Trotsky's letters on the subject is in *Writings of Leon Trotsky (1937–38)* and the transcript of his discussion with the SWP leaders is in *The Transitional Program for Socialist Revolution*. For the text of the SWP statement issued after it changed its position from abstention to support, see page 367.

to advocating the formation of an independent labor party although it recognized the need to work inside labor party formations already in existence.[26] A large majority of the SWP leadership was won over by Trotsky to the position that we should advocate and campaign for the formation of a labor party, but a large part of the membership was not convinced and wanted to stick with the antiadvocacy position adopted at the SWP founding convention. As a result, a party referendum was arranged by the National Committee and an internal discussion of the labor party question was held for several months in the middle of 1938. The Transitional Program was also debated in this prereferendum discussion.

A majority vote in the referendum supported both the new labor party position and the Transitional Program. These issues were again brought up at the SWP's second convention, in July 1939, and reaffirmed by the delegates there. Also taken up at that convention were issues that had not received much attention at the founding convention, such as our first resolution on the Black struggle and a resolution on workers' defense guards to fight the fascists. In the light of these important changes and additions it is clear that, programmatically at least, the

---

26. The national conference of the Communist League of America in 1929 adopted a platform that advocated the formation of an independent labor party; since there was little sentiment for a labor party being expressed in the unions at that time, it was understood that the CLA's advocacy of a labor party would be limited, for the time being, to educational and propaganda explanations rather than agitation or action campaigns. Two years later, at the CLA's second national conference, the advocacy position was rejected and replaced by a statement declaring that it was impermissible for revolutionists to advocate the formation of a party that could only be reformist. Most of the cadres of the future SWP were trained to think along these lines during the next seven years.

founding of the SWP only began at the first Chicago convention and that it actually extended throughout the period up to and through the second convention. So I think it is correct to say that we not only had the best program of the time, but the capacity to make it better.

ISR: Did Trotsky express any opinion about the first SWP convention?

BREITMAN: Yes, favorably, as can be seen in *Writings of Leon Trotsky (1937–38)*. He followed the preconvention discussion closely and wrote articles for the discussion bulletin himself. Then, after getting various reports, he said in a January 1938 letter to the French section, "They have made very remarkable progress. The level of the discussion was very high and the convention ended with nearly complete agreement and heightened authority of the leadership. . . . [T]he American section is the only one that made appreciable progress [in the last year or two] and has shown real political maturity."

It was on this basis that Trotsky collaborated closely with the leaders of the SWP in planning the founding conference of the Fourth International and in writing the basic programmatic documents of the conference. In Trotsky's view the SWP was the strongest section of the new International politically as well as in other ways.

ISR: How do you answer people who say, "What's the relevance for today of all this old stuff?"

BREITMAN: "If you don't know your own history, how you became what you are and how you got where you are, it's harder to become what you want to be and get where you want to go." The women's, Black, Chicano, and other movements have discovered this truth recently. It's just as true for the Marxist movement.

The convention of the new party[27]

by the editors of the 'New International'

The convention of the revolutionary militants expelled from the Socialist Party and those who are in solidarity with them, will take place in Chicago during the New Year weekend. It will mark an impressive milestone in the building of the revolutionary workers' party of the United States. The event is of international importance, for in the strongest center of world imperialism the convention will establish the largest section of the Fourth International.

The expulsion of the left wing from the Socialist Party is a decisive culminating point in the development of both the former and the latter. Under the impact of the catastrophic defeats of the working class in Central Europe in

---

27. Reprinted from the *New International*, January 1938. Its editors at that time were James Burnham, Max Shachtman, and Maurice Spector; this article was probably written by Shachtman in November or December 1937.

1933–34[28] and of the terrific crisis of world capitalism, the then moribund Socialist Party of America acquired a new lease on life by the infiltration of several thousand young and militant left-wing elements whom the bureaucratic adventurism of the Communist Party repelled. The pressure of these left-wing forces was strong enough to produce a split in the Socialist Party, as a result of which the incorrigible Old Guard separated itself from the organization. The right-wing Bourbons, stubbornly repeating the stereotyped formulas of the bankrupt Social Democracy and refusing to assimilate a single one of the obvious lessons of international events, retired to the comforts of a little Fabian society dedicated to maintaining a couple of municipal socialist election machines and to beseeching the labor bureaucracy to build them a labor party shelter.

With all their immaturity and confusion and despite their haphazard leadership, the left-wing militants were seriously striving to build a revolutionary party based on Marxian principles and participating actively in the class struggle. It was quite clear that with the centrist leadership of these militants continuing at the head, the energies of the movement would be dissipated and the movement itself end up in a state of disintegration. The best elements among the militant left were therefore constantly at loggerheads with the New York centrist leaders who, from the days before the Detroit convention of 1934, operated on the theory that capitulation to such congenital right-wingers as came from the Milwaukee sewer-socialism school—to say nothing of capitulation to Norman Thomas and his entourage of muddleheads,

---

28. This refers to the Nazi victory in Germany in 1933 and the crushing of the Social Democratic workers' movement by a right-wing government in Austria.

Fabians, pacifists, Industrial Democrats, and other nice people—was always preferable to an honest fight for revolutionary principle.

Nevertheless, revolutionary ideas were making their way in the party, and the desire to have them prevail was concretized in the growing demand that all revolutionists not members of the SP should be invited to join its ranks with full rights, obligations, and privileges, including the right to defend their point of view. In order to break down any organizational barriers between the revolutionary workers inside the party and those outside of it, and to effect a fusion of the two, the Trotskyists, organized at that time in the Workers Party of the United States, decided more than a year and a half ago to join the Socialist Party.

The affiliation of the Workers Party members to the SP (and of the Fourth Internationalist Spartacus Youth League to the Young People's Socialist League) coincided with the departure of the Waldman-Oneal-Lee-[Jewish Daily] Forward gang at the Cleveland party convention. Almost automatically, the split of the main bulk of the right wing, followed shortly thereafter by its Bridgeport and Reading contingents, caused a shift of position within the ranks of the party. A consistent left wing, standing on principled grounds and meaning business, was soon crystallized around the *Socialist Appeal* at its Chicago Institute in the winter of 1936.[29] It was achieved by a harmonious fusion of all the genuinely left-wing elements—the former members of the Workers Party and those revolutionary socialists who had been carrying on a fight for left-wing

---

29. This date is wrong. The members of the Appeal Association in the SP held a two-day national institute (caucus meeting) in Chicago in February 1937.

policies before the Workers Party was dissolved.

At the opposite pole of the party, the right-wing forces effected a concentration of a loose but nonetheless effective kind, united on no clear-cut political program, but animated by a violent antagonism to the principles of revolutionary Marxism to which, like the Stalinists, they applied the general tag of "Trotskyism." The concentration included both groups of Wisconsin reformists, the Porter-Berger Stalinist crew and the Hoan-Benson good-government people; the pacifists, the Fabians of the League for Industrial Democracy, and other good folk for whom the socialist movement begins and ends with Norman Thomas; liquidators of the Alfred Baker Lewis school, who favor the dissolution of the party into an educational institute; the deadwood, the right-wing remnants, young trade union officials on the make, and assorted imponderabilia organized in New York under the leadership of an ambitious officeholder by the name of Altman; and a frankly Stalinist group in Connecticut organized under the fitting, memory-stirring name of Committee of Correspondence.

Between these two currents stood the Hamlets of the Clarity group, organized as a separate entity following the split that occurred in the New York left-wing group when the centrists—Zam, Tyler, Delson—found themselves in a minority. It set itself the not at all modest and not at all mean task of reconciling the irreconcilable, thus underwriting its own certain collapse.

The first blow dealt the left wing was delivered at the special convention in Chicago early this year,[30] when a motion by Thomas was adopted prohibiting the publication of any separate group organs. The left wing being excluded from participation in the official party paper,

---

30. The SP's special convention in Chicago was held in March 1937.

Delegates at March 1937 Socialist Party special convention in Chicago.

which was the monopoly of the right wing and the centrists, the decision was tantamount to a gag, especially when the convention pledge to publish a generally accessible internal discussion paper was nonchalantly scrapped by the first meeting of the National Executive Committee following the convention.

The second blow at the left wing in particular, and at the leftward development of the party in general, was delivered at the Philadelphia meeting of the NEC,[31] which finally adopted a resolution on Spain. Although the convention had taken a position against People's Frontism, the resolution on Spain was a political endorsement of the Caballero People's Front and, worse than that, covered up the regime that massacred the revolutionary workers during Barcelona's May days.[32] Noteworthy is not the fact that the right-wingers throughout the party and on the NEC voted for this resolution, but that it was sponsored and carried by the Clarity group majority on the committee, which, then as now, made no modest claims to radicalism.

The reply of the rank and file of the party and the youth organization was a fear-inspiring reminder to the right wing and its centrist allies of the growth of the left-wing movement. In one party and youth organization

---

31. The SP National Executive Committee's Philadelphia meeting was held in May 1937. Supporters of the Clarity group were in the majority.

32. Barcelona in May 1937 was the site of a plot engineered by the CP to smash CNT and POUM influence in Catalonia. It began with an attack to seize the telephone exchange operated under workers' control by the CNT since the start of the civil war. When thousands of workers resisted in the streets, the question of political power was posed. Unwilling to carry the fight to a finish, the anarchists and POUM restrained the workers and agreed to a truce with the People's Front government. At the first opportunity the government violated the truce and outlawed the POUM in June.

after another, the membership voted down the miserable resolution on Spain and called upon the NEC to discard it in favor of a revolutionary document. This evidence of left-wing growth was answered by the Clarity-right-wing combination with one of the most stupid decrees known in the radical movement. As one Clarity statesman said, martial law was established in the party. Others called it the gag law. And so it was. It prohibited the membership from discussing party policies—nothing less. It forbade any attempt to call upon the NEC to initiate a new policy or alter an old one. It established an *index prohibitorum* for heretical literature—i.e., the literature of the left wing—which party institutions might sell only upon peril of excommunication and consignment to the fires of hell. The whole idea met with the approval of everybody but the membership, and it might still have worked if the NEC could have gotten enough cops to enforce it, or if it really had the power to issue letters of mark and reprisal. But the more desperate and arbitrary the prohibitory decisions of the NEC, the more clearly was its futility and impotence revealed.

The general rebellion of the membership against the infamous gag law was only widened by the notorious Altman-Thomas-Laidler proposal to support the bourgeois blatherskite, LaGuardia, candidate of the Republican Party for mayor of New York, to support him not only in the contravention of solemnly adopted convention decisions, but by the peculiarly craven step of withdrawing the socialist candidate for LaGuardia's benefit without giving him a "formal" endorsement. The right wing took the offensive on this proposal, and as was always the case when confronted by a serious offensive, the Clarity National Executive collapsed and endorsed the proposal by a majority vote.

Simultaneously, a fox-hunt was organized by the right wing against the left, which had roused the bulk of the active membership against the odious sell-out in New York, and therefore stood in the way of its execution. More than a hundred supporters of the left-wing Appeal Association were brought up on charges by the Altman administration for the crime . . . of belonging to the Appeal Association and owing fealty to an alien organization, namely, the Fourth International. In a word, the crimes charged were not acts of indiscipline, but the facts of association and belief, that is, a "conspiracy indictment." Speaker of the Assembly Sweet, who haled the five socialist assemblymen before him in 1920 in order to deprive them of their seats, charged them with no greater crimes.[33]

It is difficult to describe what followed in temperate language. What passed for a trial of the left-wingers was at once ludicrous and obscene. The Altman group functioned imperturbably as plaintiff, prosecuting attorney, judge, jury, court of appeals, and executioner, thus economizing time and energy. The no less austerely impartial National Executive Committee, after resolving to turn over the party to the People's Front combination of Alfred Landon's party + the Fusion Party + the Progressive Party + the American Labor Party + the Communist Party + the Lovestone group, devoted itself for an hour to hearing the appeal of the left wing and then endorsed the expulsion, the Clarity group vying with all the other right-wingers for the dubious honor of torpedoing the Socialist Party. To guarantee its sinking beyond the efforts of divers, a resolution was unanimously adopted calling upon all members to cease and desist from any continued

---

33. This refers to the New York legislature's lower house, which refused to seat five legally elected socialists.

support of the left wing or its organ on pain of immediate expulsion. Provision was made for the prompt lifting of the charters of all organizations which failed to execute the mass expulsion order.

The lamentable collapse of the Clarity diplomatists in face of the right-wing offensive in New York and Wisconsin was matched only by their effrontery and virulence in proceeding to cut the party to pieces so as to dislodge the left wing. But that proved to be no simple matter. Despite all kinds of shady manipulations, rigging, and dues-fixing, the left wing received an overwhelming majority of the votes for the Young People's Socialist League convention, which adopted a left-wing program, elected a revolutionary leadership, and endorsed the Fourth International.[34] In New York, the majority of the active members stood firm with the left wing; likewise in Chicago; likewise in Ohio. In states like Minnesota, California, and Indiana, the left wing was supported by anywhere from 75 to 95 percent of the membership. In reply to the LaGuardia party-wreckers, the left wing issued a call for a special convention in Chicago over the signatures of the National Executive Committee of the YPSL, the executive committees of the New York and Cook County left wing, and the state committees of the Ohio, Minnesota, Indiana, and California party organizations. The convention call has since been endorsed by numerous important party centers, like Rochester, N.Y., Bucks County and Allentown in Pennsylvania, Kansas City and St. Louis County in Missouri.

While the left wing is consolidating its forces for the re-formation of the revolutionary Marxian party in the United States, the remnants of the old Socialist Party are

---

34. After this Ninth National Convention in Philadelphia, September 3–5, 1937, the YPSL added the words (Fourth Internationalist) to its name.

disintegrating apace. In the traditional stronghold of New York, the party simply did not exist as a factor in the current election.[35] In Philadelphia, it endorsed the candidates of the Communist Party. Its Stalinist wing is breaking off and moving formally to the CP, as foreshadowed by the affiliation to the latter by the SP's star of hope among the students, Lash; by a tour which Hilliard Bernstein, an SP wheelhorse among the unemployed, is making for the Stalinists; and by the approaching desertion of David Lasser, president of the Workers Alliance. The number of members who have become indifferent or dropped out entirely runs into the hundreds. The Jewish section is secretly negotiating for fusion with the Jewish section of the Old Guard, and does it with impunity despite the tearful protests of the demoralized Clarityites. The latter's tenure in the party is itself tenuous, if the SOS cry of their latest faction circular is to be credited; some of them are already up on charges and others are threatened with removal from posts or from membership. The activity of the national office in the past period has been confined largely to the not very profitable business of taking in charters—not members. Attempts to resuscitate the "official" YPSL with hypodermic injections of Altmanite subsidies, in lieu of members, have proved vain. The only organization still left in the SP that is worth shaking a stick at—Wisconsin—will not be long in solving the enigma of continued affiliation that has puzzled so many observers. The paladins in the great war against the "sectarian left" have ended by reducing the old SP to a sect, and a disintegrating one to boot.

The future of the revolutionary political party of labor in the United States lies with the left-wing conference in

---

35. This refers to elections held in November 1937.

Chicago. It has no need to look back to the moribund movement that is left in the hands of Thomas and Tyler. The revolutionary possibilities of the old SP have been exhausted. Substantially all that was life-worthy in it, capable of assimilating revolutionary ideas, and carrying out serious socialist action, is now associated with the left wing. The tasks before the new party which will be established in Chicago are truly enormous, and the difficulties not less so. But the prospects of growth are sure, and the convictions of the revolutionists are firm.

The new party will not have to invent new formulas or new principles. It starts with the principles that have withstood the assault of time and the test of the class struggle. It will appear as the American section of the Fourth International, which stands on the granite foundation of the experiences and lessons of almost a century of the revolutionary movement. Its ideas are invincible and, once fused with the rising American working class, they will create a movement that marches irresistibly to the final triumph.

The new party is founded[36]

by James P. Cannon

All the experience of the class struggle on a world scale, and especially the experience of the past twenty years, teaches one lesson: the most important problem of the working class is the problem of the party. Success or failure in this domain spells the difference between victory or defeat every time. The struggle for the party, the unceasing effort to construct the new political organization of the vanguard on the ruins of the old one, concentrates within itself the most vital and progressive elements of the class struggle as a whole. From this point of view every concrete step in the direction of a reconstructed party has outstanding importance.

---

36. Reprinted from the *New International*, February 1938. The author had been elected national secretary of the SWP by the National Committee chosen at the Chicago convention. It was written in January 1938.

The convention of the left-wing branches of the disintegrated Socialist Party at Chicago over the New Year's weekend, which resulted in the formal launching of a new organization—the Socialist Workers Party, section of the Fourth International[37]—thus claims first attention from the revolutionary internationalists throughout the world. For them—and their judgment is better than any other because they foresee and prepare the future—it marks a new milestone on the historic road of workers' liberation.

The reconstruction of the revolutionary labor movement in the form of a political party is not a simple process. In the midst of unprecedented difficulties, complications, and contradictions, the work goes ahead, like all social movements, in zigzag fashion. The new movement takes shape through a series of splits and fusions, which must appear like a Chinese puzzle to the superficial observer. But how could it be otherwise? The frightful disintegration of the old movements, on a background of worldwide social upheaval, disoriented and scattered the revolutionary militants in all directions. They could not find their way together, and draw the same basic conclusions, in a day. The new movement is fraught with catastrophic reverses, forward leaps, and deadening periods of seeming stagnation. But for all that, it is a movement with an invincible historic motor force, and it moves along. The Chicago convention, which brought all the preceding work of the Fourth Internationalists in the U.S. to a

---

37. Strictly speaking, the SWP was not yet a section of the Fourth International since the latter organization was not founded until September 1938. Both Trotsky and the SWP leaders used this formulation even though technically the SWP was a section of the Movement for the Fourth International (MFI) between January and September.

fruitful culmination, is a forceful reminder of this fact.

The Chicago convention itself was a striking illustration of this contradictory process of fusion and split—and a step forward. It crossed the last *t* and dotted the last *i* on the split of the moribund Socialist Party. At the same time, it recorded the complete fusion of the left-wing socialists with the former members of the Workers Party, just as the Workers Party earlier came into existence through a fusion of the Communist Left Opposition and revolutionary militants of independent origin. The invincible program of the Fourth International is the magnet which attracts to itself all the vital revolutionary elements from all camps. It is the basis, and the only basis, on which the dispersed militants can come together and forge the new movement.

This was demonstrated once again at the Chicago convention when the resolution for the Fourth International was carried without a single dissenting vote. The two currents—former Workers Party and "native" socialists, which were about equally represented—showed complete unity on this decisive question. The 76 regular and 36 fraternal delegates[38] from 35 cities in 17 states, who constituted the convention, came to this unanimous decision after due consideration of the question and ample preconvention discussion. Although the great bulk of time and discussion at the convention were devoted to American affairs—and properly so—the great matters of principle embodied in the international question inspired and guided everything.

This significant victory of the Fourth International in America cannot be without far-reaching influence on the

---

38. A more accurate list of the number of delegates at the Chicago convention appears in Cannon's letter on page 79 of this book.

international arena. The brief period of struggle as a faction within the Socialist Party comes to a definite end, and the American section of the Fourth International takes the field again as an independent party, with forces more than doubled, without any losses or splits, and with a firmer unity than ever before. Principled politics in this case also have proved to be the best and most effective kind of practical politics.

Those too-clever politicians of the centrist school have sought to avoid clear-cut answers to the international question in the hope of keeping divergent forces together. They have nothing to show for it but disintegration and splits and the creeping paralysis of blind-alley pessimism in their ranks. The "Trotskyists," on the other hand, have held their own ranks firm, and have united with other serious revolutionary forces in an expanding movement inspired by enthusiasm and confidence in its future. That is, first of all, because they put the main question of internationalism squarely. Experience showed that the left-wing socialists who mean business—and they are the only ones worth counting—preferred this kind of politics.

When our plenum-conference last July[39] decided to take up the impudent challenge of the gag-law bureaucrats of the SP and fight the issue out without compromise, some comrades questioned the wisdom of this strategy, fearing disintegration in our ranks. The

---

39. The plenum-conference of the Appeal Association, held in New York in July 1937 when the SP leadership began to suspend and expel the leaders of the Appeal group, was made up of members of the National Action Committee that had been elected at the Chicago institute in March and delegates sent by local Appeal groups from around the country. In SWP parlance *plenum* refers to full meetings of a national or international committee.

convention removed all ground for argument on this score. In the five-month campaign from July to New Year's we not only held our own, but gained. Numerous branches not affiliated to the organized left wing in July were represented by delegates at the convention. Denver; Salt Lake City; Kansas City, Joplin, and St. Louis in Missouri; Rochester; Quakertown, Sellerville, and a third branch in Pennsylvania—these were among the new branches enlisted under the banner of the new party at the convention. As for the remnants of the Socialist Party, it did not claim the attention of the convention in any way. Nobody felt the necessity for discussion on this dead issue of the past. All attention was directed to the future—to the problem of penetrating the mass movement of the workers and the struggle against Stalinism.

The outstanding point on the agenda, and the one allotted the most time in the discussion, was the trade union question. And even this discussion was pretty much limited to the narrower question of practical work and tactics in the trade unions and the exchange of experience in this field. The principles and strategy of Bolshevism in regard to the trade unions were regarded as clearly established and taken for granted.

The predominance of the trade union question in its practical and tactical aspects corresponded to the most pressing needs of the hour, and to the composition and temper of the convention. The slogan "To the masses" dominated the convention from beginning to end. The conception of the Fourth Internationalists as primarily a circle of isolated theorists and hairsplitters—a conception industriously circulated by the centrists who maneuver all the time with nonexistent "mass movements" in a vacuum—could find little to sustain it at Chicago.

The great bulk of the delegates consisted of practical and qualified trade unionists who have done serious Bolshevik work in the labor movement and have modest results to show for it.

The discussion and reports from the various districts clearly showed that we already have a good foundation of trade union activity to build upon. Our positions and influence in various unions—such as they are—have not been gained by appointment or sufferance from the top, but by systematic work from below, in the ranks. That is all to the good. What is ours is ours; nobody gave it to us and nobody can take it away.

It must be admitted that the preoccupation of our national movement with problems of theoretical education carried with it a certain neglect and even a minimizing of trade union work—a serious weakness and a danger which should not be concealed. The Chicago convention was one continuous warning and demand to correct this fault and to do it by drastic measures. But if systematic national organization and direction of our trade union work have been lacking, our comrades in various localities and unions, guided by a sure instinct and a firm grasp of their theory, have gone to work in the unions with a will and have achieved good results. In some cases the fruits of their work stand out conspicuously. The convention heard matter-of-fact reports from all sections of the country. In sum total this work and its results, considering the size of our movement and its freedom from "big" pretensions, impressed the convention as fairly imposing.

This discussion, and the concrete program which issued from it, gave the convention its tone and its buoyant spirit of proletarian optimism. Revolutionary activists in the class struggle, in general, have no time for skeptical speculation and pessimistic brooding. Our proletarian convention reflected no trace of these diseases, so fashionable now on the intellectual fringes of the movement. The trade union discussion was a striking revelation that the revolutionary health of a party, and of its individual members, requires intimate contact with the living mass movement, with its struggle and action, its hopes and aspirations.

The whole course of our convention was turned in this direction. It was decided to "trade unionize" the party, to devote 90 percent of the party work to this field, to coordinate and direct this work on a national scale, and to establish the necessary apparatus to facilitate this design.

Our trade union work in the days ahead is concerned, of course, not as an end in itself—that is mere opportunism—but as a practical means to a revolutionary end. In order to aim seriously at the struggle for power a party must be entrenched in the sources of power—the workers' mass movement and especially the trade unions. Our convention could devote itself so extensively to the practical side of this question only thanks to the fact that the theoretical ground had been cleared and firm positions on the important principled questions consciously worked out.

The party arrived at these positions by the method of party democracy. Six months of intensive discussion preceded the convention. Three months of more or less informal discussion on the Spanish, Russian, and international questions after the July plenum, were followed by another three-month period of formal discussion. This discussion was organized by the National Committee. Internal discussion bulletins were published, membership meetings were held, etc. All points of view were fairly presented. The bulk of the space in the bulletins and approximately equal time in the membership meetings were given over to minorities—which turned out in the end to be tiny minorities.

In a live and free party, where members do their own thinking—and that is the only kind of a party worth a fig—everybody does not come to the same conclusion at the same moment. Common acceptance of basic principles does not ensure uniform answers to the concrete questions of the day. The party position can be worked out only in a process of collective thought and exchange of opinion. That is possible only in a free, that is, a democratic, party.

The method of party democracy entails certain "overhead charges." It takes time and energy. It often interferes with other work. On occasions it taxes patience. But it works. It educates the party and safeguards its unity. And in the long run the overhead expenses of the democratic method are the cheapest. The quick and easy solutions of bureaucratic violence usually claim drawn-out installment payments in the form of discontent in the ranks, impaired morale, and devastating splits.

Discussions among the Bolsheviks, sometimes taking the form of factional struggle, are carried on in dead earnest, corresponding to the seriousness of the questions and of the people involved. A philistine reading one of our preconvention discussion bulletins, or listening by chance at a membership meeting, might well imagine our party to be a mad-house of dissension, recrimination, revolts against the leadership, and, in general, "fights among themselves." But, to get a clear picture, one must judge the democratic process at the end, not in the middle. True, Bolsheviks are in earnest and they readily dispense with polite amenities. They put questions sharply, because as a rule, they feel them deeply. And nobody ever thinks of sparing the sensibilities of leaders; they are assumed to be pupils of Engels, who warned his opponents that he had a tough hide.

But it is precisely through this free democratic process, and not otherwise, that a genuine party arrives at conclusions which represent its own consciously won convictions. The discussion is not aimless and endless. It leads straight to a convention and a conclusion—in our case a conclusion so close to unanimous that its authority is unshakable. Then the discussion can and must come to an end. The emphasis in party life shifts from democracy to centralism. The party goes to work on the basis of the convention decisions.

The resolutions submitted to the convention by the National Committee on all the important questions, formulating the standpoint which has been advocated in our press, were all accepted by the convention without significant amendments. Much preconvention discussion had been devoted to the Russian question, as a result of the unspeakable Moscow trials and the subsequent blood purges. Some comrades challenged the designation of the Soviet Union as a workers' state, although frightfully degenerated, which can yet be restored to health by a political revolution without a social overturn. This minority opinion, however, found little echo in the ranks.

The resolution of the National Committee, which calls for the unconditional defense of the Soviet Union against imperialist attack—a position which necessarily presupposes an uncompromising struggle against the Stalinist bureaucracy in war or peace—was adopted by a vote of 66 against 3 for one minority position and 2 for another. This virtual unanimity is the best assurance for the future theoretical stability of the party. A false position on the question of the Russian revolution, now as always since 1917, spells fatal consequences for any political organization. The revolutionary Marxists have always said they would be at their posts and be the best fighters for the Soviet Union in the hour of danger. As this crucial hour draws near, the American soldiers of the Fourth International have renewed this declaration and pledge.

With a firm theoretical position and a decisive orientation to mass work, the new party of the Fourth International has every right to face the future with confidence. This confidence is also fortified by the objective political situation and by the present state of affairs in the radical labor movement. All signs point to a mighty acceleration of the class struggle as the country slides into another devastating crisis and the inevitable war draws ever nearer to the point of explosion. Meanwhile, the situation among the radical labor groupings and tendencies is clearing up. Stalinism is self-disclosed as the movement of jingo-traitors. The Socialist Party of Altman, Thomas, and Company—having expelled its vitalizing left wing—presents only the pathetically futile spectacle of an opportunist sect, lacking the merit of consistent principle on the one side or of mass support on the other. The Lovestoneites, the one-time unacknowledged attorneys of Stalinism, are now merely the attorneys and finger-men of pseudoprogressive labor bureaucrats in a couple of important unions. The various groups and cliques which challenged the bona fide movement of the Fourth International and attempted to fight it from the "left" have all, without exception, fallen into pitiful disintegration and demoralization.

The Socialist Workers Party, unfurling the banner of

the Fourth International from the hour of its birth, has no rival in the field. It is the only revolutionary party, the heir of the rich traditions of the past and the herald of the future.

Leon Trotsky, 1937.

A letter to the International Secretariat[40]

by James P. Cannon

To the International Secretariat

Dear Comrades,

By this time you will have received the minutes of the national convention. This will give you the possibility of checking over the work done there more precisely.

Here I want to give you a few personal impressions which you can take together with the reports you have heard from other comrades and eventually arrive at a general impression of your own.

1. *Representation*: According to the final report of the

---

40. Reprinted from *International Socialist Review*, a supplement of *The Militant*, January 13, 1978. This letter was undated but was attached to another letter, for the International Secretariat of the Movement for the Fourth International, dated February 9, 1938. This account of the Chicago convention, not published at the time, contained more confidential information and personal opinions than the public report that was printed in the *New International*.

Credentials Committee we had 76 regular delegates, 37 alternate delegates, and 24 fraternal delegates. This makes a total of 137. In addition, I estimate there were a couple of score of comrades and very close sympathizers from other cities who were admitted into the convention sessions. The delegates came from thirty-five cities in seventeen states. From these figures one can get a fairly clear impression that our organization, despite its comparatively small size, is spreading out over the country and has already the fairly good framework of a national organization. In this respect—which I consider very important for the future—we have long outstripped the Lovestoneites, for example, who remain primarily a New York group. The same is true of all the other groups and cliques with which we have had conflicts in the past. Among all the radical groupings ours alone is developing a really national composition.

2. *Composition of the Convention*: Precise statistics of the social composition, age, and background of the convention delegates were not compiled, unfortunately. This was contemplated but overlooked in the rush of things. However, I can state that the large majority of the delegates were proletarian activists and trade unionists. Not only that, the work of the Trade Union Commission and the discussion of the trade union question showed that we have a large number of comrades sufficiently experienced and qualified in mass work to be able to discuss all sides of the trade union question, including its most practical aspects, with the fullest assurance, as a result of their experience. I think the composition, and general character of the convention, must prompt you to make a certain revision in previous impressions of the composition and general character of the party membership which, it seems to me, you entertained. Tourists and letter-writers

can give certain impressions of the American movement, and valuable and necessary ones too. But these impressions by no means are representative of the party and the movement as a whole. The proletarian activists, as a rule, do not have the time and the means for extensive travel. And as a rule their correspondence is confined to laconic reports. One can also get a one-sided impression of the party from the Chicago and New York organizations which, despite their merits, have serious shortcomings on the side of social composition and trade union activity. It is necessary to see the party as a whole, in a representative convention, to get a clear picture of what it is made of.

3. *International*: This point on the agenda did not provoke very much discussion. This can be accounted for, to a certain extent, by the fact that no differences of opinion were manifested. The decision to affiliate to the Bureau of the Fourth International was unanimous, and likewise the provision to apportion a definite percentage of the party dues to International Bureau expenses met with universal approval. It was interesting to note, especially on this point, that the divisions between the old cadres of the Workers Party and the cadres of "native" Socialists have pretty well been obliterated in the course of a common work and discussion. Such objections and reservations on the question of 100 percent "Trotskyism" as we have encountered, have come from individuals of the older cadre and not from the former Socialists. I do not at all wish to maintain that the party is thoroughly internationalized. But theoretically the victory on this score is already complete in the united organization.

4. *Orientation*: The convention showed quite clearly that the orientation toward mass work, which began at the time of the French turn, has developed quite consistently. I think it can be said that more progress has been

made up till now in this respect in the ranks than in the leadership. While it is true that the general lead was given by the National Committee, the delegates more or less ran away with this issue and gave it real life at the convention. During the year or so of our work in the Socialist Party, the leadership put too narrow a construction on the purely factional side of this work and tended to overlook the coordination of the internal faction work with practical activity in the class struggle on a broader scale. Of course, I'm stating here my personal opinion but I do not make much of a secret of it. I consider the leadership on the whole to have been very remiss during the past year in this respect, especially during the period of our intense preoccupation with the internal struggle.

However, the locals and branches, on their own initiative, in various localities developed trade union activity, established contact, and broadened their experience and connections in this field. The most hopeful side of the convention revelations, in this respect, was not the work that has already been accomplished but the fact that it was accomplished pretty largely on the initiative of the local comrades themselves. This gives ground to think that with a more decisive orientation on the part of the party as a whole, and with a serious attempt at coordination and centralized direction, we can hope for still more gratifying results in the next period. Two postconvention items give special grounds for encouragement: the first is the result of the elections in the Marine Firemen's Union on the West Coast. No doubt you have heard that the progressive slate swept out the Stalinites by a three-to-two majority all along the line. The second item was the reinstatement of one of our comrades to his position as international organizer of the automobile workers' union at Cleveland. In the reactionary drive of the general executive board of the automobile workers' union, he was removed from his position about three weeks ago. Thereupon the locals in the district raised such a furor, bombarded the national office with so many truculent resolutions of protest, that they were compelled to reinstate him in his position. I think this is a very interesting case. The comrade, who is still a very young man—only twenty-four years old—got his political education in our New York movement.[41] Then, in the early days of the Workers Party, he was sent out in the field to see what he could do in the line of mass work, without previous experience. The leadership, perhaps, deserves credit for encouraging him to start out on this course. All the rest he did by himself.

5. *Political Firmness*: The discussion and the vote on the principal questions in dispute should be an eye-opener for anyone who thinks that fundamental positions can be lightly discarded in our party. After all the furor that was raised around the Russian question in the pre-convention discussion, with all the groups and grouplets that came forward with new revelations in this respect, and despite the fact that a minority of the National Committee came forward with an opposition point of view—despite all this—the convention supported the line of the National Committee with a crushing unanimity. On page 14 of the minutes you will see the record of the vote; for the majority, 66; for the NC minority, 3; for the Glee opposition, 2; for a special position of Heisler, 1. On page 19 the minutes show the Spanish resolution adopted by a vote of 56 against 4 abstentions.[42]

---

41. This refers to Bert Cochran (see glossary).

42. The minutes of the Chicago convention begin on page 91. The roll call vote on the Russian resolutions starts on page 111; the result of the vote on the Spanish resolution is on page 117.

It will be interesting for you to study the roll call on the Russian question and see the solid lineup of delegates, delegation after delegation. And they are not routine votes either. There was more than ample preconvention discussion and the delegates showed in the discussion that they understand their positions very clearly. *The various sections of our International, who may have got the impression of deep cleavages over the Russian question from our Internal Bulletin, should be apprised of these votes.*

The decisions of the convention on the disputed questions have naturally had a stabilizing effect on the internal life of the party, and have put a stop completely to discussion and controversy. It appears that most of the comrades who have been in opposition are disposed to let the matter rest now until another period of party work and experience intervenes. On the other hand, it can be said that the party rank and file are in no mood to tolerate any infringement of the convention decisions. The slightest signs of such a tendency would be dealt with promptly and without ceremony. Although all the opposition tendencies appeared at the convention, more or less, as isolated individuals, nevertheless there was nothing resembling a crushing or terrorizing policy. Everybody who had a dissenting point of view was given ample time to explain his position to the convention, in most cases, equal time with the majority reporters. Although we maintained, and still maintain, that advocacy of defeatism with respect to the Soviet Union is incompatible with adherence to our movement for the Fourth International, we found it possible, in view of the unanimity of the convention, to refrain from any organizational measures in this respect. Consequently, all the opposition comrades, including even the three or four who defended a defeatist point of view, have the opportunity to reflect further on the matter and to adjust themselves to the firmly established position of the party.

6. *Party Democracy*: The action of the convention, overruling and censuring the Chicago City Executive Committee in the cases of Becket and Most, should be noted. This is recorded in the minutes, under the report of the Grievance Committee, on pages 8, 9, and 10 and again on page 17.[43] Here it was not so much a question of correcting a real injustice, as of insisting on the most scrupulous observation of regularity and formality in disciplinary cases. The convention action gained added force from the fact that the individuals involved, Becket and Most, were without any support whatever in the convention. I consider these decisions very important from the point of view of establishing precedent: that no kind of summary action is to be encouraged in disciplinary matters. The delegates were very "touchy" on this point and did not hesitate to demonstrate it, even though our political friends of the Chicago City Executive Committee were involved and censured.

7. *Leadership*: The convention made a little shakeup in the leadership when it came time to elect the new National Committee. Several comrades who had been members of the committee for two years were eliminated and new forces were added. In one or two cases members of the NC were reduced to the ranks of alternates; in other cases, members of the Political Committee were elected to the National Committee but not to the Political Committee this time. In this case also some new blood was infused into the body. Provisions were made for quarterly meetings of the plenum of the National Committee. The Political Committee is to be subject to alteration at each

---

43. See pages 101–4, 122–23 in this book.

plenum of the NC. The national staff is strengthened by the addition of a fulltime trade union secretary.

In my opinion, these measures were imperatively necessary. Some of them were considered drastic and produced a certain shock. But that is good for the party and also for the individuals concerned, perhaps. Some comrades who are inclined to take a personal view of things have seen in the action of the convention, on this point, only a shuffling of the NC slate. However, it had a far profounder meaning. It marks, I hope, the beginning of a process which is to be carried out relentlessly under a slogan: The subordination of the leadership to the ranks. The isolation of a part, at least, of the national leadership from the rank and file of the party, the encumbrance of the leadership with honorary and inactive members, the tendency of the leadership to develop into a sort of officers' club whose members never offend or discipline each other, and who are free from the discipline of the ranks—all this sort of thing had developed into a crying evil in the party.

It appeared obvious to me in such a situation that matters could not be remedied by a mere reshuffling of the slate, with the polite agreement of all concerned. It was necessary to deal a blow at the whole system. This could only be done by direct intervention of the active comrades in the ranks themselves. For that reason I declined to participate in the making up of a slate. But I did frankly encourage, and even instigate, the leading proletarian delegations to take matters into their own hands and rearrange the leadership in accordance with merit and activity. I am inclined to think that an error was made here and there in the selection or rejection of this or that individual, but the whole course initiated at the convention was right and salutary.

The necessary transformation from the propaganda circle to the mass work is finding its full reflection only belatedly in the leadership itself. And since the initiative, for a variety of reasons, could not, or at least did not, come through the National Committee, it had to come from below. Perhaps this is best in the end. I look forward to the next convention with the hope that a still more vigorous and determined supervision, and if necessary, overhauling of the leading personnel, will take place.

In my judgment, this is the most important question. That the convention delegates showed an alertness to the problem, and a readiness to tackle it head-on, gives me more confidence for the future of the party than anything else. When it becomes clearly apparent to all that the rank-and-file activists are watching the leadership all the time—not merely the leadership as a whole but each individual member of it—and requires of them continuous activity and responsibility, we will be on the road to the eventual selection of a leadership that is worthy of its task. The convention showed very clearly that we have much promising material in the ranks, that we are developing a strong second line of leadership who know how to keep a vigilant and critical eye on those immediately above them, and, if necessary, to substitute for them.

Best wishes,

Fraternally,

James P. Cannon
NATIONAL SECRETARY

P.S. Today's mail brings news of a new branch at New Castle, Pennsylvania, and possibly, a new one (from the Stalinists) at East St. Louis, Illinois. We are gaining recruits from the Stalinists steadily.

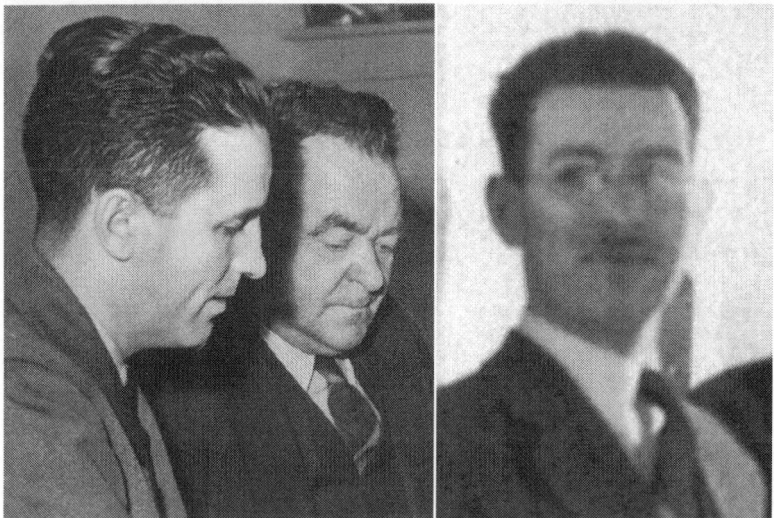

Above: Martin Abern, James P. Cannon, Max Shachtman.
Below: Farrell Dobbs, Carl Skoglund, Maurice Spector.

PART 2

Minutes, First National Convention of the Socialist Workers Party

Minutes, First National Convention of the Socialist Workers Party

Chicago, December 31, 1937–January 3, 1938[1]

FIRST SESSION, FRIDAY, DECEMBER 31, 1937

Convention called to order by James P. Cannon at 10:15 a.m.

Organization of Convention

Comrade Cannon, reporting for the NAC, made the following proposals:
1. A presiding committee of five—Cannon, Burnham, Abern, Trimble, and Dunne. Motion to concur. Carried.

---

1. These minutes, which were prepared by the convention secretary, Bill Sherman of New York, were issued in mimeographed form within a month after the convention. For security reasons, the names of National Committee members and alternates nominated and elected at the convention were deleted from the mimeographed minutes. Fortunately, a copy of the original minutes was found in the James P. Cannon archives at the Library of Social History in New York, enabling us to insert that information in this fuller version. The convention was opened at the Harrison Hotel in Chicago, and then was transferred to the Majestic Hotel.

2. Secretary of convention, Sherman. Motion to concur. Carried.
3. Sergeant at arms, Leeds. Motion to concur. Carried.
4. Agenda as outlined in Internal Bulletin No. 6[2] with the following changes:
   a) Move youth report to follow the internal. Motion to concur. Carried.
   b) Conflicts and grievances to follow party press. Motion to concur. Carried.
   c) Add Resolution Committee's report before NEC elections. Motion to concur. Carried.

Motion to adopt the entire agenda as amended. Carried.

5. Time schedule proposals for convention agenda:
   1. Address of welcome. Goldman, 20 minutes.
   2. Political report. Shachtman. Presentation, 60 minutes. Discussion, 90 minutes (10 minutes per speaker). Summary, 20 minutes.
   3. Trade union report. Cannon, 60 min. Supplementary—Trimble, 20 min.; Widick, 20 min.; Dunne, 20 min. Special viewpoint, Swabeck, 45 min. Discussion, 180 min. (8 min. each). Summary, 20 min.
   4. Unemployment report. Presentation, 20 min.

---

2. The convention agenda proposed by the Convention Arrangements Committee in an internal bulletin was: (1) Opening address; (2) Organization of the convention; (3) Political resolution—reporter: Max Shachtman; (4) Trade union resolution—reporter: J.P. Cannon, supplementary reports: Glen Trimble, B.J. Widick, V.R. Dunne; (5) Unemployed resolution; (6) Russian resolution—reporter: Max Shachtman; (7) Spanish resolution—reporter: Albert Goldman; (8) International resolution—reporter: Maurice Spector; (9) Youth resolution; (10) Declaration of Principles—reporter: James Burnham; (11) Internal situation; (12) Report of Committee on Conflicts and Grievances; (13) Party organization and constitution—reporter: Martin Abern; (14) Party press—reporter: Martin Abern, supplementary report: Robert Browne; (15) Election of National Committee.

Discussion, 60 min. (5 min. each). Summary, 20 min.
5. Russian report. Shachtman 45 min.; Burnham (NC minority), 45 min.; Glee, 20 min. Other viewpoint, 20 min. Discussion, 120 min. (8 min. each). Summaries, 30-30-15-15.
6. Spanish resolution. Goldman, 45 min.; Glee, 20 min. Other viewpoint, 20 min. Discussion, 120 min. (8 min. each). Summaries, 30-15-15.
7. International resolution. Spector, 45 min. Discussion, 60 min. (8 min. each). Summary, 20 min.
8. Declaration of Principles. Burnham, 45 min. Discussion, 90 min. (5 min. each). Summary, 20 min.
9. Internal situation. Cannon, 60 min.; Burnham (NC minority), 60 min. Discussion, 120 min. (8 min. each). Summaries, 30-30.
10. Youth resolution. Reporter, 30 min. Discussion, 60 min. (5 min. each). Summary, 15 min.
11. Party organization and constitution. Abern, 30 min. Discussion, 60 min. (5 min. each). Summary, 15 min.
12. Press. Abern, 20 min. Supplement—Browne, 10 min. Discussion, 60 min. (5 min. each). Summary, 15 min.
13. Conflicts Committee. Report, 45 min. Discussion, 90 min. (5 min. each). Summary, 20 min.
14. Resolutions Committee. Report, 30 min. Discussion, 60 min. (5 min. each). Summary, 15 min.
15. NEC elections.

Motion by Selander (Toledo): Add reporter on Midwest trade union conference, 20 minutes.

Amendment by Goldman (Chicago): That 20 minutes of trade union discussion be assigned for report on Midwest conference. Carried.

Motion to adopt time schedule as recommended. Carried.
6. Session Schedule: Dec. 31 first session, 10 a.m. to 2 p.m.; second session, 2 p.m. to 9 p.m. All other days: first, 10 a.m. to 2 p.m.; second, 3 p.m. to 7 p.m.; third, 8 p.m. to 11 p.m. Motion to adopt. Carried.
7. Convention rules: Robert's Rules of Order with the exception that motions need no seconds and subject to any other modification the convention may decide. Motion to adopt. Carried.
8. Resolutions: All resolutions printed in bulletins are before the convention. New resolutions must go to Resolutions Committee first. Motion to adopt. Carried.
9. Convention committees:
    a. Credentials and Conflicts & Grievances Committee of five. Motion to adopt. Substitute motion by Abern: Divide into two committees. Carried.
    b. Credentials Committee of five.
       Nominations: Saunders (St. Louis) declined, Breitman (New Jersey), Smith (Kansas), Glotzer (Chicago) declined, Ettlinger (New York), Widick (Ohio) declined, Ferguson (Ohio), O'Brien (Salt Lake City). Motion: The five stand. Carried.
    c. Conflicts and Grievances Committee.
       Presiding Committee nominated McCormack (Colorado), Whiteside (Kansas), Dullea (Ohio), Curtiss (Cal.), Cochran (Cleveland), Lear (Ohio). Motion to confirm. Carried.
    d. Resolutions Committee of five.
       Nominations: Swabeck declined, Shachtman, Spector, McCormack (Col.), Trimble (Cal.), Preis (Ohio), Burnham, Pemble (Minn.), Hudson (Minn.), Saunders (St. Louis), Graves, Goldman declined. Motion: Committee of seven stand. Carried.
    e. Convention Arrangements Committee. Elected by

NAC. Abern, Lewit, Wasserman, Bern, and Satir. Motion to confirm. Carried.
f. Constitution Committee of five.
Nominations: Retzkin (N.Y.), Abern, Glee (N.Y.), Burnham declined, Goldman declined, Swabeck declined, Most (Chi.), Ettlinger declined, McKinney declined, Miller declined, Schultz declined, Satir (Chi.), Furth (Cal.). Motion: The committee stand as nominated. Carried.
g. Trade Union Committee of seven.
Nominations: Swabeck, Widick, Trimble, McKinney, Dobbs, Rasmussen, Cochran, Farrell, Mills, Selander declined, Poulos, Dunne declined, Skoglund declined, Revyuk (Chi.), Lear declined, Breitman.
Motion to vote by hand on candidates. Carried.
Motion by Skoglund to reconsider. Carried.
Motion by Skoglund to ballot for candidates.
Motion by Giordano to vote by show of hands. Carried—26 for, 24 against.
On the vote being taken, the first seven as listed in these minutes were elected.
h. Unemployment Committee of seven.
Nominations: Mills (Ind.), Preis (Ohio), Geldman (Minn.), McKinney (N.Y.), Orgon (Minn.), Breitman (N.J.), Kujac (N.Y.), Kuehn (Minn.). Motion eight stand. Carried.
10. Seating arrangements: Delegates at tables, visitors in the rear. Carried. No smoking. Carried.
11. Fraternal delegates. National Action Committee and Convention Arrangements Committee to be seated with voice and no vote. Canadian delegates referred to Credentials Committee. Two representatives of Marxian Labor College to be seated as observers. Motion to concur. Carried.

Greetings to convention
Telegrams of greetings were read from David Sallume, Yellow Springs, Ohio, and from the San Francisco maritime fraction. Received with applause.

Opening address, Goldman.

Credentials Committee, Ettlinger. No report of challenges due to absence of parties involved. Will meet at 2:30 p.m., Room 818, to hear all contests and to take up question of fraternal delegates with Arrangements Committee. Report will then be given. Accepted.

Motion by Most: That resolutions presented to Resolutions Committee be mimeographed for the delegates.

Motion: To refer to Resolutions Committee. Carried.

Political resolution. Reporter: Shachtman, 12:05 to 1:05. Discussion: Most, Lear, Glotzer, Curtiss, Abern, Clarke. Session adjourned for lunch.

SECOND SESSION, DECEMBER 31, 1937

Convention reconvened at 3:30 p.m. Abern in chair.
Political resolution discussion continued. Speakers: Stern, Glee.
Summary, Max Shachtman.
Voting on resolution postponed until after Credentials Committee report. Wasserman for Convention Arrangements Committee announced that on January 2 the session would be held at the Majestic Hotel.

Grievance Committee. Reporter: McCormack. Committee proposed to Becket that they meet and take up his case tonight at 9 p.m. Becket then presented a statement attacking the whole organization in the sharpest terms.

He did not appeal against the decision of the Chicago organization, but threatened to resign unless his case was heard at once. The committee recommends that the case of Becket be heard at 9 p.m. All interested persons to be present. Motion to concur. Carried.

Credentials Committee. Chairman Ettlinger reporting. (Complete list of delegates attached [See page 133].)

Motion by Cannon: To accept report on uncontested delegates. Carried.

Canadian delegates. The committee recommends seating regular delegates as fraternal, minority delegates as observers. Motion to accept. Carried.

YPSL. Regular delegates Draper, Erber, and Gould with voice and vote. Motion to accept. Carried.

Heisler appeal. Motion that he be seated as a regular delegate. Carried.

Newark. Mendelson asked to be seated because he had five votes in Central branch. Committee recommends to reject.

Motion by Shachtman: That the three appeals—Newark, Lower East Side branch (N.Y.), and Upper West Side branch (N.Y.)—be heard now. Carried.

Committee reports:

Lower East Side branch minority contested the seating of one of the delegates from that branch on the grounds that members present but not voting should be considered in the percentage tabulation. On this basis the majority would not have received 67 percent of the vote required for three delegates. The committee rejected the appeal.

Upper West Side (N.Y.) Similar to the Lower East Side with the exception that the view presented by the minority on the Lower East Side case was taken as the basis for the election of delegates in this branch. Majority appealed against the seating of one minority delegate. Committee recommended acceptance of the appeal.

Substitute proposal by Shachtman: That in each of the three cases—Upper West Side, Lower East Side, and Newark—decisions of branch be upheld, which means Lower East Side delegate goes to majority, Upper West Side to minority, Newark minority delegate not seated. Motion carried unanimously.

Motion by Shachtman: That the three contesting delegates be seated as fraternal delegates. Carried.

South Chicago. Committee recommends that pending the decision of the Grievance Committee on the South Side case, the delegates be seated with fraternal status.

Amendment by Swabeck: That the convention accept seating of one delegate from each branch pending report of Grievance Committee. Carried.

Amendment to the amendment by Most: That no delegate of branch no. 2 be seated fraternally or otherwise because branch was organized since convention call. Lost.

Washington, D.C. Left-wing minority in SP branch sent a delegate. Recommend to seat. Carried.

Montana. Motion to seat two delegates. Carried.

Motion: To accept Credentials Committee report as amended. Carried.

Voting on political resolution.
Amendments to political resolution by Stanley:
1. That on page 8, second paragraph following the sentence ending "but will work toward the defeat of the American capitalist class and its war regime by the proletarian revolution," add the words: "that is, the fundamental war position as advanced in the thesis

'War and the Fourth International.'" Lost.
2. That the resolution should contain the same statement as in the Declaration of Principles, page 36, second paragraph, "The ISP will advocate the continuance of the class struggle during the war regardless of the consequences on the capitalist war front." Accepted by the reporter and voted on along with the rest of the resolution.[3]

Amendments by Most:
1. On democratic centralism:
   i) Page 17. Paragraph 1. Change sentence 5 to read: "Democratic centralism is based in the first place upon the common participation of the entire membership in the activity, the initiative, the information, and the control of the party, while adhering to its fundamental program."
   ii) In sentence 6 change "the unimpaired right" to "the absolute equality and unimpaired right."
   iii) In sentence 7 change end of sentence beginning with "upon the basis" to "upon the basis of the regularly adopted program and policies of the party under the direction of a party leadership expressing the will of the party as a whole; and the subordination in action of the minority to the majority, which cannot be interpreted, however, that any group shall be given 'power' in the party."
   iv) Page 18. Par. 1 (beginning "Our conception,") In sentence 1 change "by discussion" to "by equality, common participation, and discussion."
2. On outside radical groups: Page 13, par. 1 (beginning "Not very fruitful . . .") For first sentence substitute:

---

3. This passage was changed slightly in the final draft of the Declaration of Principles, which reads "regardless of the consequences for the outcome of the American military struggle." See page 328.

"The ISP extends an invitation to all unattached radicals, groups of radicals, and members of other parties, who accept its fundamental principles, to join it and loyally assist in the work of building the revolutionary party, with the assurance that they will be accorded full party privileges and rights while the ISP thus holds..."

3. On the war question: Motion that the Resolutions Committee be instructed to bring out a separate resolution on war.

Amendments voted on and defeated.

Amendment by Glotzer: That the incoming Executive Committee organize a permanent war commission as a subcommittee of the EC to plan and direct the antiwar and antimilitarist work of the party, subject to the control and supervision of the EC. Defeated.

Motion by Shachtman: To adopt resolution on political perspectives presented by the NAC with the second amendment by Stanley. Carried 56 to 4.

Statements:

McCormack voted against the resolution due to its attitude on Russian and war questions.

Most voted against on account of attitude on democratic centralism.

Glee voted against because of its inadequacy on war.

Zimmerman of Kentucky voted against on account of attitude on democratic centralism.

Heisler not voting. Was unable to hear discussion.

Motion for 5-minute recess. Carried.

Convention called to order 6:20 p.m. Chairman: Abern.

Trade union resolution. Reporter: James P. Cannon, 45 minutes. Supplementary: on Pacific Coast, Trimble; on rubber, Widick.

Motion to adjourn. Carried.

FIRST SESSION, JANUARY 1, 1938

Session opened at 10:45 a.m. with Trimble in chair.

Trade union report continued.
Supplementary report on Minneapolis: Dunne, 20 minutes.
Special viewpoint: Swabeck, 45 minutes.
Discussion: Poulos (Lynn), Carson (Boston), Farrell (N.Y.), Clarke (Detroit).
Motion to adjourn. Carried.

SECOND SESSION, JANUARY 1, 1938

Session opened at 2:03 p.m.

Grievance Committee. McCormack reported on Becket case. Submitted the following recommendation: The Grievance Committee, having convened in two sessions totaling three and one half hours and having heard representatives from both sides of the Becket case, has the following statement and recommendations to make to the convention:

Becket, in presenting a political line contrary to ours at open meetings of the party, in attacking party comrades at open meetings, in maintaining relations with members of the Oehler group, in conducting party polemics in an uncomradely and provocative fashion, has revealed himself as one who does not feel himself an integral part of our organization, but rather as a representative of an opponent organization, who seeks the floor of the convention to disseminate his views.

This estimation of the character of Becket was confirmed to the hilt by the amazing conduct of Becket at the committee hearings, where he conducted himself in an ultimatistic fashion. Becket, who has previously made no appeal to the convention, suddenly appeared at noon Friday with a demand for an immediate hearing on his case. When the committee proposed nine o'clock, at which time a full review of the case could be held, Becket stigmatized this as a symptomatic act which confirmed the nature of the party as a representative of the bourgeoisie. Despite the anti-working-class nature of the party, however, Becket appeared at the appointed time. He refused to appeal his expulsion, stating that the major issue was his right, as the only revolutionary tendency in a party which pretends to be revolutionary, to appear on the floor of the convention to present his views. Upon questioning, Becket refused to affirm or deny his willingness to go along with the decisions of this convention.

All of these actions, the committee feels, are not those of a comrade working seriously, loyally, and in a disciplined fashion for the dissemination of his views within our ranks, but those of a member of an opponent group seeking to make a demonstration at the convention.

For these reasons, therefore, the Grievance Committee unanimously decided to sustain the action of the Chicago organization.

The sole serious charge against the action of the Chicago comrades is that with the exception of charges contained in a letter from the NAC formal, written charges were not preferred against Becket. This argument the committee did not hold to be very ponderable for the following reasons: (1) That there is every reason to believe that written charges were preferred, if not in a legalistic sense at the hearings which culminated in the expulsion of Becket, then in the hearings which had preceded the final one; (2) That a legal technicality has been blown up to obscure the real content of the case; and (3) That the entire Chicago organization sustained the action, which, being on the scene, is best able to appreciate the role of Becket.

The committee is sensible of the fact that now, as never before, vigilance must be exercised in preserving the utmost democracy in our party. We do not construe this, however, to mean the demagogic exploitation of a technicality to obscure the real issues of a case, at the expense of a large and serious group of comrades.

We think that the Chicago organization was somewhat remiss in the method of conducting the charges against Becket. In the future, throughout the party generally, scrupulous attention should be given to every aspect, not only of the actual content of the charge but formal conduct of such proceedings to insure to the limit the rights of every comrade involved.

In this light, therefore, comrade chairman, the committee presents this statement and the two following motions to the convention:

(1) That the convention concur in the action of the Chicago organization in expelling Becket; and

(2) That the incoming NAC be instructed to inform the membership of the circumstances surrounding the action of the convention.

Discussion: Most, Pemble, Lear, Satir, McCormack, McKinney, Cannon.

Motion by Cannon:
A. Censure the Chicago City Executive on two grounds:
(1) Failure to observe the strict formality of presenting Comrade Becket with written charges in advance

of his trial; (2) Refusal to accept the recommendations of the NAC to reconsider its actions and refer the whole matter to the convention.
B. The convention hands this case back to the City Executive Committee with instructions to conduct a proper trial of Comrade Becket and take action in accordance with the facts established.

Vote on the Cannon substitute: 49 for, 1 against.

Heisler abstains: "because the majority was misled by the letter from the NAC."

Comrade Cannon on special privilege replied to Heisler by reading the letter referred to.

Credentials Committee. Ettlinger, reported at this time 74 delegates, 36 alternates, and 18 fraternal.

Trade union discussion continued. Cochran reporting on Ohio trade union conference.

Ricco (California).

(At this time, during Ricco's talk, Comrade Becket, who was now eligible to attend the convention on the basis of the motion previously passed, entered the hall and immediately demanded the floor. The chairman ruled him out of order on the grounds that (1) Ricco had the floor; and that (2) Becket was not a delegate.)

Motion by Heisler: That we reconsider our rules on this point and give Becket the floor. Motion lost.

Becket announced that he was withdrawing from the organization and left the hall.

Trade union discussion continued. Ricco concluded, Browner, Ettlinger, Furth, Brown.

Motion by Cannon: That Most, the last speaker on the list, be given the floor, and then the discussion be closed. Carried.

Report of Trade Union Commission by Dobbs (Attached [Page 139]).
Summary by Cannon, 30 min.
Motion: To accept the resolution of the NAC with the recommendations of the Trade Union Commission. Motion carried unanimously.
Amendments by Most: Page 38, before paragraph beginning at bottom of page ("Precisely because . . .") insert the following two paragraphs:

The development of rank-and-file initiative on the part of party members working in the trade unions is essential for the effectiveness of their work, as well as for party welfare generally. Our main trade union emphasis must be directed toward the union ranks through direct contact with them by party members in the unions. Revolutionists can only combat the bureaucratic measures of a reactionary union leadership or maintain their revolutionary policies when they themselves are in the leadership, by organized rank-and-file backing, developed from below by party union workers.

It is necessary to guard against party members in the unions waiting upon the personal advice of a few leaders for their actions. Rank-and-file initiative must be developed through fraction and party discussion, along guiding lines set down by general directives, which it is the duty of the leading bodies to issue. The party must avoid the error of underemphasizing the arenas of union activity in which leading members do not happen to be engaged.

Both amendments defeated.
Amendments by Trimble:
1. Eliminate second sentence in last paragraph on page

36 (characterizing IWW). Lost.
2. Eliminate last sentence in the above-mentioned paragraph. Carried.
3. In first two lines of the first paragraph of page 31, replace "exist neither" with "are at a minimum," change "nor" to "and," insert between "the" and "leadership" the three words "bulk of the." Carried.

Motion for a 10-minute recess. Carried.
Session resumed 5:50 p.m. Trimble in chair.

Unemployed Commission. Reporter: Art Preis (Attached [page 135]). Commission recommends that the report be referred to the National Committee as the basis for a final resolution on unemployed work.
Discussion: Kujac, McCormack, McKinney, P. Rasmussen, Burnham, Dobbs, Glee, Selander, Sherman, Heisler.
Summary, Preis.
Motion: To adopt recommendation of Unemployed Commission. Carried.
Session adjourned.

THIRD SESSION, JANUARY 1, 1938

Convention opened at 9 p.m. Trimble in chair.
Comrade Burnham for the Presiding Committee proposed that due to the fact that programmatic questions dealt with in the Declaration of Principles are covered in other resolutions, therefore the Declaration of Principles and amendments to it should be referred to the Resolutions Committee. Motion to concur. Carried.
Telegram from Comrade C. Claston Tennem of Rochester, N.Y., greeting the convention, regretting hospitalization made it impossible for him to attend. Wishes

to be recorded in favor of all advance resolutions of Arrangements Committee except internal. Favors Burnham-Carter internal resolution.

Russian resolution. Reporter: Shachtman, 45 min.
NC Minority: Burnham, 45 min.
Motion for 5-minute recess. Lost.

Russian resolution reports continued.
Glee for Glee group, 20 min.
Motion by McCormack to extend Glee's time for 20 minutes.
Amendment for 5 minutes. Carried.
Motion to extend time for adjournment to 12:30. Carried.
Russian discussion: Abern for majority, Mendelson for minority, Stirling (Ill.)—majority, Retzkin—minority, McCormack, Glee, Wright—majority, Carter—minority.
Session adjourned at 12:30 a.m.

FIRST SESSION, JANUARY 2, 1938

Session called to order at 11 a.m. McKinney in the chair.

Grievance Committee. McCormack: Unable as yet to take up Most case, and therefore proposed all contested delegates from South Side branches be seated pending report of Grievance Committee.
Chairman ruled previous decision of convention covering South Side delegates stands pending final report of Grievance Committee.

Russian resolution discussion continued.
Heisler—minority, Goldman—majority, Brooks (N.Y.)—minority, Dobbs—majority, Trimble—majority, Giordano (N.J.)—majority, Glotzer—majority, Draper, YPSL—majority.

Chair announces time for discussion exhausted.

Motion by Ettlinger to continue discussion until list is exhausted.

Amendment by Stern: To extend discussion for 30 minutes, removing superfluous N.Y. comrades who now make it one hour. Lost.

Chairman rules that questions from floor should be written and handed in to reporters.

Summaries on Russian question: Glee, 15 minutes; Burnham, 30 minutes; Shachtman, 30 minutes.

Motion to extend Shachtman's time 10 minutes. Carried.

Burnham proposed that the vote for his position on the Russian resolution be taken on the basis of a counterresolution consisting of the Russian resolution as amended by the Burnham-Carter amendment.

Chairman rules accordingly.

Amendment by Heisler to the Burnham resolution: (Insert in par. 20 at the end of first subparagraph [Page 234].)

> The temporary conflict which existed in the USSR between the economy and the state, has—in principle—been resolved against the workers' state. The conflict was resolved by means of the counterrevolution carried forward by the bureaucracy, accomplished in principle and essentially in accordance with the nature of all counterrevolutions, but in a form hitherto not thought of.
>
> A new form of the counterrevolution was made possible because of the progressive degeneration of the Soviet state brought about by bureaucracy which in its dual role as the protector of the state and the destroyer of the Soviet economy, did take to the road of counterrevolution. The bureaucracy being in control

of the state and its machinery (i.e., the large number of functionaries, the GPU, the judiciary, and the army) could and did accomplish the counterrevolution against the Soviet economy by the oppressive means of the Soviet state.

This new, bureaucratic form of counterrevolution differs from a counterrevolution as it would be conducted by the bourgeoisie from without, in those particulars which follow from basic difference in the position occupied by the two possible counterrevolutionary groups. Counterrevolutionaries from without (bourgeoisie) must resort to force throughout, to obtain the control of the machinery of the state. Counterrevolutionaries from within (bureaucracy) need no resorting to force to get control of the state machinery, since it is in control of it already, having obtained it originally as the representatives of the working class. The bureaucracy could and did accomplish the counterrevolution by means of the state's machinery, whose machinery during the existence of the workers' state was the protector of the socialized economy.

A consideration of the two forms of counterrevolution, i.e., the form of a counterrevolution from without (overthrow of the Paris Commune in 1871, of the Hungarian soviets in 1919) and the form of the counterrevolution from within (accomplished by the bureaucracy of the USSR) is of vital importance to understand the role and character of the present Russian state.

It is of no less importance to consider whether or not the counterrevolution has been accomplished wholly or in part only. Such consideration will determine the conclusion to be arrived at with reference to our proletarian duty towards the defense of Russia. While the workers' state has been—programmatically and essentially—destroyed by the internal and external policy of the bureaucracy, a formal and juridical restoration of the bourgeois state did not as yet take place. A formal restoration of the bourgeois state is consciously avoided by the bureaucracy precisely because of its counterrevolutionary purpose. The bureaucracy desires to maintain amongst the proletariat a false ideological conception concerning the role of the bureaucracy and the character of the Russian state. One of the methods by which such a false conception is maintained, the bureaucracy is forced to carry on an apparent and sometimes virtually progressive role. Such an apparent and, in part, progressive role stands in the way, at the present, of the reestablishment of the formal bourgeois state and is responsible for the unstable appearance of the Russian state.

(Here follows the paragraph beginning: "However, in this temporary and extremely unstable form of the state . . .")

Burnham rejects Heisler amendment without commenting on content: he considers it unnecessary.

Motion by Carter: That a consultative vote of fraternal delegates be taken. Carried.

Motion by Shachtman: That a roll-call vote be taken. Carried.

Vote: majority 66, minority 3, Glee 2, Heisler 1, abstaining 1, absent 3. Fraternal delegates consultative vote: majority 18, minority 4, abstentions 2.

Comrades Kohler and Cannon, who were absent at time of vote, recorded their votes in favor of majority as fraternal delegates. Comrades Trbovich (Ind.) and J. Roberts (Wash.), regular delegates, recorded their votes for majority. Comrade Hildegarde Smith, who had abstained on the vote, recorded her vote for the majority.

ROLL CALL VOTE ON RUSSIAN QUESTION

State	Delegate	Maj	Min	Glee	Others	Abst
California						
Fresno	Al Furth	X				
L.A.	Charles Curtiss	X				
	Harry Fishler					
	(proxy)	X				
San Diego	Frank Ricco	Absent				
San Fran.	Glen Trimble	X				
	Flo Wyle	X				
Colorado						
Denver	Paul McCormack			X		
Member-at large	Hilde. Smith (proxy)	X				
Illinois						
Chicago	Casano	X				
	Heisler				Heis.	
	Herman (alt.)	X				
	Most	X				
	J. Stirling	X				
Indiana						
E. Chicago	Manuel Trbovich	X				
Indianapolis	Cecil Allen (Birchman)	X				
Kansas	G. Whiteside		X			
Kentucky						
Louisville	P. Zimmerman	X				
Massachusetts						
Boston Cent.	Dan Carson	X				
	John Taber	X				
Lynn	John Poulos	X				
Michigan						
Detroit	George Clarke	X				

State	Delegate	Maj	Min	Glee	Others	Abst
Minnesota						
Austin	Julius Shade	X				
Minneapolis	O. Coover	X				
	F. Dobbs	X				
	V. Dunne	X				
	Clem Forsen	X				
	M. Geldman	X				
	Arthur Hopkins	X				
	Carlos Hudson	X				
	Roy Orgon	X				
	C. Skoglund (Tibbets)	X				
Olivia	J. Enestvedt	X				
St. Paul	Grace Carlson	X				
	Theodore Dostal	X				
Missouri						
Joplin	Al Hargis	X				
Kansas City	Daniel Noyes	X				
St. Louis	R.S. Saunders	X				
St. Louis County	Sam Hill	X				
Montana						
Billings	R.M. Hansen	X				
	Rodney Salisbury	X				
Plentywood	John Boulds	X				
New Jersey						
Newark	George Breitman	X				
	Felix Giordano	X				
	Jack Weber (Katz)	X				

State	Delegate	Maj	Min	Glee	Others	Abst
New York						
Astoria	Retzkin		X			
Boro Pk.	Sam Gordon	X				
Brownsv.	Sam Friedman	X				
Chelsea	Bill Farrell	X				
E. Side	R. Browne	X				
	J. Kujac	X				
	J. Wright	X				
L.E. Bronx	B. Morgenstern	X				
L.E. Side	Abe Miller	X				
U.E. Bronx	Max Sterling (proxy)	X				
U.W. Side	G. Brooks		X			
	Lyman Paine	X				
Village	Dick Ettlinger	X				
Wash. Hts.	S. Stanley	X				
W. Bronx	Fred Browner	X				
Williamsburg	Herman Stern	X				
Minority	M. Glee				X	
Ohio						
Akron	Blake Lear	X				
	B.J. Widick	X				
Cleveland	Bert Cochran	X				
Toledo	Arthur Preis	X				
Youngstown	Les Reid	X				
Pennsylvania						
Allentown	Walter Huhn	X				
Philadelphia	Carl Hartman	X				
	Max Shachtman (proxy)	X				
Quakertown	Howard Stump	X				
Sellerville	L. Shoemaker	X				
Utah						
Salt Lake	O'Brien	X				

State	Delegate	Maj	Min	Glee	Others	Abst
Washington, D.C.						
	J. Roberts	X				
YPSL NEC	H. Draper	X				
	Ernest Erber	X				
	N. Gould	X				
TOTALS[4]		69	3	2	1	0

FRATERNAL DELEGATES

Name	Locality	Maj	Min	Glee	Others	Abst
M. Abern	New York	X				
Black	Toronto	X				
Brown	Toronto	X				
J. Burnham	New York		X			
J.P. Cannon	New York	X				
Joe Carter	New York		X			
Drake	New York	X				
Dullea	Cleveland	X				
Garrett	New York		X			
A. Glotzer	Chicago	X				
A. Goldman	Chicago	X				
Graves	New York	X				
Lester Kohler	Minneapolis	X				
M. Lewit	New York	X				
E. McKinney	New York	X				
Mendelson	Newark			X		
Harry Milton	New York	X				
Carl Pemble	St. Paul					X
H. Rasmussen	Indianapolis	X				

---

4. The totals here do not correspond exactly with those announced as soon as the roll call was taken because afterwards some delegates who had been out of the convention hall were allowed to register their vote and at least one changed her vote.

Name	Locality	Maj	Min	Glee	Others	Abst
Ted Selander	Toledo	X				
Bill Sherman	New York	X				
Spector	New York	X				
A. Swabeck	Chicago	X				
Wasserman	New York	X				
Total Fraternal vote		19	4	0	0	1

Session adjourned.

SECOND SESSION, JANUARY 2, 1938

Session called to order 3:40 p.m. McKinney in chair.

Spanish Resolution. Reporters: Goldman, 45 min.; Glee, 20 min.

Grievance Committee. Cochran reporting findings on conflict over division of South Side branch as follows:
1. Find the Chicago Executive within its rights in reorganizing the branch.
2. The Chicago Executive divided the branch without consulting the officers of the branch or its general membership. The committee condemns this procedure as bureaucratic.
3. The Chicago Executive kept the South Side branch and the Most group ignorant of the recommendations of the NAC. We condemn this as bureaucratic.
4. Delegates: (a) the committee finds that the Most group is entitled to two delegates and recommends the seating of these delegates; (b) that the comrade seated temporarily as a delegate from the number 2 South Side branch be seated as a fraternal delegate.
5. The committee recommends that the Chicago Executive Committee call all members involved to a meeting

to discuss the whole matter and arrive at a solution that would be in the best interests of the party.

The above decisions were unanimously adopted by the Grievance Committee.

Comrade McKinney proposed that the discussion be postponed until the delegates now absent at committee meetings be present.

Motion by Cochran: To proceed with discussion on grievance report. Carried.

Discussion: Goldman.

Motion by Morgenstern for 5-minute time limit. Carried.

Amendment by Swabeck for a 10-minute time limit. Lost.

Motion by Most that two speakers, one from each side in the controversy, be given the floor.

Amendment by Browne (N.Y.) that these be the only two speakers. Carried.

Comrade Dullea for committee explained one or two points of the report.

Heisler asked floor on personal privilege.

Chair recognizes Swabeck for the Chicago Executive Committee in opposition to the Grievance Committee report.

Comrade Most spoke for the South Side branch no. 1 side of the case.

Motion by Preis to reconsider the question of the limitation of speakers. Carried.

Motion by Morgenstern for a 3-minute limit on speakers. Carried.

Motion by Gordon that total time for discussion be 15 minutes.

Discussion continued. Ettlinger, Heisler, Pemble, Stanley, Preis, Zimmerman.

Motion by Retzkin: That we substitute for points two and three of committee report the following: that it is the sense of the convention that the Chicago Executive Committee acted wrongly in not observing the strict formalities of democratic procedure in dividing the South Side branch.

Cochran summed up for the Grievance Committee.

Voting on Grievance Committee report:

Retzkin amendment: Lost—21 for, 25 against.

Report of Grievance Committee: point 5 carried unanimously; point 4, section (b) carried with 1 against; point 4, section (a) carried—32 to 13; point 3 carried—22 for, 20 against; point 2 carried—35 for, 17 against; point 1 carried—57 for, none against.

Motion by Cochran that we adjourn session for supper. Carried.

THIRD SESSION, JANUARY 2, 1938

Session called to order 8:05 p.m. McKinney in chair.

Spanish resolution discussion.

Motion by Stanley: Six speakers 5 minutes each, and summaries. Carried.

Speakers: Heisler, McCormack, Carson, Giordano, Miller.

Summaries: Glee 15 min.; Goldman 30 min.

Motion: To adopt Spanish resolution of the NAC. 56 for, 4 abstaining.

Amendment by Giordano: On page 81, line 12, insert: "in practice this means that wherever possible we try to direct all support of the antifascist struggle into the channels of the proletarian mass organizations in Spain (UGT, CNT) in preference to direct support to the Loyalist government." Amendment lost.

Amendment by Carson: Insert between paragraphs 17 and

18: "while as revolutionists we do not stand in the way of material aid to the Loyalist government so long as its role is progressive, neither do we independently undertake in the United States to raise such aid in the immediate period. Nevertheless, units of the party may make united fronts with other organizations to raise material aid for the Loyalists, provided that such united fronts afford us opportunities we should not otherwise have for putting our position on Spain fully and effectively before significant numbers of workers. In labor and fraternal organizations we support material aid to the People's Front government only as a last choice, and then only when it is inexpedient or impossible to win support for the Bolshevik-Leninists or for the oppressed Spanish workers." Lost.

McCormack stated he would abstain on the resolution but asked the reporter to include in paragraph 12, page 79, third line between "allies" and "for" the following: "poorer section of peasantry." Goldman rejected the proposal.

Motion by Glee: That the convention instruct the NEC to start a united-front campaign to aid the antifascist forces being persecuted by the Stalinists and government forces in Spain. Referred to the NEC.

Presiding Committee recommends adjustment of agenda: press report to be taken up now. Motion to concur. Carried.

Press report. Abern, 20 minutes; Browne, 10 minutes.
Discussion: Most.
Motion by Most to approve the resolution on the press in the January 1938 issue of *Left Wing Correspondence* (no. 5).
Discussion continued: Wasserman, Sherman, Heisler.

McKinney reporting for the Presiding Committee: The majority and minority have reached an agreement on the resolution on the character of the party and the internal situation. A united NAC internal resolution will be presented to the convention. This will enable us to cut down on the time allotted for presentation and discussion on internal question. Some delegates are forced to leave in order to return to their jobs, therefore the Presiding Committee proposes: (1) To terminate the press discussion now; (2) Adjourn for one hour to give delegations an opportunity to discuss composition of new NEC; (3) Immediately thereafter take up the election of the NEC.

Discussion: Wasserman in opposition to the proposals. Favors completion of the discussion on the press. Dunne for the proposal. Most against.

Motion by Birchman (Ind.): To accept the proposals of the Presiding Committee. Carried.

Session adjourned for one hour.

Session resumed. McKinney in chair.

Chairman appealed for funds. Collection taken.

Dobbs for Presiding Committee proposed:
1. An NEC of 25, 24 to be elected by the convention and one representative of the YPSL. Ten alternates. Motion to concur. Carried.
2. Plenary sessions of the National Committee to be held quarterly in important centers of country. Carried.
3. Political Committee to be subject to change at each plenum by National Committee. Carried.

Speaking for the Minneapolis, Ohio, California, and Michigan delegations, Comrade Dobbs nominated a slate of candidates. This slate had already been taken up with various other delegations separately.

NEC: Abern, Bardacke, Burnham, Cannon, Carter, Clarke, Cochran, Dobbs, Dullea, Dunne, Goldman, Kerry, Lewit, McKinney, Morrow, Rosenberg, Saunders, Shachtman,

Skoglund, Spector, Swabeck, Trimble, Weber, Widick, youth (YPSL).

Alternates in the following order: Glotzer, Farrell, Stevens, Erber, Curtiss, Sherman, Selander, Milton, McCormack, Turner.[5]

Nominations from the floor. For National Committee: Most, Wright (declined), Pemble (declined), Glotzer. For Alternates: Allen (Ind.).

Discussion on NEC and method of nominations: Retzkin, Ettlinger.

Motion by Stern: 3-minute time limit. Carried.

Discussion: Dunne, Wright, Kujac, Miller, Morgenstern, Mendelson, Preis, Birchman, Stern.

Summary: Dobbs.

Motion by Skoglund: To vote by ballot. Carried.

Chair appointed Ettlinger, Saunders, and Secretary Sherman as tellers.

Secretary announced the vote as follows: Abern 64, Bardacke 63, Burnham 65, Cannon 65, Carter 61, Clarke 63, Cochran 61, Dobbs 62, Dullea 63, Dunne 63, Goldman 64, Kerry 60, Lewit 59, McKinney 64, Morrow 59, Rosenberg 60, Saunders 63, Shachtman 64, Skoglund 61, Spector 62, Swabeck 61, Trimble 62, Weber 62, Widick 61, Glotzer 4, Most 4, Selander 1, Shoenberg 2 (no such name nominated; an error might have been made on Rosenberg's name—Sherman, Secy.).

The first 24 were declared elected. Alternates: Glotzer 44, Farrell 46, Stevens 45, Erber 44, Curtiss 45, Sherman 43, Selander 44, Milton 44, McCormack 41, Turner 45, Allen 4, Wright 1.

Session adjourned.

---

5. Stevens was the pseudonym of Esther Lieberman of New York City, Turner that of Larry Trainor of Boston.

FIRST SESSION, JANUARY 3, 1938

Session opened at 11:30 a.m. Trimble in the chair.

Comrade Abern for Presiding Committee proposed to close discussion on press report and refer the report to the NEC for further decisions on the basis of recommendations made in report and discussion. Motion to approve. Carried.

International report: Spector, 45 minutes.

International resolution and resolution on practical work read by Spector.

Amendment by Most: That in paragraph 3 of the international resolution we replace "to set up a half-way house between the Second and Third Internationals" with "to set up a centrist international realignment."

Discussion continued: Heisler, Widick, Preis, Browner, McCormack.

Spector in summary accepts amendment of Most with provision that it be extended to cover more completely the general idea contained.

Motion to adopt the international resolution as amended. Carried.

Internal resolution

Presiding Committee proposes in view of the fact that the minority resolution had been withdrawn, Comrade Cannon will restrict his presentation to 20 minutes with 10 minutes each for other groups. Motion to concur. Carried.

Shachtman takes over the chair from Trimble.

Chairman of the Resolutions Committee reported that a resolution on the internal situation had been handed in by Comrade Glee. The committee recommended that Comrade Glee be allowed to represent his resolution if he so saw fit.

Internal report by Cannon:
1. Changes in resolution. The NAC had agreed on the following changes in the internal resolution: (a) Delete the last sentence, first paragraph on page 5 [264]: "In this sense the program itself automatically delimits and excludes from the party all elements hostile to the party and its basic conceptions." (b) In the last two lines of the next-to-last paragraph replace the words "dilettantes, do-nothings, phrase-mongers, triflers, and windbags" with "irresponsible elements."
2. The minority resolution is withdrawn.
3. A separate motion is introduced as follows: "Positions taken in the preconvention discussion which have not been specifically prohibited by the convention cannot be prohibited by the subsequent decisions of the National Committee or any subordinate party unit without specific decision of the party membership recorded by referendum vote or by another convention."

Carter, 10 minutes.

Comrade Shachtman presented a statement on the censure of the Chicago Executive Committee in the name of Cannon-Shachtman:

> We wish to make it clear that our vote for the censure of the Chicago Executive Committee in no sense implies a declaration that a subordinate body is bound in discipline to carry through automatically a recommendation of a superior body as if it were an instruction. Nor does our vote imply any questioning of the loyalty and motives of the leadership of the Chicago organization, or a condonement of the disloyalty of

Becket or the irresponsible acts of Comrade Most. Our vote was cast solely for the purpose of calling the attention of the Chicago committee to the imperativeness of the most scrupulous regard for democratic procedure, especially towards critical minorities and irrespective of provocation. We urge the convention to associate itself with this statement in order to eliminate to the last degree all misunderstanding and unnecessary friction.

Most, 10 minutes.
Motion by Most: That statement on democratic centralism in *Left Wing Correspondence* no. 4, be added as a supplement to the internal resolution:

Democratic centralism, the synthesis of centralism and workers' democracy, in its true Leninist sense, is based wholly and unexceptionally on a community of ceaseless activity and initiative common to the whole of the party. It is a democracy of action, centralized only in the sense that that action must be collective.

In the centrist and reformist working-class parties, reflecting the organization of capitalist society, this community of action, which is the prime characteristic of workers' democracy, is replaced by a centralization of activity and initiative in the hands of the party functionaries, while the membership is either passive or in the position of subordinates carrying out instructions.

Democratic centralism means the overcoming of this dualism and this differentiation between the leaders and the ranks. It is the application of the methods naturally adopted by the masses in the social revolution, to the party which is the advance representative of that revolution.

In this way the experiences of the rank and file in their daily contact with the masses are freely transmitted to the party organization, assuring the greatest adaptation to conditions.

Following the collapse of the original principles of the Communist International, there has been an almost universal corruption of the true meaning of democratic centralism, taking it to mean a body of administrative forms and methods for the direction of the revolutionary party.

Such formalism is completely contrary to democratic centralism. Formal democracy or centralism, as long as there is a dualism of activity and initiative in the organization of the party, can only mean either anarchism or bureaucratism internally, and either centrist tail-endism or sectarian isolation externally. Democratic centralism is not an administrative form but a condition of completely mutual relations between the leadership, the party, and the masses, each of the former giving guidance to, but at the same time drawing its inspiration from, the broader group; a twofold relationship which is possible only through activism and enterprise, pervading the party as a whole.

Glee made oral statement on the internal situation. Burnham given floor on special point (Stalinist frame-ups). Internal discussion continued: Ettlinger, Preis, Goldman. Motion to limit discussion to 3 minutes. Carried. Session adjourned.

SECOND SESSION, JANUARY 3, 1938

Session called to order at 3:00 p.m. Shachtman in chair.

Internal discussion continued: Carson, Revyuk, Zimmerman. Presiding Committee proposed summaries as follows:

Most 5 min., Carter 5 min., Cannon 10 min. Motion to concur. Carried.

Summaries: Most; Carter; Cannon.

Motion to accept the internal resolution as amended. Carried.

Amendment by Martin. That in order to provide real internal democracy an internal bulletin be issued regularly. Lost.

Saunders for the Resolutions Committee: Recommends that Most's supplementary resolutions on democratic centralism be submitted to the NEC for favorable study and consideration. Most records his vote in favor of the adoption of the above resolution by the convention.

Motion by Hill: To concur in the Cannon-Shachtman statement on the censure of the Chicago Executive Committee in Most and Becket cases. Carried.

Most: Oral statement on the Cannon-Shachtman statement demanded the exclusion of the section branding Most as irresponsible.

Shachtman in the chair ruled that reference to Most included in the Cannon-Shachtman statement was a personal opinion with which anybody was free to associate himself or not, and that no action taken by the Chicago organization or any other body in connection with Comrade Most could be taken retroactively.

Resolutions Committee: Comrade Graves moved adoption of the colonial resolution ["The Present War in the Far East and the Tasks of the Party," page 275].

Motion by Abern: To refer to the NEC for final action and to issue it in the name of the convention. Carried.

Motion for 10-minute recess. Lost.

Motion by Most: That the NEC appoint a subcommittee to

investigate allegations of Cannon-Shachtman statement in reference to Most. Lost.
Statement by Pemble. (Attached [page 151].)
Statement by Most. (Attached [page 151–52].)
Statement by Revyuk, alternate, South Side branch, and Zimmerman, delegate, Louisville. (Attached [page 153].)

Constitution.
Name of party. Proposal: International Socialist Party, Socialist Workers Party, Workers Party, Independent Socialist Party, International Workers Party.
Motion that only one comrade speak for each name. Time for each speaker 3 minutes. Carried.
Speakers: Shachtman ISP, Trimble SWP, Sherman WP, Glee Ind. SP, Abern IWP.
Voting: IWP-9, WP-0, Ind. SP-1, Int. SP-19, SWP-34.
Final vote: SWP-41, ISP-25.
Abern recorded as voting against SWP.
The proposed constitution was read and adopted with the following amendments:
Article II—Purpose amended: Change last part following "abolition of capitalism" to read "and the establishment of a workers' government to achieve socialism."
Article III—Emblem, left to NEC.[6]
Article VII, section 3—NC of 24 members, alternates 10.
Article VIII—YPSL, section 4 to be taken up by the NC with the NC of the YPSL for final wording.[7]

---

6. This article, proposing that the new party have an emblem of an unspecified character, was deleted when it was referred to the incoming National Committee. This deletion affected the numbers assigned to subsequent articles.

7. The proposed draft of this article, which called the YPSL "the youth organization of the party," said: "Members of the YPSL over the age of twenty, who have been members of the YPSL for six months, must

Article IX, section 2—Eliminate "minimum" from first line.

Article X—Discipline, section 3, change to read as follows: "Charges against any member shall be made in writing, and the accused member shall be furnished with a copy in advance of trial. Charges shall be filed and heard in the branch to which the member belongs. Where the member is also a member of any higher body charges may be filed either in the branch or in any body of which he is a member. Charges filed before the branch shall be considered by the branch executive committee (or a subcommittee elected by it) at a meeting to which the accused member is summoned. The branch executive committee shall submit a recommendation to be acted upon by the members of the branch. Charges considered by higher bodies of the party shall however be acted upon by the said bodies."

Article XII—National Conventions. Convention shall be held once a year. The NC may by a two-thirds vote postpone the national convention for not more than six months provided that a notice of such postponement be given not later than one month before the time for the convention call. Such action may be nullified on the demand of branches representing at least one-third of the membership.

Article XII, section 2—Internal bulletin shall be issued during convention discussion period.

Article XIII deleted.[8]

---

apply for membership in the party." After consultation between the two national committees the age for mandatory application for SWP members was changed from twenty to twenty-one.

8. The proposed Article XIII—Leagues—read as follows:
"*Section 1.* Members of the party in trade unions and other nonparty

Amendment by Retzkin: Article XII, section 3—add the following: At least one month prior to the convention call notice be given to members of coming convention call. Lost.

Motion: Branches organized after convention call shall have fraternal representation. Carried.

Comrade Shachtman for the Presiding Committee proposed that alternates be listed in order as follows: Glotzer, Farrell, Stevens, Erber, Curtiss, Sherman, Selander, Milton, McCormack, Turner. Motion to concur. Carried.

Resolutions Committee. Saunders reporting: Declaration of Principles, page 36, paragraph 2 [page 328]: eliminate "on the capitalist war front," replace with "for the outcome of the American military struggle." Motion to concur. Carried.

Motion by Glee: Substitute "regardless of the war front of America or its allies." Lost.

Motion: Add to follow the paragraph at the bottom of

---

organizations and institutions shall organize themselves into leagues for common work within such organizations.

"*Section 2.* The work of a league within a given mass organization shall be under the direction and control of the party body having jurisdiction over the party members constituting the league. The members of a league must work as a unit under all circumstances. Violations of league discipline shall be reported to the proper organization of the party for action."

Leagues was the word used in the SP in 1937 to denote what the WP and the communist movement generally called *fractions*. Deletion of the article reflected dissatisfaction with the SP term; the practice of disciplined coordination of party members' work in the unions and other organizations was not in question. A few minutes later in the convention the Resolutions Committee introduced a resolution apparently endorsing the principle of trade union work contained in the already deleted Article XIII, and the convention adopted this. But the term *fraction* became and remained standard in the SWP.

page 36 [page 329]: "the practical steps which our party will take in the course of its opposition to such a war will be decided in light of the consideration of the need of facilitating the utmost aid to the Soviet Union's armed forces against an imperialist power in conformity with our position of defense of the Soviet Union from imperialist assault." Carried.

Motion: Refer last two sentences, paragraph 2, page 15 to the NEC for rewording. Carried.[9]

Motion: That revisions of the Declaration of Principles of an editorial and literary character be made by the NC on condition that the line not be altered. All amendments of this character be submitted to the NEC. Carried.

Statement of Stern: Had twenty amendments to submit to the NEC and not all of a literary character. Shortness of time made it impossible to present them to the convention.

Glee: Is in conflict with the Declaration of Principle on a number of points.

Resolutions Committee continued.

Moved vote of thanks to Jac Wasserman and Lillian Reynolds for their work on technical arrangements for the convention. Carried.

Propose that the convention send a telegram of greetings to Leon Trotsky. Carried.

---

9. These two sentences were not changed in the published document: "They [the principles of the revolutionary party] have been concretized in the basic documents of the first four congresses of the Communist International and the fundamental programmatic documents put forward by the Movement for the Fourth International in the past fourteen years. The SWP stands upon the main line of principle developed in these documents." See page 305.

That the letter of the League for a Revolutionary Workers Party be referred to the NEC with instructions to deal with it in accordance to the reference to such groups in our political resolution. Carried.

Motion to reconsider the question of the name of the party. Lost.

Motion to send greetings to Paula Aragon, Ed Parker, and Tom Mooney. Carried.

Resolution by Stern on antiwar campaign is embodied in Far East resolution.

Resolutions on agriculture, by Salisbury and St. Louis, referred to the NEC with recommendation for a survey of the agricultural situation.

Resolutions on the *Socialist Appeal*, by (1) St. Louis; and (2) Most, reported favorably by the committee. Motion to adopt. Carried.

Resolution by Chelsea branch on name referred to Constitution Committee.

Resolution by Chelsea branch on war dealt with in Declaration of Principles.

Resolution by Trimble on setting up of a committee to study and expose specific Stalinist organizations. Referred to NEC.

Resolution that Article XIII of constitution regarding trade union work be endorsed. Motion to concur. Carried. Motion to refer to the NEC. Lost.

Statement: Curtiss in opposition to the resolution on trade union leagues.

Motion by Most: To recommend to the NEC that full proceedings of the convention be published and made available to the membership. Carried.

Motion by Most: To publish internal discussion bulletin on the work of the convention. Lost.

Motion by Most: That the NEC be empowered to draw

up a clause in the constitution on referenda in accordance with the internal resolution. Carried.

Motion: Refer the youth report to the NEC for action. Carried.

Comrade Farrell Dobbs in the closing address urged all delegates to carry out the decisions of the convention in the same spirit which animated the convention sessions.

Convention closed its sessions with the singing of the "Internationale."

ATTACHMENT

Delegate list

Used by Credentials Committee

Branch	Number of members	Delegates	Alternates
California			
Fresno	150	Al Furth	Harold Rakoczy*
Los Angeles Branch Central	47	Charles Curtiss	
		Harry Fishler (proxy)	
San Diego	10	Frank Ricco	
San Francisco	39	Glen Trimble	
		Flo Wyle	
Colorado			
Denver	9	Paul McCormack	
Members at Large	5	Hildegarde Smith (proxy)	

---

* Denotes delegates who had not registered when this list was compiled although their credentials had been received by mail; some never did arrive or register.

133

Branch	Number of members	Delegates	Alternates
Illinois			
Evanston branch	5	Francis Heisler	Hayes
South Side branch no. 1	10	Melos Most	Harry Paine
			Emil Revyuk*
South Side branch no. 2	15	J. Stirling	C. Kahn*
West Side branch	200	Norman Satir	Paul Herman*
		Rose Casano	
Indiana			
East Chicago	9	Manuel Trbovich	Herbert Martin
Indianapolis no. 1		Cecil Allen*	Robert Birchman
Kansas	6	George Whiteside	Hildegarde Smith
Kentucky			
Louisville	6	P. Zimmerman	L. Hamilton
Massachusetts			
Boston Central	32	Dan Carson	
		John Taber	
Lynn	14	John Poulos	Joseph Steele*
Michigan			
Central		George Clarke	Harold Robins
Minnesota			
Austin	23	Julius Shade	
Minneapolis	175	Oscar Coover	R. Tibbett
			Paul
		Farrell Dobbs	Rasmussen
		Vincent R. Dunne	A. Pease*
		Clem Forsen	Wilbert Houchin

Branch	Number of members	Delegates	Alternates
		Max Geldman	Karl S. Kuehn
		Arthur Hopkins	
		Carlos Hudson	
		Roy Orgon	
		Carl Skoglund	
Olivia		J. Enestvedt	
St. Paul	30	Theodore Dostal	Jules Geller
		Grace Carlson	Dorothy Shultz
Missouri			
Joplin	6	Al Hargis	
Kansas City		Daniel Noyes	Ronald Larsen
St. Louis	20	Robert S. Saunders	David Burbank
			Robert Warner
			Harry Von Romer
			Everett Washburn
St. Louis County	15	Sam Hill	Eugene Hoffman
Montana			
Billings	35	R.M. Hansen	
		Rodney Salisbury	
Plentywood		John Boulds	
New Jersey			
Newark Central	38	Felix Giordano	Dorothea Katz
		Jack Weber	Carl Ford
Lenin		George Breitman	Reuben Plaskett
New York			
New York City			
Astoria	18	Alex Retzkin	

136 / FIRST SWP CONVENTION

Branch	Number of members	Delegates	Alternates
Boro Park	20	Sam Gordon	
Brownsville	11	Sam Friedman	
Chelsea	23	Bill Farrell	Bill Sherman
East Side	55	Robert Browne	E. Stevens*
		Paul Kujac	Sterling
		John G. Wright	
Lower East Bronx	18	Bernard Morgenstern	
Lower East Side	26	Abe Miller	
Upper East Bronx	20	Max Sterling (proxy)	
Upper West Side	32	G. Brooks	Freddie Drake
		Lyman Paine	
Village	23	Dick Ettlinger	
Washington Heights	16	Sherman Stanley	
West Bronx	29 (?)	Fred Browner	Martin Abern
Williamsburg	13	Herman Stern	
Minority Group	7	Martin Glee	
Ohio			
Akron-Friday branch	8	Blake Lear	Richard Ferguson
Saturday branch	10	B.J. Widick	Robert Stiler
Cleveland	26	Bert Cochran	Robert Dullea
Toledo	12	Art Preis	
Youngstown	7	Les Reid	Al Adler
Pennsylvania			
Allentown-Lehigh local	16	Walter Huhn	
Philadelphia	27	Carl Hartman	
		Max Shachtman (proxy)	
Quakertown	8	Howard Stump	John Knisley

Branch	Number of members	Delegates	Alternates
Sellerville	11	L. Shoemaker	Howard H. Besch
Utah			
Salt Lake City	8	Vaughan T. O'Brien	
Washington, D.C.		J. Loewy	
YPSL NEC		Hal Draper	
		Ernest Erber	
		Nathan Gould	

FRATERNAL DELEGATES

Name	Locality
Martin Abern	New York
George Black	Toronto† (Alt. Smith)
Tom Brown	Toronto (Alt. Jones)
James Burnham	New York
James P. Cannon	New York
Joseph Carter	New York
Freddie Drake	New York
Robert Dullea	Cleveland
Manny Garrett	New York
Albert Glotzer	Chicago
Albert Goldman	Chicago
Frank Graves	New York
Lester Kohler	Minneapolis
Morris Lewit	New York
Ernest R. McKinney	New York

---

† The two Canadians, Black and Brown, representing a minority in the Canadian group, were seated without decisive vote. One of these was Ross Dowson.

Name	Locality
Saul Mendelson	Newark
Harry Milton	New York
Carl Pemble	St. Paul
Hugo Rasmussen	Indianapolis
Ted Selander	Toledo
Bill Sherman	New York
Maurice Spector	New York
Arne Swabeck	Chicago
Jac Wasserman	New York
Total delegates	76
Alternates	36
Fraternal delegates	24

Report of Trade Union Commission

(Adopted by the convention)

1. National registration of party and YPSL membership as to union affiliation.
2. Recommend to committee on party constitution that paragraph be included making trade union membership compulsory for all party and YPSL members who can be made eligible for such membership.
3. General questionnaire to be sent all party branches by national trade union department calling for report on extent of union organization in the area by CIO, AFL, and bona fide independent unions, strength of the party branch in the unions, extent of Stalinist influence, level of political action in mass movement, i.e., labor party, LNPL, etc., together with report of future perspectives of party branch union work.
4. Preliminary questionnaire to be circulated at convention by trade union committee of BJW, BF, and ERM [B.J. Widick, Bill Farrell, E.R. McKinney].
5. Whenever two or more members of the party or YPSL

belong to the same trade union, they are to constitute a party trade union fraction, which will work under the political direction of the party branch and shall be responsible to the directing trade union committee of the branch and the national trade union department.

6. Individual trade union fractions should meet at least once a week and all of the trade union fractions in the branch shall meet jointly at least once a month.

7. The party branch shall transmit regular reports on trade union activity to the national trade union department.

8. National fractions in the various industries shall be created as rapidly as material conditions will permit. It is especially recommended that national fractions be created in the auto, steel, maritime, and trucking industries at the earliest possible date.

9. As one of its first tasks the national trade union department shall issue general directives to the party branches on trade union fraction work.

10. It shall be the general policy of the party to concentrate its trade union work in those industries and geographical centers where the party has its strongest roots in the mass movement. The most qualified party members available shall be sent into these centers of activity in the largest possible numbers.

11. The incoming NEC shall establish a national trade union department and designate a full-time national trade union secretary. The national trade union department and its functionaries shall work under the direction of the NEC.

12. Each party branch shall set up a trade union committee to conduct the registration of the party membership and to carry out the directives of the national trade union department in the campaign to activize thoroughly the party membership in the mass movement.

13. The national labor secretary shall issue regular

bulletins to the party branches on the trade union activity of the party.

14. National, regional, and district conferences shall be called from time to time by the party for the purpose of strengthening our trade union work.

15. Cheap popular pamphlets dealing with trade union matters shall be issued by the NEC at the earliest possible date.

16. It is specially recommended that immediate aid be given to the maritime and agricultural fractions by the incoming NEC due to certain urgent and pressing problems.

17. Note to NEC: At least two capable comrades must be made available by January 15 for work in the maritime unions on the Gulf Coast to issue regular bulletin and colonize party cadre to prevent the development of serious complications on the West Coast.

An immediate survey must be made of the agricultural industry on the West Coast and a definite policy adopted on the question of national affiliations.

Farrell Dobbs
Reporter

Report of Unemployment Commission

(Referred to National Committee)

I. Unemployment and the unions

The underlying threat to the trade union movement in the present economic crisis has created a genuine stirring within the ranks of organized labor. The rank and file is exerting increasing pressure upon the leadership to undertake action for the securing of relief and government work-relief jobs.

The union bureaucracy itself, particularly in the less stable CIO, realizes that unless the unemployed members are aided, they face a depletion of their membership and a loss of prestige. This is reflected in many parts of the country by the establishment of welfare committees in union locals, particularly CIO groups. For example, in Ohio, the CIO initiated a statewide conference to be followed by local conferences on the relief problem, set up permanent committees, etc. The Workers Alliance was invited to this statewide conference and is being invited to send fraternal delegates to local CIO councils. The national leaders of the CIO have sent out instructions to all affiliates to immediately set up committees and undertake action for the protection of their unemployed members. *The CIO has become a major factor in the unemployed movement.* However, inexperience and the characteristic class-collaboration policies are being expressed in their methods, with the Stalinists giving the tone to policy and program.

Nevertheless, once the unions enter into a conflict, even poorly expressed, with the government apparatus as such, we have the beginning of a struggle with the capitalist state itself. In other words, the union bureaucracy will experience increasing difficulty in maintaining the illusion that the state is an impartial agency between conflicting classes, for in the unemployed struggle the government assumes directly the role of the agency of the ruling class. This factor places before the revolutionists a powerful springboard with which to project directly into the union movement the Marxist conception of the class nature of the state.

A further serious consideration is that the unemployed as a group, even with the best type of organization independent of the organized employed workers, have but limited weapons with which to coerce the ruling class. The main bargaining power of the workers is in their ability, through control of the means of production, to curtail and limit the profits of the bosses through strikes. The unemployed can riot or demonstrate, but they cannot hurt the ruling class at its most vulnerable point, production and profits. Thus, only by effective collaboration between employed and unemployed can the unemployed gain access to this one final weapon of bargaining power.

II. The Workers Alliance

The WAA, the only existing national independent organization of unemployed, at this moment should be giving militant leadership to this development within the unions. Unfortunately, its entire national leadership as well as most state leaderships are either Stalinists or Stalinized right-wing Socialists. The once militant policies of the organization have degenerated into mere legislative lobbying, and the organizational program is saturated with class-collaboration, People's Frontism, etc. Membership, never large, has fallen off by at least two-thirds.

Despite the fact that the Stalinists have mechanical control of the organizational apparatus, within the ranks of the organization are thousands of independent and militant workers, and many of the local organizations throughout the country are beginning to resist the servile policies of the leadership in this period. Moreover, the demand for militant action will grow rapidly in the ranks, even among the rank-and-file Stalinists who are beginning to take the natural path of militant action despite the party line when that line presents the prospect of accepting for themselves starvation and misery without a fight. Hungry workers who demand immediate action to satisfy their most naked needs despite all the blandishments of Stalinism, are driven by their stomachs to follow a militant class-struggle leadership which responds to their own needs and demands. Stalinists may divert and hinder for a brief while the development of the inevitable struggle for existence, but the *necessity for quick results,* characteristic of the unemployed movement, will force the workers to force the Stalinists aside in favor of decisive leadership.

However, the WAA is becoming rapidly attached to the CIO. State and local bodies of the WAA are sending official delegates to CIO councils and are collaborating on welfare and grievance committees. Thus, in wide sections of the country, the WAA is becoming a ready-made channel to the CIO apparatus and is in direct contact with large sections of rank-and-file unionists in mass-production industries. These unionists are exerting increasing pressure upon their leadership for immediate action and results, but such leadership is not forthcoming from their own top ranks but only from the ranks of revolutionary socialism.

III. The role of revolutionary socialists in the unemployed movement

Our group in the past period has not attempted in a serious or organized fashion to activize itself within the unemployed movement. Here and there throughout the country, on a local and isolated basis, our comrades have functioned well within the WAA or within the local independent groups such as the Federal Workers Section in Minneapolis. The little real work we have done has demonstrated the possibilities, within certain limits, for us within this field.

Our failure to achieve more influence within the unemployed movement is due to two factors. First, the period of our existence within the SP tended to exert an organizationally disintegrating effect upon our mass organization fraction work. The comrades in the unions and in the WAA were constantly hamstrung and tied by the necessity of observing discipline to vacillating SP policy and of working with hodgepodge elements within the SP. This of course was required by political expediency, but it is no longer so. Secondly, during the upswing in employment and production and the inception of the CIO movement, when younger and more militant workers were being called back temporarily to private industry, many militants left the WAA for the CIO movement. In such a period, conservatism and class collaboration came to the fore in the unemployed movement and simplified the aims of the

Stalinists to seize the reins of the organization.

The new strata of the unemployed are not the devitalized elements who make up a good portion of the WAA at present. The new unemployed are like the young and potentially militant industrial workers. Great numbers of them belong to unions, and are *pressing the unions for assistance*. This group can and will fight. These are the workers we must approach and orient ourselves toward in our unemployed work in the next period.

IV. 'Our own' unemployed organization

Present economic developments, the growing relations between the WAA and the CIO, the CIO, the pressure on unions, the character of the new strata of unemployed—all point to the folly of attempting to set up "our own" unemployed organization.

Even from a technical standpoint such an undertaking would be out of the question for our group at this time. The organizing personnel required, the finances, and every other technical consideration make such a step absolutely out of the question even if it were desirable, except under the most abnormal and acute circumstances. Further, such a movement would tend to isolate us from the main trend of the organizational developments of the unemployed movement—*toward the trade union movement*. In other words, the unemployed movement will eventually be incorporated into the trade union movement and there is a strong possibility that it will have no independent organizational structure.

Such a move would be, moreover, a retreat from a head-on struggle with Stalinism and reformism at a time when all the economic and social factors have provided the preconditions for the successful exposure of the Stalinists before the working class.

Finally, it is not true that we have exhausted the possibilities of fraction work within the WAA. The truth is that we have scarcely even explored these possibilities. Local factors have prevented the Minneapolis comrades from working within the WAA, but in almost every other section of the country where we have had even the smallest group of active comrades, results have demonstrated the possibilities of earnest fraction work if conducted on a genuinely organized and directive basis. We need point only to the work of a handful of comrades in Newark, Toledo, Allentown, New York City, etc.

V. Our tasks

1. Our main task is to utilize our limited personnel and resources to gain access to the workers in the trade unions. We must make the question of protecting the unemployed a direct responsibility of the unions themselves. Where feasible and where our comrades have a leading role in progressive unions, we should work towards the establishment of unemployed organizations under the guidance of the union or a union local patterned after our experience in Minneapolis.

2. We should begin immediately to undertake serious fraction work within the WAA. Every unemployed comrade who is not a union member should be required to join and become active in the WAA. Under exceptional circumstances where the unemployed have no means of expression whatsoever, that is, neither a Workers Alliance nor trade unions, and where the question of protecting the unemployed is posed, independent organization of the unemployed, in a local sense, should be undertaken. This latter must be subordinated, however, to our basic policies of directing our energies toward the trade unionists. Wherever our comrades work in the Workers Alliance,

they should establish broad progressive blocs organized after the fashion of our comrades in New York City.

3. The convention should appoint one comrade in the center who shall act as the national secretary on unemployed organizations to coordinate the work of our unemployed fractions within the WAA and the work of the unionists in relief actions. The secretary should coordinate his work with the trade union committee and labor secretary and should act as a center for correspondence, information, and discussion.

Art Preis
Reporter

Statements

JANUARY 3, 1938

At this Chicago convention of the *Socialist Appeal* Association, Comrades Shachtman and Cannon submitted a statement which included a reference to the "irresponsible actions of Most." This constituted a serious charge against Comrade Most. He was given no opportunity to defend himself against these charges nor was any evidence whatever submitted to the convention.

In spite of this, the convention voted to concur in the statement. This was a violation of the rights of a member and a violation of the constitution adopted at the convention. The undersigned delegate to the convention disassociates himself from this convention action.

Carl Pemble
FRATERNAL DELEGATE,
ST. PAUL

I wish to enter the following statement into the minutes directly after the record of my motion asking for a hearing on the Cannon-Shachtman statement by the National Committee:

The factional allegation against me contained in the Cannon-Shachtman statement on Chicago, steamrollered through the national convention without permitting any amendments from the floor, I regard as one of the most serious charges ever made by an official body against a member. The fact that the convention voted down a motion to investigate the truth of a charge which is calculated to debase the party standing of a member—the fact that it refused to have a regular hearing on such a charge—proves that the supporters of the statement were not interested in determining the truth, but were factionally motivated.

Whereas the censures of the Chicago organization were only made after a careful hearing, a slightly less severe censure of myself was made without even permitting discussion on the motion. This amounts to disciplinary action without charges or a trial.

The decision of the convention was a reward for factional gossipmongers who, being unable and unwilling to discuss the position of *Left Wing Correspondence* in a political fashion, have diverted attention from this position by unprincipled personal attacks on its supporters. I emphatically deny having ever acted contrary to the interests of the tendency, and wish to declare that I have been singled out for this unwarranted attack purely because of my political position in the preconvention discussion, and repeat my request of the incoming National Committee that it determine the facts in the case. I shall cooperate in every way with such a hearing.

The entire effect of the statement is to place stress on personalities instead of political positions, and is an insult to the intelligence of the membership.

Melos Most
DELEGATE, CHICAGO

We consider the action of the convention in concurring with an opinion of two comrades (Cannon-Shachtman) as to the irresponsibility of a comrade (Most) without either giving the criticized comrade a hearing or demanding the grounds for this opinion a direct violation of democratic centralism.

We consider the convention's acceptance by a vote of the unexplained opinion of comrades, no matter how important, an example of conformance to some of the forms of democracy and at the same time an unprincipled violation of its spirit.

E. Revyuk
ALTERNATE,
SOUTH SIDE BRANCH,
CHICAGO

P. Zimmerman
DELEGATE, LOUISVILLE

PART 3

Chicago convention resolutions

The political situation and the tasks of the party[1]

The capitalist world crisis

The political and economic situation in the United States is developing in the midst of a convulsive evolution of a world capitalist society in a state of crisis and decay—a world crisis with which the United States is inextricably connected and from whose effects it cannot exempt itself by a policy of either economic or political "isolation."

The world bourgeoisie has been able to surmount the violent crisis that shook its whole economic structure

---

1. The first draft of this resolution was printed in *Bulletin Number 6*, Organizing Committee for the Socialist Party Convention, January 1938, which was available to the delegates when the convention began at the end of December 1937. With minor changes made by the convention it was reprinted in *Socialist Appeal*, January 22, 1938. Max Shachtman and James P. Cannon were assigned by the National Action Committee to prepare the first draft. The convention adopted this resolution by a vote of 56 to 4.

beginning with the stock market crash in the United States in 1929. In countries such as Germany, a purely conjunctural improvement has been achieved by a sharp reduction of the standard of living of the masses and by a tremendous increase of operations in the armaments and related industries, resulting in a partial consolidation of the fascist regime. In France, the People's Front movement has been able to survive and to perpetuate its democratic illusions on the basis of a temporary prosperity, or more accurately, of a slowing down of the more violent pace of economic decline which harassed the country a few years ago. England too has been able to arrest a more catastrophic economic fall by virtue of the unprecedented armaments program inaugurated by the government.

None of the big powers, however, can achieve that level of economic stability which was attained, for example, by France after the World War, except by resolving, at least on a capitalist basis, the conflict between its productive forces and the national boundaries and the limitations imposed by its share of the world market. This is especially true of those powers, like Germany, Italy, Japan, and Poland, whose need of economic expansion comes into the sharpest and most immediate conflict with the present divisions of the world market. The present period may be characterized as one in which all the imperialist powers are jockeying for best position, from the standpoint of the advancement of their economic and military (armaments) strength, in preparation for the inevitable struggle for the redivision of the world among the big imperialist bandits, i.e., for the second world war.

In this sense, the second world war has already begun. More exactly, the big preliminary skirmishes have already taken place. The conquest of Ethiopia by Italian imperialism[2] strengthened the latter's position along the lifeline of British imperialism, in the Mediterranean, the Red Sea, and northeastern Africa. The mineral wealth and strategical importance of Spain are the object of a duel between Italy-Germany and England-France, the accompanying shadow of the civil war on the peninsula. The invasion of China by Japan only heralds the war in which not only these two countries, but also the Soviet Union, the British empire, and the United States will be inescapably and directly involved as active belligerents.

If the inevitable world war has not yet broken out, this is due to the large elements of uncertainty represented by the dense crisscrossing network of conflicts, rivalries, and contradictions among all the powers of the world. The deliberately simplified Stalino-reformist division of contending forces into "democracies" and "dictatorships" does not seriously correspond to any reality save that of the need to prepare the working masses to act enthusiastically as cannon fodder for "democratic" imperialism. The rivalry of the two great imperialist monsters, the United States and Britain, continues to be deepgoing, in spite of the recent mitigation of its sharpness by momentarily coinciding interests (opposition to Japanese expansion). The British conflict with Japan over the domination of China and, prospectively, of India, is presently sharper than the antagonism between Japan and the United States for the hegemony of the Pacific. However, the conflict between England and Italy for control of the Mediterranean is of secondary importance and does not necessarily signify the occupation of opposite sides by these two countries

---

2. The Italian imperialists invaded Ethiopia in 1935 and still remained in control of the country when World War II began in 1939. The Italian troops were driven out in 1941.

in the coming war, any more than it did in the last war.

It would be erroneous, also, to conclude that because England and Germany were opposed in the last war, they will inevitably be opposed in the next. The bonds making for an alliance between these two powers are far stronger than, for example, the bonds making for an alliance between France and the Soviet Union. It is inconceivable, practically speaking, that France would engage in a large-scale war without the assured and direct support of Great Britain, for whom all her present allies of the small "democratic" countries (Poland, Rumania) can scarcely substitute from the standpoint of strength or importance.

An additional element of uncertainty, which serves in a way to postpone the actual outbreak of the war for a period of time, is the "military unpreparedness" of two of the principal decisive powers, England and Germany. But the "completion" of the armaments programs of these two countries involves such a diversion and squandering of economic strength as to sap their otherwise none-too-stable economic bases. The impending economic crisis, presaged by the recent convulsions in the New York, London, and Paris stock exchanges, will not only be more devastating, from all indications, than the preceding crisis, but will in all likelihood serve as the principal direct factor to precipitate the outbreak of hostilities in the international struggle to redivide the world. In this sense, a war boom alone can arrest the most disastrous development of the crisis.

The Soviet Union occupies a singular position in the present world situation. The fragility of its alliances with capitalist powers (France, etc.) is only a reflection of the still existing irreconcilability between the world of imperialism on the one side, and the yet remaining achievements of the Bolshevik revolution on the other. It is conceivable, of course, that for a given period the conflict between two imperialist camps may become so sharp as to cause one side to enter into a real military alliance with the Soviet Union. But it is no less likely that the rival imperialist camps will find it more expedient to postpone a settlement of the conflicts among themselves, involving not only the risk of the defeat of one set of imperialists by the other and their reduction to a secondary status by the victor, but also the defeat of all of them by the proletarian revolution.

A postponement of the interimperialist war for a redivision of the capitalist world market is conceivable only in the form of a joint imperialist struggle to destroy the Soviet Union and to divide it among themselves as colonies, spheres of influence, and protectorates. The imperialist "haves" would thereby not only preserve their present forces in the world market (colonies, etc.) from being snatched up by victorious "have-nots," but, in the event of a defeat of the Soviet Union, would even extend their powers along with their present threatening rivals. It would therefore be the greatest blindness to imagine that the plans of Germany and Japan, who are ready to forego for the time being their demands for a larger share of the world market of the other imperialist powers if the latter consent to a partitioning of the Soviet Union, are unacceptable to countries like France and England because of their adherence to the renowned principles of democracy. It is not at all out of the question that the imperialist powers may seek to compose their own differences at a feast over the body of the Soviet Union.

U.S. imperialism and the coming war

It is entirely inconceivable that American imperialism can succeed in resisting the inexorable tendencies that are pulling it into the vortex of the coming world war. The United States is today the strongest world power. The bases of its economic and political strength extend over every continent, and the shocks and convulsions of capitalism anywhere in the world have their immediate, direct or indirect, effects upon this country. This is expressed in military terms by the fact that, despite the virtually invulnerable geographic position of the United States, its armaments program today is the largest in its peacetime history, adjusted to the objectives of world conquest rather than to the myth of self-contained isolation. Politically, it was expressed in the clearest terms in the aggressive, interventionist speech of Roosevelt in Chicago, announcing the determination of American imperialism to take the leadership in the struggle to keep its present most dangerous rival, especially in the Far East, from increasing its ration of the Asiatic market; earlier, in Cordell Hull's efforts to consolidate the dominant position of American imperialism at the Latin American conference in Buenos Aires; and subsequently by the sharp notes to Japan which are only a reflection of America's dogged intention of keeping the "Open Door" open in China and preventing any other power from shutting off the United States from expansion upon the Asiatic continent.[3]

The direct economic and territorial (colonial) expansion of the United States in the rest of the world is entirely out of proportion to its own economic-financial strength. The position occupied by foreign trade in the economic life of

---

3. The Open Door for China policy was elaborated by the U.S. government in 1898. Under a facade of helping China by preventing that country's exclusive domination by any particular imperialist power, the policy sought to "open the door" of China to unlimited exploitation by U.S. capitalism.

the country, while comparatively small in percentage, is nevertheless decisive, particularly in the form of the continued export of capital. The efforts to solve the devastating economic crisis in the United States on "national soil" have not succeeded in yielding lasting results. Quite the contrary. Although the United States has shared in the general world recovery from the crisis which reached its lowest point in 1932, it has not been able to attain the production level reached at the 1929 boom peak. The "New Deal" recovery has not even been as strong as the recovery experienced by other countries, due largely to the heavy armaments program of U.S. imperialism. The United States in the "Roosevelt era" has not only benefited from an extensive system of government spending, of liberal credit facilities, of a substantial increase of production made possible by the employment of public funds which facilitated the reorganization of capitalist enterprises, but to a certain extent, from the armaments program both of the United States and the rest of the world.

The recovery has undoubtedly reduced the size of the army of the unemployed and mitigated the conditions of the working class in general by an increase in its purchasing power. But this increase in the purchasing power of the masses has not kept pace with the increase in their productivity; the opposite—that is, a widening of the gap between actual output and purchasing power—has occurred. The degree of capitalist prosperity attained in 1929 has thus not yet been reached and from all indications will not be attained before the outbreak of another ravaging crisis. The first symptoms of that crisis are already obvious, and they mark the collapse of both the "New Deal" and the "New Deal" ideology which captured the minds of the masses in the period just elapsed.

It is possible that the full development of the present

recession into a deep crisis may be temporarily arrested by a certain period of economic upturn, but the line of development toward a raging crisis is already unmistakable. While neither the rate of development of the crisis, heralded by the present slump, nor the moment of its cataclysmic outbreak can be accurately predicted, it is safe to say that it will break at a lower level than in 1929 and will be of greater scope, depth, and duration.

Along with it will break the illusion of a speedy and lasting recovery which accompanied the preceding crisis as a hangover of the American "prosperity" ideology. The American ruling class will be compelled to intervene in the most brutally aggressive manner outside its own borders in order to maintain its own power and profits. The role of "pacifier" of Europe played by the United States in the past will necessarily be replaced by an attempt to reduce the European powers (and Japan) to a poor relation's share of the world market, corresponding to the unpostponable need of expansion of American imperialism. It is entirely excluded by reality that the older imperialist powers, themselves desperate and driving relentlessly to war to expand or even retain their resources at each other's expense, will give way to American encroachments merely as a result of purely political or financial pressure. Such decisive changes of the world map as the United States must seek to accomplish, can be obtained only at the cost of war.

It is most unlikely that in the event of an inter-imperialist war, the United States will be one of the original belligerents. At the same time, it is just as unlikely that she will wait, as was the case in the last world war, for thirty-two months before entering the hostilities in order to emerge as the decisive victor. The comparative poverty of the European imperialist powers, as well as the speedier and more general destruction promised by the coming war, will determine the earlier intervention of American imperialism for the purpose of delivering, as in 1917, the decisive blow in the war and of having the decisive word in the division of the spoils.

It is just as unlikely that the United States will precipitate the world war by immediately starting a duel with Japan, as is hoped by British imperialism, which is still unprepared for a war in Asia, and by the Stalinist bureaucracy. Under the concrete conditions, a direct military struggle against Japan at the present time would signify that American imperialism is pulling British chestnuts out of the fire and acting as a bulwark protecting the eastern flank of the Soviet Union—and the American bourgeoisie does not intend to enact either role. It may be said with practical certainty that the United States will engage in a war with Japan only under such circumstances as would make it possible not only to deliver a stiff blow at Japanese imperialism in China, but also to strengthen American imperialism at the expense of British. Similarly in the case of the Soviet Union. Unless the latter guarantees vast concessions to the United States in advance, American imperialism would in all likelihood permit itself a direct war alliance with the Soviet Union in a struggle against Japan only after it was well under way, and when the entry into the conflict of the United States would permit it to dictate the terms both to its enemy and its ally.

Position of the SWP

If the working class is unable to prevent the outbreak of war, and the United States enters directly into it, the SWP stands pledged to the traditional position of revolutionary Marxism. It will utilize the crisis of capitalist rule engendered by the war to prosecute the class struggle with the utmost intransigence, to strengthen the independent labor and revolutionary movements, and to bring the war to a close by the revolutionary overturn of capitalism and the establishment of proletarian rule in the form of the workers' state. Combating the chauvinistic wave, it will not only reject any and every form of class collaboration, support of the war and of the capitalist government, but will work toward the defeat of the American capitalist class and its war regime by the proletarian revolution.

The SWP will advocate the continuance of the class struggle during the war regardless of the consequences to the military front of American capitalism; and will try to prepare the masses to utilize the war crisis for the overthrow of U.S. capitalism and the victory of socialism.

Even if the United States were to be allied with the Soviet Union in a war against another imperialist power, this circumstance would not for a minute alter the imperialist character and aims of the war so far as the United States is concerned; neither, therefore, would there be any alteration in the position of the SWP with regard to American capitalism and its government and in our irreconcilable hostility towards them. The practical steps which our party would take in the course of its opposition to the war would, however, have to be decided in consideration of the need of facilitating the utmost material aid to the Soviet Union's armed forces in their war against an imperialist power, in conformity with our position of defense of the Soviet Union from imperialist assault.

Changes in American politics

The impending economic crisis will not only propel the United States sharply along the road to imperialist war, but will be accompanied by a radical change in the political situation at home. Up to the present time, the

"People's Front" movement has assumed the form of support of the Roosevelt regime, and to a greater or lesser extent of its policies, not only by the bulk of the Democratic Party and sections of the progressive Republicans, but by the Farmer-Laborites, the trade unions (CIO and AFL), the Stalinists, and the Social Democrats. But this form, expressed in the field of legislation through the official, but internally torn, Democratic Party, is already proving inadequate for a perpetuation of the class-collaborationist illusions fostered to a large extent by the partial recovery. Under the impact of the already present economic decline and the inevitable crisis, it will prove to be entirely unable to fulfill its function.

The blow struck at the masses by the crisis will undoubtedly produce a new political orientation among them. If the revolutionary party measures up to its task, it will gain great strength from increased support of sections of the working class. But it is virtually certain that in the first period, the growing radicalization of the masses will be expressed predominantly in reformist channels, for even if the full force of the crisis should be felt before the end of the Roosevelt term in office, the Republican Party will benefit to a far lesser extent than did the Democratic Party as a result of the crisis that broke out during Hoover's term in office.

Three main courses of development are possible of realization in the coming period of political reorientation.

1. Throwing the responsibility of failure to prevent or solve the crisis upon Congress, and consequently upon the official Democratic Party, Roosevelt seeks to retain political control by splitting the party into conservative and progressive camps, allying the latter with the progressive Republicans, and basing himself upon the organized labor movement, either in the form of trade unions or of local,

statewide, or national labor parties, similar to the American Labor Party in New York during the last elections. Roosevelt would thus seek to reconstitute a majority in the country by converting a "managed" labor party movement into an appendage of a reorganized Democratic Party, the reactionary sections of which (South, etc.) would tend to merge with the reactionary bulk of the Republican Party.

2. The New York labor party movement spreads to the rest of the country and constitutes itself as a national middle reformist party based on the trade unions allied with various petty-bourgeois politicians and political grouplets, dominated by middle-class demagogues of the LaGuardia type and by labor leaders like Lewis or Green or both; and breaking either partially or completely with the Roosevelt and Democratic Party machine much in the manner in which the ALP broke with the Lehman and Democratic Party machine in New York in the recent mayoralty campaign.

3. The labor party development takes on a more radical form in appearance, namely, a policy and leadership determined by the Lewis bureaucracy and the Stalinist party. In a word, the unfolding of the economic crisis would scarcely result in any mass movement of fascism in the United States, but because of the still unexhausted "democratic" reserves in America, the present diffused and unorganized "People's Front" movement would shift to the left and assume more clearly delimited forms.

Faced with the prospect of the formation of a national labor party of one kind or another, the SWP has no need of altering the fundamental revolutionary Marxian position on the labor party question.[4] The revolutionary party can-

---

4. Later in 1938, a few months after the adoption of this resolution, the SWP did alter its conception of what the fundamental revolution-

not take the responsibility for forming or for advocating the formation of a reformist, class-collaborationist party, that is, of a petty-bourgeois workers' party. At the same time we must be aware that under certain conditions the movement for a labor party would not only draw into its ranks the great mass of the organized workers of the United States, but would even absorb most of the progressive, advanced, and semirevolutionary tendencies in the labor movement. The SWP could stand completely apart from such a movement only at the risk of complete isolation and ineffectiveness in the class struggle.

It would be wrong to conclude from this that even if a national labor party, based on the trade unions, were formed, the SWP would or should seek to affiliate with it. Whether or not the revolutionary party in this country would pursue the same tactics toward the labor party that Lenin recommended at one time in England, cannot be determined in advance and could be decided only on the basis of the concrete reality of the given labor party, of the general political situation and the relationship of forces. Even if such a tactic is not eventually adopted, it would be totally false to remain completely aside from a labor party if it has a mass basis in the trade unions. The primary and principal means of retaining and extending our contact with the masses under such conditions would be not so much directly through the political branches of the labor party as through the trade unions themselves. All considerations therefore point to the imperative necessity facing the SWP of making systematic, organized, concentrated efforts to root itself in the factories and in

---

ary Marxist position on the labor party was. See page 356 for "The problem of the labor party," the document approved by a referendum vote of the SWP membership in the summer of 1938.

the trade unions, and to participate to the fullest extent in the daily struggles of the workers and in mass work in general. Therein lies the main line of our preparation for the period to come.

Opponents in the workers' movement

The SWP is the product of the fusion of the elements formerly organized in the Workers Party with the revolutionists in the SP and the YPSL in the course of the struggle to win the membership of these organizations to the principles of Marxism and the banner of the Fourth International. In the split provoked by the reformists and centrists, the Fourth Internationalists rallied the overwhelming majority of the members of the Young People's Socialist League and the bulk of the active membership of the Socialist Party. What remains of the latter is an opportunistic sect, confined to a few localities, having no real and solid connections with the labor movement, and completely dominated by a confused combination of municipal Social Democrats, pacifists, utopian reformers, second-rank labor bureaucrats, and a demoralized appendage of centrists. The experience with the Thomas-Hoan-Tyler Socialist Party is at an end; it is behind us. The SWP would be disorienting itself completely if it concentrated any efforts in the direction of the old SP under the illusory impression that there are still substantial numbers of militants within the ranks who can be won to the revolutionary program.

The Lovestone group, which since its inception has led the existence of an unacknowledged attorney for Stalinism, and has maintained itself thanks primarily to the adaptation of some of its trade union functionaries to the class-collaborationist bureaucracy, now finds itself compelled to unload the responsibility for the crimes and policies of Stalinism, above all in the Soviet Union, which it defended up to yesterday. This is not only eloquent testimony to the degeneration of the counterrevolutionary Stalinist bureaucracy, but a sign of the shift which is taking place to one extent or another throughout the working-class movement. The fact that the Lovestoneite leadership is forced to make so radical a retreat from its previous position, and to adopt many of the criticisms and programmatic points of our movement, even if in a distorted form, testifies to the possibilities of winning to the ranks of the revolutionary party a number of workers in its organization. While this possibility of recruitment cannot be ignored, it must nevertheless be borne in mind that the Lovestone group still remains a tiny sect confined essentially to a very few localities.

Not very fruitful would be the expenditure of any energy in a hunt for recruits from or fusion with the variety of disintegrating ultraleftist sects (Oehler, Weisbord, etc.) which have doomed themselves to sterility and have become reactionary, even if insignificant, obstacles on the road to the building of the revolutionary party in the United States. While the SWP holds the door wide open to all the sincere revolutionary elements still affiliated with such sects, and is ready to admit them to membership on the basis of acceptance of the party program and without the slightest prejudice to the rights or obligations which they would share in common with all other members, it considers it wasteful and futile to engage in a series of "negotiations" looking towards "fusion" with the sects themselves.

The Communist Party presents a different problem. Although it has grown enormously in the recent period as a result of the influx of large numbers of middle-class elements, attracted by its petty-bourgeois line, it has also succeeded in recruiting thousands of militant and even revolutionary-minded workers. The interests of the counterrevolutionary Stalinist bureaucracy, which dictate the position and activity of the Communist Party in this as in all other countries, come into increasingly sharp conflict with both the historical and the immediate interests of the working class. As the economic and political crisis sharpens in the United States, the Communist Party will be more clearly revealed not as a defender of the working class but as a decisive prop of the American bourgeoisie and its class rule—a position determined by the desire to win American imperialism, at all costs, to an alliance with the Soviet bureaucracy.

The revelation of the reactionary role of the Stalinist party and its leadership will serve to drive a wedge between the latter and the worker-militants in its ranks. The sharpening of the class struggle in the United States, as well as the horrible results of Stalinist policy in the Soviet Union and Spain, will therefore bring with it sharp internal conflicts and crises in the ranks of Stalinism, the first signs of which are already present at the periphery of the Stalinist movement. These will open up to the SWP the prospect of winning many former Stalinist workers to its ranks, and under favorable circumstances, of a split in the CP, even the prospect of the fusion of a section of the Stalinist party with the SWP on the basis of the program of the Fourth International. The party must therefore pay close attention to this field and prepare the most favorable situation by patient and systematic activity among the Stalinist rank and file, and elements under their influence, above all in the trade union movement.

Firm adherence to Marxism necessary

The world situation and the perspectives of development in the United States thus confront the SWP with tremendous tasks, which it can accomplish only with the greatest responsibility and seriousness. The party must prepare itself consciously and deliberately for these tasks. It must be aware especially of the fact that it faces not only a great sharpening of the class struggle in the United States, but above all the early prospect of an imperialist war, which will be the severest test of all organizations and policies. It can meet this test only by the rigid safeguarding of the Marxian principles of revolutionary internationalism upon which it is founded.

The truly revolutionary party, especially in the present period, must be able to defend the immediate and historical interests of the working class not only on the economic and political field, but also on the theoretical field. The most active participation in mass work, which is mandatory upon the party, does not conflict with but rather presupposes the most militant defense of the party's program and its theoretical principles from the assaults of all other currents and ideologies in the labor movement.

The party cannot close its eyes to the fact that the almost unbroken series of defeats and setbacks suffered by the world labor movement, especially in the past fifteen years, and above all the tragic disintegration of the Russian revolution (the phenomenon of Stalinism), have produced a widespread reaction not only against Stalinism but against the principles and organization of revolutionary Marxism. This reaction has manifested itself, both in the realm of theory and political action, in the almost universal attempted substitution of all sorts of reformist and revisionist doctrines, programs, and movements for the doctrine and movement of scientific socialism. The attempts to eliminate the latter from the working class represent at bottom the pressure of a reactionary petty-bourgeois ideology upon the ranks of the labor movement in general and of the revolutionary movement in particular. The degeneration of the socialist movement, which celebrated its triumph in the Second International upon the outbreak of the World War, has succeeded in the past decade in completely destroying the Third International as a revolutionary or progressive force.

It would be absurd to imagine that the Marxian wing of the movement, represented by the Fourth International throughout the world, could be completely immune from this petty-bourgeois, disintegrating tendency. Fortified though our movement here and abroad is by the assimilation of the rich lessons of the last twenty years, and standing uncompromisingly though it does on the granite foundation of the principles of revolutionary Marxism, which the reformists and turncoats jeer at as "obsolete" or "superorthodox," our International and our party have felt the effects of the current of degeneration at their periphery.

This current can be counteracted by the party waging a consistent struggle for the defense of those revolutionary principles upon which it is built and by which it must guide itself in all its daily activity. The party today must become the rallying center of all revolutionary and class-conscious workers. Unless the party is to fall victim to a sectarian, self-satisfied rigidity, it must take into account the prospect that in the coming period it will draw into its ranks many workers, not only from the Stalinist camp, but in general, who have not passed through the years of political and theoretical training that the main core of the party has experienced. In a sense, these new elements will bring with them, unconsciously, confused and distorted ideas. The utmost patience and the broadest inner-party democracy are required in assimilating all new forces, especially militant proletarians, but the task can be successfully performed only if the party itself maintains an unyielding firmness in its own principles and its own theoretical conceptions. Otherwise, the party will gradually decline into a formless mass of conflicting and contradictory currents which will not only negate its basic program but render it ineffective as a revolutionary force in the class struggle.

Democratic centralism

The SWP sees the fundamental causes of the degeneration of the other workers' parties in their departure from the principles of revolutionary Marxism and the adoption of petty-bourgeois reformist policies and theories. This process has always been accompanied by the imposition of bureaucratic regimes inside those organizations. Precisely because our party is based upon the tested principles of Marxism and is inflexible in its defense of the program of revolutionary internationalism, it stands foursquare upon the basis of democratic centralism in its structure. The party that stands for the triumph of workers' democracy cannot tolerate a bureaucratic regime and structure in its own midst. Democratic centralism is based in the first place upon a common adherence to the fundamental program of the party. It implies the free interchange of opinion, the right of discussion, presentation, and defense of views within the framework of the principles of revolutionary Marxism, the unimpaired right of the membership freely to decide the policies of the organization and to select its leadership. It further implies the most rigid discipline in action on the basis of the program and policies of the party, under the direction of the party leadership and the subordination in action of the minority to the majority.

The "democracy" of the Stalinist parties is confined to the "right" of the party membership to carry out unquestioningly all the decisions arbitrarily arrived at by a bureaucratically appointed leadership over which the ranks of the party have absolutely no control. The "democracy" of the "all-inclusive" Thomas-Tyler party is a miserable fraud. Our whole experience has demonstrated that it consists in the fullest freedom for the opportunists and reformists to act as they please, even in the violation of the formal policy of the party, and in the most brutal bureaucratic suppression of the revolutionary left wing for the crime of fighting inside the party for a Marxian program. The "all-inclusive" party conception of the present leaders of the Socialist Party is a gross deception, which has ended with the inclusion of all right-wingers and the exclusion of all revolutionists.

Our conception of democratic centralism, which makes possible the richest and most fruitful inner life in the organization and the mutual influencing of all its component parts by discussion, definitely excludes, however, the conversion of the party into a bohemian talking shop which discusses interminably without ever coming to a decision and acting upon it. The revolutionary party is primarily a party of action and not an intellectualistic discussion club where everybody may come and go as he pleases. Democratic centralism is the means which enables the party to arrive in the freest, most untrammeled, and speediest manner at those decisions and at that practice which makes possible the party's most effective participation in the class struggle.

Party must be rooted in the unions

We cannot ignore the fact that the past development of the Fourth Internationalist movement in this country has prepared it to meet the great tasks that now face it chiefly in one sense, namely, in that it has provided the party with its thought-out and proven principled foundations. At the same time, it must be recognized that the intensely political and polemical life of the movement in the past, its enforced isolation from the mainstream of the working-class movement, has produced not only certain sectarian tendencies (Oehler, etc.), but also a tendency towards an exclusively internal existence unconnected with the living movement of the working class. It is imperative that this tendency be overcome and that the party turn its full energies towards rooting itself in the labor movement.

The SWP proceeds in its tactics and activities not merely from the standpoint of what it ought to be and must become, but primarily from the realistic consideration of what it is at the present time, what forces are at its disposal, and what tasks it can reasonably accomplish in the coming period. We are not yet a mass party and therefore cannot assume all the responsibilities incumbent upon such a movement. It is only in certain localities—and they are not numerous—that our party has firm contacts with the organized labor movement. For the most part, however, the party still operates as a large propaganda organization. It is necessary to take deliberate measures to pass beyond these confines. The main task of the party in the coming period is not the impossible one of becoming the leader of the American working class; that would be a vain illusion, and would bring both disappointment and disorientation into our midst. Our main task is to entrench ourselves in the labor movement, above all in the trade unions, to gain important bases in the labor movement, to consolidate them, and to proceed from them to our next tasks.

The accomplishment of this simple, prosaic, but indispensable task means a radical improvement of the composition of our party. We will not succeed in rooting the party in the working class, much less to defend the revolutionary proletarian principles of the party from being undermined, unless the party is an overwhelmingly proletarian party, composed in its decisive majority of workers in the factories, mines, and mills. We cannot blind ourselves to the fact that this is not the case at the present time. The party must therefore steer a deliberate course towards recruiting above all from the factory proletariat, especially those engaged in heavy industry. It is a perilous weakness of our party that it has a very small representation in the mining industry, in steel, in automobile, etc. Our attention must therefore be turned to the most patient and systematic agitational activity in the industries, in the shops themselves. The winning of a thousand factory proletarians to the ranks of the party would be a triumph which would change the whole complexion of the movement and both the nature and effectiveness of its work in the class struggle. What is said about the social composition of the party applies with at least equal force to the organization of the youth, which, precisely because of the decline of youth in industry, has a far too small proportion of proletarian elements in its composition.

No effective work can be done in the trade unions—and consequently no effective work in the class struggle—unless the party is directly connected with these elementary organizations of the working class. This means that the party must not only demand a minimum of activity of all its members, but that it demands of every worker in its ranks immediate adherence to his corresponding trade union, and activity inside of it if he is already a member. The most correct trade union policy in the world has little or no significance if the party is not in a position to apply it where it is meant to be applied.

These elementary measures, which are indispensable for the transition from a propaganda group to a mass party in the American working class and its struggle, will, if carried out in an organized, systematic form, enable the party to ward off the danger of being sapped by triflers and dilettantes, by purely literary radicalism, and to become a serious and significant factor in the great struggles and decisive tests that lie ahead on the road to the proletarian revolution.

The trade union movement and the Socialist Workers Party[5]

The most important single field of activity of the revolutionary proletarian party is the trade unions. Unless the party is deeply rooted in the basic economic organizations of the working class, and is inseparably associated with them in their daily struggles, it can be, at best, a literary propagandist group but not a living revolutionary political party of the proletariat, able to lead the latter in the decisive struggle for power. The party that is divorced from the trade union movement and its daily work, is doomed to sterility and disintegration. This is especially true in the United States at the present time.

---

5. The first draft of this resolution was printed in *Bulletin Number 6*, Organizing Committee for the Socialist Party Convention, January 1938. It was reprinted in three installments in *Socialist Appeal*, February 5, 12, and 19, 1938. The National Action Committee assigned James. P. Cannon and Ernest Rice McKinney to prepare the first draft, but when Cannon was sent out of town on an assignment it set up a new committee of B. J. Widick, Bill Sherman, and McKinney. Max

The outstanding characteristics of the working-class movement in the United States in the recent period are the enormous growth of trade union movements, which now embrace millions of workers never organized in the past; the development of the CIO as the movement of the workers in the basic key and mass-production industries, organized in industrial unions, as contrasted with the classic AFL form of craft unions; the violent conflict between the AFL and the CIO, and the recent trend towards the unification of the two bodies; and the expansion of the powers and role of the federal government as "mediator" in the conflict between the workers and the employers.

The growth of industrial unionism

Most significant and promising of all recent phenomena in the working class is the speedy growth of the CIO movement among the hitherto unorganized workers.

Essentially the AFL always was, and today especially is, the organization of the skilled worker or the aristocracy of labor. With the exception of a few of its affiliates or of certain periods in its history, it pursued a deliberate policy of ignoring the great mass of the unorganized proletarians in the basic industries of the country. So far as organizing the mass-production industries was concerned, the craft union structure of the AFL made the achievement of that task practically impossible.

The CIO movement represents a radical break with this reactionary tradition. Under the banner of this movement hundreds of thousands of hitherto unorganized workers have swelled the ranks of organized labor, demonstrating the practicability, and even the ease, of organizing

---

Shachtman edited their draft before its first publication. The convention adopted this resolution unanimously.

1937 labor battles: **above**, Flint GM sit-down strike; **below**, Memorial Day massacre during Little Steel strike.

the masses of unorganized once the doors of unionism are thrown open to them. Moreover, the CIO movement has grown on the basis of the organization of the key and mass-production industries of the country controlled by the most powerful financial oligarchs (rubber, auto, steel, packinghouses, etc.). Still more, it has shown that the only possible and feasible means of organizing big industry and of preserving the unions is the industrial, or vertical structural form.

Contrary to the obsolete craft union structure of the AFL, which is thoroughly reactionary and divisive, the industrial union corresponds entirely to the modern organization of industrial life, made possible by the tremendous technological progress and consequent leveling of skilled workers to the plane of semiskilled or unskilled. Finally, the organization by the CIO of the unskilled mass-production industrial workers, the most poorly paid and the least subject to petty-bourgeois influences, produced a decisive change in the social composition of the organized labor movement.

Up to that time, the latter was dominated overwhelmingly by the labor aristocracy, closely interwoven with the bourgeois political parties, and presided over by a reactionary bureaucracy which never encountered any really perilous proletarian opposition in the ranks. Now, the organization of several million truly proletarian elements into unions drastically alters the relationship of forces in the organized labor movement. The unskilled, truly proletarian forces are the predominant element in the union movement for the first time, and thus constitute a formidable power not only against the conservative labor bureaucracy but also against capitalism itself.

This is already indicated by the fact that, immediately upon their organization into unions, and despite the fact that their employers represented the most powerful groups of the bourgeoisie (or rather, precisely because of that fact), these masses in the basic industries adopted the most advanced fighting tactics, encroaching directly upon the "sacred" property rights of the bourgeoisie (sit-in strikes), and conducted their struggles in the most militant and aggressive manner, often in disregard of the restraining hand of the CIO bureaucracy.

It is indicated also by the fact that, scarcely having entered the field of economic organization, they already showed their inclination to arm themselves with independent political organizations as well, to break with the traditional bourgeois parties (which are also the traditional alternatives of the AFL political policy), and to create their own party. This highly significant political tendency is weakened or checked—but its existence is not disproved—by the attempts of the CIO leadership to direct it back into old party channels or to distort it in the form of petty-bourgeois labor and farmer-labor parties.

All these considerations underline the fact that, on the whole, the CIO has been and remains the more progressive force in the organized labor movement.

The growth of the CIO movement has not, however, eliminated the AFL as a factor in the labor movement. Quite the contrary. The AFL has not only succeeded in maintaining virtually intact all the forces it had after the departure of such CIO organizations as the United Mine Workers and the Amalgamated Clothing Workers, but has even registered an increase in membership, in vitality, and even in strike activity. The unionization of the American working class in the recent period has not, by and large, taken place in one section at the expense of the other, but has proceeded along parallel lines, both in the CIO, which has recorded the greatest and most significant gains, and in the AFL.

The preservation and even growth of the AFL is accounted for by a number of important factors. In the first place, it still remains the organization primarily of the skilled workers, the aristocracy of labor. The AFL, furthermore, is the "traditional" organization of union labor, with strong craft traditions. In many industries and trades, its solidity is based upon the fact that it has regular contracts with the employers. Moreover, its main basis is constituted by more or less stable unions of long standing, having a strong apparatus, regular dues systems, and ample treasuries, a firm bureaucracy, regulated local and national organizations, with their own regular meetings, conventions, constitutions, elected officialdom, etc., etc.

In addition, under the irresistible influence of the patent successes of the industrial form of organization, certain sections of the AFL and its bureaucracy have relented from their stiff insistence on the craft union form of organization, and organized new unions on an industrial basis. Finally, the fact that the once apparently unhalting sweep of the CIO has been checked, and even driven back by the employers, has served to strengthen the feeling among certain sections of the working class that the AFL is not outlived and can be utilized as well as or even better than the CIO for the defense of labor interests. The flagrantly undemocratic system of leadership instituted by the CIO in the new unions organized by it has also been skillfully exploited by the AFL bureaucracy to its own advantage.

Growing desire for unity

A whole series of circumstances has now brought prominently to the fore the question of the unification of the AFL and the CIO. The main responsibility for the split two years ago unquestionably lies on the shoulders of the AFL bureaucracy. By its reactionary control of the labor movement, the Executive Council of the AFL sought to stifle every attempt to modify the obsolete craft union structure upon which it is based, and actively sabotaged all efforts to organize the unorganized, especially in the mass-production industries, on an industrial, that is, on the only conceivable basis.

The formation of the CIO, its fight against the Green-Woll-Frey machine, its decisive plunge into the work of organizing the masses of the unskilled in the key industries, were progressive steps and more than warranted the active support given by the revolutionists to the CIO as the progressive section of the labor movement. In its fight against the CIO, the leadership of the AFL played a disloyal and reactionary role. Instead of facilitating the work of organizing the big industries of the country, it stood in the way at every turn, joining in the union-breaking chorus of the employers and their apologists. In many cases, the AFL leadership even resorted to downright strike-breaking in an effort to stem the sensational advances made by the CIO.

However, notwithstanding the wide rift that developed between the two sections of the labor movement, there are now strong forces at work for their unification. The setbacks suffered by the various sectors of the union movement in most recent times have strengthened the feeling that one united organization, instead of two antagonistic ones, would make it easier to win labor's battles against the employers. The defeat registered by the workers in the "Little Steel" and similar strikes has only served to emphasize the need for putting an end to the division in labor's camp.[6]

---

6. The U.S. Steel Corporation signed a contract with the CIO in March 1937, without a strike, but its leading competitors, known as "Little

On top of this is the ominous deepening of the new crisis, which weakens labor's hold on industry and foreshadows an employers' offensive to reduce the workers' standard of living, annul all the gains made in the past period, and wipe out whatever union control has been established. The dangers of the crisis are reflected in the mounting sentiment among the organized workers throughout the country for a speedy unification of the AFL and the CIO so that labor may be able to present a sorely needed common front against the capitalist class.

Contributing to this inexorable trend are a number of subsidiary factors. The Roosevelt regime is not antagonistic to unity, but rather favorable. In its systematic work of preparing the country for war and extending the militarization of all institutions, it understands that the trade unions can be more smoothly coordinated into a war machine if friction in their ranks is eliminated and if they are a single unit led and controlled by a single reactionary leadership.

In addition, a certain section of the employers is exerting pressure in the direction of unification because it finds the "raids" conducted by the CIO on the AFL, and vice versa, with their consequent effects on industrial production, to be more unprofitable to the employers than dealing with a single, conservatively led union would be. The financial drain upon both CIO and AFL in the violent

---

Steel" (Bethlehem Steel, Republic Steel, Youngstown Sheet and Tube, Inland Steel, and Weirton Steel), refused to recognize the CIO and forced its 75,000 members at the plants of the first four companies out on strike in May 1937. Eighteen strikers were slaughtered, scores injured, and hundreds arrested in militant battles by the steelworkers. The strike was virtually defeated by late June, but lingered on into October. It was the first major defeat for the CIO. Little Steel was not unionized until 1941.

struggles against each other is also a factor of some influence in bringing unity closer to realization.

Finally, the original point in dispute, namely, the question of organizing the mass-production industries on an industrial (vertical) basis, has already been settled by the realities of the auto, rubber, steel, and electrical unions now in existence and functioning. Not even the most hardened Bourbon of craft unionism in the AFL leadership would seriously propose today to dissolve the United Automobile Workers, for example, into the twenty-two craft unions which existed under the Green dispensation prior to the CIO's advances.

Apart from face-saving considerations, the principle of industrial unionism, at least as applied to the mass-production industries, may be considered generally acknowledged throughout the organized labor movement, and reluctantly accepted even by the Green-Woll machine. What stands chiefly in the way of the successful conclusions of the unity negotiations now under way is the struggle for power in the united organization between the old AFL and the new CIO bureaucracies. The main point in dispute is not the right of industrial unionism, but such a form of reunification as will give the one or the other bureaucratic machine the greatest number of supporters and the upper hand in the united organization.

Our party, together with every revolutionary and class-conscious worker, takes a clear-cut position in favor of the earliest and completest possible unification of the AFL and the CIO, and also the hitherto unaffiliated railroad brotherhoods. The only condition, practically speaking, under which such a unity would be a step backward would be one binding the former CIO unions to abandon the industrial form of organization and to divide themselves into scores of impotent craft unions. Unification on such a basis is, however, scarcely conceivable.

Unity would be a tremendous step forward for a number of reasons. The united trade union membership in the United States today is the largest ever reached in all its history, far larger than at the postwar peak. Unity of all the unions into one would mean a common, organized union front of approximately eight million workers,[7] with a tremendous attractive power for the still unorganized, with almost inexhaustible forces capable of withstanding the offensive of the employers and of advancing aggressively the demands of the workers on all fronts. The unification would overcome the present, thoroughly reactionary division between the unskilled, proletarian elements in the unions, on the one side, and the skilled labor aristocracy on the other. Finally, a united union organization is, in general, a better field for the work of the revolutionary vanguard than a union movement divided against itself.

The reactionary role which the AFL leadership has played is clearly established in the minds of the class-conscious workers. From this it should not follow that the revolutionary vanguard makes a fetish of the CIO and worships unquestioningly at its shrine. Prior to the establishment of the unity of the two organizations, which the revolutionists must advocate as their general line, they work in either organization, according to specific local circumstances.

The revolutionist does not withdraw from a union just because it may be conservative in policy or leadership; on

---

7. In September 1937 the CIO claimed a membership of 3,718,000 and the AFL claimed 3,600,000 (later the AFL became the larger organization). The members of the international unions in the railroad brotherhoods that were affiliated to the AFL were included in the AFL figure; the unaffiliated rail and other independent unions must have brought the total figure to around 8,000,000, out of a labor force of around 31 million employed in nonagricultural jobs.

the contrary, such a condition is usually all the greater reason for revolutionary activity in the union, always provided, of course, that the union embraces the decisive sections of the workers (employed or unemployed, as the case may be) in its particular field. But even where concrete circumstances dictate working in an AFL or craft union, the revolutionary militant must always bear in mind the need of stressing the obsoleteness and ineffectualness of the craft union form and the demonstrated superiority of the industrial form of organization, be it achieved by direct organizing of the unorganized, or by the amalgamation of craft unions already in existence in a given industry.

Although it is impossible for us at the present time to influence decisively the course of events, or to determine the pace and method of trade union unity, we are nevertheless bound to concentrate our propaganda and agitational activity among the workers in favor of the most desirable basis for unity, that is, democratic organization and a wide measure of autonomy for the affiliated unions, especially such a measure as would facilitate the organization of the basic industries into industrial unions and preserve the integrity of those already in existence. Every attempt to carve up the industrial unions into craft formations must be stubbornly resisted as thoroughly reactionary.

While the general line of all militants in the labor movement must be based upon the speediest consummation of unity, it does not follow that each and every single concrete question can be solved by the abstract consideration of unity at all costs. Prior to the complete unification of the two main bodies of labor, a number of cases have already appeared where the bald slogan of unity would actually set back the militant and progressive movement. While the tactical line in each particular case must be subordinated to the general line of complete unification of the trade union movement, it does not follow that the two coincide in every instance or at every given moment.

The militant vanguard must constantly stress the fact that neither industrial unionism nor unity, by themselves, solve the problems of the working class and its struggle. In its way, each is a step forward for labor which facilitates its further progress. Unification is always desirable because it enables labor to present a more solid and effective front. Industrial unionism aids in the development of rank-and-file democratic control and in militant mass action, and promotes the best functioning of the organized workers in the modern big machine industries.

But unless the industrial unions, or the union movement in general, function as class-struggle organizations, they present to the working class no decisive and lasting advantages. Class collaboration under whatever form or structure finally yields only defeat for the working class. The correct basis for the union movement can be found only in the theory and practice of the class struggle, in the widest inner-union democracy, in rank-and-file control, and in a leadership and policy based upon the class struggle and workers' democracy.

The trade union bureaucracy

Class-struggle policies and leadership, and union democracy, are at a minimum in the AFL and in the CIO. The bulk of the leadership of both sections of the union movement have in common the fact that they both serve as the labor lieutenants of the capitalist class and are the defenders, basically, of the capitalist system. All the difference between the two movements notwithstanding, this common fundamental feature of the leaderships can be ignored only at the greatest peril to the proper orientation of the militant vanguard. The AFL bureaucracy is the classic representative of class-collaboration policies in the labor movement, with its theory of the "harmony of interests" of employer and employee, and the acceptance of capitalism implied in the slogan of a "fair day's pay for a fair day's work." The same bureaucracy has, consequently, not recoiled from the most arbitrary and repressive measures against every militant and revolutionary minority that has threatened its rule and its policies.

Fundamentally, the role of the CIO leadership has been no less reactionary. It has performed the function of steering the spontaneous and independent class action of the workers organized under its banner back onto the road of class collaboration, of employer-employee "harmony," of reliance upon the Roosevelt, i.e., the capitalist government, its institutions and its "impartial mediation." The failure of the "Little Steel" strike only emphasized the ruinous results of this course. The most elementary requirements of strike organization were ignored. No real strike committees or mass picket lines were organized. The workers were not given to understand that the strike was to be a real and vigorous class action and that victory depended upon their own might, their own militancy, their own organization.

Aided and abetted by the Stalinists, who follow their line, Lewis and Murray repressed the militant forces in favor of an appeal to and dependence on official action by the president and the governors involved. The idea that Roosevelt, and not the workers, would win the victory for the union proved fatal, as was to be expected. Class collaboration was carried to the limit of welcoming the Ohio National Guard in Youngstown. The leaders and their subordinates poisoned the minds of the workers with assurances that the governor had sent the guard to keep the plants closed, and thereby help the workers defeat the employers.

The bureaucratic management of the new CIO unions is notorious. The Lewis-Hillman-Murray clique, aware of the danger to their leadership and policies represented by the mass unionization of the aggressive unskilled workers in the large-scale industries, sought to paralyze rank-and-file control in advance by establishing a bureaucratic guardianship over all the unions they organized. Neither the leadership nor the policies were voted by the union membership. No regular organization has been set up in most cases. Officials are appointed in the worst traditions of the United Mine Workers of America.

The CIO itself is a self-appointed committee of leaders which has never been ratified by the rank and file. The inability of the latter to determine their leadership or decide upon the policies of the various "organizing committees" has already produced a bad reaction in the organizations, manifesting itself in a decline of interest, falling into indifference, reduced attendance at meetings, etc. The CIO can be restored to its full strength and effectiveness, and put in a position to exploit all the possibilities of growth before it, only in a relentless struggle against the poison of class collaborationism and bureaucratism, and against the leadership that represents them.

If neither industrial unionism, nor unity, as such, are a solution of the problem, they are nevertheless steps in that direction. The problem itself may be summed up as follows: the triumph of a militant leadership in the unions, basing itself on class-struggle policies, union democracy, and rank-and-file control.

Political tendencies in the workers' movement

Of all the labor political groups in the trade unions today, which one is indicated to promote a solution of this key problem?

The Communist Party was once the organizer of the progressive and left-wing movement in the trade unions. It has completely abandoned this role today. In the period of its reactionary degeneration, it has been reduced to the position of an agency in the American trade unions representing the interests and responding exclusively to the commands of the anti-Soviet bureaucracy of the Kremlin.

Throughout the trade unions, but above all in the CIO, the Stalinists are the most servile and venomous assistants of the reactionary bureaucracy. They outshout the most vehement in their advocacy of class collaboration, of reliance on the Roosevelt regime, of subservience to the union officialdom. At the same time, it must be emphasized that they nevertheless have a different basis than that of the CIO or AFL bureaucracy. The latter, though they act as the labor lieutenants of the bourgeoisie, and base themselves on bourgeois democracy—whose left, reformist wing they constitute—cannot preserve their own power as a bureaucracy without, to one extent or another, preserving the source and foundation of that power, namely the trade unions. Their policies, in the long run, do, it is true, help destroy the very trade unions upon which they rest; but in doing so, as shown by the German, Italian, and Austrian experiences, they are themselves destroyed.

The Stalinist bureaucracy, even in the trade unions, is, however, primarily an instrument of the counterrevolutionary Stalin bureaucracy in Russia, and serves its interests first of all. The preservation and advancement of the interests of the trade unions, and the working class in general, are entirely secondary considerations, subordinated to the Stalinists' main function. For them, the trade unions are primarily institutions to be converted into instruments for the People's Front, for the successful propagation of the war of the "democratic" imperialists against the "reactionary" imperialists in defense of the Stalin regime. The most consistent class collaborationists and social patriots[8] in the working class, and in the trade union movement, are the Stalinists. Hence, they are the most violent and bureaucratic enemy of all revolutionary and truly progressive forces in the unions. Hence, their chief slogan: "Drive the Trotskyists out of the labor movement," which means, drive out of the labor movement all those who stand for the class struggle, who oppose imperialist war and the reactionary bureaucracy which is already part of the capitalist government machine today and the war machine tomorrow.

The idea that the Communist Party represents a progressive factor in the trade union movement is based upon outworn memories of the past. The CP today is a reactionary force in the labor movement and must be dealt with as such. It is a pernicious influence which the vanguard elements and militants in general must fight tooth and nail to eliminate from the working-class movement.

Blocs with the Communist Party in the trade unions are, as a rule, entirely inconceivable for the revolutionary Marxists, and are permissible only under the most extraordinary and exceptional circumstances, and provided only that the utmost vigilance is maintained towards them and the most rigid political independence is insisted upon. Ninety-nine times out of a hundred, collaboration with the CP forces will prove permissible only under exceptional circumstances where they are part of a much more broadly organized general progressive or left-wing movement of which we may also form a part.

---

8. Social patriotism is a term used by Marxists to refer to socialists who abandon internationalism and other revolutionary principles in the interest of patriotism to the ruling class.

In those unions which are under the control of the Stalinists, and in which left-wing minority work is particularly difficult, it is the special duty of the revolutionists to remain doggedly at their task, to avoid and fight against expulsion, and not to leave the rank and file under the uncontested leadership of the CP cliques.

The Thomas-Tyler-Altman Socialist Party cannot be counted as a decisive progressive force in the trade unions. The SP is a right-wing propaganda sect without direct influence of its own in the labor movement. Wherever individual members of that party occupy official or leading posts, they were gained, as a rule, not by the advancement of a militant socialist position, but as a result of adaptation to the policies and rule of the conservative union bureaucracy. This has, in fact, been the traditional method of "rooting themselves in the unions" pursued by the SP reformists.

Even over these officials, the SP has no control, nor does it seek to exercise any. Party discipline is employed only against those few rank-and-file militants who do seek to conduct a militant struggle against class collaborationism and bureaucratic leadership in the unions. However, because of the number of rank-and-file SP members who are ready to go part of the distance in a consistent struggle for left-wing policies, it is permissible and necessary for the revolutionists to form blocs with them in specific instances and for specific ends.

With insignificant changes, what has been said about the SP applies to the Lovestone group. The positions occupied by some of its members in the trade unions have been acquired or maintained, generally speaking, by the surrender of working-class principles and adaptation to the conservative bureaucracy and its policies. Examples of this are to be found in the International

Ladies Garment Workers Union, the shoe workers' union, and the auto workers' union. As with the SP, blocs are permissible under certain conditions with the Lovestone group.

To the extent that the Lovestoneites also come into conflict with the Stalinists and their murderous red-baiting drive against all militants, the Lovestoneites will be compelled to seek a common front at least on such elementary questions as the rights of minorities in the unions. Actuated though they are by the interest of self-defense and self-preservation, temporary blocs with clearly limited aims are quite conceivable between the revolutionary Marxists and the Lovestoneites.

From the standpoint both of its membership and its sympathizers, the IWW plays only a limited role in the labor movement today. As an organization, it is a reactionary sect, dominated by a narrow-minded anarchist clique imbued with a deep hatred of the Marxists and the Russian revolution, and animated by the narrowest factional interests. On the other hand, as a general movement, in the sense of those former members of the IWW who are still influenced by its ideology, it has a distinct importance in certain fields, notably in the maritime industry. Most of these elements have splendid traditions behind them and are permeated by an irreconcilable spirit of class struggle and militance. In the maritime industry, the building of a broad progressive and militant movement requires a sincere cooperation with the best elements among the syndicalist-minded workers.

At the same time we must conduct a persistent and stubborn—though patient and comradely—struggle to break down the antipolitical, anti-Marxist prejudices inculcated into these militants and fostered by the corrupt parliamentarism and reformism of the Social Democracy and by the bureaucratism, deceit, fakery, and treachery to principles of the Stalinists.

Reorient the party

The only consistent revolutionary and progressive force in the trade union movement is represented by our party, the party of the revolutionary class struggle. It can begin to accomplish its tasks only by understanding its present relationship to them. The party is woefully weak in general, and especially weak in the trade unions. Its influence and leadership is either local, episodic, or accidental. Very little systematic trade union work is done, and what is done is not properly organized or centralized. Our press only casually reflects the American class struggle. News of the trade union movement, of its struggles and internal life, is accidental in its columns, dependent largely upon chance contributions of isolated comrades.

A complete reorientation of our party, from the membership up to the leadership and back again, is absolutely imperative and unpostponable. No less drastic a reorientation is required of our weekly press. The attention of the party must be focused primarily upon the American labor movement. The energies of the party must be devoted mainly to rooting itself in the trade unions, becoming an inseparable part of the trade unions and their struggles. *The bulk of the party's work must be directed to this vital field of the class struggle.* Unless this slogan is translated speedily into life, the party is doomed to vegetate as an impotent sect which will be washed away by the waves of the first serious social crisis.

The party membership must be rooted deeply in the trade unions. The first demand for activity that the party must make on every member is that he join the union in which he is eligible for membership. The sweep of unionism, covering virtually every craft, trade, and industry, ensures the possibility of virtually every worker becoming a unionist today. It should be borne in mind that if our party is to be a genuinely proletarian party, both in its composition and its ideology, it must be composed, in its decisive majority, of proletarians and trade unionists. Above all, it should be borne in mind that if the party is to survive the coming war, with its certain persecution and hounding of the revolutionary movement, if the party is to fulfill its great tasks during the war, if it is not to be dispersed and its efforts rendered nugatory—the party membership must be solidly and inseparably connected with the organized working class. There is no better way of accomplishing this connection than by every member becoming an active, responsible, and influential trade unionist.

Guidelines for trade union work

Precisely because of the intensely political and polemical environment in which our party has developed, it is necessary to emphasize a number of fundamental, elementary guiding lines for our trade union work.

The party is the leader and guide of all the work of its members in the trade unions. Without party leadership and guidance, all trade union work inevitably degenerates into opportunism and becomes a hindrance to revolutionary progress. In his mass work, the party member must not become a "mere trade unionist," or forget the need of imbuing the trade union movement with a revolutionary political class consciousness. However, in order effectively to pursue his work in the trade union movement the revolutionist must understand keenly the importance of approaching his fellow unionists and their problems not so much on the basis of his own consciousness and experience but rather on the basis of the level of consciousness and the degree of experience of the average trade unionist.

To approach the trade unionist, trade union problems, or even the trade union leadership in exactly the same manner in which one political organization deals with a rival political organization would result in self-isolation. The revolutionist must be conscious of his political role, but at the same time also of the fact that he is dealing, in the first place, with trade union problems and with workers who have not as yet developed beyond a trade union consciousness.

The excellent work which our comrades have already done in various unions shows the vast, untapped possibilities for participation in the class struggle and recruitment to the revolutionary party which are opened up before us by a serious and systematic work in the trade unions.

A serious approach to the trade unions and their problems, and not a hypercritical one, is the need; a responsible attitude toward the work of building the trade unions and our influence within them, and not a lightminded, "experimental" one; an attitude of methodical, patient enlightenment of the politically undeveloped worker on the basis of his day-to-day experiences in the unions and in the class struggle, and not a supercilious, "high political" approach to him.

The present period also calls for a highly responsible attitude in the key question of strikes in general, and particularly sit-down strikes. It is imperative to combat the defeatist, reformist propaganda that strikes are impossible in a period of economic crisis or decline. Strikes, and victorious ones, are possible even under such difficult circumstances; only it is more important than ever that they be carefully organized, the moment and the place deliberately chosen, and the struggle conducted in the most militant and determined manner. In this connection it is important to be aware of the danger of strikes or other actions confined to small minorities, harmful in general, and always tending to degenerate into adventuristic movements which only antagonize the bulk of the organized workers.

The sit-down strike is not a universal substitute for the classic form of strike action (quitting the plant, mass picket line, etc.), but it is indubitably a proven contribution to proletarian tactics and an effective weapon in their struggle. Its initiation and extension are a tribute to the resourcefulness of the proletariat in finding new and powerful methods of fighting its class oppressors. It has served, moreover, the important end of breaking down an awesome respect for bourgeois private property which the ruling class instills in the proletariat from its childhood onward. It is our duty to defend this weapon against all attempts to suppress, discredit, or outlaw it. This does not signify that we advocate the indiscriminate use of the sit-down at all times and in all cases. We judge its feasibility on the same general considerations which determine our tactics in strikes: general objective conditions, the state of the union, mood of the membership, position of the employers and the state, possibilities of achieving the objective, etc., etc.

The sit-down strike, has, however, an even more significant future before it than the ordinary strike. Precisely because it challenges the fundamental tenet of capitalism, the inviolable right of private property in the means of production, the sit-down strike seems to be one of the main indicated means of mass action—by virtue of the seizure of the plants and their temporary control by workers' committees—for realizing in the coming period the slogan of "Workers' control of production." The deepening of the present crisis will push this slogan to the foreground and properly directed by the revolutionary party, it may become the decisive popular slogan with the masses of the workers and above all the militant trade unionists.

We reject contemptuously the arguments against the sit-down strikes advanced by the government authorities, the employers, and the trade union bureaucrats. On their lips, this opposition is simply one way of formulating their opposition to strikes in general, as well as to all militant mass action of the workers. At the same time, it is necessary to point out that, as a rule, any attempt by a small minority in a given plant or industry to impose a sit-down strike upon the big majority of the workers involved, without consulting them or obtaining their agreement, or at a time when the majority of the workers either have no acute grievances or are not as yet conscious of them—will lead inevitably to a reaction against sit-down strikes, ordinary strikes, and even unionism in general on the part of the more undeveloped workers.

A serious and responsible attitude in this question is absolutely imperative. While we do not join in the reactionary chorus of condemnation of so-called outlaw strikes—the responsibility for which usually reposes upon the bureaucracy, which cynically ignores the legitimate demands and grievances of the workers—and while we remain steadfastly on the side of any group of workers once they are engaged in a struggle with the capitalist class or any section of it, we are conscious of the responsibility that reposes upon us as a vanguard force, and therefore counsel against the indiscriminate or promiscuous use of the sit-down strike into which workers are often provoked by the brutal exploitation to which they are subjected by the employers.

The same general propositions hold true of so-called

unauthorized strikes. The left wing strives to obtain the maximum amount of support both from the officialdom of its own union and from working-class organizations as a whole, for all the actions which it advocates, strikes included. We oppose the bureaucratic conception that the calling of strikes is the exclusive prerogative of the international officials of a given union, and we advocate the widest democratic control of the strike weapon by the rank and file, vested, in the first place, in the hands of the local and district unions and in the shop committees, which must be set up everywhere and which must have the most immediate charge of protecting the interests of the workers and enforcing the provisions of any agreement entered into between the employers and the employees.

While taking proper cognizance of the fact that the rules of many trade unions require official permission from the international officials before a strike may be called, and orienting ourselves accordingly, we cannot ignore the fact that the international officialdom of the various unions is not only opposed, generally speaking, to the use of the strike weapon, but sabotages it when it is employed. Situations are therefore quite conceivable in which the only way the rank and file can obtain legal permission for a strike at certain times is by forcing the hand of the officialdom by what the latter often start by condemning as an "outlaw" strike.

The immediate tasks of the party

The party sets itself the following immediate tasks for its work in the trade unions:

The immediate registering of all party and YPSL members in order to have a complete record of the trade or profession of each member, union affiliation or eligibility, position in the trade union, etc., etc.

Every effort must be made immediately to have every eligible non–trade unionist in the party join the union of his trade or industry and take an active part in its life.

Wherever two or more members of the party and the YPSL belong to the same union, they are to constitute themselves a party trade union fraction, to work under the direction of the trade union department of the party.

Where no union exists for a given trade or industry, in a given locality, our comrades must take the initiative in organizing the unorganized.

The need of a nationally connected left wing in the American trade union movement is the most urgent problem in that field today. None exists at the present time, since the old left-wing movement organized by the Communist Party[9] has been completely liquidated and dissolved into the trade union bureaucracy. Without a left-wing movement standing on the militant platform of the class struggle, the trade union movement in this country is doomed to the demoralizing effects of class collaborationism and the dead-hand control of the reactionary union bureaucracy. Our party must take the leadership in organizing and integrating nationally the left-wing movement.

Where such groups do not yet exist, we must take the initiative in forming them on the widest possible basis compatible with the formation of a genuinely progressive

---

9. This probably refers to the CP-led Trade Union Educational League before 1929. The TUEL organized left-wing groupings inside the AFL and it also attempted to start independent unions where the AFL was inactive or dormant. In 1929, when the Stalinist "third period" was initiated in the U.S., the CP changed the name of the TUEL to the Trade Union Unity League, denounced the AFL as "social fascist," and took all of its members out of the AFL unions and shunted them away from the mainstream of the labor movement in an unsuccessful attempt to build its own "red" unions.

movement having a basically class-struggle platform. Progressive groups should be conceived of not only as fields of recruitment for the revolutionary party, but as the means for setting in motion the largest number of workers at a given time for the advancement of a left-wing position and a left-wing leadership. It is not a precondition for our participation that from the outset we have the leadership of such groups, but it is an absolutely minimum condition that we have the right to advocate and defend our own position in the ranks of the general progressive group.

Platform of the left wing

The left-wing movement should stand on the following general platform:

Against class collaboration and for a policy of class struggle.

For the fullest inner-union democracy for all members of the union and for all groups. Against the attempt to illegalize and suppress all minority groups in the unions, such as has been done in the International Ladies Garment Workers Union, and for the system of group rights in the union such as prevails, for example, in the International Typographical Union.

For the normal functioning of all unions and against bureaucratically appointed organizers and leaderships such as prevail in most of the "organizing committees" of the CIO. For immediate holding of conventions, adoption of constitution and policies, and democratic selection of the leadership.

For the shop steward and shop committee systems throughout the industries, integrated into the trade unions.

Against any attempt to "incorporate" the trade unions, against all "government regulation" of the trade unions, and in general, against all attempts to deprive the unions of their complete class independence by subordinating them to the apparatus of the government, which is only a machine for defending the interests of the capitalist class.

For the defense against the government, the employers, and the trade union bureaucracy of the vital weapon of the strike, including the sit-down strike.

For the amalgamation of all craft unions in a given industry into industrial unions.

Against high initiation fees and prohibitive dues systems, especially in the present period of unemployment and crisis. Against the dropping of unemployed members from the rolls for inability to pay the regular dues required.

For the defense by the trade unions of the interests of the unemployed. For the organization of the unemployed by the trade unions themselves. For the affiliation in a body of the unemployed workers of a given trade or industry to the corresponding union, and for full rights of voice and vote for those workers on all questions directly affecting them and their specific problems (the system employed by project workers associated with the Teamsters union in Minneapolis).

For special attention to the defense of the rights and interests of the young workers and apprentices, and for the annulment of the exceptional legislation against them now existing in the unions, which prevents them from participating in the trade union movement and its struggles with full rights.

In order that these tasks may be carried out in a systematic, efficient, and centralized manner, the convention instructs the incoming National Executive Committee of the party to establish immediately a regular trade union department, with a responsible and functioning trade union secretary. The National Executive Committee of the YPSL shall appoint a representative to function in the party's trade union department.

Resolution on the Soviet Union[10]

1. The twentieth anniversary of the Bolshevik uprising marks the completion of a cycle of degeneration in the Russian revolution and the inauguration of a new stage in its development. The unbroken series of sanguinary purges represent a one-sided civil war in which the Bonapartist bureaucracy has succeeded in wiping out virtually every single representative of two generations: the generation which was the bearer of the ideas and traditions of the October revolution itself (the old guard of Leninism), as well as the Thermidorian generation, representing the petty-bourgeois reaction against the October revolution,

---

10. The first draft of this resolution was printed in *Internal Bulletin*, number 2, Organizing Committee for the Socialist Party Convention, November 1937, and was reprinted in *Bulletin Number 6*, January 1938. Maurice Spector and Max Shachtman were assigned to prepare the first draft. The convention vote was 69 in favor of this resolution against 6 in favor of other positions. This resolution has never been printed publicly before now.

which beginning with the recession of the world revolution after 1923, undermined the social and political conquests of the Russian revolution. In the civil war in Spain, the Stalinist bureaucracy has appeared for the first time on a large, decisive scale as the principal and direct counterrevolutionary force in the labor camp operating for the preservation of capitalism and against the proletarian struggle for power and emancipation. In international politics, perverting the slogan of "Defend the Soviet Union," the Stalinist bureaucracy has subordinated itself to one of the two main imperialist camps and is busily engaged in preparing the world proletariat to serve as cannon fodder for the "democratic" imperialists in the coming world war.

This new stage in the development of the Russian revolution requires a new statement of position by the revolutionary Marxists.

2. The degeneration of the Russian revolution has met with a mixed reception in the international bourgeois and working-class world. The bourgeoisie, in actuality, warmly welcomes the break of the Soviet bureaucracy with all the principles of revolutionary socialism and internationalism. Where it permits itself a criticism of the bloody purges and the economic maladministration of the Soviet Union, it is only for the purpose of breaking down the faith of its "own" working class in the idea of socialism and proletarian struggle and of promoting the idea of the superiority of "democratic" capitalism over the new social order. The revolutionary Marxists, however, will continue to unmask the revolting hypocrisy of the bourgeoisie, whose criticisms are designed to make the workers continue to tolerate and to uphold a social system under which "democracy" is a gross fraud lightly discarded for a most barbaric and open dictatorship against the masses as soon as the latter threaten the privileges and profits of private property—a

social system which, in the advanced countries, condemns the bulk of the population to unemployment, misery, and war in the midst of unexampled abundance.

3. The complete disintegration of Stalinism has prolonged the lease on life of all varieties of social reformism. While bolstering up the Second International by taking over its classic position in favor of class collaboration, participation in coalition governments for the purpose of suppressing the revolutionary aspirations of the masses, and support of one's "own" national bourgeoisie in case of war, the Stalinists, by their course in the Soviet Union, have afforded the Social Democrats the occasion for advertising their pretended moral and political superiority over "Bolshevism." The revolutionary Marxists reply to these pretensions by associating themselves proudly with the great principles, traditions, and achievements of the movement represented by Lenin and Trotsky, and condemn Stalinism precisely because it represents the very antithesis of that movement. The Social Democrats and reformists of all kinds seek to identify Stalinism with Leninism and Bolshevism, to designate the former as the direct, legitimate successor of the latter. They attempt thereby to utilize the just antipathy of the class-conscious vanguard towards Stalinism both for the purpose of covering up their historical crimes and of justifying, in retrospect, their betrayal and struggle against the October revolution and against the principles of revolutionary Marxism, that is, the principles of Leninism. Rejecting or perverting the principles of revolutionary Marxism, the Social Democracy led the international working class into the charnel house of the last world war, and afterwards, along the road that plunged the Italian, the German, the Austrian, and now—almost—the Spanish proletariat into the hideous abyss of fascism. Refusing to follow the path of the

"adventuristic Bolsheviks," the Mensheviks and Social Revolutionists feverishly sought to prop up the regime of Kerensky and the Russian bourgeoisie, to prosecute the war on behalf of Anglo-French imperialism, to crush the Russian proletarian revolution both before and after its triumph. Spurning the theories of Marxism, the philosophers of petty-bourgeois anarchism have led the Spanish proletariat from one needless defeat after another, capitulating lamely to the bourgeois People's Front at a time when the real power was actually in their hands. The basic political purpose which all these historically discredited currents in the labor movement pursue, with their argument that Stalinism is only a synonym for Leninism, is expressed substantially in these terms: "We never opposed a proletarian revolution in Russia—it was Stalinism we always fought. We never fought revolutionary Marxism—it was Stalinism we have been fighting from 1914 to 1937."

4. The revolutionary Marxists of the Fourth International cannot make the slightest concession to the attempts to rehabilitate any of the varieties of social reformism. Quite the contrary, these attempts must be vigorously and vigilantly resisted; otherwise the Fourth International will be affected at its very heart by the disintegrative poisons now flowing through the veins of the working-class movement. Hence, the necessity of a merciless and uncompromising struggle in our own ranks against those liquidators of the revolutionary Marxian movement who seek to compound an abstract condemnation of Stalinism with a rejection of the fundamental principles of Marxism, thus breaking down the line dividing revolution from reformism—as well as against the "ultraleftist" liquidators who have shown, in the vital question of the civil war in Spain, their failure to make a prompt and unambiguous choice between the camp of imperialism and the camp

of revolution, thus forecasting their position with regard to the no-less-vital question of the Soviet Union.

The revolutionary Marxists combat Stalinism not because it has continued the line of Leninism and of the Russian revolution, but because it has brutally broken that line. The revolutionary Marxists combat Stalinism not because they have become reconciled by a hair's breadth with the Social Democracy and the Second International, but precisely because it is Stalinism that has effected such a reconciliation. Only such an approach to the problem makes it possible to draw the lessons of the Russian revolution, both in the period of its upsurge and decline, in such a way as to build up in this country and everywhere else a solidly founded party of the proletarian revolution.

The October revolution

5. The war of 1914–18 marked the close of the epoch of capitalist expansion, and the opening of the epoch of wars, fascism, and revolution. Capitalism, along with the continuance of the periodic crises, entered the stage of its general crisis as a social system. The alternative of social progress and development through the overthrow of capitalism and the socialist revolution, or cumulative social decay, misery, wars, and fascist barbarism through the maintenance of capitalism was posed directly to mankind, with no third solution.

6. The Russian revolution was the direct product of the world war, which in turn was the inevitable explosion of the productive forces against the barriers of private property and national frontiers. With the outbreak of the war, the epoch of capitalist expansion and bourgeois democracy yielded to the epoch of wars and revolutions. Humanity was faced by the alternatives of socialist progress on the road of the revolutionary overthrow of capitalism, or

reversion to barbarism under the heel of fascist dictatorship. The Russian revolution was the first stage of the world revolution. Under the leadership of Bolshevism, the Russian proletariat victoriously struck at the weakest link in the chain of world capitalism. The Russian bourgeoisie proved incapable of solving the problems even of the "bourgeois" revolution; its democratic pose masked its imperialist aspirations. Russian Menshevism and the Social Revolutionists vainly sought to prop up the coalition with the bourgeoisie.

The Bolshevik Party, founded and built upon the principles of Marxian internationalism, alone proved equal to the demands of the revolutionary crisis. Under the leadership of the Bolshevik Party, and only through that road, did the workers take and defend the state power. The revolution of 1917 thus provided a conclusive vindication of the principles, strategy, and tactics of Marxian internationalism.

The workers' state

7. The revolution of 1917 established as the state form the dictatorship of the proletariat, in which control by the working class was exercised through the soviets, the basic institutions of the workers' state, and through the factory committees, the army committees, the trade unions, and the revolutionary party expressing the fundamental historical interests of the proletariat. The dictatorship was exercised uncompromisingly against the bourgeoisie, both national and international, and against all irreconcilable enemies of the workers' regime. Though the circumstances of the early years of the revolution, the civil war, and the imperialist intervention made impossible the extension of the fullest degree of workers' democracy, nevertheless genuine accounting and control by the workers was maintained

to an unprecedented and sufficient degree.

8. As its major economic measure, the workers' state nationalized all important factories, banks, mines, railroads, means of communication, and established a state monopoly of industrial enterprise and foreign trade. In agriculture, the expropriation of the landlords was followed by the distribution of the land to the peasants, a partial attempt to nationalize the land directly in the form of state farms, and eventuated in the present form of collectivization as the general basis of agricultural economy.

9. From its first days, the workers' state took those social measures possible to it in the light of material conditions, and looking forward to the social expansion of the future: provisions for universal education, social insurance, recreation, cultural development, right of self-determination, and full cultural freedom for separate nationalities and national minorities.

10. The founders of the workers' state from the beginning recognized clearly the international character of the revolution. They understood that the revolution in Russia was simply the first stage in the international revolution; and that the success of the Russian revolution depended in the last analysis upon the extension of the revolution internationally.

Isolation and degeneration of the revolution

11. Following a great upsurge of the workers in all countries, electrified by the Russian revolution, which brought the workers to the threshold of victory in Germany, Hungary, Poland, and Italy, the revolutionary wave was beaten back. Everywhere except in Russia, the revolution was defeated. The causes of this defeat are to be found in the still remaining strength of imperialism, the exhaustion of the masses following the war, but above

all, in the treachery of the Social Democracy which, as in 1914 and 1917, proved in the crisis to be the servant of the bourgeoisie and the enemy of the revolution; and which handed back the power to the bourgeoisie even where the workers, as in Germany, had virtually conquered it. Through these defeats, the proletarian revolution was temporarily isolated within the Soviet Union. The Social Democracy is thus mainly responsible for laying the social basis for the subsequent rise and triumph of the Stalinist bureaucracy.

12. The rigors of the imperialist war and the civil war, the famine, the industrial and financial breakdown, and the spectacle of the temporary defeat of the international revolution brought the Soviet masses to a state of physical and moral exhaustion.

13. The economy, culture, and social traditions bequeathed to the workers' state by tsarism were the most primitive and backward of Europe.

14. The circumstances of the early years of the Soviet state had made necessary, as indispensable and entirely justifiable prerequisites for the defense of the workers' regime, certain temporary checks and limitations upon the free democratic control exercised by the working class as a whole over the regime.

15. When, following the conclusion of the civil war, the defeat of the internal counterrevolution, and the consolidation of the regime, the time came to remove these checks and limitations on workers' democracy, to undertake the more positive tasks of the revolution, and to elaborate a policy for the Soviet state in accordance with the general strategy of the world revolution, the task proved too great. In the face of the exhaustion of the masses, the breakdown of the economy, and the defeat of the world revolution, the revolutionists, gathered in the so-called Left

Opposition, and their policy—representing unambiguously the interests of the proletariat—were defeated. Stalinism—representing both in its program and its ruthless bureaucratic tactics precisely the defeat of the revolution internationally, the exhaustion and backwardness of the masses and the Russian economy—was able to win control of the party and of the state apparatus. Summing up its abandonment of revolutionary internationalism in the reactionary and in the last analysis counterrevolutionary theory of socialism in one country,[11] Stalinism proceeded to extend and solidify its control through the destruction of party and workers' democracy.

The present character of the Soviet state

16. During the process culminating in the present purge and executions and in the imposition of the new constitution,[12] the Stalinist bureaucracy has usurped political control of the Soviet state. It has completely eliminated workers' control. The organs through which that control was exercised—the soviets, the factory committees, the army committees, the trade unions, the revolutionary party—have been either destroyed or remain as mere forms stripped of all power.

---

11. "Socialism in one country" was Stalin's theory, introduced into the communist movement for the first time in 1924, that a socialist society could be achieved within the borders of a single country. It later was incorporated into the Comintern's program and tactics and, serving as the ideological cover for abandoning proletarian internationalism, was used to justify the conversion of CPs throughout the world into docile pawns of Soviet foreign policy. Trotsky's major critique is in his 1928 book, *The Third International After Lenin* (Pathfinder, 1974).

12. Trotsky's analysis of the new Soviet constitution adopted in 1936 will be found in *The Revolution Betrayed* (Pathfinder, 1972) and *Writings of Leon Trotsky (1935–36)* (Pathfinder, 1977).

17. Crushing the independent organizations and institutions of the working class, the bureaucracy has not only lifted itself to ever greater heights from the masses out of which it came, but has replaced the appeal to the masses for arbitrament of all social and economic conflicts and disputes with an appeal to a supreme arbiter whom it has brought forth from its own midst, and who maintains the dominance of the bureaucracy by the props of the army, the police, the labor aristocracy, the better-off collective farmer, and by allowing the masses to vote "yes" from time to time in the Bonapartist plebiscites of the regime. In this way, the bureaucracy has established a radically new *political regime*. The Bolsheviks in 1917 conceived the political regime of the dictatorship of the proletariat to be the most democratic the world had yet seen, a dictatorship exercised against the bourgeoisie and an extensive democracy for the toilers expressed through workers' control of all social and economic life. It can now be said that the complete destruction of the revolutionary party, the Communist youth organization, the trade unions, the soviets, the factory committees, etc., and the bloody annihilation of the two revolutionary generations, have climaxed the replacement of the political regime of the proletarian dictatorship by a Bonapartist dictatorship of the counterrevolutionary bureaucracy. Only a political revolution can remove the bureaucratic incubus which has left the Russian proletariat no peaceful or legal means whereby to discharge it.

18. It is the outstanding contradiction in Soviet life that while this radical political change has occurred, the basic economic structure established by the October revolution has remained substantially unaltered. The expropriation of private property in the means of production and exchange, and their nationalization as state property, is

the fundamental and indispensable characteristic of the proletarian revolution which inaugurates the transitional regime between capitalism and socialism known as the dictatorship of the proletariat (workers' state). To the extent, therefore, that the nationalization of the means of production and exchange and the monopoly of foreign trade remain basically in effect, the Soviet Union retains the socioeconomic foundations of a workers' state. More accurately, the Soviet Union today represents a bureaucratically degenerated workers' state, whose basic structure must be defended by the Russian and international proletariat against world imperialism and against the anti-Soviet bureaucracy of Stalinism. It would be fatal to revolutionary strategy to identify the tendency to degeneration with the accomplished fact, the betrayal of the principles of October with the consummation of its overthrow. The positions of the Soviet proletariat and the security of its economic successes have been placed in the utmost danger by the destruction of workers' democracy and the revolutionary Leninist party. But the traditions of October are still anchored in the hearts and minds of the masses, and what is decisive, the property relations established by the October revolution still obtain. A social regime may find expression in various political forms. The bureaucracy is the product of political and social reaction, just as the democratic soviets were the product of the revolutionary upsurge. But the social content of the bureaucratic dictatorship is still determined by the economic structure and the productive relations created by the October revolution.

With this economic structure, and despite the carryover and subsequent further intrusion of capitalist features, the Soviet Union has been able during the past decade to record a far greater rate of economic expansion than has ever been accomplished in a capitalist nation. That this was achieved without the Soviet Union benefiting fully from participation in world economy, and in spite of the ever retarding effect of the Stalinist bureaucracy, demonstrates the immense superiority of planned economy, of even embryonically socialized as against capitalist economy.

19. However, the bureaucratic political dictatorship runs into ever increasing conflict with the needs and interests of the nationalized economy. This conflict to an ever greater degree takes the form of the sabotage of production by the bureaucracy, through the interference of bureaucratic arbitrariness in the administration of industry; through the protection of bureaucratic privileges against the needs of the economy; through inefficiency, corruption, falsification of plans and statistics; through dislocations introduced among the various branches of industry and agriculture; manipulation of the currency; and the necessarily vain and demoralizing attempt to solve economic problems by the administrative terror of the GPU. Secondly, in order to secure and increase its privileges and the privileges of those united with it in the upper strata of Soviet society, the bureaucracy is led to the introduction of more and more potentially capitalist features in the economy: partial rights of inheritance, piecework, huge wage differentials, interest-bearing bonds and savings accounts, inalienable peasant private property, extension of the free market—all added to those features such as the bourgeois system of payment for work necessarily carried over from capitalism in the early stages of the revolution.

20. In the social life, also the bureaucracy constantly increases the sources of conflict through the mighty and growing differences in the standards of living, the luxuries provided for the privileged at the expense of necessities for

the masses, the restoration of ranks, and the all-pervasive police-terror frame of mind inspired by the activities of the GPU.

21. The present crisis in the Soviet Union is not only terribly witnessed by the executions, imprisonments, and exiles, but is deeply characterized by them. The wiping out of the entire revolutionary generation, occurring simultaneously with the complete deprivation of all democratic rights of the masses and the sanctification of the Bonapartist regime of absolutism, has been carried through by the Stalinist bureaucracy with the deliberate purpose of creating all the political preconditions for a fundamental assault upon the economic basis of the workers' state, namely, the nationalization of the means of production and exchange. Just as the revolutionary proletariat, in seizing power in 1917, created the political conditions for the expropriation of private property, so the counterrevolutionary bureaucracy, by consummating its dispossessing of the proletariat from political power, has created the political conditions for the destruction of nationalized economy and the restoration of private property.

The Soviet bureaucracy is not a class, nor is the labor aristocracy upon which it relies. But both contain the elements of a new, i.e., a capitalist class. The evolution of the Stalinist bureaucracy represents a long process of shifting from one class base to another. Under the pressure of its world imperialist allies, of the labor aristocrat and the bureaucrat, of the factory director and the well-to-do farmer, the Stalinist bureaucracy not only seeks a new class base under its political domination, but must inevitably seek to establish the economic foundations for such a new class. This can mean nothing else but an intensified drive in the coming future to wipe out the socioeconomic foundations of the workers' state.

The Russian and international proletariat, therefore, in fulfilling their elementary duty of defending the Soviet Union from all reactionary assaults, must be conscious of the fact that the anti-Soviet bureaucracy is now the principal hindrance in the Soviet Union to the revolutionary defense of the conquests of the October revolution.

22. The present crisis in the Soviet Union thus results from the conflict between its policy and its economy, the conflict between the military-bureaucratic dictatorship and the nationalized industry, that is to say, between the Stalinist bureaucracy and the Soviet masses. *The outcome of this crisis is not yet decided.* The definitive victory, in all spheres, of the bureaucracy over the masses and the economy will mean necessarily the consolidation of a new ruling class and the restoration of capitalism. The victory of the masses over the bureaucracy will reestablish the workers' state and regain unequivocally the road toward socialism.

23. The insolent claim made by the bureaucracy of the "final and irrevocable victory of socialism" within the Soviet Union is manifestly false, and disproved in the first instance by the existence of the bureaucracy itself. Socialism is much more than the nationalization of the means of wealth production and the successes of industrialization and collectivization; socialism is a balanced system of production and distribution developing harmoniously without the shock of crises, and able to satisfy human needs on a level of productivity superior to that of the most advanced capitalism. Socialism is a classless, stateless social order based on the highest achievements of technique and the international division of labor. From this Marxian viewpoint, Soviet reality has as yet barely entered the threshold of socialism. Soviet economy is in a state of transition between capitalism and socialism, marked

by all the deepgoing contradictions between socialized property relations and bourgeois norms of distribution, by the opposites of privilege and want, by the social differentiation and antagonisms in the ranks of the proletariat and in the collectivized village. The piece-work system of wage payment, leading to further differentiation between a Stakhanovite labor aristocracy and the great mass of the workers, is itself a capitalist principle of payment. As long as living standards in the USSR continue to be still inferior to those in the West, the poverty in goods of consumption is a source of bureaucratic rule. The evidences of a transitional economy are apparent on every hand, in the disproportion between the means of production and of raw materials, between transport and industry, between quantity and quality, and in the chronic danger of monetary inflation. And these contradictions are still further sharpened by the bureaucratic and reckless police methods of administrative compulsion in place of rational economic direction. The claim of the bureaucracy is only a libel on the whole ideal and conception of socialism.

24. Likewise is it false to conclude that capitalism has been restored within the Soviet Union. Though many incidental features of capitalist economy are present, and the possibility of capitalist restoration is present and growing, nevertheless the basic structure of the nationalized economy is incompatible with the capitalist mode of exploitation and the existence of a consolidated bourgeois class.

25. It would be false, further, to conclude that there has yet developed within the Soviet Union a "new" socioeconomic class in the full Marxist sense of the term. Though the privileged layers of the society—the bureaucracy itself, the upper stratum of the army, the members of the wealthy collectives, the Stakhanovites, some of the technicians, the professionals—contain the elements of

a class, they have not yet solidified social and economic forms or constructed a class ideology in such manners as to constitute a socioeconomic class. Moreover, the further development and consolidation of these groups would, in virtual certainty, transform them not into a "new" and hitherto unknown class, but simply into a new bourgeoisie. Though the new constitution, by its explicit statement of the liquidation of the political power of the soviets and its assertion of the political monopoly of the bureaucracy masquerading as the Communist Party, gives juridical form to the usurpation of political power by the bureaucracy, the constitution is cautious and secondary in its invasion of the economic structure and property relations established by the revolution.

26. The situation of the Soviet Union, considered as a whole, is still transitional in character, capable of development back to capitalist restoration, or forward toward socialism through the reestablishment of the political rule of the proletariat, that is, proletarian democracy. In its political phase it is a Bonapartist dictatorship of the bureaucracy; based economically upon the state monopoly of industry and foreign trade and upon the collectivized agriculture.

The solution of the present crisis of the Soviet Union

27. The present crisis in the Soviet Union will eventuate either in capitalist restoration, which will follow with certainty as the immediate result of successful imperialist attack, or in the long run, with equal certainty, from the continued rule of the Stalinist bureaucracy; or, on the other hand, in the reconquest of power by the workers, the reestablishment of their own democratically controlled dictatorship as the state power, the reform of the economy, and the reassertion of unambiguous progress toward

socialism. The character and methods of the present dictatorship, its armed suppression of all opposition or suspicion of opposition, has done away with all possibility of the peaceful reform of the state, and leaves the masses only the road of political revolution.

28. The outcome of the present crisis in the Soviet Union will be decided by international forces. The Soviet Union is an integral part of the world economy and polity, and cannot be artificially isolated from the rest of the world, in spite of all the pretenses of the theory of socialism in one country. The economic and social conflicts within the Soviet Union are reflections and expressions of the conflicts of international economy and of the international class struggle. The dependence of the Soviet Union and its destiny upon international forces is most strikingly of all shown in the preparations for and probable events of the coming imperialist war. Indeed, the internal policies of Stalinism are inescapably bound up with its foreign policy, resting upon alliances with the democratic imperialist powers and the social-patriotic betrayal of the masses and of the workers' revolution.

The defense of the revolution

29. The military victory of one or more of the imperialist powers over the Soviet Union would guarantee the immediate restoration of capitalism within the Soviet Union. The unconditional defense of the Soviet Union against imperialism is therefore the imperative duty of the international proletariat.

Stalinism, however, likewise in the long run guarantees the complete defeat of the revolution and the restoration of capitalism within the Soviet Union. The revolutionary defense of the Soviet Union, that is, the defense of the remaining conquests of the revolution of 1917—above all of the nationalized economy and the mighty foundation it provides for workers' rule and progress toward socialism—therefore requires no less imperatively the struggle against Stalinism. This means, within the Soviet Union, the political struggle to win the decisive sections of the Soviet masses to the revolutionary program and upon that basis the overthrow of the Stalinist bureaucracy and the reestablishment of the democratically controlled workers' state. The struggle against Stalinism, far from being inconsistent with the unconditional defense of the Soviet Union against imperialism, is a necessary part of such defense. The struggle for the revival of the Russian proletariat and for the overthrow of the Stalinist dictatorship that will ensure the socialist progress of the Soviet Union, is impossible without the fullest political and material aid to the Bolshevik-Leninists in the Soviet Union in their work to reconstitute the revolutionary proletarian party of Marxian internationalism, section of the Fourth International.

30. The defense of the Soviet Union, of the Russian revolution, is inseparable now as always from the international revolution. The success of the revolution internationally, in at least certain of the advanced capitalist nations, is the only assurance for the socialist development of the Soviet Union, the only way in which to root out Stalinism and regenerate the Russian revolution. Defense of the Soviet Union therefore excludes support of any imperialist government or capitalist government within any imperialist coalition in the coming war, whether or not allied with the Soviet Union; but requires the vigorous prosecution of the class struggle within every country with the aim of the overthrow of the capitalist government and the establishment of a workers' state. Only such a state can in actuality defend the revolutionary interests of the Soviet Union.

31. Within the Soviet Union and internationally, the indispensable condition of the extension of the revolution is the building of the new party of Marxian internationalism, the Fourth International. The task of the defense of the Soviet Union, the revolutionary struggle for workers' power and for socialism throughout the world, are summed up in the building of the Fourth International and its sections throughout the world.

Amendment to resolution on the Soviet Union[13]

The following amendment to the Convention Arrangement Committee's resolution on the Russian question is submitted by Burnham and Carter:

Delete section 18 in the committee resolution, and insert the following, changing the subsequent section numbers accordingly:

18. The experiences of the Russian revolution show that the class rule of the workers (i.e., the dictatorship of the proletariat or workers' state) is, like other types of class rule, able to express itself in a number of different governmental forms. The material conditions, both national and international, of the Russian revolution, made

---

13. This appeared first in *Internal Bulletin*, number 2, Organizing Committee for the Socialist Party Convention, November 1937, and was reprinted in *Bulletin Number 6*, January 1938. It received 3 votes out of the 75 cast at the convention. It has never been printed publicly before now.

impossible in Russia the healthiest and most progressive form of proletarian class rule: namely, full workers' democracy through control by the soviets and the other mass organs and institutions of the proletariat. Nevertheless, during the early years of the revolution, the soviets and other mass institutions did have a considerable and important function as organs of class power. But it was in particular and decisively through the commanding position of the Bolshevik Party, expressing clearly the fundamental historical interests of the proletariat, that the class domination of the proletariat, the workers' state, was assured and maintained.

The cumulative destruction both of the mass organs of proletarian rule (the soviets, trade unions, factory committees, etc.) and of the revolutionary Bolshevik Party by the Stalinist bureaucracy meant the weakening and degeneration of the workers' state, of the class rule of the proletariat. This process proceeded by stages, reaching one crisis in 1927 with the smashing of the Left (revolutionary) Opposition, and another in the subsequent smashing of all remaining oppositions. During this same period the remaining power of the mass organs of the workers was being steadily reduced toward zero.

However, the ascendancy of the bureaucracy did not in itself destroy the dictatorship of the proletariat. In a distorted and much weakened form, the dictatorship functioned through the governmental rule of the bureaucracy; and the conflicts still going on within the bureaucracy even constituted a certain form of workers' democracy. During this period the bureaucracy thus played a dual role: a reactionary role in its undermining of the workers' state by the destruction of workers' democracy and control, and in its bureaucratic arbitrariness; but also a progressive role in its protection and, in fact, development, of the nationalized economy, the socioeconomic foundation of the workers' state. The vast superiority of such an economy over capitalist economy is demonstrated in the fact that the first Five Year Plan, carried out during this period of the bureaucratic distortion of the workers' state, even in spite of the bureaucracy and the inability of the Soviet Union to participate fully in world economy, recorded a far greater rate of economic expansion than ever accomplished in a capitalist nation.

In the most recent period, the beginnings of which were marked externally by the signing of the Franco-Soviet pact and the entry of the Soviet Union into the League of Nations,[14] and which was completed by the trials and executions of 1936–37 and by the adoption of the new constitution, the character of the regime has again altered.

The dual character of the bureaucracy—reactionary and progressive—has now ended. *The bureaucracy, taking its actions as a whole, now functions solely as a reactionary force.* The bureaucracy no longer expresses, even in distorted form, the interests of the proletariat; but, on the contrary, expresses anti-working-class interests, thus in the last analysis bourgeois interests—the interests of the privileged layers of Soviet society, now in the process of transformation into a new bourgeois ruling class, and of the sections of the international bourgeoisie toward whom Stalinism gravitates.

This characterization of the bureaucracy is indicated by the new constitution, which gives juridical form to the accomplished liquidation of the soviets as organs of class

---

14. The Franco-Soviet nonaggression pact, signed in May 1935, was accompanied by Stalin's statement that he "understands and fully approves the policy of national defense made by France in order to keep its armed strength at the level of security." The Soviet Union entered the League of Nations in September 1934.

power; and is proved (a) by the present purge, which is wiping out what remains both of the generation which made the revolution and that which carried the dictatorship through the first stages of its bureaucratic development; (b) by the fact that the institutions of state power (army, police, courts, prisons . . .) now function directly against the interests as well as against the persons of the proletariat; (c) by the fact that during the past year the bureaucracy has definitely entered the road of the destruction of the planned and nationalized economy; (d) by the alteration in foreign policy revealed in the difference between the role of Stalinism in Spain today and its role in China in 1926–27—the difference between hindrance and obstacle and historically implicit counterrevolution, on the one hand, and direct and explicit counterrevolution on the other.[15]

19. The change in character of the Soviet regime, the development of the bureaucracy together with the privileged layers of Soviet society (Stakhanovites, well-to-do peasants, administrators, technicians, professionals, etc.) toward their transformation into a new ruling class, brings the bureaucracy into ever increasing and deepening conflict with the needs and interests of the nationalized economy. The Soviet economy, established through the expropriation of the basic means of production, distribution, and communication by the state in the chief socioeconomic action of the revolution, has, of course, always contained

---

15. The clumsy arrangement of things being contrasted in this passage may obscure the point being made—that the Stalinist policy in China in 1926–27, when the Communist Party's subordination to the Kuomintang brought about the crushing of the revolution, was not deliberately counterrevolutionary while the Stalinist policy in Spain a decade later, when the CP's People's Front policy was opening the road for Franco's victory, was deliberately counterrevolutionary.

conflicting features: in general because of the fact that there is no distinctive economic structure in the social regime intermediary between capitalism and socialism—the economy partaking of the nature of both capitalist and socialist economy, and more specifically because of the actual circumstances of the state of development of Russian economy. However, the decisive control by the state was assured through the monopoly in the basic industries, and this made possible the elaboration and achievement—even if uneven and incomplete—of the plans.

During this last period, however, and in particular during the last year, the actions of the bureaucracy are actively sabotaging the plan and disintegrating the state monopoly. Agriculture has never, to any considerable extent, been fully nationalized; and the extension of the free market, the return of larger amounts of private property to individual peasants, the partial rights of inheritance—all give an ever more capitalist character to the collectives, the basis of the agricultural economy. Interest-bearing bonds and bank accounts, though still minor, are increasing. Certain rights of inheritance hold generally. The new methods of cost accounting tend to atomize the various branches of industry and to set up greater conflicts among them. The necessarily bourgeois character of the mode of distribution of income is intensified by the growing and by now enormous wage differentials. The attempt to solve difficulties in production by police terror and administrative methods, and the bureaucratic arbitrariness employed with reference to management and technique, are a constant and growing source of economic disruption. Though the failure to publish careful statistics makes impossible an exact estimate, it is clear that today for almost the first time, the plan as a whole is far behind schedule; and even—which would be altogether unprecedented since the institution of the first plan—that production today is behind that of a year ago.

20. These considerations make it impossible any longer to regard the Soviet Union as a workers' state in the traditional sense given to this term by Marxism. The concept of the dictatorship of the proletariat (or workers' state) is not primarily an economic but predominately a political category. The class rule of the proletariat, however carried out—through full soviet democracy, the revolutionary party, several workers' parties, or through a distorting but still proletarian bureaucracy—is an essential aspect of a workers' state, if we are to retain any significant political and historical meaning in our use of this term. All forms, organs, and institutions of the class rule of the proletariat are now destroyed, which is to say that the class rule of the proletariat is destroyed.

However, in this temporary and extremely unstable form of the state, though proletarian rule has been destroyed, bourgeois rule is not yet reestablished. The state is controlled by the bureaucracy for and in the interests of itself and the other privileged strata of Soviet society, and to a certain extent in the interests of the sections of the international bourgeoisie toward which the bureaucracy gravitates. These privileged strata do not *yet* constitute a class in the full socioeconomic sense, and it would be an error, leading to political disorientation, to consider their consolidation as a class already completed.

21. Nevertheless, in spite of the political rule and the change in the nature of the Soviet state, and in spite of the intrusion into the economy of more and more alien features, the economic structure as established by the October revolution still remains basically unchanged. It is true that the bureaucracy will, if its course is unchecked, carry through a basic change. But it has not *yet* done so, and

here again it would be altogether incorrect to anticipate what may possibly or even probably occur in the future. This economy—the state monopoly in the decisive means of production—is an indispensable step for the proletarian revolution and an indispensable means toward the achievement of a fully socialized economy and a socialized society. Therefore, so long as this economy—the socioeconomic foundation of a workers' state—endures, it is the imperative and inescapable duty of the Russian and the international proletariat *to defend it*, both against any and all imperialist powers—whose military victory in a war against the Soviet Union would guarantee the destruction of the economy and the restoration of capitalism—and likewise against the Stalinist bureaucracy, whose continued rule in the long run also guarantees the destruction of the economy and the restoration of capitalism.

Resolution on the Russian question[16]

(Note: The following resolution is a minimum statement of agreement of the undersigned. Any documents appearing over individual signatures of members of the group represent individual opinions and not the opinion of the group as a whole. This resolution is offered as a minimum basis of discussion. The elaboration and formulation of a definitive position on this question should result from the party discussion.)

The nature of a society is determined by the relations of production. The possession, property, or ownership of the means of production determines the class in power. The forms of possession, property, and ownership are expressed in control of and benefit from the means of

---

16. This was printed in *Internal Bulletin*, number 2, Organizing Committee for the Socialist Party Convention, November 1937. It received 2 of the 75 votes cast at the convention. It has never been printed publicly before now.

production. Possession, property, or ownership of the means of production without control or benefit is a legal fiction, and of no importance in determining the real nature of the society. The lords controlled the means of production in feudal society; the bourgeois, the means of production in capitalist society; the workers must control the means of production in a workers' society. Without workers' democratic control of the means of production there can be no workers' economy, no workers' rule, and no workers' state. There is no workers' democratic control of the means of production in Russia; hence there is no workers' state.

J. Carlo	M. Kirschbaum	E. Margolin
M. Goddard	M. Moriarity	I. Stern
J. Bitner	J. Rosenberg	M. Glee
N. Harrison	E. Deren	G. Milton
R. Grote	M. Miller	D. Eastman
H. Ross	M.J. Bernstein	S. Gilbert
W. Cohen	H. Gourin	
A. Bienstock	S. Cyons	

Resolution on Spain[17]

1. The events of the first week of May in Barcelona came as a crucial phase in the long process which started a few weeks after the outbreak of the civil war: the process of the liquidation of the forms of dual power which, to one degree or another, came into being during the first days

---

17. This was printed in *Internal Bulletin*, number 1, Organizing Committee for the Socialist Party Convention, October 1937, and reprinted in *Bulletin Number 6*, January 1938. Max Shachtman and James P. Cannon were assigned to prepare this document, which was never printed publicly until now. The convention vote was 56 for the resolution against 4 abstentions. This document was written at the halfway point in the 33-month civil war in Spain, and its authors assumed that its readers were well acquainted with the many developments in this struggle up to that point. A much more detailed account of the same period will be found in Felix Morrow's *Revolution and Counter-Revolution in Spain* (Pathfinder, 1974), which was completed, except for a 1938 preface, around the same time as this resolution. Trotsky's analysis of the civil war will be found in *The Spanish Revolution (1931–39)* (Pathfinder, 1973).

Above, POUM militiamen on Huesca front during Spanish civil war, March 1937. **Below**, courtroom during 1938 Moscow trial.

of the civil war.[18] The events began with the defensive actions of the anarchist workers holding the telephone exchange—which they had occupied since July 1936 (an occupation legalized under the decree of October 24)—taken against the attack of a Stalinist-controlled company of the police of the Catalan government. In actuality, however, the armed resistance of the workers was the long-delayed reply to the cumulative series of persecutions, repressions, and invasions of rights carried out by the government against the workers. The repercussions of the initial incident spread throughout the city, and the action changed from a defensive to a potentially insurrectionary character. The workers were in the streets, and armed. There is good reason to believe that firm revolutionary leadership would have brought the workers to power, first in Barcelona, then throughout Catalonia, and subsequently in Spain as a whole. Such leadership was lacking. Through vacillation and delay, the strength of the workers' movement was dissipated, and the government collected its

---

18. "Dual power" is a Marxist term for contending centers of power and authority that arise in revolutionary situations. After the fall of tsarism in Russia of 1917, for example, there were two bodies that different sections of the population recognized as representing their interests—the Provisional Government on one side, the soviets on the other. Neither was able to exercise full hegemony until the Bolshevik-led October insurrection gave all power to the soviets. In Spain dual power was not that well developed during the civil war, but the workers and peasants did have their own militias, union committees, peasant committees, and other bodies independent of the government that performed revolutionary functions on a local scale and that represented embryonic dual power. With a revolutionary leadership, these bodies could have been extended and united into a force capable of playing the same role in Spain that the soviets had played in Russia. The People's Front and its parties did all they could to dismantle these bodies or to render them harmless while concentrating all power in the capitalist central government.

forces. Hundreds of the best militants were slaughtered through the spinelessness and treachery of their own leaders; the workers left the streets defeated.

2. The Barcelona events were a decisive test for every political tendency. In these events, the Popular Front regimes were compelled to come fully into the open, and thereby to reveal unmistakably their fundamentally counterrevolutionary nature. Both the Barcelona and the Valencia governments[19] sent their troops *against* the workers. In doing so they only expressed more bluntly their consistent role during the entire course of the civil war: their role as liquidators of the organs of workers' power in order to accomplish the reconsolidation of bourgeois power.

3. The provocation to the Barcelona events was furnished by Stalinist-controlled police, led by the Stalinist minister of police, [Rodríguez] Salas, just as the governments relied upon the Stalinist divisions to complete the suppression. In general, the Stalinists in Spain, supported by the blackmail tactics of the Soviet bureaucracy, have been the leading force in charting the reactionary course of the governments' policy. In Loyalist Spain, by their actions both within and outside the governments, the Stalinists have been the chief enemies of the workers' revolution. In order to permit Stalin to demonstrate to French and British imperialism his fitness as an ally in the coming war, Stalinism in Spain has acted unswervingly to repair the tottering structure of capitalism within Loyalist Spain, to smash all of the

---

19. The central government of Spain, controlled by the People's Front, was in Madrid until September 1936 when Largo Caballero became premier, and it then was moved to Valencia. The "Valencia government" refers to Caballero's regime. In May 1937 Caballero was replaced by Negrín, who transferred the central government to Barcelona in October 1937. That was the "Barcelona government." The fascist seat of power was in Burgos.

achievements, institutions, and organizations of workers' power, and to annihilate all revolutionary militants who can be neither misled nor corrupted.

4. The policy of the right-wing Socialists (Prieto-Negrín) in Spain has been distinguished from that of the Stalinists only by its slightly more hypocritical covering and by a somewhat greater devotion to "legal" formalities. The right-wing Socialists took their places alongside the Stalinists, together with the bourgeoisie of the Esquerra and the Estat Catala, to support and carry out the assassination of the Barcelona workers. The Barcelona events prove the Stalinists and right-wing Socialists to be not merely the lackeys but the direct allies of the bourgeoisie.

5. At the time of the Barcelona events, the left-wing (Caballero) Socialists were nominally in control of the Valencia government through the premiership of Caballero. Caballero, advertised for years as the "Spanish Lenin," had, after the outbreak of the civil war, accepted the call to head the bourgeois coalition government of the People's Front, had, that is to say, become the director of a capitalist government. No "good intentions" on his part nor any misgivings, therefore, can enable him to avoid political responsibility for the development which followed and led inescapably to the Barcelona events themselves. It was under the premiership of Caballero that the workers' committees in the factories were steadily deprived of power; that control by elected councils in the armies was eliminated; that the proletarian police in the cities lost power to a rehabilitated bourgeois police; that the reactionary and counterrevolutionary Civil Guard was reconstituted as the Republican Guard; that the press of the anarchists and POUM was censored and in numerous cases suppressed; that revolutionary militants were imprisoned and shot; that the government propaganda

attacked the perspective of the socialist revolution in favor of "defense of capitalist democracy"; that the POUM was ousted from the Catalan government; that the division of the land among the peasants was hindered and blocked; that no action was taken to raise the all-important slogan of "Freedom for Morocco";[20] that the defense of Malaga was entrusted to incompetents and traitors; that the Aragon front was sabotaged for the sake of a political blow at the anarchists and POUM, whose forces held it. It was, finally, while Caballero was still premier that the troops of the Valencia government marched into Barcelona to shoot down the workers. If, as is doubtless the case, the initiative in many or even most of these developments was taken by the republicans, Stalinists, and right-wing Socialists, and not by Caballero himself, that by no means absolves Caballero from political responsibility, but simply traces that responsibility in such cases to passivity and default rather than to overt action.

6. In the case of the anarchists and the anarcho-syndicalists, the Barcelona events only revealed more strikingly what had been demonstrated by the entire preceding year: namely, the petty-bourgeois, reformist character of anarchism and anarcho-syndicalism in practice. In Catalonia, the bulk of the militant workers were, and still are, assembled in the

---

20. This slogan was important because Franco launched his fascist uprising in July 1936 from Morocco, then a colony partly of Spain and partly of France. He would have been unable to do this if the People's Front government elected in February had granted freedom and independence to its Moroccan colony. But the Spanish government refused to do this because it did not want to antagonize the bourgeois components of the People's Front (just as the French People's Front government, also elected in 1936, refused to free its Moroccan colony). Even after the civil war began in Spain, Franco's army, which included many Moroccan mercenaries, would have been undermined or weakened if the Loyalist government had proclaimed the liberation of Morocco.

anarchist and anarcho-syndicalist organizations. These workers have shown a hundred times that they are prepared to fight, and to fight for the proletarian revolution. Nevertheless, the whole course of anarchist policy has turned them aside from revolutionary struggle. Above all, the entry of the anarchist leaders into the governments both of Barcelona and of Valencia made impossible the correct struggle for the extension of the dual power, and introduced a disastrous disorientation into the minds of the workers. The cowardice of the anarchist leaders was irrevocably shown when they failed to take action after the ousting of the POUM from the government. The "antipolitical" ideology of the anarchists proved to be opportunist and reformist politics in action. The majority of the workers who manned the barricades in May were members of the anarchist organizations. But far from receiving any clear revolutionary directives from their leaders, they at first were given no directives whatever, and were then told to conciliate peacefully, to lay down their arms if necessary, above all not to fight, and to leave the barricades. The anarchist leaders turned their backs on the workers and the revolutionary insurrection, and preferred to rely upon compromise and maneuvers with the Stalinists, the republicans, and the bourgeois government.

7. Likewise did the crisis of the Barcelona events sum up the entire past course of the POUM. The members of the POUM were alongside the anarchist workers at the barricades, and with them were prepared to fight. Nevertheless, the POUM leadership hesitated, delayed, and finally decreed capitulation. In actuality, the POUM leadership trailed behind the leadership of the anarchists, excusing their own failure to take the initiative—which would have swept the anarchist ranks along with them—by the capitulation of the anarchist leaders. In the Barcelona events, as

during the previous months, the POUM refused to take, in a determined, uncompromising, and really serious manner, the road toward proletarian power. As in the case of every centrist party, its revolutionary words and resolutions have turned into compromise and vacillation when put into practice. Its disastrous error in entering the coalition government of Catalonia—when every dictate of history demanded the extension of the organs of workers' power in complete independence of the government and in political struggle against it—was made fatal by the failure of the POUM to learn from this error: participation in the bourgeois government is *still* defended by the POUM. Its exclusion of the Bolshevik-Leninists was only another decisive indication of its refusal to learn from past experience and to launch upon an independent Marxist course. Like the anarchist leaders, and indeed for the most part trailing the anarchist leaders, the leadership of the POUM in practice has put its faith not in the proletariat and in the perspective of the workers' revolution, but in impermissible compromises with People's Frontism, with republican and reformist "allies," in maneuvers, delays, and hesitations. There is, it is true, a deep gulf separating the vacillations and compromises of the anarchists and the POUM from the direct treachery of the Stalinists and right-wing Socialists—the gulf of the Barcelona barricades—but, nevertheless, the anarchists and POUM leaderships again demonstrated in the Barcelona events their inability to lead the revolution in Spain to victory.

8. The only political groups which measured up, to any considerable degree, to the test of the Barcelona events were the two small and comparatively recently formed organizations, the Bolshevik-Leninists (Fourth Internationalists) and the left-wing anarchist group called the "Friends of Durruti." The militants of both groups were in

the forefront of the fight on the barricades; the Bolshevik-Leninists responded with concrete and specific slogans applying a revolutionary perspective as raised by the potentially insurrectionary character of the action: and the Friends of Durruti, though less clear and precise in their perspective and slogans, showed their great development away from the anarchist and anarcho-syndicalist ideology of their parent organizations and toward the Marxist course. Neither of these groups, however, had sufficient mass influence to avail against the capitulation of the anarchist and POUM leaderships.

9. The direct result of the Barcelona events was the downfall of the Caballero government, and the formation of the Negrín government. In self-defense of its own bureaucratic position resting upon the UGT and the so-called Socialist Left, and in part upon political support from the anarchists and POUMists, the Caballero group was unable to carry through the repression as fully and as rapidly as the Stalinist-bourgeois reaction demanded. But the program of the reaction had been carried through by the Caballero group to a sufficient extent in the months from September to May to have undermined its own bulwark from the left against the right, and had so weakened its own position as to enable the reaction to dispense with the services of Caballero and the trade union federations in the new government, at least for the present. Caballero, the anarchists, the UGT, and the CNT were excluded. The new government represents a coalition between the bourgeois parties, including the Basque Catholics and Nationalists, the right-wing Socialists, and the Stalinists. In terms of the Barcelona events, thus, the new government is a government of the coalition of the assassins of the Barcelona workers. The Negrín government represents a great political shift to the right as compared with the

Caballero government, a shift which shows the success with which the bourgeoisie has strengthened and reinforced the capitalist character of the People's Front regime, and at the same time enables steps to be taken against the remnants of the dual power and against the revolutionary workers in a more firm and ruthless manner than was possible under Caballero.

10. The Negrín government launched itself under the central slogan of "Win the war," expanding this slogan as: "Win the war *first*, social reform afterwards." In practice, this slogan has meant: Smash the social revolution and its adherents *now*. The two tasks of winning the war and achieving the social revolution are, in fact, inseparable. The *only* method of winning the war against Franco in the interests of the workers and peasants is *through* the extension and finally the victory of the revolution. The policy of the Negrín government can result only in one of three possible alternatives, none of which is in the interests of the Spanish masses: (1) the military victory of Franco; (2) a "compromise" settlement, engineered by the military staffs of both armies and supervised by the imperialist powers, with the institution of a military dictatorship; (3) a barely conceivable Loyalist military victory which would find in power a military-bureaucratic regime scarcely distinguishable in social and political content from an outright fascist regime under Franco. The *only* solution for the Spanish masses is the extension of the revolutionary struggle and, by seizing power, the transformation of the present war against the fascists into a revolutionary war for workers' power throughout Spain.

11. During the months since May, the Negrín government has shown that it is far more efficient in smashing the proletarian revolution than in winning the war against Franco. Its success in the moves taken against the

revolution and revolutionists has been much more distinguished than its success on the military front. Except in a few localities, the POUM has been outlawed. Virtually the entire leadership of the POUM has been arrested and imprisoned. The censorship exercised against the anarchist press has been greatly increased. Hundreds and even thousands of militants have been jailed, including large numbers of the international volunteers. Secret military tribunals have been set up. Workers' demonstrations on the anniversary of the outbreak of the civil war were prohibited. The reconstitution of the army on a bourgeois basis has been nearly completed. Most of the remaining units of proletarian police in the cities have been eliminated. The bourgeoisie is reappearing more and more boldly. Workers' control in the industries has been cut to a minimum. The land is administered in the interests of the richer peasants and farmers and against the interests of the poorer peasants. Under Negrín, the agents of the Soviet bureaucracy have transferred bodily into Spain the system of the Moscow trials, and have completed the building up of a Stalinist GPU which—with the sanction of the People's Front regime—maintains its own jails and torture chambers and carries out its own raids, jailings, frame-ups, and executions, climaxed by the lynching of Andrés Nin. A campaign of slander and frame-up against Caballero and the anarchists only waits fuller preparation before being carried to the lengths of the campaign against the POUM.

12. During the months since the establishment of the Negrín government—though already started long before that time—a change in the character of the Spanish struggle has been taking place with increasing rapidity. This change is expressed simultaneously in two related phases: (1) the difference in social and political content between

the Franco and Loyalist regimes is more and more narrowed—a fact attested by the apparently growing apathy of the masses on both sides, resulting in desertions, unwillingness to fight, sporadic movements of discontent, etc.; (2) the ever greater subordination of the conflict considered simply as a civil war within Spain to the interimperialist conflicts in a world scale—a development strikingly witnessed by the Nyon conference.

From the beginning, of course, the class struggle which lay at the root of the Spanish events did not express itself as a direct and clear-cut struggle of the working class and its allies for workers' power against the bourgeoisie and its allies defending bourgeois power. From a fundamental historical point of view, there is no ultimate class differentiation separating the Loyalist from the Franco regimes: both were and are bourgeois governments. Likewise, from the beginning, as shown most obviously by the direct intervention of numerous powers, the Spanish civil war was necessarily interconnected with the imperialist rivalries. Up to the present, however, the dominant character of the Spanish conflict has been that of a civil war against fascism, in substance a defense by the Spanish workers and peasants of their organizations, their rights, and positions against the certain and immediate annihilation of these by the victory of the fascists. There can, therefore, be no doubt of the *progressive* nature of the military struggle against Franco, in spite of the fact that this struggle was conducted under the sovereignty of the bourgeois People's Front government and necessarily worked to the advantage or disadvantage of the various imperialist powers. There could, therefore, be no doubt that the road to the proletarian revolution lay through practical support of this struggle, just as it lies in support of *every* progressive struggle.

Now, however, there is a danger that the progressive

character of the war between the People's Front and fascist governments will be eliminated by virtue of the narrowing gap between the Franco and the Loyalist regimes and by the interimperialist rivalries and struggle becoming the dominant feature of the struggle in Spain, or on an extended international field of operations. In that event, of course, the tactics of the Marxists with reference to the Loyalist government would undergo a radical alteration, for the struggle of the Valencia-Barcelona regimes against the Burgos government would then have become an indistinguishable part of the struggle of one imperialist group against another. Support of any kind to the People's Front government by the proletariat would then be a crime, for it would be the duty of the working class to follow, with reference to that government, the same defeatist policy which it now adopts with reference to Franco.

13. In any case, the increasingly reactionary regime established by the People's Front makes a vigorous struggle for democratic rights indispensable precisely in the territory of the People's Front government. Although the leaders of the People's Front suppress the struggle for a *socialist* revolution on the grounds that the masses must confine themselves to a struggle for "democracy," they have in practice systematically deprived the masses of their most elementary democratic rights and institutions. In the same sense that the struggle against fascism is determined by an uncompromising defense of all the democratic conquests of the masses, so the struggle for a revolutionary policy and movement has as an indispensable precondition the struggle for the maintenance of democratic rights and institutions which are being broken down by the pseudodemocratic People's Front.

So long as the civil war in Spain, on the side of the Loyalists, maintains a progressive character, Marxists both within and outside of Spain are confronted with two simultaneous and integrally related duties: to join in the united front of struggle against Franco; and at the same time to press forward the revolutionary program, both in propaganda and wherever possible in specific action, in order that, by winning the majority of the masses to that program, it will be possible to go on to the transfer of power.

Within Spain, the united front of struggle against Franco, from the Marxist point of view, has meant and could only have meant technical and military aid to the Loyalist government; a support of course, unaccompanied by the slightest political confidence or support, and given not to strengthen or bolster up the government itself, but in reality to enable the masses to learn through their own experience that the coalition bourgeois government could not conduct a consistent and effective war against Franco and that if they wish to smash fascism they must go on to take power for themselves. Such support presupposes revolutionary (thus "antigovernment") propaganda and agitation, and the advancing of specific demands and taking of specific actions in accordance with a revolutionary perspective.

Outside of Spain, the united front of struggle against Franco dictated the cooperation of Marxists with other groups, parties, and individuals in joint efforts for material and financial aid to the Loyalist forces, which meant under the given circumstances, material and financial support to the Loyalist government. Once again, of course, such united front activities presuppose no political confidence in the government, and they go along with propaganda and agitation for the full revolutionary program, the sharpest criticism of all activities of the government militating against the furthering of the revolution, and the effort to influence the course of events in Spain in the direction of the revolution, and thus, in the long run, toward the overthrow of the government itself in favor of a proletarian regime.

14. Even from the point of view of material and technical support, however, the duty of revolutionists, whether within or outside of Spain, has never been confined to the united front struggle against Franco, any more than would be the case in any other united front activity. Not merely by propaganda, but in action, it is the duty of the revolutionists in Spain to prosecute the revolution, and therefore to support materially the building up of the revolutionary party, the strengthening and extension of revolutionary forms and institutions (workers' or soldiers' councils, even in embryonic form, proletarian police, etc.), and to defend by every practical as well as propagandistic means workers' rights against the encroachments of the government. Similarly, revolutionists outside of Spain have the special and peculiar duty to render this same material support, and in particular, to give technical and financial aid to the revolutionists in Spain.

15. When a decisive section of the Spanish masses shall have been won to the concrete slogans and program of the revolution, it then becomes the duty of the revolutionists to render all technical, material, and military support to the revolutionary masses and their potential organs of power *against* the People's Front government, and for the overthrow of that government in favor of workers' power. Under such circumstances, any form of material support of the government loses all progressive character and becomes directly counterrevolutionary. To achieve the conquest of power by the workers, which under such circumstances would be both possible and compulsory from a revolutionary point of view, far from involving a weakening of the military struggle against Franco, would

reinforce it—since only through the triumph of the workers' revolution can the military struggle against Franco be carried to a conclusion in the interests of the workers. Similarly, where revolutionary organizations or institutions, revolutionary workers or their rights, are attacked by the government, it is the duty of all revolutionists to defend these workers and their rights and the revolutionary organizations and institutions, not merely by propaganda but with material and, if necessary, armed support, as against the government—even where a revolutionary situation does not exist. From both of these aspects it follows with respect to the May events that unconditional support and defense of the Barcelona workers *as against* the government is given by all revolutionists.

16. In spite of the repressions of the government and of the Spanish GPU, the proletarian and revolutionary opposition to the Negrín government, in one or another degree of development, is by no means wiped out. Quantitatively speaking, such opposition is most widespread within the two great trade union federations (the UGT and the CNT), among the followers of the anarchists and of Caballero. Indeed, it is probably the case that the majority of the Spanish workers have little confidence in the government and would be prepared to follow a determined opposition to it led by Caballero and the anarchists. Under such circumstances, their failure to lead such an active movement is a sufficient indication of the criminal nature of the vacillating and passive policies of Caballero and the anarchists. The recent pact signed by the trade union federations is likewise significant of the extent of the opposition movement. Though the POUM has, except in a few localities, been illegalized, it still functions underground, though on a basis gravely handicapped both by the smashing and imprisonment of its leaders, and its own past errors in

policy. The Bolshevik-Leninists, formed into a separate organization during the spring, though small and driven underground, were better prepared for illegal activity than any of the others, and their influence is growing. The great weakness in the opposition movement is, of course, that with the exception of the Bolshevik-Leninists, no section of the opposition is operating in terms of a correct and adequate revolutionary program; nor does the entire past course of the leaders of the opposition movements give any grounds to expect that their policy will be correctly revised in the future.

17. Under the given and immediate circumstances of the Spanish struggle, the duty of revolutionists, while as always putting forward the full revolutionary program and supporting each concrete step in the defense or advance of that program, is to concentrate their rendering of material support on: (1) direct aid to the Bolshevik-Leninists (Fourth Internationalists) of Spain, the only group in Spain adhering to a program capable of solving the Spanish crisis in the interests of the Spanish masses; and (2) aid for the defense of revolutionary workers persecuted by the Loyalist government, and of workers' rights violated by that government. The first task, by the nature of the case, is largely confined to revolutionists themselves; in the second task, as broad a united front of organizations and individuals consistent with the task should be sought.

18. Political support is given by Marxists only to the revolutionary program and its adherents. Material support is given to *every* progressive struggle, of every class, group, nation, or colony, since such struggles coincide with the historical interests of the working class and therefore of mankind as a whole. If in Spain a decisive section of the masses is prepared to support one or another of the opposition movements, such as that of Caballero or of a

Caballero-anarchist alliance, against the Negrín regime, then the revolutionists will also support such a movement. They will do so without giving such a movement political confidence, which is ruled out by the past history and present policies of the leadership of these oppositions, but because such a movement would represent a step forward, and perhaps an unavoidable step, on the road toward the proletarian revolution in Spain; and the masses may well have to learn in terms of their own experience the inadequacy of the solutions offered now by Caballero and the anarchists, just as they are learning the inadequacy and treachery of the Negrín government. To stand aside from such movements would be to condemn the revolutionists and their program to sterility, since only in the actual process of struggle, a struggle conducted not in terms of a priori formulas but of the conditions imposed by life and by history, will the masses learn the superiority of and necessity for the revolutionary solution of their problems.

19. It cannot be anticipated that the success of such opposition movements would achieve the victory of the revolution. The Spanish revolution can be victorious only on the basis of the revolutionary program and the carrying out of that program in practice. For this, the indispensable instrument, and the key to the solution of the Spanish crisis, is the revolutionary party. Such a party, and such a party alone, will bring the Spanish workers to victory. The elements for the creation of such a party are present in Spain through the fusion of the Bolshevik-Leninists, the left anarchists, the left Socialists, and the left wing of the POUM, on the foundation of the revolutionary program, the program of the Fourth International. The answer to the Spanish events will be given by the success or failure in the task of bringing this party into being.

20. The task of forging the new party in Spain is, however,

inseparable from the task of building the new party internationally. The disastrous and treacherous policies of the Socialist and Communist parties of Spain are integrally related to the disastrous and treacherous policies of the two Internationals with which they are affiliated. Throughout the Spanish struggle, the Second and Third Internationals have demonstrated anew that they are not the revolutionary leaders of the working class, but are the greatest obstacles to the revolution and act within the working class as agents of the class enemy. Their policy of reliance upon the democratic imperialisms—exactly in accord with the People's Front reliance upon the republican bourgeoisie within Spain—is directly counter to the interests of the Spanish revolution and is part of the preparation for the betrayal of the masses to the democratic imperialisms in the coming war. The Spanish workers can be defended only by the world proletariat. The struggle against fascism can be supported and advanced not by the good will of Eden, Chautemps, Stalin, or Roosevelt, but only by the deepening and extension of the revolution internationally. For this, the Second and Third Internationals, committed irrevocably to class collaboration and social patriotism, are useless and worse than useless: history has demonstrated that under their leadership there can be no victory, but only betrayal. The problems of the Spanish revolution, thus, as all the great problems of our epoch, demand as their answer the worldwide building of the new, Fourth International, the International of the triumph of the world socialist revolution.

The internal situation and the character of the party[21]

The Socialist Workers Party is a revolutionary Marxian party, based on a definite program, whose aim is the organization of the working class in the struggle for power and the transformation of the existing social order. All of its activities, its methods, and its internal regime are subordinated to this aim and are designed to serve it.

Only a self-acting and critical-minded membership is capable of forging and consolidating such a party and of solving its problems by collective thought, discussion, and experience.

From this follows the need for assuring the widest party democracy in the ranks of the organization.

---

21. The first draft of this was printed in *Bulletin Number 7*, January 1938. After amendment at the convention, the final draft was printed in *Socialist Appeal*, February 26, 1938. It was written by James P. Cannon and Max Shachtman. The precise vote by which the convention adopted this resolution was not recorded in the minutes.

The struggle for power organized and led by the revolutionary party is the most ruthless and irreconcilable struggle in all history. A loosely knit, heterogeneous, undisciplined, untrained organization is utterly incapable of accomplishing such world-historical tasks as the proletariat and the revolutionary party are confronted with in the present era. This is all the more emphatically true in the light of the singularly difficult position of our party and the extraordinary persecution to which it is subjected. From this follows the party's unconditional demand upon all its members for complete discipline in all the public activities and actions of the organization.

Leadership and centralized direction are indispensable prerequisites for any sustained and disciplined action, especially in the party that sets itself the aim of leading the collective efforts of the proletariat in its struggle against capitalism. Without a strong and firm central committee, having the power to act promptly and effectively in the name of the party and to supervise, coordinate, and direct all its activities without exception, the very idea of a revolutionary party is a meaningless jest.

It is from these considerations, based upon the whole of the experience of working-class struggle throughout the world in the last century, that we derive the Leninist principle of organization, namely, democratic centralism. The same experience has demonstrated that there are no absolute guarantees for the preservation of the principle of democratic centralism, and no rigid formula that can be set down in advance, a priori, for the application of it under any and all circumstances. Proceeding from certain fundamental conceptions, the problem of applying the principle of democratic centralism differently under different conditions and stages of development of the struggle can be solved only in relation to the concrete situation, in the course of the tests and experience through which the movement passes, and on the basis of the most fruitful and healthy interrelationship of the leading bodies of the party and its rank and file.

The leadership of the party must be under the control of the membership, its policies must always be open to criticism, discussion, and rectification by the rank and file within properly established forms and limits, and the leading bodies themselves subject to formal recall or alteration. The membership of the party has the right to demand and expect the greatest responsibility from the leaders, precisely because of the position they occupy in the movement. The selection of comrades to the positions of leadership means the conferring of an extraordinary responsibility. The warrant for this position must be proved, not once but continuously by the leadership itself.

It is under obligation to set the highest example of responsibility, devotion, sacrifice, and complete identification with the party itself and its daily life and action. It must display the ability to defend its policies before the membership of the party, and to defend the line of the party and the party as a whole before the working class in general. Sustained party activity, not broken or disrupted by abrupt and disorienting changes, presupposes not only a continuity of tradition and a systematic development of party policy, but also the continuity of leadership. It is an important sign of a serious and firmly constituted party, of a party really engaged in productive work in the class struggle, that it throws up, out of its ranks, cadres of more or less able leading comrades, tested for their qualities of endurance and trustworthiness, and that it thus ensures a certain stability and continuity of leadership by such a cadre.

Continuity of leadership does not, however, signify

the automatic self-perpetuation of leadership. Constant renewal of its ranks by means of additions and, when necessary, replacements, is the only assurance that the party has that its leadership will not succumb to the effects of dry-rot, that it will not be burdened with deadwood, that it will avoid the corrosion of conservatism and dilettantism, that it will not be the object of conflict between the older elements and the younger, that the old and basic cadre will be refreshed by new blood, that the leadership as a whole will not become purely bureaucratic "committee men" with a life that is remote from the real life of the party and the activities of the rank and file. Like leadership, membership itself in the party implies certain definite rights.

Party membership confers the fullest freedom of discussion, debate, and criticism inside the ranks of the party, limited only by such decisions and provisions as are made by the party itself or by bodies to which it assigns this function. Affiliation to the party confers upon each member the right of being democratically represented at all policy-making assemblies of the party (from branch to national and international convention), and the right of the final and decisive vote in determining the program, policies, and leadership of the party.

With party rights, the membership has also certain definite obligations. The theoretical and political character of the party is determined by its program, which forms the lines delimiting the revolutionary party from all other parties, groups, and tendencies in the working class. The first obligation of party membership is loyal acceptance of the program of the party and regular affiliation to one of the basic units of the party. The party requires of every member the acceptance of its discipline and the carrying on of his activity in accordance with the program of the party, with the decisions adopted by its conventions and with the policies formulated and directed by the party leadership. Party membership implies the obligation of 100 percent loyalty to the organization, the rejection of all agents of other, hostile groups in its ranks, and intolerance of divided loyalties in general. Membership in the party necessitates a minimum of activity in the organization, as established by the proper unit, and under the direction of the party; it necessitates the fulfillment of all the tasks which the party assigns to each member. Party membership implies the obligation upon every member to contribute materially to the support of the organization in accordance with his means.

From the foregoing it follows that the party seeks to include in its ranks all the revolutionary, class conscious, and militant workers who stand on its program and are active in building the movement in a disciplined manner. The revolutionary Marxian party rejects not only the arbitrariness and bureaucratism of the CP, but also the spurious and deceptive "all-inclusiveness" of the Thomas-Tyler-Hoan party, which is a sham and a fraud. Experience has proved conclusively that this "all-inclusiveness" paralyzes the party in general and the revolutionary left wing in particular, suppressing and bureaucratically hounding the latter while giving free rein to the right wing to commit the greatest crimes in the name of socialism and the party. The SWP seeks to be inclusive only in this sense: that it accepts into its ranks those who accept its program and rejects from membership those who reject its program.

The rights of each individual member, as set forth above, do not imply that the membership as a whole, namely, the party itself, does not possess rights of its own. The party as a whole has the right to demand that its work not be disrupted and disorganized, and has the right to take all the measures which it finds necessary to assure its regular and normal functioning. The rights of any individual member are distinctly secondary to the rights of the party membership as a whole. Party democracy means not only the most scrupulous protection of the rights of a given minority, but also the protection of the rule of the majority. The party is therefore entitled to organize the discussion and to determine its forms and limits.

All inner-party discussion must be organized from the point of view that the party is not a discussion club which debates interminably on any and all questions at any and all times, without arriving at a binding decision that enables the organization to act, but from the point of view that we are a disciplined party of revolutionary action. The party in general not only has the right, therefore, to organize the discussion in accordance with the requirements of the situation, but the lower units of the party must be given the right, in the interests of the struggle against the disruption and disorganization of the party's work, to call irresponsible elements to order and, if need be, to eject them from the ranks.

The decisions of the national party convention are binding on all party members without exception and they conclude the discussion on all those disputed questions upon which a decision has been taken. Any party member violating the decisions of the convention, or attempting to revive discussion in regard to them without formal authorization of the party, puts himself thereby in opposition to the party and forfeits his right to membership. All party organizations are authorized and instructed to take any measures necessary to enforce this rule.

The internal situation and the task of the party[22]

Minority resolution submitted by Burnham, Carter, and Draper

The ISP takes form primarily through the fusion of the revolutionists formerly belonging to the Workers Party with the revolutionary wing of the Socialist Party.

The ISP begins this new period in the development of the revolutionary party in the United States as an enlarged propaganda group striving to become a mass workers' party. The specific problems and tasks of the ISP flow not merely from its general program, but also from a correct understanding of its present and actual character in relation to the labor movement and to political conditions as a whole.

---

22. This was printed in *Bulletin Number 7*, January 1938, through which it came to the consideration of the convention. Since it was withdrawn in return for concessions in the resolution adopted by the convention it was not voted on. Although it was withdrawn, several of the ideas in it were reintroduced a year and a half later, at the second SWP convention, and in the factional fight that began soon after that convention. "ISP" were the initials used in all the resolutions before the conventions decided on the name of the new party.

Among the primary assets of the ISP are to be found: (1) its revolutionary Marxist program, the indispensable condition for the building of a revolutionary party and the achievement of the socialist revolution; (2) a core of loyal and politically trained revolutionary militants; (3) the skeleton of a national organization; (4) a substantial trade union base in at least one locality (Minneapolis) and significant trade union influence in a number of other localities (the West Coast, Ohio, New Jersey, Massachusetts); (5) a militant and growing youth organization.

As against these, a sober and realistic estimate must set a number of weaknesses and liabilities: (1) the small size of the organization in relation to the magnitude of its tasks; (2) the presence within the organization of unassimilable ideas and individuals, tending to disrupt and disorient the positive work of the organization; (3) the fact that the organization is not yet genuinely national in scope, and does not function as a welded national unit; (4) the fact that the organization is only in program and not yet in fact the vanguard of the American working class; (5) the poor social composition of the organization in many localities shown by the far too large percentage of nonproletarian members; (6) the presence within the organization as a whole—and not merely in certain groups within the organization—of sectarian habits of thought and practice carried over from the past; (7) the extremely ineffective and inefficient administrative and organizational habits, often negating the fruitful application of policies correct in the abstract and almost always interfering seriously with the positive results accomplished; (8) a systematically insufficient attention to concrete and specific issues, particularly American issues, revealed both in propaganda and in action.

In general, these weaknesses and liabilities, though

contributed to by personal incapacities and unavoidable technical difficulties, are, of course, the actual features of an enlarged propaganda group in the process of transition.

The problem of the ISP is precisely to carry through its transformation from propaganda existence into an active and vigorous functioning as a mass revolutionary Marxist workers' party. It must, however, be understood that this transition cannot be completed at a single leap. It would be a disorienting illusion to imagine that the ISP is *already* a mass workers' party; its problem is to *become* one. It must endeavor to reach out toward ever broader strata of the working class, but in this next stage it will still make its chief appeal to and draw its most numerous recruits from the *advanced* workers. Both the present reality and the future perspective thus condition the character of its activities, campaigns, and propaganda.

In carrying through this transition, the first and central task is to extend the amount and depth of trade union activities. Unless the ISP is firmly and widely rooted in the trade unions, its transformation into a mass workers' party is entirely out of the question. Every eligible party member, unless specifically assigned to other work, must be an active member of his appropriate trade union. The party as a whole must, through its press, its concrete directives, and its planned campaigns advance itself and its members within the trade union movement. Every contact and possibility for trade union work must be systematically utilized, through entering into shops and industries, securing jobs as union organizers and officials, building up local opportunities, and planning trade union work as a whole through a national trade union staff. It would be a mistake, however, to suppose that trade union activity will be built up by spreading activities into any and every direction. The most fruitful approach in the period ahead will be, as a rule, to deepen and extend trade union work in those localities and industries where there is already some contact or some partial base, rather than to try artificially to penetrate altogether new fields. This approach is indicated amply by the experience of our own organization. It should not, of course, be taken to exclude the utilization of new opportunities when and where these arise.

Along with the trade union work, and inseparable from it, must go the recruitment of new proletarian members into the party. Though a revolutionary party does not and should not consist exclusively of proletarians, nevertheless its stability both in action and in program, and its decisive influence, are best achieved with a high proletarian composition. The proletarianization of the membership must be made a *conscious* and directed aim of the ISP. There is, however, no *special* means by which this aim can be attained, and it is an illusion to suppose that a proletarian party can be built merely out of the desire to have it proletarian. The proletarianization of the membership will follow naturally and normally from the extension and deepening of genuinely proletarian activities, especially from trade union activity, and without this is impossible.

The ISP must likewise recognize as a major task the preservation and advance of the theoretical tradition of revolutionary Marxism, its defense against non- and anti-Marxist ideas and theories, and the education both of its own membership and of the working class generally in this theoretical tradition.

It is, further, necessary for the ISP to break decisively out of its routine, irresponsible, and in part sectarian organizational habits; and at the same time to devote systematically increased attention to concrete and specific issues and especially to the issues of American politics and the American revolution. Unless this is done, the ISP cannot hope to become a serious force in this country. Accomplishment here is not by any means a mere matter of decisions and resolutions, but requires sustained effort on the part of individuals, and conscious resolve to overcome the inertia of the past. The leadership in its entirety must bear a considerable measure of responsibility both for the grave lacks in this respect during the past and for correction in the future. Two important and necessary technical steps toward this end are: (1) the systematic departmentalization of activities, both in order to gain increased administrative efficiency, and also in order to utilize more fruitfully the special abilities and talents of individual members; (2) the allotment of responsible tasks to a far greater number of members than has been the case in the past. The restriction of responsible tasks to a comparatively small number of persons has been a serious and conspicuous weakness in our work during the past, and must be corrected even at the risk of having certain tasks temporarily carried out in a less able manner. This is the only way in which to carry on wider activities, and to develop a genuine and ample leadership.

In achieving its transition, the ISP must also reckon with non- or anti-Marxist currents within its own ranks. Only by decisively overcoming such tendencies with the program and practices of revolutionary Marxism can the party be built.

One of these tendencies, developed into a system of ideas and actions by the Joerger group, is that of ultraleftist sectarianism. The views and practices of this type of sectarianism are incompatible with the views and practices of Marxism, and experience has shown that if consistently held and carried out they lead necessarily to a definitive organizational break with Marxism. This has already been demonstrated in practice by the conduct of the Joerger group, which during these past months has been disloyal, disruptive, and destructive in the extreme.

This ultraleftist sectarianism, in its own perverted way, represents a withdrawal from the concrete tasks of the revolutionary movement, and is thus in actuality and in result by no means wholly distinguished from a second incompatible tendency within our ranks: the tendency most strikingly expressed by Glee. The given policies held at any moment by Glee are as a rule in direct opposition to the policies of Marxism. However, it would be an error to judge Glee merely by his policies, which, in point of fact, he constantly shifts with the shifting winds. Glee represents in his activities a petty-bourgeois dilettantism, a fundamentally light-minded gossip- and rumor-psychology, a corridor and playboy "revolutionism" which, if not rooted out of the ISP, would doom it to utter sterility.

From such tendencies as these the current of revolutionary Marxism must be firmly and unambiguously defended. It is necessary to warn the Joerger group, Glee, and those other individuals or groups inclining toward their conceptions and practices, that those conceptions and practices are incompatible with the conceptions and practices of revolutionary Marxism; that they will, if consistently carried out, result in a definitive organizational break with the ISP. And in particular it is necessary to warn the Joerger group and Glee in the sharpest manner, that disloyal and disruptive conduct, a failure to carry on the work of the ISP, a refusal to carry out loyally the decisions reached by this convention, will result in their immediate, unconditional, and unceremonious expulsion.

The internal regime of the revolutionary party must be understood as following, in general, from its historical task and its program, in relation to the given specific circumstances. However, the internal regime may itself assume independent significance, and neither program nor determination can guarantee the building of the party and the successful fulfillment of the historical task without the proper and necessary conception of and attention to the internal regime.

This regime is based upon democratic centralism, upon the fused principles of democracy and discipline: the fullest possible democracy in the discussion of points of view, the determination of policy, the selection and control of leadership; the supplying at all times of ample and adequate information to the membership, without which democracy is meaningless; the most concentrated and unified discipline in action, in the carrying out of decisions, in the accomplishment of specific tasks. These two principles are integrally related, and neither can be understood in separation from the other.

Party democracy, it must be clearly pointed out, does not mean anarchic individualism. Genuine democracy can take shape only within proper bounds and limits. The revolutionary party cannot be turned into a discussion club; nor can democracy be made the excuse for disruption and sabotage of necessary party activities. This is particularly important in the light of the approaching war crisis, which will impose upon the party the need for the strictest discipline.

At the same time, discipline must not be allowed to mean, or act as the excuse for, bureaucratism. There are within our organization potential sources of bureaucratic tendencies. These are found, in part, in incorrect conceptions of the nature of the revolutionary party derived from misunderstandings about the traditions of revolutionary Marxist organizations (for example, the Russian Bolshevik Party) or from illicit generalizations from practices of former revolutionary organizations designed, rightly or wrongly, to meet particular and special circumstances (for example, the Zinovievist "Bolshevization" plans[23]). In part they arise from an understandable but still improper *impatience* in the face of either general organizational inertia or the particular opposition of some manifestly false oppositional group. And in part, also, they may be traced to the lack of material means in our movement, which unquestionably hinders the effective and broad participation of the full membership in all phases of political life.

The test for genuine democracy occurs precisely in the face of determined and forceful opposition, and is not at all confined to differences of opinion revolving over secondary questions of practical means or shades of opinion defined in the light of identical common general conceptions. While recognizing that the revolutionary party cannot pretend to comprise individuals holding any and all types of opinion, cannot and should not aim to be an all-inclusive party in the reformist sense, and especially that the revolutionary program must be kept clear from all compromise and conciliation with reformism or centrism, yet it is impossible to set up a priori standards to define beforehand allowable limits of difference. The general aim of the ISP must be to include within its ranks, and extend the obligations and rights of membership to all

---

23. When Gregory Zinoviev was president of the Communist International in the mid-1920s, a campaign was begun at his initiative to "Bolshevize" all of the national sections of the Comintern except for the section in the USSR. The alleged aim of this campaign was to elevate the standards of the national parties by indoctrinating them with the lessons learned from the history and practice of the Russian Bolshevik Party in Lenin's time. In fact the result was to restrict proletarian democracy in those parties and to encourage the development or hardening of bureaucracies that would carry out the dictates of the Kremlin.

those who will join loyally, seriously, and in a disciplined manner to build the revolutionary party.

These conceptions, which are those of the best and healthiest traditions of revolutionary Marxism, including those of the Bolshevik Party, and which are of peculiar and imperative urgency under the present and given circumstances of the development of the revolutionary movement, demand the rejection of the doctrine expressed by the committee majority, namely, that advocacy of a defeatist view on the Soviet Union is, in and of itself, incompatible with membership in the ISP. Such a rejection in no way implies the slightest weakening of political opposition to such defeatist views; nor does it contradict the conviction that if consistently carried out such views will in actuality lead to organizational break. Nevertheless, the basis of the break must be found in experience and practice; and no other demand can be put upon those members holding defeatist views than the universal demand from all members for loyalty and discipline.

No action taken by this convention proposes or contemplates the expulsion or disciplining of any members for the advocacy, within the authorized periods and mediums of discussion, of those views which have been the subject of preconvention and convention controversy.

The doctrine of the committee majority would, if accepted by the convention and subsequently carried out, provide a major precedent for the future bureaucratization of the party, the purely administrative solution of political issues, the suppression of minority opinion and of intelligent critical thought on the part of the membership as a whole, and in the end the destruction of party democracy. It would be a step toward a "monolithic" party in which disputes, if allowed at all, would never extend beyond minor points of application and technique.

Our aim must be to go forward to a genuinely democratic, genuinely disciplined, revolutionary workers' party; neither a discussion club nor an amorphous coalition nor a bureaucratic machine. The closest relationship between the leadership and the membership, the fullest participation of the membership in the political life of the party, the most determined unity of action in loyal and serious work—are all means toward the building of such a party. And only such a party can achieve or hope to achieve the *socialist* revolution.

The present war in the Far East and the tasks of the party[24]

The war in the Far East between China and Japan lays bare some of the principal symptoms of the crisis of world capitalism in its final, most highly developed, imperialist stage, and opens up perspectives of great revolutionary developments in a decisive part of the globe. On the one hand, Japan, weakest link in the chain of world imperialism, is seeking to overcome the maladies of its decline by a war of colonial conquest. On the other hand, by their invasion of China, the Japanese imperialists have provoked a defensive campaign which, despite its initial weakness and inadequacy under the leadership of the Kuomintang, assumes the character of a war for national liberation. At the same time, in pursuing their predatory aims in China, the Japanese imperialists have accentuated the interimperialist antagonisms, which are forcing mankind to the brink of a new world war.

---

24. This was printed in *Socialist Appeal*, January 29, 1938. The National Action Committee assigned Frank Graves and Harold Isaacs to prepare

Revolutionary Marxists have always drawn a sharp line of distinction between imperialist wars and wars of national liberation. In the case of the former, our policy is one of revolutionary defeatism in all the warring countries as the only means of advancing the international socialist revolution. In the case of the latter, we unconditionally support the oppressed country against the imperialist oppressor, since every blow struck against imperialism, whether on a national or international scale, serves the interests of the international proletariat, and at the same time facilitates the revolutionary advance of the peoples of the colonial and semicolonial countries. In accordance with this conception it is the duty of our party to aid China's defense against Japanese imperialism in every way possible.

China, a semicolonial country, because of its importance as a great market and field for capital investment, has become an arena of struggle between the big imperialist powers. Japan's aim is to forestall her rivals and to make of China her own exclusive colony. The Chinese national bourgeoisie, due to historic belatedness and ties of mutual interest with imperialism, proves incapable of conducting, with energy and consistency, China's struggle against Japan in the only way that is possible: namely, by mobilizing and arming the masses and drawing them into the war. The Chinese bourgeoisie and its government fear the masses more than they do imperialism. This explains the weakness of China's defensive campaign and the comparative ease with which Japan has been able to win a series of important military victories. It also explains the capitulatory mood of the Chinese bourgeoisie and its

---

the first draft. The convention referred it to the National Committee for final action and publication in the name of the convention.

government, which, dismayed by a succession of military defeats, would like to lay down its arms and come to terms with the Japanese imperialists.

China's liberating struggle against imperialism can be carried to a successful conclusion only by the exploited masses of that country, united under the leadership of a revolutionary Marxist party, and aided by the exploited and oppressed of all other countries. But in order to be able to build a revolutionary party which will have the support of the overwhelming masses, the revolutionary vanguard in China is obliged to participate actively in the struggle *now*—at a time when the leadership is in the hands of the bourgeois Kuomintang and its Stalinist allies. A revolutionary party and a revolutionary mass movement cannot be conjured up out of thin air. The Chinese Bolshevik-Leninists can bring them to life only by a tireless and self-sacrificing participation in the war against Japan, in the course of which they explain events to the soldier and civilian masses, expose the weakness and treachery of the bourgeoisie and its government, and mobilize the masses for independent revolutionary action. Our party does not hold aloof from the trade unions because they are dominated by a reactionary bureaucracy which frequently betrays the workers. With such a policy, our party would condemn itself to a sterile sectarian existence. Similarly in China: If the Bolshevik-Leninists were to stand aside from the war struggle on the ground that the Kuomintang leadership is reactionary, treacherous, and ineffectual, they would condemn themselves to complete isolation from the masses. The workers and soldiers would turn a deaf ear to their criticism of the Kuomintang's conduct of the war, and all hope for building a revolutionary party and a revolutionary mass movement would be lost.

Support of and active participation in China's struggle while it remains under Kuomintang leadership does not, however, require the Chinese revolutionists to lower their own banner, renounce their own independent revolutionary program, merge themselves in a politically amorphous "People's Front," abdicate the right of criticizing the Kuomintang's conduct of the war. This is the line of the Stalinist traitors. Political self-renunciation of this kind not only fails to advance China's struggle but prepares in advance its betrayal and defeat. The Chinese Bolshevik-Leninists keep aloft the revolutionary class-struggle banner of the Fourth International while taking part in the war, in the front lines and at the rear. They seek to effect the mobilization of the Chinese masses around independent revolutionary slogans corresponding to each given stage of the struggle and to the life interests of the masses themselves. Thereby they advance the indissolubly united tasks of the class struggle and the national war against imperialism.

Japanese imperialism, by its predatory invasion of China, threatens the position of all its rivals in the Pacific, including the United States. The present actual interests of American imperialism in China are relatively small, both in comparison with British and French interests and with American interests in Latin America. Trade with China accounts for only 3 percent of America's total foreign trade while American investments in China amount to less than $200 million, which is only one-tenth of American interests in Mexico. But it is the historic or future imperialist interests of the United States, rather than the immediate stake involved, which determine the Far Eastern policy of the Washington government. If Japan's aims in China should be realized, this would signify not only the loss of the present stake, but the closing of the door to future

American trade and investments in that country. More, it might also mean the loss of America's lucrative trade with Japan, since Japan hopes through the conquest of China to achieve a considerable degree of economic self-sufficiency. The Washington government is alive to these perils. Recurrent breakdowns in American economy, occurring at shorter intervals, serve warning that American capitalism, throttled by the national frontiers, must extend its markets and investments abroad or resign itself to permanent decay.

Recognizing that ultimately Japan can only be stopped by war, which was the sense of Roosevelt's Chicago speech, American imperialism and all its agencies seek to unite the working class of this country for support of the coming armed struggle. The aim of this struggle will be to establish American domination of the Pacific as a stage toward world domination. With variations, the different shades of bourgeois opinion all sing the same song: "Preparedness." The active war preparations of the Washington government, including arrangements for "parallel" action with Britain in the Far East, are shrouded in a smokescreen of pacifist propaganda in order to render easier the mobilization of the masses for war in defense of "freedom and democracy" and the "independence of weak nations"— in reality, to establish the position of the United States as the world's greatest imperialist power. In the work of drugging proletarian consciousness, the Stalinists and the reformists of every stripe, including the trade union bureaucrats, play an important role, with the Stalinists in the vanguard. The latter, newest exponents of twentieth-century social patriotism, sow base illusions concerning the "peaceful character" of American imperialism and call upon the imperialist government in Washington to help save China from Japan in the name of "collective security."

They brazenly offer services as recruiting sergeants in the war that the American imperialists are preparing to undertake against "military-fascist" Japan.

When American imperialism intervenes in the Far Eastern struggle, it will do so, not in order to save China for China's sake, but in order to preserve and extend its own predatory interests in China and the Far East. With these aims, the working class of America has nothing in common, while the Chinese masses would be just as badly off as the slaves of Wall Street as they would be as the colonial slaves of imperialist Japan. In such a war, the only policy which can possibly serve the interests of the American workers and the Chinese masses will be the policy of revolutionary defeatism. Our party, at the head of the working class, will seek to convert the imperialist war into civil war for the overthrow of the imperialist bourgeoisie and the establishment of workers' power. Only a workers' government in this or any other country can serve the interests of the workers and at the same time befriend and help the masses of China and other oppressed countries.

The American working class is not yet prepared to take over power. It can, however, invoke its own class sanctions against imperialist Japan and in this way bring effective aid to China's struggle. Our party has the duty to point out to the workers their close community of interests with the struggling Chinese masses and to carry on an agitation for the application of working-class sanctions. Such action by the American workers will advance the class struggle in this country, promote international working-class solidarity, and further the cause of the worldwide socialist revolution.

The campaign for a consumers' boycott of Japanese goods, sponsored by the Stalinists, pacifists, and trade union bureaucrats, is becoming an instrument of chauvinist propaganda. The boycott is a characteristically petty-bourgeois, and by itself an extremely ineffectual, weapon against Japanese imperialism. The present consumers' boycott receives tacit support from the Roosevelt government in line with its war mobilization plans. If the boycott remains the sole form of popular action against Japanese imperialism, it can only play into the hands of the imperialist warmongers and become a point of support for "national unity" and class collaboration. In order to combat this danger and to assure the effectiveness of the boycott as a weapon against Japanese imperialism, it is necessary to utilize the boycott sentiment as a basis upon which to agitate for independent working-class action. The "boycott" of Japanese goods in Shanghai in 1931–32 became effective only when it ceased being a simple boycott, that is, when bands of pickets raided shops and warehouses and seized all Japanese goods found on the premises—in other words, when mass "sanctions" were applied at the source of distribution. The party does not *oppose* the consumers' boycott, but regards it as secondary to the urgent need to impose active *working-class* sanctions against the Japanese imperialists.

Specifically, in order to aid China's progressive struggle against Japanese imperialism it is the duty of our party:

1. To propagandize the progressive character of the Chinese war among the widest layers of the workers and to build a strong sentiment of working-class solidarity with the exploited Chinese masses in their struggle against Japanese imperialism. In this connection, we condemn the criminal attitude of all the ultraleft sectarians who stubbornly refuse to recognize the difference between a predatory, imperialist war and a war of national liberation. Their attitude, which has nothing in common with revolutionary Marxism, can only give aid and comfort to

the Japanese imperialists.

2. To carry on a tireless campaign in the trade unions, through the medium of the party nuclei, for the invocation of working-class sanctions against the Japanese imperialists. These sanctions should take the form of:

(a) Refusal of maritime workers to sail vessels transporting cargoes to or from Japan.

(b) Refusal by longshoremen to load or unload cargoes destined for or coming from Japan.

(c) Refusal by workers in industry to use materials, either crude or partly processed, that have been made in Japan.

3. To extend to the Communist League of China (Chinese section of the Fourth International) the fullest material and moral aid in order thereby to assist our Chinese comrades in discharging the great revolutionary responsibilities which have fallen upon them.

4. To unmask the predatory aims and war preparations of American imperialism.

5. To conduct an agitation for the withdrawal of American warships and forces from China, where they are stationed solely to protect the interests of the American imperialists, and to link this up with a nationwide campaign against the growing danger of world imperialist war.

Constitution of the
Socialist Workers Party[25]

Article I. Name
The name of the organization shall be the Socialist Workers Party (hereinafter referred to as "the party.")

Article II. Purpose
The purpose of the party is set forth in its Declaration of Principles: its purpose shall be to educate and organize the working class for the abolition of capitalism and the establishment of a workers' government to achieve socialism.

Article III. International affiliation
The party is affiliated to the International Bureau for the Fourth International. Its National Committee is

---

25. The first draft of this was printed in *Bulletin Number 7*, January 1938. The committee assigned to prepare it consisted of James P. Cannon and Joseph Carter. The final draft, after being amended and adopted by the convention, was printed in a pamphlet, *Declaration of Principles and Constitution of the Socialist Workers Party* (SWP, 1938).

empowered, subject to approval of the International Bureau, to enter into fraternal relations with groups and parties in other countries not affiliated to the bureau with the aim of drawing them closer to or into the movement for the Fourth International.

Article IV. Membership

Section 1. Every person who accepts the Declaration of Principles of the party and agrees to submit to its discipline and engage actively in its work shall be eligible to membership.

Section 2. Applicants for membership shall sign an application card reading as follows: "I hereby apply for membership in the Socialist Workers Party. I accept the Declaration of Principles and constitution and agree to abide by the discipline of the party and to engage actively in its work."

Section 3. Every member must belong to a duly constituted branch of the party in the territory where he resides, or at his place of work, if such a branch exists. In territories where no branch exists, applicants shall be admitted as members-at-large.

Section 4. All applicants for membership shall be endorsed and recommended by two persons who have been members for not less than three months. Action by the party branch on applications for membership takes place in the absence of the applicant.

Section 5. An official membership card shall be issued to each member.

Section 6. A member desiring to leave one locality for another must apply to his branch for permission and receive a transfer card, which is to be deposited with the branch of the locality to which the member moves. If no branch exists in the new locality, the member shall remain a member-at-large.

Section 7. The National Committee is empowered to accept groups or organizations of individuals, eligible under Section 1 of this article, as members en bloc, and to assign them to the proper branches.

Article V. Units of organization

Section 1. The basic unit of the party shall be the branch, formed on a territorial or occupational basis. A branch shall consist of not less than 5 nor more than 50 members. When a branch achieves a membership of 50, it shall be subdivided into two branches. Exceptions can be made only by permission of the National Committee.

Section 2. Wherever two branches exist in the same locality, a local executive committee shall be formed by elections at a joint membership meeting. Where three or more branches exist in the same locality, a local executive committee shall be elected at a city convention.

Section 3. In such cases as may be decided by the National Committee, state or district executive committees, elected by state or district membership meetings or by local or district conventions, shall be formed.

Article VI. Administration

Section 1. The highest governing body of the party is the national convention. Its decisions shall be binding upon the entire membership.

Section 2. Between national conventions, the authority of the convention, subject to the decisions of the convention itself, is vested in the National Committee elected by the convention.

Section 3. The National Committee shall be comprised as follows:

Par. 1. There shall be 24 members, elected by the national convention, plus one member selected by the NEC of the YPSL.

Par. 2. The national convention shall also elect 10 alternates, to fill vacancies in the National Committee in the order decided upon by the convention.

Par. 3. Members of the National Committee may be dropped from the committee and/or from the party only by vote of the national convention. Members of the National Committee may, however, for cause be suspended from membership and be barred from all rights as members, pending final decision of the party convention, by vote of two-thirds of the membership of the National Committee.

Section 4. The National Committee directs all the work of the party, decides all questions of policy in accord with the decisions of the convention, appoints subordinate officers and subcommittees, including the Political Committee, and, in general, constitutes between conventions the functioning authority of the party.

Section 5. The local governing body of the party shall be the local executive committee, or where only one branch exists, the branch executive committee. Where state or district executive committees shall be constituted, the National Committee shall decide their relation to the local and branch executive committees.

Section 6. The branch executive committee shall be elected by the membership of the branch, and is subordinate to the branch membership. Its duties are to direct the activities of the branch, and to act with full powers for the branch between branch meetings. This section applies likewise to local executive committees.

Article VII. Young People's Socialist League

Section 1. The Young People's Socialist League is the youth organization of the party for work among the young workers, young farmers, and students.

Section 2. The YPSL is guided in its activities by the Declaration of Principles of the party, party policies and decisions.

Section 3. The YPSL is politically subordinate to the party but enjoys autonomy to decide its own organization problems, and to elect its own officers and committees.

Section 4. Members of the YPSL over the age of twenty-one, who have been members of the YPSL for six months, must apply for membership in the party.

Section 5. In all corresponding organs of the party and the YPSL, there shall be an exchange of representatives, each enjoying full rights (voice and vote).

Article VIII. Initiation fees and dues

Section 1. Each applicant for membership (other than charter members) shall pay an initiation fee of fifty cents, which shall be receipted for by an initiation stamp furnished by the national office. The entire initiation fee shall be paid to the national office.

Section 2. Each member shall pay a monthly dues of fifty cents, which shall be receipted for by dues stamps furnished by the national office through the branch treasurer (or local or district treasurer), and affixed to the membership card of each member. In addition, all members are expected to make regular voluntary contributions according to their means.

Section 3. Unemployed members or housewives not otherwise employed, shall pay ten cents per month, which is receipted for by a special stamp issued by the national office.

Section 4. Where branches are joined in local or district committees, one half of all regular dues payments (twenty-five cents) shall go to the national office; three-tenths (fifteen cents) shall go to the local or district committee; the remainder (ten cents) shall go to the branch. Where local or district committees do not exist thirty-five cents of each fifty cents dues shall go to the national office. Dues of members-at-large and unemployed members shall go in full to the national office.

Section 5. Members of the youth organization who are simultaneously party members shall pay party dues of ten cents per month, the entire amount going to the national office.

Section 6. A special international assessment of ten cents per member per month shall be paid by all members and receipted by a special stamp; to be sent to the International Bureau for the Fourth International.

Section 7. Members who are three months in arrears in payment of dues shall cease to be members in good standing, and shall be so notified by the branch executive committee. Members six months in arrears shall be stricken from the rolls of the party.

Article IX. Discipline

Section 1. All decisions of the governing bodies of the party are binding upon the members and subordinate bodies of the party.

Section 2. Any member or organ violating the decisions of a higher organ of the party shall be subject to disciplinary actions up to expulsion by the body having jurisdiction.

Section 3. Charges against any member shall be made in writing and the accused member shall be furnished with a copy in advance of the trial. Charges shall be filed and heard in the branch to which the member belongs. Where the member is also a member of any higher body charges may be filed either in the branch or in any higher body of which he is a member. Charges filed before the branch shall be considered by the branch executive committee (or a subcommittee elected by it) at a meeting to which the accused member is summoned. The branch executive committee shall submit a recommendation to be acted upon by the membership of the branch. Charges considered by higher bodies of the party shall, however, be acted upon by said bodies.

Section 4. Action by any unit or organ in disciplinary cases deemed improper by a higher unit, may be changed by direct intervention of a higher body.

Section 5. Any member subjected to disciplinary action has the right to appeal to the next higher body, up to and including the national convention. Pending action on appeal, the decision of the party body having jurisdiction remains in full force and effect.

Article X. Qualifications for elections

Section 1. Except in the case of newly organized branches, members of local and branch executive committees must have been members of the party for at least three months, and members of the district committee must have been members of the party for at least six months.

Section 2. Members of the National Committee must be members of the party for at least one year.

Article XI. National conventions

Section 1. The national convention of the party shall be held once a year. The NC may by two-thirds vote postpone the national convention for not more than six months, provided that a notice of such postponement be given not later than one month before the time for the convention call. Such action may be nullified on the demand of branches representing at least one-third of the membership.

Section 2. The call for the convention, together with

an agenda and the proposals of the National Committee shall be issued at least sixty days before the date of the convention for discussion in the local organizations and the official publications. An internal bulletin shall be issued during the convention discussion period.

Section 3. Representation at the convention shall be proportionally based upon the dues-paying membership in good standing at the time of the convention call. Branches organized after the convention call shall have fraternal representation.

Article XII. Amendments

Amendments shall be made to this constitution by majority vote of the national convention.

Article XIII. Press

All organs of the party are subject to and under the direction of the party and National Executive Committee.

Declaration of principles[26]

PART I

The decline of capitalism

Capitalist society, based upon the private ownership of the means of production and exchange and upon the free exploitation of labor by the bourgeoisie, came into being through the revolutionary struggle of the bourgeoisie, supported by the workers and peasants, against

---

26. The preconvention draft of this was printed in *Bulletin Number 7*, January 1938. James Burnham prepared the first draft, after which it was turned over to a committee consisting of Maurice Spector, Max Shachtman, and Burnham. The latter's dissatisfaction with the draft presented to the convention was expressed the day before it began when he urged a plenum of the National Action Committee in Chicago not to select him as the convention reporter on the Declaration of Principles "in view of amendments made to original draft, with which he is in disagreement." The amended draft adopted by the convention was printed in a pamphlet, *Declaration of Principles and Constitution of the Socialist Workers Party* (SWP, 1938).

the feudal lords and their retainers. In its initial periods, capitalism was a mighty progressive force, shattering the outmoded social and political forms of feudal society, vastly expanding the productive mechanism, and encouraging on an unprecedented scale the development of science and technique. The achievements of capitalism have brought mankind, for the first time in history, to the point where the material conditions are present which would enable all men to be supplied with the means for a full and ample life. Food, clothing, shelter, and the marvelous products of modern invention, could be provided in such abundance as to remove forever hunger, material want, and insecurity; and thereby form the foundation for a new and magnificent age of social and cultural development.

Now, however, the social and political forms of capitalism, effective once in the struggle against feudalism, themselves constitute an insurmountable obstacle to the utilization of further advance of the productive forces. The capitalist property relations, the subordination of production to profit instead of the fulfillment of human needs, the artificial restrictions imposed by national boundaries and national politics, not merely block the development of production, but actively sabotage it. Capitalism has entered the stage of its decline on a world scale. The successive cyclical crises of capitalist economy extend their scope and depth; and the intervening boom periods are unable to shake off the devastating effects of the preceding crisis. Capitalism is unable even to make use of the latest inventions and scientific products. The declining rate of profit pushes the bourgeoisie to desperation, to the attempt to place the entire burden upon the masses, and to efforts at adventurist solutions in foreign wars. Wide-scale unemployment becomes a permanent feature. The relative standard of living of the masses is progressively lowered, and is grotesquely out of line with what is made possible by the productive mechanism. The fear of insecurity is common to all except the most privileged. War is an ever present threat when not an actuality, and the weight of the armament programs adds to the oppression of the masses. And in its insane and frantic attempt to preserve the rotted system which supports its power and privilege, the bourgeoisie and its agents systematically destroy every social and human value, imposing upon men a moral regime of lies and viciousness and maddened terror.

Wars and revolutions

The period of the decline of capitalism is marked by an almost constant series of wars and revolutions. The imperialist powers, confronted by the inadequacy of their internal markets and the decline of the rate of profit, are compelled to seek new outlets for surplus capital and new possibilities for capital accumulation, as well as cheaper raw materials and profitable markets for the goods which their own populations cannot purchase. The peace of exhaustion following the war of 1914–18 lasts only long enough to permit sufficient preparation for the new war. In a world divided up and farmed out among the great powers, the mutual struggle for capital outlets, raw materials, and markets, becomes ever more intense.

The nations are plunged into economic, tariff, and exchange struggles, and armament competition, finally issuing in the armed struggle of worldwide imperialist war. At the same time, the masses, driven to desperation by the lash of the crisis, by the weight of exploitation, tyranny, and war, fight back in widespread wars for liberation on the part of the colonial peoples and in the revolutionary struggle of the working class for its emancipation.

Fascism

In the period of capitalist decline, the bourgeoisie is able to maintain a sufficient measure of profits and its own position of social privilege only by constantly reducing the general living standards of the dispossessed majority, by imposing upon it unemployment, insecurity, curtailed social services, and periodically resorting to war. The resistance generated among the masses by this course completes the material preconditions of revolutionary crises, and poses the question of the overthrow of the capitalist order as the sole solution. When such crises near a climax, and the working class, because of the lack of a strong revolutionary party, fails to act decisively for the revolutionary solution, it suffers internal demoralization and loses the confidence of the middle-class masses ruined by the crisis. Under the domination of finance capital, a fascist movement is then able to succeed in mobilizing the desperate middle-class elements and even certain demoralized sections of the working class on a wholly reactionary basis. Capitalist rule is reconsolidated through the victory of fascism; and capitalist society is temporarily "saved" by the destruction of the workers' organizations, wholesale terror and violence against working-class militants, and the suppression of all forms of independent class expression.

Under the totalitarian regime of fascism democratic rights are done away with, and the institutions of democracy are either abandoned or made inoperative. The trade unions, political parties, and all other independent organizations of workers and farmers, and even many independent bourgeois organizations, are smashed or compelled to become a passive part of the state machinery. The right to strike is abrogated. Terror is exercised not only against revolutionists, but against any workers engaged in a militant struggle for their own defense. Divisions are sown among the people by appeals to the basest racial prejudices and nationalistic passions. Science, art, and education are perverted to the degenerate service of the totalitarian state. Through its iron control fascism is able to drive down the standard of living of the masses and thrust upon them the costs of the crisis; and at the same time to head unchecked toward the wars made inevitable by the depth of the internal social crises. Thus, in the period of its decline, capitalism allies itself with everything that is archaic and destructive and reactionary, and threatens to drive whole nations, perhaps mankind itself, back into barbarism and savagery.

The position of the United States

In spite of its magnificent natural resources and its unparalleled industrial plant, the United States is in no way exempt from the influences of the world decline of the capitalist order. On the contrary, as has been proved by the war of 1914–18 and by the economic crisis of 1929, and is being further proved in the rapid approach of the new war and the new economic crisis, the United States is inseparably interlocked into the system of world imperialism. With the war of 1914–18, the United States rose to the position of the leading imperialist power at the very time when capitalism everywhere had entered its decline and conflicts between the great powers were therefore intensified. American imperialism cannot expand further, or even maintain its existing world position, without cutting deeply into the share of world power now in the hands of the other imperialist nations, as well as into the living standards of the masses in the United States itself, in Latin America, South America, Europe, and Asia, whom it exploits directly or from whom it exacts tribute. The economy and politics of the United States are inextricably connected with crises, wars, and revolutions in all parts of the world. The phenomena of capitalist decline—economic crises unprecedented in their depth, mass unemployment, inability to utilize inventions and technological improvements, insecurity, violations of democratic rights, the ever present threat of war—are all present, many to an exaggerated degree, in the United States. Nor can the United States, under capitalism, escape the more dire extremes of the new war and of fascism. In the very nature of the power of United States imperialism lie the irrepressible conflicts that herald its collapse.

The only road

For capitalism there is no way out, no alternative to the perspective of crises of cumulative intensity, growing unemployment and impoverishment, insecurity, political tyranny, fascism, war, and chaos, ending in collapse of the social order and a relapse into barbarism. And there is only one alternative to capitalism. That alternative is to do away with capitalism itself, to wipe out its central and insurmountable conflict by taking the ownership and control of the natural resources, the productive plant, and means of exchange, out of the hands of private individuals and corporations, and placing that ownership and control in the hands of society itself, to be used for the fulfillment of human needs and not for profit. The only alternative, the only possible solution, is to build a socialist society. Thus, and only thus, can men achieve plenty, security, peace, and freedom.

The role of the working class

In the struggle against capitalism and for socialism, the central role, following both from its key position in the process of production and likewise from the coherence and discipline imposed upon it by the methods of production, must be filled by the working class, in particular by the industrial working class. The working class will, however, require the support of other sections of society who are also exploited and oppressed. Large sections of the middle classes, the debt-ridden small farmers, the Negroes as a persecuted race, colonial and semicolonial peoples fighting against imperialist exploitation, these must be won by the working class as its allies. Only through the social revolution and socialism can all of the oppressed and exploited, and indeed all of mankind, find deliverance from insecurity, want, and tyranny.

The capitalist state

In any society, the real power is held by those who own and control the means whereby that society lives, the instruments of production, distribution, and communication. In capitalist society, such ownership and control is held and exercised by the big bourgeoisie, by the bankers and industrialists. Through its hold on the major natural resources, the factories, mines, banks, railroads, ships, airplanes, telegraph, radio, and press, the big bourgeoisie effectively dominates capitalist society, runs society in such a manner as to secure and maintain its own interest and privilege, and upholds the system of the exploitation of the great majority. The state or government, far from representing the general interests of society as a whole, is in the last analysis simply the political instrument through which the owning class exercises and maintains its power, enforces the property relations which guarantee its privileges, and suppresses the working class. In these essential functions all of the organs and institutions of the state power cooperate—the bureaucracy, the courts, police, prisons, and the armed forces. The particular political forms of capitalist society (monarchy, democracy, military dictatorship, fascism) in no way affect the basic social dictatorship of the controlling minority, and are only the different means through which that dictatorship expresses itself. The belief that in such a country as the United States we live in a free, democratic society, in which fundamental economic change can be effected by persuasion, by education, by legal and purely parliamentary methods, is an illusion. In the United States, as in all capitalist nations, we live, in actuality, under a capitalist dictatorship; and the possibilities for purely legal and constitutional change are therefore limited to those which fall within the framework of capitalist property and social relations, which later are severely curtailed by the circumstances of the decline of capitalism and in the long run, if the capitalist dictatorship continues, involve fascism for the United States as elsewhere. Genuine freedom can be realized only in a society based upon the economic and social equality of all individuals composing it, and such equality can be achieved only when the basic means of production, distribution, and communication are owned and controlled, not by any special class or group, but by society as a whole.

The conquest of power

Since the capitalist state is the political instrument of capitalist dictatorship, and since the workers can carry out socialization only through the conquest and maintenance of political power, the workers must, as the necessary political phase of the change of ownership and control of the productive mechanism, take control of state power through the overthrow of the capitalist state and the transfer of sovereignty from it to their own workers' state—the dictatorship of the proletariat.

Opportunities for the workers to take power have come and will come in the course of the disintegration of material life and of culture under capitalist dictatorship. The masses find themselves faced with growing hunger, impoverishment, curtailment of social services, and the threat or actuality of fascism and war. When the profound social discontent generated by the crisis of capitalism extends to a decisive majority of the working class and of the productive sections of the population generally, and when these have been won to the perspective of revolutionary change, the workers will be in a position to take power and to put an end to the destructive course of capitalist dictatorship.

The fundamental instruments of the workers' struggle for power cannot be the existing institutions of the governmental apparatus, since these represent basically the interests only of the capitalist minority. They must, on the contrary, be class organs, arising out of the class struggle, forged in the course of united actions of the workers and their allies, and representing genuinely and democratically the interests of the great majority, of the workers and their allies. Such organs the Russian workers found in the soviets or councils of the workers, soldiers, and peasants. The exact form which the workers' councils, or soviets, will take in any given nation cannot of course be predicted in advance, since this will depend in part upon the special experiences and traditions of the class struggle within the given nation—in the United States, for example, the councils could conceivably be a development from general strike committees. Nevertheless, it can be certain in advance that it will be through these councils, alone democratically representing the interests of the workers and of the great majority, that the workers will overthrow the capitalist class, and through a transfer of sovereignty from the existing governmental apparatus to the councils, will take state power. The workers will destroy the whole machinery of the capitalist state in order to render it incapable of counterrevolutionary activity and because it cannot serve as the instrumentality for establishing the new social order. Its place will be taken by a workers' state, based upon the workers' councils.

The workers' state

The workers' state is a temporary political instrument making possible the transition to the classless socialist society. Its task is to defend the workers' revolution against its enemies, both within and without, and to lay the foundations for socialism and the final elimination of all classes and class rule. Like every other state, therefore, the workers' state is, under one aspect, a dictatorship. Unlike every other state in history, however, it is a dictatorship exercised by the great majority against the counterrevolutionary minority. And, equally unlike every other state, its aim is not the perpetuation of its rule, but on the contrary, through the provision of material plenty for all and through education, to abolish the remains of class division in society and thus to eliminate the necessity for state coercion, that is, to do away with itself, with any form of state whatever. In an industrially advanced nation, the workers' state will be able from the outset to assure and continually extend far more genuine and substantial democratic rights to the masses than ever accorded to them under capitalism. Through the councils, the masses will exercise free and democratic control over all the policies of the workers' state, not merely in political questions but in the vital plans for socialist construction, will freely elect all officials and maintain the permanent right of recall. Salaries of officials will have the level of a skilled worker as their maximum. Through factory and other types of industrial and agricultural committees, the workers will participate in the fullest possible degree in social and economic administration. The workers' state will not have a professional army, but will depend upon a mass workers' militia, in which distinctions other than those required for technical efficiency will be abolished and democratic control over officers will be exercised by the ranks. While the workers' state will necessarily reserve to itself the indispensable right to take all requisite measures to deal with violence and armed attacks against the revolutionary regime, it will at the same time assure adequate civil rights to opposition individuals, groups, and political parties, and will guarantee the opportunity for the expression of opposition through the allotment of press, radio, and assembly facilities in accordance with the real strength among the people of the opposition groups or parties.

The most important of the socioeconomic measures to be taken by the workers' state in its initial period is the expropriation and socialization, without compensation, of all monopolies in industry and land; all mines, factories, and shipping; all public utilities, railroads, airplane systems, and other organized means of communication; all banks, credit agencies, gold stores; and all other supplies and services that the revolutionary government finds it necessary to take over in order to lay the foundations of a socialist society. This socialization of the means of production and exchange will injure only the small handful of financiers, landlords, and industrialists whose private control of the resources of the country is the source of hunger, unemployment, and insecurity for the bulk of the people. The policy of socialization pursued by the workers' state will make possible the guarantee to every willing worker of a well-paid job, security against unemployment, insurance against industrial risks, old age, and sickness; and will further provide adequate educational, recreational, and cultural opportunities for the entire population. There will be no need for the workers' state to impose arbitrary, premature, and oppressive measures upon small individual proprietors, craftsmen, and small-scale farmers. The example of the social and personal advantages of the socialist organization of production, and assistance from the workers' government, can be trusted to lead them to voluntary collectivization. Socialism will release the productive forces to serve the needs of men, and will enable production to be planned rationally in terms of actual social requirements. It will allow the utilization of every technical improvement. The leisure and educational opportunities which will accompany these material advantages, together with the removal of the deadweight of the perverted capitalist culture, will offer every individual possibilities for the fullest creative development.

The socialist society

With the provision of material abundance through planned socialist production, and the great educational and cultural advances thereby made possible, the socially useless and parasitic classes, as well as the remnants of capitalist ideology, will be eliminated. The entire population will be transformed into a community of free producers owning and controlling the total productive wealth and resources of society, and freely and consciously working out their own destiny. The need for the coercion and repression of socially alien classes will disappear with the disappearance of these classes, and together with them, of all classes. With it will vanish the need for a state machinery—even for the workers' state. The state as an institution for the domination, repression, and coercion of men will be replaced by a purely technical administration for the handling of the general business of society. The noblest objective of the human race—communism, the classless socialist society—inaugurating a new era for all of mankind, will be realized.

The working class can build a complete socialist society only on the basis of a world division of labor and resources, and world cooperation. The revolutionary party in this country does not aim merely to lead the working class of the United States in revolution, but to unite with the workers of all other countries in the international revolution and the establishment of world socialism. Modern forces of production have compelled capitalism itself to transcend national boundaries; and the conflict between the world economy of capitalism and the outlived, constricting national political boundaries is a major source of the disastrous evils which confront the modern world. Capitalist imperialism cannot, however, achieve a harmonious society. World socialism is the only solution for the conflicts and disorders of the modern world, as well as for the major conflicts within a single nation. A socialist society will rationally and scientifically utilize the natural resources and productive machinery of the earth in the interests of the people of the earth, and will solve the conflict between the efficient development of productive forces and the artificial restrictions of national boundaries. It will grant the rights of free cultural self-determination to all nations. In these ways, world socialism will remove the causes of international wars, which under capitalism now seriously threaten to send mankind back into barbarism or complete destruction.

PART II

The revolutionary party

The working class, under capitalism and in the initial stages of the socialist revolution, is neither economically nor socially nor ideologically homogeneous. It is united in terms of fundamental historical class interest, and by the urgent needs of the daily class struggle. However, it still remains divided by different income levels and working conditions, by religion, nationality, culture, sex, age. Through the perverting influence of capitalist oppression and propaganda, it is further divided by conflicting ideologies, and weakened by the low cultural and educational level of many of its members. There are, moreover, the divisions between various sections of the working class and its potential allies in the revolutionary struggle. For these reasons, the working class cannot, as a whole or spontaneously, directly plan and guide its own struggle for power. For this, a directing staff, a conscious vanguard, arising out of the ranks of the proletariat and based upon it, participating actively in the day-by-day struggles of the workers and in all progressive struggles, and planning clear-sightedly the broader strategy of the longer-term struggle for state power and socialism, is indispensable. This staff and vanguard constitutes the revolutionary party.

The entire experience of our epoch demonstrates irrefutably that without the leadership of the revolutionary party the lasting victory of the workers is impossible. Without an adequate, firm, and strong revolutionary party, the magnificent heroism, militancy, and self-sacrifice of the workers lead and can lead only to sporadic and unconnected battles for partial aims which achieve no lasting conquests and prepare the ground for defeats.

The revolutionary party must be forged in active struggle. Its leadership cannot be imposed from above. It can be won only by demonstrating in action the correctness of its program and the superiority of its tactics. The support of the party cannot rest upon demagogy—the universal instrument of all other political parties. It cannot be imposed on the masses by force and against their will, but must be based upon free acceptance by the decisive sections of the masses. The membership of the revolutionary party comprises the most advanced, determined, and devoted militants in the struggle for socialism, voluntarily united on the basis of tested principles and welded together in rigorous discipline.

The program of the revolutionary party rests upon the great principles of revolutionary Marxism expounded by Marx, Engels, Lenin, and Trotsky, and representing the summation of experience of the working class in its struggle for power. These principles have been verified in particular in the experiences of the last world war and by the victory of the Russian proletarian revolution. They have been concretized in the basic documents of the first four congresses of the Communist International and the fundamental programmatic documents put forward by the movement for the Fourth International in the past fourteen years. The SWP stands upon the main line of principle developed in these documents.

The organizational structure of the revolutionary party, enabling the party to carry through its historic task, rests upon the principle of democratic centralism. This means the fullest inner-party democracy combined with centralized direction and rigid discipline in action. Inner-party democracy guarantees full and free discussion of all party problems, and freedom of criticism both of policies and of the leadership. The leadership, up to and including the highest bodies, is freely and democratically elected by the membership, and subject to its control and removal. The administration of the party is centralized, with lower units subordinate to the higher units. In public and in action, all members are required to carry out the discipline of the party.

Capitalist economy and politics are today worldwide in their basis and scope. The great crises of the modern world—economic crisis, war, revolution—are international in character. The struggle against capitalism and the solution of the problems of the modern world in a world socialist society are likewise international. Consequently, the revolutionary party, if it is to be able to lead this struggle, must itself be an international party, planning its course in terms of an international strategy applied tactically in terms of the local conditions and circumstances of any given nation, and organized in national sections adhering to a single unified national center.

The working class can conduct partial defensive actions and even achieve certain offensive gains on the basis of the united front and a nonrevolutionary perspective. It can take and maintain power, however, only when a decisive majority has been won to the concrete program of the revolution; and this is possible only through the firm and active leadership of the revolutionary party. Similarly, the leadership of the revolutionary party is required to secure the defense of the workers' state and to carry out the organization of socialist economy. The role of the revolutionary party as the leader of the class continues until all forms of class organization, including both the state and all political parties, have disappeared, giving way to the classless socialist society.

The Second International

The Second International (now known as the Labor and Socialist International), answering at one time the needs of one stage in the development of the working class, performed a great progressive function in the mass organization of workers and in the spread of the ideas of socialism. During the period of relative prosperity and stability of capitalism at the beginning of this century, however, and with the rise of imperialism, which fostered the growth and dominance of a labor aristocracy and a conservative trade union and party bureaucracy associated with it, the Second International and all of its major constituent parties were corrupted, and degenerated into patriotic props of bourgeois democracy. The leadership abandoned the road of revolutionary class struggle for power in favor of class collaboration and purely reformist activities aiming at partial demands sought within the framework of capitalism. It accepted, in principle and in practice, the policy of participation in bourgeois coalition governments: that is, of service as political executives for the bourgeoisie.

The extent of the degeneration was fully revealed in 1914, when the parties of the Second International in Europe went over in a body to full-blown social patriotism, and within each country became the recruiting agents within the working class for the imperialist war. Following the war, these parties and the International became the chief bulwark of capitalism against the rising tide of proletarian revolution; in Germany, the leading party of this International drowned the revolution in blood, and handed the power back to the German bourgeoisie. The intervening period has only confirmed the lessons of those years. From instruments of reforms, especially for the labor aristocracy, they were converted, after the war, into agencies for wiping out the previously conquered social reforms of labor, whose existence was no longer tolerable by a declining capitalist order. Everywhere, the Second International and its parties have functioned as a brake set against the workers' revolution, and have proved not merely their inability to lead the workers to victory, but—as in Italy, Germany, and Austria—their certainty of condemning the workers to defeat and finally to fascism. At the present time, the most important remaining parties of the Second International (Great Britain, France) have already proclaimed their social patriotism in the coming war, have voted for the imperialist armament budgets, and are making ready once again to lead the masses to slaughter for the cause of "democratic" imperialism; and in Spain the party of the Second International, administering the bourgeois government of the People's Front, is making impossible the success of the military struggle against the fascists by subordinating the working class to the bourgeoisie and at the same time liquidating the revolutionary conquests of the workers within the Loyalist territory. Organizationally, the Second International functions merely as a bureaucratic secretariat; and the apparatus of all of the major parties is firmly in the hands of hidebound reformist bureaucracies.

Experience thus proves that the Second International is an International of defeat and betrayal, and is totally bankrupt as an actual or potential leader of the revolutionary movement. Its reform is excluded on both political and organizational grounds. The development of the revolutionary party in the present era requires the complete and absolute break, both organizationally and politically, with the Second International.

The Third International

The Third, or Communist, International, was projected by Lenin immediately following the betrayal of the Second International to the war, and founded in the fire of the October insurrection in Russia. In its early years, under the guidance of the leaders of the mightiest triumph of the working class, the Third International was the flaming inspiration of the oppressed masses of the entire world. The workers' state in Russia was successfully defended against its enemies, its power consolidated, and the foundations of a socialist economy established; mighty battles were fought everywhere by the working class on the international arena; the programmatic documents of the early years of the International summed up the great and permanently valid principles of revolutionary Marxism, and applied those principles to the conditions of our time.

But the failure of the revolution in the advanced nations and the physical and moral exhaustion of the masses as the result of the imperialist war and the revolutionary struggles enabled the Stalinist clique to gain control of the Soviet state apparatus, the Communist Party of the Soviet Union, and subsequently the Communist International and all of its sections. With Stalin and his adherents in control, and proceeding from the reactionary and anti-Marxist policies of attempting to build a pretended socialism within the national confines of the Soviet Union alone, in independence of the international revolutionary struggle, and of suppressing Soviet, workers', and party democracy in the interests of bureaucratic control and privilege, the history of the Third International and its sections became one of decline, degeneration, and decay.

The entire Third International has become a mere appendage of the Stalinist bureaucratic machine, utilized as an instrument to serve the interests of the bureaucracy, and against the interests of the working class both of the Soviet Union and of the entire world. The events of the past four years—the collapse of the German Communist Party at the advent of Hitler; the proceedings of the

Seventh Congress of the Communist International;[27] the adoption of the policy of the People's Front; the new constitution of the Soviet Union; the policies currently pursued within Spain and China; and above all the unprecedented series of trials, executions, and purges beginning within the Soviet Union but now being extended by the GPU throughout the world[28]—these events make clear the extent and profundity of the degeneration of the Third International. The Third International is now being used to enlist the masses within the "democratic" imperialist countries to support one of the imperialist coalitions in the approaching world war, and to smash all opposition to the new war. The Third International stands within the international working class as the chief bulwark of capitalism and the chief obstacle to the socialist revolution.

The organization of the Third International and its sections is rigidly monolithic in character. No slightest semblance of party democracy remains. The control of

---

27. The Seventh Congress of the Comintern, held in Moscow July–August 1935, turned out to be its last congress. None other was held in the next eight years before Stalin liquidated the Comintern as a concession to his imperialist allies in World War II.

28. To name only a few victims of the Stalinist purges extended into other countries in the months preceding the SWP convention: Andrés Nin, POUM leader, was kidnapped by the GPU in June 1937 in Barcelona and murdered soon after. Erwin Wolf, a Czech national and member of the International Secretariat of the Movement for the Fourth International, was kidnapped by the GPU in Spain in July 1937 and was never seen again. Ignace Reiss, a veteran officer of the GPU who broke with Stalinism after the first two Moscow trials, was murdered by the GPU in Switzerland in September 1937. The GPU plan had been to murder Leon Sedov, Trotsky's son, on the same occasion, but by accident Sedov did not show up for a meeting with Reiss and thus lived another half year before being murdered by the GPU in a Paris hospital in February 1938.

bureaucratic absolutism extends from top to bottom. Its regime is compounded of lies, frame-ups, treachery, and terrorism.

No hope whatever of the reform of the Third International or its sections remains. In policy and organization, in ideas and practices, it is hopelessly and utterly bankrupt. The development of the revolutionary party, the continued defense of the remaining conquests of the Russian revolution, the struggle for proletarian power, are inseparable from an uncompromising break with and intransigent struggle against the Third International.

Centrist parties and groupings

From time to time within nearly every country in the modern world, parties or political groupings develop in terms of a program which seeks an intermediary position between revolutionary Marxism (representing the unequivocal historical interests of the working class) and reformism (representing in the last analysis the interests of the bourgeoisie operating within the working class). Prominent examples of such parties include the British Independent Labour Party, the German Socialist Workers Party (SAP), the Spanish Workers Party of Marxist Unification (POUM), the Brandler-Lovestone groups—and many of them have during recent years been affiliated to the so-called London Bureau. These centrist parties and groupings, which attempted to straddle between the two major class forces in modern society, are by their very nature sterile and incapable of leading an effective and successful struggle for the socialist revolution. Though progressive as a stage in the evolution from reformism to revolutionary Marxism, centrism, stopping short of transformation into revolutionary Marxism, functions in practice to disorient the workers, acts as a cover for reformism both of the Social

Democratic and Stalinist varieties, and blocks the revolutionary struggle for workers' power. Revolutionary Marxism, therefore, cannot tolerate any conciliation with centrism.

The new International

War, fascism, the economic crises of capitalism, are international phenomena. The conflict between the restrictions which national boundaries place upon the development of the productive forces and the international character of economy is a world problem. Socialism by its very nature is an international social order. So too, if the workers' movement and the workers' revolution are to succeed, must they be international, and directed in terms of an international strategy. Because of the unequal development of the countries of the world, and since state power is national under capitalism, its conquest must begin in some given nation or nations. But the seizure of power in one country can endure and can go forward toward socialism only by the extension of the revolution to the entire world, and by the building of socialism as a world system. The SWP therefore rejects the utopian and anti-Marxian theory of "socialism in one country."

The revolutionary party must thus be an international party, with sections in every country. Its strategy must be worked out in terms of an international perspective, with national tactics adapted to the specific peculiarities and conditions within each nation, but all flowing from the international strategy.

The recognition of the hopeless bankruptcy of the existing Internationals of the working class, of the Second and Third Internationals, and of the impossibilities of their reform, is consequently inseparable from the recognition of the imperative need for building the new, Fourth International, based upon the uncompromising principles of revolutionary Marxism. The rebuilding of the revolutionary party in the United States is an integral part of the rebuilding of the revolutionary party internationally, of the formation of the Fourth International.

The revolutionary party in the United States collaborates in the fullest measure with all groups, organizations, and parties in all other countries standing on the same fundamental program as our own; and cooperates with them in the elaboration of a complete world program. The SWP, therefore, is affiliated with the Bureau for the Fourth International as its section in the United States.

Parties in the United States
1. The Socialist Party

Following the split of the world's working-class political movement by the social-patriotic betrayal of the Second International and the subsequent organization of the Communist International, the Socialist Party of the United States entered a long period of stagnation. Politically it stood at the right wing of the parties of the Second International, but, unlike the European parties, it had little mass influence. Its policies were class collaborationist and thoroughly reformist in character. Its perspective was based upon the achievement of petty reforms within the framework of capitalist society, and its activities were confined largely to trivial parliamentary contests chiefly within the sphere of municipal politics. Within the trade unions, so far as it functioned at all, it acted only as a prop for the reactionary old-line bureaucrats. Internationally, it restored and maintained its affiliation to the Second International; that is, to the organization which engineered the social-patriotic betrayal to the war and which smashed the socialist revolution in the West European countries.

Following the victory of Hitler in Germany, a progressive

ferment set in among the membership, the active section of which was resolved to learn from and profit by the lessons of the German defeats. This ferment took form as an organizational struggle of the Militant faction against the stranglehold of the Old Guard, representing reformism in its most crass and reactionary expression. The struggle reached a head at the Cleveland convention in 1936, as a result of which the main sections of the Old Guard split away from the Socialist Party to form the Social Democratic Federation, through which their policies continue in operation.

Both before and after the Cleveland convention, there was an influx into the Socialist Party of unaffiliated revolutionists, and of an entire revolutionary group, the former Workers Party. The revolutionists already within the party fused with these incoming revolutionists, joining in the common struggle for an uncompromising revolutionary policy and a genuinely revolutionary party. The spectacle of the rapid advance of the revolutionary current, however, dismayed and alarmed the centrists and right-wingers who were still in control of the apparatus of the Socialist Party. Resolved to prevent at all costs the transformation of the party into a clear-cut revolutionary organization, they called the Chicago convention in March 1937, in an attempt to cut off the revolutionary current. Failing in this attempt because of the resistance of the membership, they took bureaucratic measures in the summer of 1937 to split the party. In flagrant violation of the convention decisions and the will of the membership, they utilized their control of the national apparatus to put an end to party democracy and then to expel the revolutionary wing. The decisive political motivation for the expulsion of the revolutionists was the determination of the old-line leadership to swing the party sharply to the right, exemplified by the treacherous decision to support the capitalist candidate for mayor of the New York People's Front, extending from the Lovestoneites and Stalinists to the Republican Party.

The entire active militant membership rallied to the revolutionary wing, and stood with unbroken ranks, firm in the resolve to carry forward the great task of rebuilding the revolutionary party in this country. The centrists and right-wingers have retained only the formal shell of the Socialist Party, a hopeless, miserable, impotent clique, already falling apart in a dozen different directions and sinking in its bulk to sterile passivity. That Socialist Party is now only a dead husk. It offers no hope; it has no policy, no perspective. There is no hope for it any longer on the American political scene. The comparatively small number of individual militants remaining within it can function in the revolutionary movement of the working class only by breaking immediately and finally with the Altman-Thomas-Tyler Socialist Party, and with everything for which it stands.

2. The Communist Party

The Communist Party of the United States is a faithful replica of the sections of the Communist International everywhere. Its main function is to prepare the mass support of the United States government in the coming imperialist war; it has already announced publicly its support of that war and its intention of acting as the lynch gang to take care of all those who oppose the war. In compliance with the policy of the People's Front, it supports capitalist candidates and capitalist parties in elections, and utilizes its full influence to direct the workers away from independent proletarian action. It acts as the propagandist for the Moscow trials and has already begun the introduction of the system of the Moscow trials into this country; a step which will lead to ever increasing attempts at the frame-up, terrorization, even assassination of working-class militants.

Within the labor movement, the Communist Party of the United States plays a reactionary role. Indeed, its policy in practice is not less reactionary than that of the old-line trade union bureaucrats with whom it is allied. The primary concern of the Communist Party is not with the immediate needs of the workers and their unions; it seeks only to manipulate the unions in accordance with the requirements of the People's Front in preparing the social-patriotic betrayal to the war. The Stalinists within the unions are ready to make any deal whatever with either bureaucrats or bosses, to engineer any type of sellout, and in general devote their energies to the crushing of every sign of progressive and militant opposition. In their use of gangsterism, lies, frame-ups, and bureaucratism, the Stalinists in the unions are distinguished from the older-style reactionary bureaucrats only by the greater skill, thoroughness, and ruthlessness of the Stalinists in applying their anti-working-class and counterrevolutionary methods.

Far from offering any hope whatever in the task of building the revolutionary party, the Communist Party of the United States is a counterrevolutionary agency, the chief obstacle within the working class to building the revolutionary party. It is true that there are at present, either within the Communist Party or its various collateral organizations, many individuals with militant and even revolutionary sentiments who, though dissatisfied with the party and its policy, do not yet realize the full implications of the policy and are not yet ready to break sharply with Stalinism. These elements will inevitably come into sharp conflict with the treacherous policies and leadership of the Communist Party. The revolutionary party will be a rallying banner for all those who break with Stalinism. But this can be accomplished only through the unremitting, constant, and uncompromising struggle against Stalinism itself in all its forms and on every field.

3. Labor and farmer-labor parties

There is at present in this country, as on other occasions in the past, a movement toward the formation of various sorts of labor and farmer-labor parties. In a few states and localities such parties are already in existence, and functioning as political organizations.

Mass labor and farmer-labor parties are all defined in political character as *reformist*. As such, the programs and activities are directed to securing reforms within the framework of capitalist society, and against the revolutionary overthrow of capitalism. The solution of the historical problems of the working class—the defeat of fascism, the abolition of war, the gaining of material security—none of them can be secured without the revolutionary overthrow of capitalism. In the present era the continuance of capitalism makes war, fascism, impoverishment for the masses, inevitable. It therefore follows—as is also demonstrated conclusively by the experience of the labor movement—that these reformist parties act in practice and in crises as bulwarks of capitalism and enemies of the socialist revolution. Their false program and perspective disorient the masses, turning them aside from revolutionary class struggle, and permit the forces of reaction to consolidate without effective opposition.

The history of the present labor party movement in this country reinforces these conclusions. The American Labor Party in New York was specifically founded by the trade union bureaucrats to gather votes for Roosevelt from those workers whom the Democratic Party could no longer dupe or attract, and who would not therefore have voted for a presidential candidate on an old-party ticket. Similarly, in 1937, it brought nearly half a million labor votes to the capitalist candidate LaGuardia. So, in the rest of the country, the labor party movement is used by the bureaucrats to bolster up and refurbish capitalist politics, to provide a new coating to make capitalist politics palatable to the masses. There is every indication that the present labor party developments, however far they may be extended, will continue the efforts to make deals and bargains with the two existing capitalist parties, perhaps even to fuse with one or another section of these parties, and will strive to maneuver to a position of holding the "balance of power" between them by playing one off against the other. Far from constituting independent class politics, the present labor party development is, from the point of view of the bureaucrats and the bourgeoisie, the method for preventing the growth of independent class politics.

For such reasons, the revolutionary party cannot for a moment compromise with the program of the labor and farmer-labor parties. It must consistently and vigorously put forward its own full revolutionary program as the *only* solution to the problems of the workers and of the masses generally; and must strive at all times to recruit directly into its own ranks. Nor can the revolutionary party properly take the initiative in advocating the formation of labor or farmer-labor parties.

Nevertheless, the labor party movement, from the point of view of the workers themselves, does reveal a progressive development in general towards class consciousness. In spite of the channels into which it is led by the bureaucrats, it shows in the masses a growing realization of the true character of capitalist politics as summed up in the Republican and Democratic parties and a striving for independent political action. To stand aside completely from such a development where it comprises the bulk of the militant and advanced sections of the workers would be hopelessly sectarian for the revolutionists. Where the labor party develops as a genuine mass movement separate from the capitalist parties, the revolutionists must remain in the midst of the workers who are passing through that experience precisely in order to make certain that the workers will draw the lessons from that experience which are required in order to go on from it to revolutionary class politics. Uncompromising, programmatic independence on the part of the revolutionary party is an indispensable precondition for any activity in which revolutionists may engage, especially through their trade unions, in broad and significant labor party movements. Whenever the revolutionists find themselves in a labor party, they will stand at each stage for those concrete policies and actions which sum up a progressive and class perspective; for complete breaks with the capitalist parties and no support of candidates on capitalist tickets; for direct mass actions and avoidance of limitation to parliamentary activities; for full internal democracy; for support and defense of concrete working-class rights against their invasion from any source, including invasions from candidates of the labor party itself; etc.

The SWP

In the light of the considerations set forth in this Declaration of Principles, and basing itself upon the great principles herein outlined, the convention of revolutionary socialists held in Chicago from December 31, 1937, to January 3, 1938, establishes the SWP as an independent organization. We call upon all revolutionary militants to join with us to build the SWP into the mass revolutionary party which will lead the working class of the United States to power; and which, together with the revolutionists of all countries united in the Fourth International, will achieve the victory of the international revolution and of world socialism.

PART III

The aim of the SWP

The main specific task of the SWP is the mobilization of the American masses for struggle against American capitalism, and for its overthrow. To this end the party will seek to win the support of the industrial and agricultural workers by its activity within their mass organizations, and to establish an alliance between the workers and farmers and other sections of the middle class ready and able to join labor in a struggle against the big capitalist class. The SWP will support and seek to give leadership to all progressive struggles, whether for immediate or more far-reaching demands, to strikes, organization campaigns, demonstrations, mass actions for relief and jobs and social insurance, mass fights against lynching, evictions, foreclosures, violations of civil rights, and against every type of reaction. While relying primarily on mass actions, propaganda, and agitation as the means for furthering its revolutionary aim, the party will also participate in electoral campaigns, though at all times contending against the fatal illusion that the masses can accomplish their emancipation through the ballot box. Election campaigns will serve primarily as a means for revolutionary propaganda; and candidates who are elected will utilize their offices first of all to expose the sham of capitalist democracy and to promote the mass movement of the workers. The party will endeavor constantly to educate the militant workers in the principles of revolutionary Marxism. Everywhere, by direct participation, it will seek to demonstrate in action the applicability of its principles and tactics and the competence of its leadership.

The trade unions

The trade unions are the elementary and basic organs of working-class defense against capitalist aggression; and of all trade unions, the most important are those of the workers in the large shops, mills, factories, and mines of the basic industries. The primary field of party work is trade union activity.

In trade union policy, the party stands for the methods of militant class struggle; the organization of the unorganized; industrial unionism, in all fields where this is feasible; and broad inner-union democracy. The party fights against policies of class collaborationism, against bureaucratism, gangsterism, and racketeering, and against reliance on the government and governmental agencies. The party, while in no degree relaxing its support of the unions and their struggles, fights also against those forces within the unions which carry out these reactionary policies; against the trade union bureaucracy and against all other reactionary tendencies in the unions—in particular against Stalinism. The party stands for the closest cooperation between the trade unions and the unemployed for their common interest, and opposes any discrimination against the unemployed workers.

The party stands for trade union unity, since a divided trade union movement weakens the defensive strength of the workers against reaction, and facilitates the coming of fascism. The party does not, however, make a fetish of "unity at all costs." While against the policy of building paper "red unions," as advocated by the Stalinists in the so-called third period,[29] and in favor of working within the genuine existing unions, which are for the most part reformist in policy and leadership, the party recognizes that special circumstances may have brought about the development of genuine unions outside the chief central trade union body or bodies, and in such cases it supports these independent trade unions while working for their reintegration into the mainstream of the labor movement; and where the existing central body or bodies refuse to organize a given field, the party favors its organization in any case on a temporarily independent basis.

In keeping with its stand for trade union unity, the party favors the unity of the AFL and the CIO on the foundation of progressive trade union policy. In the division of the labor movement into AFL and CIO, the party recognizes the historically more progressive character of the CIO movement in its policies of industrial unionism and organization of the unorganized. Nevertheless, the CIO does not have an exclusive claim to support, both because of its own reactionary features—its extreme violations of trade union democracy and its class collaborationism—and more especially because the AFL remains a genuine mass organization of a section of the American working class. Consequently, in the case of concrete disputes between the two and in questions of conflicting fields of operation for party members, there is no universal formula in favor of either organization; each such

---

29. The Stalinists did not actually *advocate* the building of *paper* "red unions" in the "third period," but most of the "red unions" they labored to build existed only on paper or in their imaginations.

issue must be settled on its own merits in the light of the specific circumstances involved.

The party supports and builds the trade unions. It is not content, however, to work in them at the level of mere and "pure" trade unionism. It seeks to build within the unions a broad progressive wing based on progressive trade union policies. And at all times it aims to raise the level of class consciousness of the trade union members, and to politicalize their thoughts and activities to the fullest possible degree.

The middle classes

Though the leadership in the revolutionary struggle for socialism can be held only by the working class, the working class cannot succeed in its struggle without winning to its side broad sections of the middle classes; of the farmers, professional workers, small shopkeepers, etc. The middle classes in modern society, occupying a social position which causes them to vacillate between the two basic decisive classes—bourgeoisie and proletariat—have no independent social perspective or program for society as a whole, and thus in crucial situations tend always in their bulk to throw their weight to one or the other of the two decisive classes. It would therefore be fatal from a revolutionary point of view for the working class to attempt to win the middle classes by abandoning its program (the program of revolutionary socialism) and accepting as substitute some specious "middle-class program" (as is done in the case of the tactic of the "People's Front"). On the same grounds, the SWP rejects the conception of a "two-class party"[30] (farmer-labor party,

---

30. The SWP was not opposed to an alliance between the working class and sections of the middle class but it held that such an alliance could

etc.), which is an attempt to put two different classes on the same plane by organizing them into a single party with a single program. Preserving its own program intact, the working class must win the middle classes, especially their lower, more impoverished, and more discontented strata, by first demonstrating to them the power and strength of the working class in action, and second, by supporting those specific demands and struggles of the middle classes which are directed implicitly against capitalism and whose full achievement requires the sharpest struggle against capitalism itself: demands for mortgage relief, tax relief in the "lower brackets," better conditions of farm tenancy, improved conditions for the lower-paid professional workers and technicians, etc.

In agriculture, the revolutionary working-class party bases itself primarily upon the agricultural proletariat, whose interests it defends at all times, even when need be, against the middle-class farmers. The living conditions of the great mass of farm tenants, sharecroppers, and smaller independent farmers are in this country at almost a subhuman level, in many instances indeed well below that of the industrial workers. In recent years also, many of the professional workers have been feeling the full weight of capitalist decline both in the lowering of their own living standards, and likewise in the growing disparity between the tasks they are trained to accomplish and the inability of capitalism to provide any way to make use of their training. These sections of the population are beginning to

---

not serve the interests of the workers unless they had their own party to represent them. The conception of a "two-class party" promoted by the Stalinists in the Far East had always been condemned by the Left Opposition as a scheme to promote class collaboration with the colonial bourgeoisie (for example, with the Kuomintang in China).

organize in defense of their immediate interests. Support of their progressive demands and struggles, linking of those struggles with the struggles of the proletariat, and a bold and vigorous policy on the part of the revolutionary party will save them from fascism—to which they will otherwise turn—and win them to the socialist revolution.

Negroes and other oppressed racial groups

The Negroes compose the most exploited and persecuted section of the population of this country. Racial differences and antagonisms, moreover, are exploited by the capitalist dictatorship to drive down the standard of living of all workers and to keep them from uniting against their oppressors. The SWP will seek to break down the vicious chauvinistic "superiority" prejudices with which the bourgeoisie systematically poisons the minds of the white workers. It will aim to convince the white workers on the one hand, and the workers of the Negro and other oppressed racial groups (such as the Japanese, Mexicans, and Filipinos) on the other, that their interests are the same. Workers, regardless of race, must be united in economic and political organizations for a common struggle. The SWP stands for the complete equality of the Negroes and all other races, and will fight against every form of race discrimination—economic, political, social, against wage differentials, lynching, Jim Crowism, the barring of Negroes and other racial groups from the trade unions, discrimination against them where they are in unions, and all other forms of racial and national chauvinism. At the same time it points out that the Negro masses cannot achieve deliverance by reliance upon Negro capitalists or middle-class Negroes or upon so-called Negro capitalism. Only by the complete abolition of capitalism will the Negroes gain freedom from discrimination, exploitation, and tyranny.

The unemployed

The enormous and largely permanent army of the unemployed during the period of the rapid decline of capitalism is a vast depository of every kind of social discontent. In a position where the conduct of their lives has lost social meaning, the unemployed will join with the movement that convincingly fights for their demands and opens to them the prospect of a new and integral place in the social order. Unless the working-class movement, by giving support to their struggles and by vigorous presentation of the revolutionary way out of the crisis, draws in the unemployed, they will be a prey to chauvinistic and military propaganda, to fake social nostrums, and to fascist demagogy. The SWP will resist all efforts to erect barriers between the employed and unemployed, will constantly stress the community of interest between them, and will show in action how the fight of employed and unemployed against their common oppressor can be united. It supports and helps organize the struggles of the unemployed masses for relief, for jobs, against evictions, for social insurance, etc. It stands for the unity of the employed and unemployed, by the organization of the latter into a movement directly associated with the trade unions.

The youth

Throughout its existence, the capitalist system has been marked by the extreme and shameful exploitation of children and youth. Today, in the decline of capitalism, it is unable even to offer jobs at starvation wages to millions of the youth, but holds out for them a life of frustration and sterility, and the destruction and degradation of fascism and war. It is particularly from the ranks of the youth, with their physical vitality, their courage, and their moral idealism, that the SWP can and must expect to recruit the best militants in the struggle for socialism. The party will champion the progressive interests, aims, and demands of the youth, and will carry out as an urgent and most important task the building of a broad youth organization, based upon the principles of revolutionary Marxism, which will embrace young workers, farmers, and students. The party, however, rejects the conception that the youth constitute a special or independent "class" in modern society, with special historical interests and program. A youth movement which will be of aid in the struggle for socialism must be an integral part of the revolutionary workers' movement, and must base itself upon the perspective of their program.

The struggle against imperialist war

Since war is inevitably bred by capitalist society, the only genuine struggle against war is precisely the struggle against the social system which breeds it, the struggle against capitalism and for socialism. Only through the elimination of the causes for war will war itself be done away with. Through socialism alone can mankind establish the foundations for enduring peace.

The SWP is against every imperialist war, and opposes all wars fought by any and all imperialist states, whether fascist or democratic, since such wars can only be reactionary in character and counter to the interests of the masses and of the revolution. In the imperialist United States, the SWP fights against war preparations and militarization; but at the same time always makes clear that war cannot be permanently prevented unless the imperialist government of the United States is overthrown and its place taken by a workers' state, that lasting peace is possible only under socialism.

Pacifism attempts to divorce the struggle against war from

the prosecution of the class struggle against capitalism. In practice, therefore, pacifism is entirely futile and powerless against war itself; and still further, spreads illusions about the nature of war which divert the masses from the genuine struggle against it and play into the hands of imperialism. The SWP, consequently, exposes the futility and illusions of pacifism. In the United States, pacifism is particularly dangerous because its ideas are so widespread and influential, and because it is in a sense the "official" imperialist doctrine—indeed, the ideological preparation for the next imperialist war bases itself largely on the notion that from the point of view of the United States it will be a "war for peace."

If, in spite of the efforts of the revolutionists and the militant workers, the U.S. government enters a new war, the SWP will not under any circumstances support that war but will on the contrary fight against it. The SWP will advocate the continuance of the class struggle during the war regardless of the consequences for the outcome of the American military struggle; and will try to prepare the masses to utilize the war crisis for the overthrow of U.S. capitalism and the victory of socialism.

The SWP opposes and will continue at all times to oppose every form of social patriotism, all advocacy of "national union" or "suspension of the class struggle" during wartime, and will make clear to the workers that no war conducted by the capitalist government of the United States can be to their interest, or can be other than a war for imperialist profit and plunder.

The policy of the SWP with respect to imperialist war holds good under all conditions: it applies if the war is conducted between the fascist imperialisms and the "democratic" imperialisms in the same manner as if the war takes place between coalitions including both fascist and "democratic" imperialisms on each side. It applies also if the United States is in military alliance with the Soviet Union. In the latter case, the SWP would unreservedly support the Soviet Union against imperialism; but would expose the treacherous imperialist aims of the United States in the alliance, would call for the overthrow of U.S. capitalism and its replacement by a revolutionary workers' government, which alone could carry forward the war in the interests of labor, of the revolutionary defense of the Soviet Union, and of the world socialist revolution. The practical steps which our party will take in the course of its opposition to such a war will be decided in light of the consideration of the need of facilitating the utmost aid to the Soviet Union's armed forces against an imperialist power in conformity with our position of defense of the Soviet Union from imperialist assault.

Colonial peoples

The struggle against imperialist war is inseparable from the struggle against imperialism in general, and therefore, from support of the wars of enslaved peoples against their imperialist oppressors, of colonies against the nations which keep them in servitude, of nationalities, races, and minorities which suffer from the yoke of oppressors, of workers' states against capitalist states. The SWP is not neutral or indifferent in such wars, but actively supports the oppressed against the oppressors.

United States imperialism, exploiting the masses within its national boundaries, at the same time and to an even greater degree, exploits the peoples of Latin and Central America, Cuba, Puerto Rico, Hawaii, Liberia, the Philippines. These people are thus the potential allies of the American workers in the struggle against U.S. imperialism, and neither they nor the American workers can expect to win freedom except in joint combat against the common enemy. The SWP supports every progressive struggle of these peoples. It stands for the immediate and unhampered right of self-determination for them, free from military, political, or economic intervention or pressure by the U.S. government. It stands for the immediate and unconditional independence of all the territories, colonies, and dependencies of the U.S. and for the withdrawal of all troops from them. It is opposed to any attempt by American imperialism, open or masked, to infringe upon the right of self-determination of any nation or people.

The revolutions in the colonies, semicolonies, and spheres of influence of United States imperialism are integrally and reciprocally related to the revolutionary struggle against that imperialism at home. A successful revolution in the United States would be decisive for the emancipation of the toiling masses throughout Latin America; while, on the other hand, a revolution beginning in one of the Latin American countries, or in one of the colonies or semicolonies of the U.S., could spread throughout the continent and powerfully accelerate the development of the class struggle and the revolution within the United States. The SWP regards it, therefore, as a central task to aid and support the revolutionary movement in these nations and colonies, and to establish the closest relations with the revolutionists and revolutionary organizations within them.

The defense of the Soviet Union

The Russian revolution, the greatest event in the history of mankind, is the guide and inspiration of the workers of the entire world. All the years of imperialist assault and sabotage, of the misrule, treachery, and finally usurpation of Stalinism, have not yet succeeded in destroying the foundations of the workers' state, nor did they prevent the Soviet Union, the product of that revolution, from demonstrating the immense superiority of the socialist organization of society over even the most developed forms of capitalism, and have not succeeded in wiping out the great social conquests of the revolution. The economy and social relations established by the revolution still remain, against the blows of Stalinism, providing the foundation, once the Soviet Union is cleansed of the poison of Stalinism, for victorious resumption of the march toward socialism. It is, consequently, the elementary and imperative duty of all workers, and especially of the revolutionary party, to defend the Soviet Union unconditionally against any and every imperialist nation. The defense of the Soviet Union cannot, of course, rest primarily upon the League of Nations or attempted alliances with capitalist nations, but is essentially based upon and inseparable from unrelenting struggle against the counterrevolutionary policies of Stalinism, which now imminently threaten to complete the betrayal and liquidation of the Russian revolution; and inseparable equally from the extension of the workers' revolution to other nations, which, in the last analysis, is the only effective defense of the Russian revolution.

Coalition governments

When a working-class party enters a coalition government of the bourgeois regime, it thereby accepts responsibility for the administration of the bourgeois state and functions thus as an agent of the class enemy. Such an action is incompatible with revolutionary class struggle, which is directed toward the overthrow of the bourgeois state and the triumph of a workers' regime. The SWP will under no circumstances whatever enter or give political support to any bourgeois government.

Democracy and fascism

The SWP stands unequivocally for the fullest and most complete democracy, possible only by the victorious achievement of socialism. Indeed, this is presupposed in the very ideal of socialism, for the fullest and most meaningful democracy is realized only with the realization of socialism. Nevertheless, it is not democracy in the abstract or mere democratic forms devoid of content to which the SWP gives allegiance. The SWP defends and aims to extend the concrete democratic rights of the masses, for these alone are of actual value and significance.

Capitalist democracy, though permitting a certain number of these concrete democratic rights, is in the last analysis a mask for the dictatorship of the bourgeoisie. At no time does it or can it permit the wide or genuine exercise of democratic rights by the masses. Under capitalist democracy, the working class must fight to extend to the maximum all democratic rights, which capitalism, especially in the period of decline, seeks to curtail. The defense of democratic rights, the defense of genuine democracy, demands in the end the social revolution, since only through the revolution will democracy for the masses be achieved. The defense of the fraud of capitalist "democracy"—which is the rule of capitalist exploitation—only guarantees in the end the crushing by fascism of even those limited democratic rights and institutions which capitalism is "normally" compelled to tolerate.

In the decline of capitalism, the growing internal conflicts of capitalism in nation after nation make it necessary for the bourgeoisie, if it is to maintain its social dictatorship and class domination, to abolish or reduce to a shell the capitalist democratic form of government and go over to fascism. Fascism does away with all of the democratic rights of the masses. But fascism also, since it is the outgrowth and product of capitalism in decline, can be defeated finally only through the socialist revolution. The effective struggle against fascism cannot, therefore, be divorced from the struggle against capitalism itself and for socialism.

Democratic rights are necessary for the masses at all times in order for them to organize, and to facilitate political education and propaganda in the ideas of socialism. The SWP therefore stands at all times for the defense and extension of the democratic rights of the masses, and advocates the broadest possible united fronts for such defense.

Though insisting upon the fundamental identity in social character between all forms of capitalist dictatorship, the SWP recognizes the rise of the conflict between capitalist "democracy" and fascism, which sometimes assumes the sharpest forms, even those of civil war. While at all times pointing out that only the socialist revolution can in the end defeat fascism, and advocating the continuance of the class struggle for socialism under all circumstances, the SWP will, as a stage in the struggle for socialism, utilize every conflict between "democratic" capitalism and fascism to smash the latter and to advance the interests of the independent class movement of the workers in their irreconcilable struggle against capitalist rule itself under any form. Such policies as the purely electoral joint support of Hindenburg against Hitler in Germany, or of Van Zeeland against Degrelle in Belgium,[31] are not a means of

---

31. The German Social Democrats supported the conservative Junker General Hindenburg against the Nazi Hitler in the presidential elections of 1932. They had opposed Hindenburg in 1925 when he was first elected, but now they called for his election as a lesser evil to keep the fascists out of office. Hindenburg was reelected in 1932 and less than a year later appointed Hitler chancellor, the post from which the latter smashed the labor and revolutionary movements and instituted fascism. A similar incident occurred in Belgium in 1937. The fascist leader Degrelle got onto the ballot in a by-election for a parliamentary seat from Brussels, where he decided to make a show of fascist strength. Van Zeeland, Belgium's premier and leader of the Catholic Party, entered the race against him, and the Social Democratic and Stalinist parties decided not to enter candidates of their own in this race in order to help Van

struggle against fascism, but of destroying the class independence of the workers, thus facilitating the advance of fascism, and are consequently contrary to the principles of the SWP. Support of one of the imperialist coalitions in the coming war on the alleged grounds that the given coalition was "democratic" and arrayed against fascism, far from being an active defense against fascism, would be social-patriotic treachery, and altogether contradictory to revolutionary principles, and to the interests of the working class. However, support of the military struggle against Franco in the Spanish civil war has been not merely consistent with revolutionary principle but the sole possible policy for revolutionists with respect to the Spanish civil war and the only road of development toward the Spanish workers' revolution. The attitude toward analogous civil wars in other countries, including the United States, which involved an armed internal war between a fascist camp and a bourgeois-democratic camp, would be the same: all technical and military support in the joint struggle against fascism as an inseparable part of the preparation for the socialist revolution.

The People's Front

The policy and tactics of the "People's Front" are merely the classic policy and tactics of class collaboration and coalitionism renamed and reapplied in the circumstances of the present time. The People's Front combats the program

---

Zeeland defeat Degrelle. This passage does not mention the fact, which embarrassed the leaders of both the SWP and the Movement for the Fourth International, that their comrades in Belgium also voted not to run their own candidate in the by-election, for the same reason as the Social Democrats and Stalinists. But the SWP leaders thought it appropriate to dissociate themselves from the position of their Belgian comrades by stating what they thought in their Declaration of Principles.

of Marxism and the class struggle for socialism: that is, it attempts to crush the independence of the working class, subordinating it ideologically, politically, and organizationally to the bourgeoisie. The People's Front, formulated and advocated in its most vicious form by Stalinism, proposes national unity and class peace on the basis of a program for the alleged defense of bourgeois democracy. The aim of the People's Front is to prepare for mass support to the coming imperialist war in the "democratic" nations. The result of the People's Front, as already proved conclusively by experience in both France and Spain, can only be the thrusting back of the revolution, the weakening and disorientation of the workers, betrayal to the war, and in the end the victory of fascism. The SWP therefore rejects and combats People's Frontism.

The united front

The working class must be united if it is to achieve victory. The most decisive unity will be gained when the majority of the working class unites on the basis of the ideas of revolutionary Marxism. Meanwhile, in spite of organizational and political differences, the workers must achieve united action in order to defend their rights and advance their interests. If they do not, wage and relief cuts, increasing abrogation of political and civil liberties, and finally, war and fascism, are assured.

United action in the interests of the workers cannot be gained through the People's Front, which is in actuality the abandonment of the workers' struggle; nor from the pseudo–united front "only from below," once advocated by the Stalinists;[32] nor from unity based on paralyzing

---

32. The "united front from below" was Stalinist double-talk designed to cover up the fact that the Stalinists were opposed to united fronts

"nonaggression pacts." The SWP stands for and advocates broad, honest, carefully defined united fronts of organizations on specific issues facing the workers, in which each organization, loyally adhering to the united front, retains its political and organizational independence, and its right to criticism either for failure to carry out the united front agreement or on questions of program and principles. Such united front actions develop the mass power of the workers, show the workers the need and value of unity, expose the weakness or treachery of reactionary and reformist leaders, and give the revolutionary party the opportunity to prove in action the correctness of its principles and tactics. United front actions are thus indispensable preparations for the revolutionary unity which, in the revolutionary crisis, will enable the workers to take power.[33]

---

with other working-class tendencies during the "third period." While contending that they favored united fronts (a popular position among the workers), they insisted that the only kind of united front in which communists could participate was one in which the Communist Party, leaders and members, got together with the members, but not leaders, of other tendencies. Excluding the leaders of the other tendencies in advance was, of course, a sure way to guarantee that there would be no united front of any kind.

33. The Declaration of Principles adopted at the Chicago convention remained in effect for three years. At the end of December 1940 the SWP held its Fourth (Special) National Convention in New York. The main purpose of this gathering was to act on a proposal from the SWP Political Committee that the SWP should formally discontinue its affiliation to the Fourth International because such affiliation opened the party to crippling persecution under the recently enacted Voorhis law. After accepting this proposal and making corresponding changes in the constitution, the convention also took up a resolution on the Declaration of Principles, which, it said, "requires some changes and additions to bring it up to date and correspond with new developments which have transpired since the foundation convention.

"This task can be performed satisfactorily only after adequate time

has been provided for consideration of proposed changes and their discussion in the ranks of the party. As a step toward the preparation of this task, the Fourth (Special) National Convention resolves:
"1. To suspend and withdraw the Declaration of Principles adopted at the foundation convention;
"2. To authorize and instruct the National Committee to prepare the draft of an amended Declaration of Principles for submission to the party for discussion and eventual decision by party convention or referendum."

A revised draft was presented, a few weeks before the Minneapolis trial, to the October 1941 NC Plenum–Active Workers Conference in Chicago. That meeting unanimously approved the NC's recommendation that a final draft should be submitted to a referendum vote of the party membership after the branches had been given an opportunity to propose amendments. Suggestions and amendments were solicited from the branches in October, a final draft was started in November, and the PC minutes of December 8 reported that a final draft would be sent out for the referendum vote "within the next few days." But December 8 was also the day that the U.S. government formally entered the war and the day when the defendants convicted in the Minneapolis trial were sentenced to prison. At that point it was not at all certain that the SWP would be able to remain a legal party and it was possible that a new declaration of principles could become a pretext for additional repressive measures against the SWP. Second thoughts about a declaration of principles and a referendum occurred, and agreement was reached in the party leadership to cancel the referendum and put aside the project of adopting a declaration of principles. Since that time the SWP has followed the practice of setting forth its basic positions in other forms, such as resolutions, statements, manifestos, etc.

SOCIALIST APPEAL

PUBLISHED WEEKLY AS THE OFFICIAL ORGAN OF THE SOCIALIST WORKERS PARTY

Vol. II. - No. 3.   401   Saturday, January 15, 1938   5 Cents per Copy

Hail the Socialist Workers Party!

House Defeats Ludlow Amendment 209 to 188-

By the narrow vote of 209 to 188, the House of Representatives in Washington, under heavy pressure from President Roosevelt, and with the solid reactionary bloc casting its ballot for the majority, defeated the amendment of Representative Louis Ludlow providing for a national referendum to be taken before war can be declared against another country by the United States.

Carrying on a vicious chauvinistic campaign against the amendment for the past several weeks, were all the forces of reaction, all the war-mongers, patrioteers, ably seconded by the American section of the Stalinist Foreign Office—the Communist Party. The Browderites stood in a single camp not only with the Big-Army-and-Navy Presidents, but with Stimson, Landon and the Old Guard of the Republican Party.

NEW FORMAT

We are glad to announce that beginning with the next issue, the Socialis Appeal will appear in a new format. This is the last of the tabloid size, and from now on we will print a full-size newspaper format.

Marxists and for the working class in general by the LaFollette-Ludlow proposed amendment to the constitution, which would make it necessary, before congress can declare war, to refer the question to a referendum, except in the case of actual invasion. It is only necessary to apply the accepted principles of evolutionary Marxism to solve the problem correctly.

Pacifist Cure-All

Revolutionary Marxists, especially since Lenin's vigorous polemics against pacifism, have consistently taken the position that any policy which pretends to solve the problem of war independently of the class struggle creates illusions and is therefore

An old problem in a new form is raised for the revolutionary

By Albert Goldman

(Continued on page 2)

Join the Struggle For Socialism!

The Chicago convention of the revolutionary socialists has established the American section of the Fourth International.

In forming the Socialist Workers Party of the United States, the convention shaped the indispensable weapon of the working class in its struggle against a powerful and merciless class enemy, the exploiter of labor and oppressor of the people. With only the trade unions at its disposal, the working class is but half-armed. With a revolutionary political party at its head, it is invincible.

The Anti-Labor Drive

The Socialist Workers Party could not have been founded at a more crucial moment. The American working class is face to face with a heavy employers' onslaught upon its standard of living, already badly undermined by years of crisis and depression. The only solution that the wisest of the capitalist statesmen, Roosevelt, has been able to offer to the problem of hunger is to cut down the production of food. Now, with a new depression leading towards an even sharper crisis, the capitalists, whose rule Roosevelt has been bent on preserving, are proceeding to throw new hundreds of thousands out of work and to cut the wages of those whom they continue to employ. The most powerful capitalist nation of the earth has proved incapable of feeding.

PART 4

Minutes, SWP National Committee plenum

Minutes, SWP National Committee plenum

New York, April 22–25, 1938[1]

FIRST SESSION, APRIL 22, 1938

Session called to order at 12:45 p.m. by Comrade Cannon. Chairman: Dullea.

---

1. This plenum was one of the most turbulent and unpredictable gatherings in the history of the SWP and its predecessors. Many of the participants were uneasy or uncertain about what to do, and some resented "pressure" to make decisions without sufficient time to think them over adequately. It was the kind of situation that occurs when a political movement is confronted with the need to make sharp turns in its policies—some inevitably make the change in their thinking faster than others. The cause of the divisions and frictions manifested at this plenum was a series of proposals emanating from Leon Trotsky in Mexico. Trotsky was writing a programmatic document for the founding conference of the Fourth International, which was held in September 1938. He wanted the SWP to sponsor this document in the preconference discussion and he wanted to discuss it with the SWP's leaders in order to get any ideas they might have for the document and to persuade them that its main line was correct. This also involved trying to persuade them that they had to change their

341

NC members present: Abern, Cannon, Carter, Clarke, Dullea, Dunne, Gould, McKinney, Morrow, Shachtman, Spector, Widick.
NC alternates present: Morgan, Stevens, Sherman.
Fraternal delegates: Butterworth, Robertson.
By invitation: Kluger, Wasserman.[2]

---

position on certain questions decided by the Chicago convention. The discussions between Trotsky and the SWP delegation (Cannon, Shachtman, V.R. Dunne, and Rose Karsner; at the Mexican border it was decided that because of citizenship problems a fifth member of the delegation, Carl Skoglund of Minneapolis, should not cross the frontier) took place in March 1938, three months after the Chicago convention. Trotsky's arguments were convincing to the SWP leaders, as Cannon and Shachtman indicated on their return to New York, where they gave reports about the discussions to the Political Committee. (See glossary for composition of the PC.) But the members of the PC were not prepared or willing at that point to take positions on the questions posed by Trotsky. That was why, on the eve of the plenum, they decided on the rather unusual procedure of referring the whole matter to the National Committee, without any recommendations other than that reports be given on the discussions in Mexico, to be followed by a question and answer period and a recess for the members to read the documents related to the discussions. These minutes were published in mimeographed form by the SWP national office for internal use only; they were circulated to the National Committee and the SWP branches. An earlier, typed, version, located in the James P. Cannon archives at the Library of Social History enables us to give, in the form of footnotes, a few passages that were omitted from the mimeographed version for security reasons.

2. The plenum voted to restrict attendance to the members and alternates of the National Committee, three representatives of the YPSL (Nathan Gould, Hal Draper, Emanuel Garrett, but Draper was absent and replaced by Robert Stiler), two fraternal delegates from the Canadian section (Bill Butterworth and Robertson [Earle Birney]), two associate editors of the *Socialist Appeal* (Frank Graves and Harold Roberts [Harold Isaacs]), and four national functionaries (George Novack and Pearl Kluger, who were assigned to the party's defense work; Jac Wasserman of Pioneer Publishers; and Sherman Stanley [Stanley Plastrik], business manager of the *Socialist Appeal*). The PC

Agenda proposed by the Political Committee:
  I. Oral reports on the thesis
  II. Questions
  III. Recess to study documents³
  IV. Concrete discussion on the separate questions:
    1. Political situation in the country and transitional demands
    2. Labor party
    3. War
    4. International conference
    5. CP
    6. Defense
    7. Pan-American conference
    8. Party press

---

had also recommended inviting "Comrade G" (John Glenner [Jan Frankel]), and he might have been present at the plenum without his name being listed. After the Chicago convention, Gregory Bardacke, an NC member, had asked to be recorded as "Jay" in the minutes, and alternates Albert Glotzer and Bill Farrell had asked to be designated as "Gates" and "Morgan," which is how the three are recorded in these minutes. Since six regular members of the NC were absent from the plenum, the first six alternates in the order designated at Chicago cast decisive votes at the plenum, in accord with the then prevailing practice.

3. The "thesis" was the draft of Trotsky's programmatic document, "The Death Agony of Capitalism and the Tasks of the Fourth International," which was distributed to the plenum participants when they arrived in New York for the plenum. It was also referred to as the "international thesis" and the "international transitional program." Other documents given to the plenum participants included "stenograms," the transcripts of the Trotsky-SWP discussions in Mexico a month before the plenum. It was to read these documents that the plenum voted to recess for four and a half hours at the end of its first session. The Trotsky-SWP discussions were transcribed by a secretary in six parts. Three of these, along with the "thesis," are in *The Transitional Program for Socialist Revolution*; the other three are in *Writings of Leon Trotsky (1937–38)*.

9. Organizational questions
   a. California
   b. General
   c. Language groups
   d. Finances

Clarke: Reports request of Comrade Cochran that important points on the agenda be held over until his arrival tomorrow morning.

Motion by Widick: That we adopt the agenda as proposed by the Political Committee. Carried.

Motion by Clarke: That we take up the organizational questions and other matters that do not hinge directly on the main report. Lost.

Motion by McKinney: That we proceed with the agenda as adopted; if there are any changes to be made they can be made after the report. Carried.

Motion by Carter: That we adopt the procedure recommended by the PC in regard to attendance at the plenum. Carried.

Comrade Cannon reports on two resolutions received from the New York City branches requesting open sessions of the plenum. Also one from Louisville condemning the proposal for a closed plenum on the ground that not only the decisions arrived at but all controversy implicit in the prior discussion of them be before the party. Also reports on procedure for attendance recommended by the PC as contained in PC minutes number 16 [April 21, 1938].

Comrade Cannon gives general report on discussions[4] on the first six points under IV on the agenda.

---

4. At this point the mimeographed minutes omitted the words "held with our comrades in the south."

MINUTES / 345

Short report by Comrade Shachtman on discussion regarding factory committees.

Question period
Questions by: Widick, Morrow, Clarke, Gould, Stevens, Morgan.
Answers by: Cannon, Dunne, Shachtman.
Motion by Morrow: That we adjourn to read the documents and reconvene at 7:00 p.m. Carried.
Meeting adjourned at 2:30 p.m.

SECOND SESSION, APRIL 22, 1938

Session called to order by Comrade Dunne at 7:30 p.m.
NC members present: Abern, Burnham, Cannon, Carter, Clarke, Dullea, Dunne, Goldman, Gould, Jay, Lewit, McKinney, Morrow, Rosenberg, Shachtman, Spector, Weber, Widick.
NC alternates present: Morgan, Stevens, Erber, Sherman, Milton.
Fraternal delegates: Butterworth, Robertson, YPSL: Stiler, Garrett. (Comrade Gould reports that Comrades Garrett and Draper were selected as the YPSL delegates, Comrade Stiler as alternate to Draper, who is out of town.)
By invitation: Kluger, Novack, Roberts, Graves, S. Stanley.

Political situation in the country and transitional demands
Motion by Lewit: That we grant the floor to anyone who is prepared to speak. Carried.
Discussion: Goldman, Abern, Burnham, Spector, Widick, Gould, Cannon.
Proposal by Lewit: That we adjourn this session after Comrade Cannon speaks and reconvene at 10:00 a.m. Carried.
Session adjourned at 11:45 p.m.

THIRD SESSION, APRIL 23, 1938

Session called to order at 11:00 a.m.
Chairman: Dullea.
NC members present: Abern, Burnham, Cannon, Carter, Clarke, Cochran, Dullea, Dunne, Goldman, Gould, Jay, Lewit, McKinney, Morrow, Shachtman, Spector, Weber, Widick.
NC alternates: Gates, Morgan, Stevens, Erber, Sherman, Milton, Turner.
Fraternal delegates: Butterworth, Robertson, Stiler, Garrett.
By invitation: Kluger, Novack, Wasserman, Roberts, Graves, Stanley.

Political situation in the country and transitional demands (contd.)
Motion by Cannon: That we adjourn for lunch at 1:30 p.m. and reconvene at 2:30 p.m. Carried.
Discussion: Weber, Clarke, Carter, Morrow, Jay, Cochran, Lewit.
Resolution presented by Spector:

> *Resolved*: That this April plenum of the SWP endorses and adopts the thesis on the "Death Agony of Capitalism and the Tasks of the Fourth International"; that we subscribe in principle to the conception of the program of transitional demands proposed therein as a strategic means of bridging the gap between the maturity of the objective revolutionary conditions and the immaturity of the proletariat and its vanguard, between the immediate demands of the daily struggle and the program of the socialist revolution; that the plenum elect a commission to draft a concrete program of action based on this Transitional Program and the

conditions and needs of the American working-class struggle; that such program of action be submitted to a referendum vote of the National Committee in the event that the commission is unable to report before the plenum adjourns; that the Political Committee shall thereupon take the necessary measures within a period to be duly determined by the committee to submit the Transitional Program to a discussion and referendum of the party membership.

Motion: To table until the end of the discussion. Carried.
Session adjourned at 2:00 p.m.

FOURTH SESSION, APRIL 23, 1938

Session called to order by Comrade Dullea at 3:15 p.m.
Chairman: Dullea.
NC members present: Abern, Burnham, Carter, Clarke, Cochran, Dullea, Dunne, Goldman, Gould, Jay, Lewit, McKinney, Morrow, Shachtman, Spector, Weber, Widick.
NC alternates: Gates, Morgan, Stevens, Erber, Milton, Turner.
Fraternal delegates: Butterworth, Robertson, Stiler, Garrett.
By invitation: Kluger, Novack, Wasserman, Roberts, Graves, Stanley.
Substitute resolution presented by Shachtman:

The plenum affirms the primary importance of adopting a program of transitional demands to help bridge the gap between the maturing social crisis and the political immaturity of the proletariat, as well as to provide the party with the means of gaining access to the workers as they actually are and feel, and giving concrete replies to immediate problems. Only in this manner can the SWP take the broad road leading away from its past as an essentially propaganda group to its future as a party of action.

The plenum endorses the general line of the thesis on the "Death Agony of Capitalism" and adopts it as a draft of an analysis of the position of world capitalism and of the tasks of the revolutionary vanguard in the mobilization of the masses for struggle against capitalist rule.

The plenum instructs the Political Committee to draw up a concrete program of action for the party, based upon the general line of the thesis and adapted to the specific objective situation in the United States, the political level of the working class, and the strength of the party, setting forth the necessary transitional demands in accordance with their appropriateness, under given conditions, as slogans for propaganda, agitation, or action.

This program shall thereupon be submitted to the National Committee for adoption or revision and then be presented to the party as a whole.

The PC shall organize and supervise the presentation and discussion of the program in the branches of the party.[5]

Motion: To table until end of discussion. Carried.
Motion on procedure by Morrow: That we proceed with the discussion, take a list of speakers, and determine

---

5. The key difference between the seemingly identical resolutions of Spector and Shachtman revolved around Spector's formulation that the party "endorses and adopts" the Transitional Program compared to Shachtman's that the party "endorses the general line" of the Transitional Program. This nuance reflected certain reservations and hesitations on Shachtman's part regarding some aspects of the program.

some time for closing the discussion on this point.
Substitute motion by Gould: That we proceed with the discussion on the labor party. Carried. (It is understood that this motion does not preclude returning to discussion on the resolutions presented.)

Labor party
Motion: That Comrade Burnham lead off the discussion on the labor party.
Suggestion by Goldman: That comrades from the field give reports on concrete situations arising on the labor party.
Burnham: Seconds that proposal.
Reports: Cochran, Turner, Widick, Clarke, Weber.
Motion on procedure: That we adjourn at 6:30 p.m. to attend the plenum dinner. Carried.
Discussion: Goldman, McKinney, Stevens, Novack (with permission from the plenum), Gates.
Session adjourned at 6:30 p.m.; to reconvene at 10:00 a.m.

FIFTH SESSION, APRIL 24, 1938

Session called to order by McKinney at 12:30 p.m.
NC members present: Abern, Burnham, Cannon, Carter, Clarke, Cochran, Dullea, Dunne, Goldman, Gould, Jay, Lewit, McKinney, Morrow, Shachtman, Spector, Weber, Widick.
NC alternates: Gates, Morgan, Stevens, Erber, Sherman, Milton, Turner.
Fraternal delegates: Butterworth, Robertson, Stiler, Garrett.
By invitation: Kluger, Novack.
Motion by Abern: That we adjourn one hour for lunch and go through the afternoon without adjournment.

Suggestion by McKinney: That the chairman who presided at last night's session take the chair and proceed with the business of the plenum. Accepted.

Comrade Dullea takes the chair.

Discussion on procedure:

Motion by Burnham: That we proceed to have informational discussions on the status of the antiwar movement and the CP in the various localities from which the comrades come. Carried.

Motion by McKinney: That we proceed with the agenda from where we left off last night. Lost.

Chairman: Sherman.

Motion by Milton: That the resident National Committee members who are not present be immediately informed that there is a plenum going on and that they be present.

Motion by Goldman: To table. Carried.

Weber on procedure: The chairman should in this case call on various comrades to report on their sections. Procedure accepted.

Reporters: Gould, Weber, McKinney, Turner.

Proposal by Burnham: That the facts given by Comrade Gould go into only one copy of the minutes; not in the mimeographed record. Carried.

Motion by Gould: (Proposed for the records of the party only—not for mimeographed record).[6]

---

6. At this point the mimeographed minutes omitted the following passage:

"1. The SWP establish a special national department to organize, direct, and coordinate our national work in the CP, to work in the closest collaboration with this department in the YPSL.

"2. At the present stage of development we do not, as a policy, withdraw adherents of the Fourth International in the CP from that party as individuals but rather strive to: (a) Get these adherents (under our

Tabled until this point on the agenda comes up.[7]

Motion by McKinney: That we resume the discussion on the labor party at this point. Carried.

Lewit: Point of order: Comrade McKinney's motion is out of order, presenting motion that was defeated.

Substitute motion by Cochran: That all speakers on the list be allowed a limit of five minutes each; that a vote be taken at the conclusion.

Chairman rules this motion out of order.

Motion by Dullea: That we adjourn now for lunch and reconvene in one hour. Carried.

Session adjourned at 2:00 p.m.

SIXTH SESSION, APRIL 24, 1938

Session called to order by Comrade Cannon at 3:15 p.m. Chairman: Lewit.

NC members present: Abern, Burnham, Cannon, Carter,

---

discipline) into strategic positions with the object of obtaining information and of gaining influence; (b) Organize a national fraction with the perspective of a national split to be executed at some propitious time.

"3. When our fraction is strong enough we issue a regular national paper of this fraction for the YCL and CP as a Leninist organ in the Communist movement.

"4. The party committee issue special material (leaflets, etc.) to direct a barrage at the CP on the issues of the Moscow trials and the war question over which question there is the greatest doubt and dissatisfaction with the CP policy."

7. The point on the agenda about the CP was never reached at the plenum; Gould's motion and other unfinished business were referred to the Political Committee. At its May 5, 1938, meeting the PC voted that work in the CP should be handled by the Secretariat rather than a special department (point 1). It concurred with points 2 and 3, but did not mention point 4.

Clarke, Cochran, Dullea, Dunne, Goldman, Gould, Jay, Lewit, McKinney, Morrow, Rosenberg, Shachtman, Spector, Weber, Widick.

NC alternates present: Gates, Morgan, Stevens, Erber, Sherman, Milton, Turner.

Fraternal delegates: Butterworth, Robertson, Stiler, Garrett.

By invitation: Kluger, Novack, Roberts, Graves.

Motion by Cannon: That we adopt our position on the general Transitional Program first; then consider the motions presented. Carried.

Weber: Motion: That we have two speakers for each of the motions, twenty minutes to each speaker, close the discussion, and take the vote.

Amendment by Shachtman: That each speaker have five minutes each on the concrete motions. Carried.

Reading of both motions—Spector's and Shachtman's.

Shachtman speaks for his own motion.

Amendment by Shachtman to his motion. (Included in record above.) [Fourth session]

Spector and Cannon speak for Spector's motion.

Goldman: Point of procedure: I think that we should not put the question of the referendum together with the other motions. I think that the vote on the referendum should be separate and apart from the other motions.

Cochran: Point of procedure: We're placed in the position of voting for two motions that are almost identical; the only question of difference I gather is the question of referendum. I suggest that these two motions be incorporated.

Burnham speaks for Shachtman's motion.

Motion by Cannon: Proposal to separate Comrade Spector's motion into three parts: (1) general direction of the motion; (2) question of commission; (3) question of referendum. Accepted by Comrade Spector.

Motion by Cochran: Substitute for the whole: Comrade Shachtman and Comrade Spector be constituted as a commission to try to bring back if possible a common motion; if not they will come back with their respective motions. Lost.

Voting on the motions

First part of Comrade Spector's motion against Comrade Shachtman's complete motion:

	Spector's motion	Shachtman's motion
Abern	X	
Burnham		X
Cannon	X	
Carter		X
Clarke	X	X (with Goldman's statement)
Cochran	X	X (with Goldman's statement)
Dullea		X
Dunne	X	
Goldman	X	X (statement)
Jay	X	
Lewit	X	
McKinney	X	
Morrow	X	
Rosenberg		X
Shachtman		X
Spector	X	
Weber	X	
Widick	X	
Gould	X	
Gates	X	
Morgan	X	
Stevens		X

	Spector's motion	Shachtman's motion
Erber		X
Sherman		X
Milton	X	
	17	11

Statement by Goldman: I consider that the motions of both Spector and Shachtman are essentially the same. Both accept the general line of the thesis and both assert the necessity of amplifying, modifying, and concretizing the transitorial demands to apply to the particular conditions of the U.S. The speeches in support of the motions may indicate a difference but not the motions themselves. I do not wish to anticipate possible future differences on the actual demands. I therefore vote for both motions.

Consultative vote	Spector	Shachtman
Butterworth	Abstains	
Robertson	X	X (with Goldman's statement)
Stiler	X	
Garrett		X
Turner		X
	2	3

Shachtman: Counterposes the following part of his motion to the second part of Spector's motion:

"The plenum instructs the Political Committee to draw up a concrete program of action for the party, based upon the general line of the thesis and adapted to the specific objective situation in the United States, the political level of the working class, and the strength of the party, setting forth the necessary transitional demands in accordance with their appropriateness, under given conditions, as slogans for propaganda, agitation, or action.

"This program shall thereupon be submitted to the National Committee for adoption or revision and then be presented to the party as a whole."

Cannon: Suggests to Comrade Spector that he substitute Political Committee for commission. Accepted by Spector.

Second part of Comrade Spector's motion: That the Political Committee draft a concrete program of action based on this Transitional Program and the conditions and needs of the American working-class struggle.

	Spector's motion	Shachtman's motion
Abern	X	
Burnham		X
Cannon	X	
Carter		X
Clarke		X
Cochran		X
Dullea		X
Dunne	X	
Goldman		X
Jay		X
Lewit	X	
McKinney	X	
Morrow	X	
Rosenberg		X
Shachtman		X

	Spector's motion	Shachtman's motion
Spector	X	
Weber	X	
Widick	X	
Gould	X	
Gates	X	
Morgan	X	
Stevens		X (statement)
Erber		X
Sherman		X
Milton	X	
	13	12

Statement by Stevens: I voted for Shachtman's motion the first time; it didn't matter to me how it went to the PC.

Motion by Cochran: That the NC decide on the question of a referendum vote after it has the program in its hands. 9 for, 14 against. Lost.

Motion by Spector: That the program shall be submitted to the party membership for referendum. Carried.

Labor party

Motion by Cannon: That we adopt the draft statement[8] distributed to the members as the position of the plenum; and instruct the Political Committee to take this as a basis, concretize it and elaborate it, and submit

---

8. In the typed minutes Cannon called the draft statement on the labor party "the draft statement of Comrade Crux" (Trotsky); the mimeographed version speaks only of the statement distributed to the plenum members. Trotsky's draft statement, mailed after the SWP delegation had left Mexico, will be found under the title "The Problem of the Labor Party," in *The Transitional Program for Socialist Revolution*. The expanded form of this article, on which the SWP membership voted in referendum, is printed on page 381.

it to the party for discussion culminating in a referendum vote.

Discussion:

Jay: Speaking for the position on the labor party adopted at the Appeal congress [SWP founding convention] in Chicago.

Motions by Burnham:

1. The SWP welcomes and supports every tendency toward independent working-class political activity.

2. Such tendencies within the U.S., increasingly stimulated by the economic and social crisis, are now being expressed within the ALP, LNPL, local labor and farmer-labor parties, various forms of and proposals for trade union and labor candidates, etc. Within these movements, ever larger masses of workers are, in a confused and partly conscious manner, striving for class intervention on the political arena.

3. The trade union bureaucrats, the bourgeois liberals, and the Stalinists, confronted with these tendencies and this movement, have as their aim the strangling of the movement, the prevention of its fruition along class lines, and the transformation of it into what would be in effect, whether or not in name, a new capitalist third party.

4. The SWP cannot remain neutral or stand aside from the clash of social forces taking place within this movement. It is its clear duty to give firm, positive, critical support to the workers in their tendency toward independent class political action, and to combat the class collaborationism, opportunism, and betrayal of the labor bureaucrats, bourgeois liberals, Stalinists, and reformists generally.

5. Where party members are already—through the

unions, other organizations, or in other ways—participants in this movement they are, by their specific actions and propaganda, obligated to attempt to further and deepen the advance to full independent working-class political action on a class-struggle foundation: through demands for independent candidates, organizational statutes permitting the fullest democracy and fullest functioning of the workers and their organizations, and programmatic demands leading at every stage toward conscious acceptance of the revolutionary perspective.

6. Where the question of adherence to LNPL or other organized expression of this movement arises within unions or other mass organizations, party members in such unions and mass organizations shall advocate adherence, and shall present and argue for adoption by their organizations of organizational and programmatic demands along the lines indicated above.

7. Within this movement the position and actions of the party members are distinguished from those of the bureaucrats, bourgeois liberals, Stalinists, and reformists by our resolute struggle for program, above all the Transitional Program, as well as the specific organizational and immediate demands.

8. It is excluded that party members or the party as such should give support in elections to candidates appearing on capitalist party tickets; in general—though here no universal rule can be given in advance—critical support in elections to candidates appearing solely on independent tickets of a labor party, farmer-labor party, labor, or union slates, can be given.

9. The party and the party press must devote increasing space and attention to the developments in this movement.

10. The PC is instructed to draw up a resolution along these lines, amplifying and motivating them, and in light of this, concretizing directions to the membership.

Discussion: Dunne for Cannon's motion, Morrow for Cannon's motion.
Motion by Jay: That we readopt the resolution that was passed at the Appeal congress in Chicago.
Discussion continued: Cannon for his motion, Cochran for Cannon's motion.
Motion by Goldman: That we adjourn for recess at the end of Shachtman's speech. Carried.
Motion by McKinney: That we take up the matter of continuing the plenum after Shachtman's speech. Carried.
Discussion continued: Shachtman for Burnham's motion.
Motion by Cannon: That we extend the plenum one more day. Carried.
Motion by Jay: That we convene tomorrow morning at 9:00 a.m. Laid over until tonight's session.
Session adjourned at 7:30 p.m.; to reconvene at 8:30 p.m.

SEVENTH SESSION, APRIL 24, 1938

Session called to order at 9:10 p.m. by Comrade Cannon.
Chairman: Jay.
NC members present: Abern, Cannon, Carter, Clarke, Cochran, Dullea, Dunne, Goldman, Gould, Jay, Lewit, McKinney, Morrow, Rosenberg, Shachtman, Spector, Weber, Widick.
NC alternates: Gates, Morgan, Stevens, Erber, Sherman, Milton, Turner.

Fraternal delegates: Butterworth, Robertson, Stiler, Garrett.
By invitation: Kluger, Novack, Wasserman, Roberts, Graves.
Discussion continued.
Turner: Speaks against taking a sharp turn without adequate thought and preparation.
Weber for Cannon's motion, Spector for Cannon's motion.
Motion by Cochran: With the exception of the makers of the motion, we pass a limitation rule of 5 minutes per speaker. Lost.
Discussion continued: Rosenberg, Abern, Goldman, Erber, Cannon.
Lewit: Proposal that we proceed with the vote.
Motion by Spector: That we do not proceed to a vote tonight; that we adjourn. Carried.
Motion by Cannon: That if any comrade cannot be here tomorrow he be given the privilege of casting his vote tonight. Carried.
Session adjourned at 12:30 a.m.

EIGHTH SESSION, APRIL 25, 1938

Meeting called to order by Comrade Cannon at 11:40 a.m.
Chairman: Weber.
NC members present: Abern, Cannon, Carter, Clarke, Cochran, Dullea, Dunne, Goldman, Jay, Lewit, McKinney, Shachtman, Spector, Widick.
NC alternates: Gates, Morgan, Stevens, Erber, Sherman, Milton, Turner.
Fraternal delegates: Butterworth, Robertson, Stiler, Garrett.
Discussion continued: Jay for his motion, Stevens, Clarke, Widick, Cannon.
Motion by Shachtman: That we vote for or against each motion. Carried.

	Cannon's motion			Burnham's motion			Jay's motion		
	For	Agst.	Abst.	For	Agst.	Abst.	For	Agst.	Abst.
Abern	X				X (statement)		X		
Burnham		X		X					
Cannon	X				X			X	
Carter		X		X				X	
Clarke	X				X (statement)		X		
Cochran	X				X			X	
Dullea		X		X (statement)				X	
Dunne	X				X			X	
Goldman		X		X				X	
Jay		X		X (statement)			X		
Lewit	X				X			X	
McKinney			X			X		X	
Morrow	X				X			X	
Rosenberg	X								
Shachtman		X		X				X	
Spector	X				X			X	
Weber	X				X			X	
Widick	X				X			X	
Gould		X		X				X	
Gates (see statement)									
Morgan	X				X			X	
Stevens		X		X			X (statement)		
Erber		X		X			X (statement)		
Sherman		X		X				X	
Milton			X			X	X (statement)		
	12	10	2	10	11	2	4	18	0

Consultative vote

	For	Agst.	Abst.	For	Agst.	Abst.	For	Agst.	Abst.
Butterworth		X			X				X
Robertson		X		X					X
Stiler		X		X				X	
Garrett		X		X			X (statement)		
Turner	X				X			X	
	1	3	1	3	1	1	1	2	2

Statement by Stevens on the Jay motion: In voting for Comrade Jay's motion, I am voting for the principled position we held at that time (the Appeal congress in Chicago); have not read the motion passed at the Appeal congress in some time. Statement endorsed by Erber, Milton, Garrett.

Statement by Dullea: In voting for Comrade Burnham's motion I consider it merely an extension of the possibilities inherent in the convention position.

Statement by Jay: I am voting for the Burnham motion with the understanding that Comrade Burnham's motions are only the practical steps of carrying out my motion.

Statement by Abern: In voting against Comrade Burnham's motion, I am voting against an opponent motion. Endorsed by Clarke.

Statement by Gates: Unable to participate fully in the discussion on the labor party, having to depart from this plenum before its conclusion, I am not ready to cast my vote on the labor party motions at this time. This is not meant as an abstention. I will send in my vote in the next days.[9]

Motion: That the members who left their vote before the actual vote was taken be permitted to complete their vote. Carried.

Motion by McKinney: That we adjourn for lunch; that we return in one hour and proceed with the discussion on the next item of the agenda, which is the war question. Withdrawn.

Motion by Cannon: That we adjourn and that we take up the international immediately after reconvening;

---

9. In June 1938, according to the SWP Political Committee minutes, Glotzer was recorded as being in favor of the Cannon motion on the labor party.

One-hour time limit on the international question and a half hour each on each of the remaining points. Carried.

Session adjourned at 2:00 p.m.

NINTH SESSION, APRIL 25, 1938

Session called to order at 3:15 p.m.
Chairman: Erber.
NC members present: Abern, Cannon, Carter, Clarke, Dunne, Goldman, Gould, Jay, Lewit, McKinney, Morrow, Shachtman, Spector, Widick.
NC alternates: Morgan, Stevens, Erber, Milton, Turner.
Fraternal delegates: Butterworth, Robertson, Stiler, Garrett.
By invitation: Kluger, Novack.

Report by Shachtman on the international situation.
Motions by Shachtman:
1. That the plenum decides to send a minimum of two delegates to the international conference.[10] Carried.
2. That members of the National Committee who will be in Europe at the time of the conference may be mandated as representatives of the American section to the international conference. Carried.
3. That the delegation shall stand for the formal launching of the Fourth International at this conference. Carried.

War
Motion by Cannon: That the plenum finds that the Political Committee took the correct principled position on the Ludlow amendment but made a tactical

---

10. In the typed minutes this sentence contained three more words: ", Cannon and Shachtman."

error in failing to give critical support to this movement without making any concessions whatever to its pacifist and illusory character. Withdrawn.

Motion by Carter: That the plenum reverses the position of the Political Committee on the Ludlow amendment and declares it incorrect; that the PC be instructed to issue a statement in support of a popular referendum on the question of war, with a critical declaration in reference to the pacifist and illusory tendencies in the pro-Ludlow movement.

Discussion: Goldman, Carter, Milton, Widick, Jay, Sherman, Spector.

Motion by Morgan: After we vote on this question we return to the international question, on the point that was not settled. Carried.

Substitute motion for the whole by Cannon: The plenum finds that the Political Committee was correct in its principled opposition to the pacifist illusions contained in the Ludlow amendment—an opposition that was fully justified. The PC nevertheless took a purely negative position which prevented the party from utilizing the entirely progressive sentiment of the masses, who supported the idea of submitting the warmongers to the control of a popular referendum before the declaration of war. The plenum instructs the PC to correct its position accordingly. Carried.

Motion by Cannon: That the stenograms of the conversations submitted to the plenum members shall be confined to the National Committee and shall not be circulated in the party. Carried.[11]

---

11. At this point the mimeographed minutes omitted an additional motion or part of a motion by Cannon: "That the inter-

Amendment by Shachtman: That members of the National Committee will be held strictly accountable for infringements on this decision. Carried.

Request from the Canadian delegates to be instructed as to whether they may be permitted to take the documents back for the NC of the Canadian comrades. Motion to refer to the PC. Carried.

International conference

Motion by Cannon: That the first comrade leave immediately upon receipt of the necessary funds; that the second delegate shall leave a few weeks later.[12] Carried.

Proposal by Shachtman: That a special fund be raised immediately to finance the above enterprises. Carried.

Motion by McKinney: That we take up the defense question next. Carried.

Report by Novack.

Motion by Shachtman: That we refer the balance of this discussion and the presentation and discussion on all other points, except those points requiring purely formal concordance by the plenum, to the PC. Carried.

---

vention of Comrade Crux [Trotsky] shall not be publicized by the party. Carried."

12. In the typed minutes this sentence read as follows: "That Comrade Cannon leave immediately upon receipt of the necessary funds; that Comrade Shachtman shall leave a few weeks later in time to join Comrade Cannon in Paris at the time Comrade Cannon finishes his work in England." Paris was the place where the delegates to the founding conference of the Fourth International were to assemble. Cannon's work in England was to try to unify different groups into a single organization that would be recognized as the British section of the International. His report to Trotsky about this work is in *James P. Cannon the Internationalist* (Pathfinder, 1980).

Pan-American conference[13]

Motion by Shachtman: Propose that the plenum endorse the following motion of the PC: That we have three delegates to the conference from the SWP. Delegates: Burnham, Abern, McKinney. Carried.

Motion by Cannon: That we gather up all the stenograms; that all the comrades who received these stenograms shall return them to the secretary before they leave town.

Motion by Shachtman: That the Political Committee be authorized to dispose of the copies of the stenogram as it sees fit. Carried.

Plenum adjourned at 5:15 p.m., April 25, 1938.

Motion by Weber (left with secretary to be brought up under language groups): That the PC immediately establish a commission to deal with this question, to draw up theses on it, and to organize planned activity with the aim of attracting the Jewish masses to the Fourth International.[14]

---

13. The Pan-American conference was held in New York in May 1938; it was also called a preconference of the All American Pacific Bureau. In attendance besides representatives of the SWP and the Latin American subcommission were delegates with mandates from Cuba, China, and Puerto Rico; another mandate came from Australia. The International Secretariat was represented by Glenner (Frankel) and Shachtman. The conference's task was to prepare a number of resolutions for the coming international conference.

14. On May 5, 1938, the Political Committee set up a commission on the Jewish question, consisting of Weber, Lewit, Spector, Sylvia Bleeker, Morrow, and Novack, with Lewit as secretary. On July 7 it voted to send the commission's theses on the Jewish question to the NC members, and on August 11, it voted to approve the theses, which are reprinted on page 403.

DOCUMENTS

On the Ludlow Amendment[15]

by the SWP National Committee

After discussing the Ludlow amendment, and the policy adopted toward it by the Political Committee, the April session of the National Committee of the Socialist Workers Party came to the following conclusion:

Though the Political Committee and the party press were correct in combating the pacifist illusions engendered by the sponsors of the Ludlow amendment and the treacherous distinction between wars of "aggression" and "defense" embodied in the amendment, they failed to estimate rightly the genuinely progressive character of the popular response to the project of a referendum on war, a response based upon the legitimate distrust which the masses feel toward the bourgeois government, their unwillingness to fight without protest in the threatening imperialist war, and their desire for democratic control of their own destiny.

---

15. Reprinted from *Socialist Appeal*, May 21, 1938.

From this failure, the Political Committee drew the incorrect tactical conclusion of a negative position with respect to the amendment itself and the general project of a popular referendum on war. Such a negative position isolates the party from the progressive mass movement aroused by the project, and tends to sterilize its active struggle against imperialist war.

The party and its press must therefore alter their line on this question. They must become the most militant advocates of a popular referendum on war. They must seek to have labor everywhere demand that the amendment be formulated to provide for a popular referendum on the undertaking of any war, be it allegedly "defensive" or "aggressive," and that all citizens from the age of eighteen upward, since from that age they are liable to military service, have the right to vote in the referendum.

They must take no responsibility for the pacifist illusions fostered in connection with the amendment and in particular must continue to expose the bourgeois politicians, including Ludlow, La Follette, and Company themselves, who seek to exploit the honest antiwar sentiment of the masses by introducing a bill in Congress and then either dropping any serious fight for it or so diluting and circumscribing it as to nullify the will and longings of the masses. They must endeavor to extend the struggle beyond the confines of purely parliamentary debate, so that workers' pressure may be brought into play by means of organized mass action. In this way, the party will not only be able to correct its tactical error, but also to deepen and solidify its connections with the genuine and progressive movement of the masses.

The decline of American capitalism and the revolutionary transitional program for the next period[16]

by the SWP Political Committee

I.

1. The American capitalist economy, now passing through a fresh period of economic crisis and depression following the 1933–37 upturn, has definitely entered its phase of general decline. For the first time in its history, the top of the boom cycle, measured by all significant indices, was substantially below the top of the preceding boom (1929). This central fact unmistakably demonstrates the

---

16. Reprinted from *Internal Bulletin*, SWP, number 2 [June 1938]. This resolution was referred to under several names: American transitional program, the national action program or theses, the program of action, etc. A week after the April plenum the Political Committee set up a subcommittee to explore the possibility of preparing a joint "concrete program of action" (American adaptation of the Transitional Program) that could be presented to the membership for referendum vote. This meant either reconciling the Spector and Shachtman motions and the Cannon and Burnham motions, or deciding that they could not be

falsity of any theory of American "exceptionalism"[17] and the truth of the Marxist contention in our international draft thesis that the United States, along with the entire capitalist world, has exhausted its progressive potentialities.

2. The economic crisis in the United States is thus no cyclical fluctuation preceding a further advance of production, but a stage in the development of a permanent and general crisis in the economic and social relations of American capitalism. This general crisis of the social order itself does not of course exclude the possibility and even probability of temporary periods of revival. But every such upturn in the future will be feverish, brief, uneven, and yield to deeper crisis and more grinding depression on a lower level. Mass unemployment, increasing insecurity, and lowering of the general standard of living have become chronic and inseparable features of American economy and insurmountable without the destruction of capitalism itself.

---

reconciled and a joint resolution could not be agreed on. For almost a month the subcommittee could report no progress, except that Spector and Burnham were each preparing their own resolutions. Finally the subcommittee, with prodding from the PC, was able to report an agreement to fuse both documents, which meant an understanding had been reached that the divisions expressed at the plenum could be bridged without sacrifice of principle on either side. Even so, it was the middle of June before the Political Committee approved an amended draft and submitted it to the membership for discussion and vote. The PC held that the resolution on the American transitional program and the resolution on the labor party were to be considered "a single document divided into two sections," which were to be discussed and voted on separately.

17. The SWP's hostility to theories of American "exceptionalism" was not based on the belief that American capitalism did not have exceptional and even unique features but on the conviction that these exceptional features could not exempt American capitalism from the laws that shaped capitalism everywhere, especially in the period of its decline and decay.

3. The gigantic technical development of the United States, its enormous material resources, and the fact that this country has risen to the relatively dominant position in world capitalism during the period when world capitalism had entered the epoch of decline, only accentuates the impact of the crisis. The roots of the American crisis are international and the fate of the United States was never more closely linked up with the destiny of world capitalism as a whole. Economic rise and slump in the United States are sharper and more devastating than in any other country; and the attempt to extricate itself from the crisis by means of the redistribution of the world market is driving American capitalism to play a leading part in the preparations for the new imperialist war.

4. The effects of the 1929–33 economic crisis, and even more the impact of the new crisis before the completion of a recovery cycle comparable to the previous boom period, produce an uneven but ever deepening and all-embracing social crisis, the continuing character of which is made certain by the insoluble nature of the economic crisis. Confronted by the ravages of the economic crisis in their own lives, the masses seek a way out. The unprecedented sweep to the New Deal was one abortive attempt to find such a way. But the realities of capitalist decline are shattering the illusions of the New Deal no less ruthlessly than they dissipated the dream of the "New Era" (1923–29). The New Deal expenditures served temporarily to prop up the sagging foundations of capitalism and "stabilize" decay by "planned" sabotage of production. Despite billions of dollars of government pump-priming, however, the boasted economic gains of three years of the New Deal were wiped out in three months of the most precipitate decline in American economic history. The army of the unemployed has once more risen to thirteen million. The

national organization of Labor's Non-Partisan League and the formation of La Follette's national Progressive Party are events of the greatest symptomatic importance as indicating the pressure of the masses trying to find their road beyond the collapsing framework of the traditional two-party system.

II.

5. As yet the discontent of the masses has not found clear and explicit expression. Nowhere in the world is there a greater gap than in the United States between the technical and material organization of economy, which have fully matured for the socialist revolution, and the backwardness of political consciousness of the masses, which still revolves within bourgeois limits. At the same time nowhere is there a greater gap between political backwardness and implicitly revolutionary anticapitalist action of the masses (the sit-in strikes). In these circumstances, to which must be added the approach of a new world war, the prospect of long drawn out, comparatively stable tendencies, such as once characterized many of the older European countries, must be ruled out.

6. This situation is fertile for the rapid and stormy political development of the masses. At the same time it provides the soil for radical and pseudoradical middle-class movements, and an unprecedentedly rapid growth of an American fascist movement, which might be a consequence of such third-party movements. To ward off the historical danger of fascism, the revolutionary party must immediately find a way of actively intervening in these developments, directing them toward the organized class political action of the workers, drawing into the struggle

the lower middle classes, and carrying through the struggle to the workers' revolution, which alone can solve the problems of the crisis.

7. From these considerations follows the urgent need of a *transitional program* to facilitate bridging the gap between the objectively matured revolutionary conditions and the lagging political consciousness of the masses. If in the period of capitalist expansion the welfare of the masses continually lagged behind the development of the productive forces, then under the conditions of capitalist decline resistance to exploitation is impossible without coming into conflict with the very foundations of capitalism. Under the conditions of the social crisis the old forms of revolutionary agitation and propaganda for the socialist goal, combined with daily agitation for immediate demands more or less realizable within the framework of capitalism, have become inadequate. Even the struggle for the so-called immediate demands is compelled to take on the character of a struggle against the confines of capitalist law and order (sit-down). The function of the transitional program is to bridge the gap between the program of immediate demands and the full program of the proletarian revolution.

8. The transitional program must be bold, decisive, and resolute. It must at every stage deepen the class consciousness of the workers and enhance their confidence in their own class organizations and political action. It must provide positive and militant answers to the burning problems with which decaying capitalism and the social crisis relentlessly confront the workers; problems arising from the contrast between the enormous productive capacity of the United States and the increasing pauperization and misery of the masses; problems of the growing danger, as the class struggle sharpens, of the rise of

a fascist movement; problems of the struggle against the imminent approach of imperialist war. In the very nature of a transitional program, of course, it cannot in advance be given final and finished form. With the changes in the mass movement and in the state of mind of the workers, the transitional program must correspondingly change, to advance or on occasion to retreat, altering the emphasis and utilization of slogans and shifting tactics through which the program is presented.

9. For the Socialist Workers Party to orient its activity around a transitional program means to enter a decisively new phase in the development of a revolutionary party in this country. It means to concentrate attention and activity principally on the mass movement. It means striving to transform the party from an enlarged propaganda group to a genuine party of action in the class struggle. It means that the entire work of the party for the next period must revolve around the objective of making our program known to the American masses. It must be carried into the unions and all mass organizations, public meetings, street-corner demonstrations, labor party organizations, and Labor's Non-Partisan League. It is primarily a program of agitation and mass action around the agitation.

III.

Without relinquishing our support also of the struggle for the immediate demands (shorter hours, higher wages, higher relief, social insurance, democratic rights, etc.) but the more effectively to mobilize the workers against the burden of the economic crisis, the danger of fascist violence, and the imminence of imperialist war, the Socialist

Workers Party proposes the following as a program of transitional demands for the next period:

A. Struggle against the economic crisis
1. Workers' control of industry

The capitalist offensive takes the form of wage cutting, ruthless speed-up, the shutting down of plants, the monopolist rise of prices; state-capitalist and bureaucratic schemes of industrial regulation and "planning" threaten the workers with economic serfdom. To counter this capitalist drive and to prepare for their own future management of industry under social ownership, the workers must extend the implications of the sit-down by demanding the right of their own independent audits and inspection of the corporation books, disclosure of business "secrets," and exposure of all other monopolistic and fraudulent methods whereby big business operates for the purpose of shifting the costs of the depression and crisis on the workers.

The organizations best fitted to cope with the problems of workers' control at the point of production are the *shop committees*. Every effort must be exerted to organize the shop committees, which may become organs of dual power in the factory and the nucleus of soviets, as the crisis takes on a revolutionary character in the future. Where these committees already exist as union organs in organized shops, they must be broadened out and infused with militant class consciousness and leadership. It is also necessary to guard against the setting up or transformation of existent shop committees into substitutes for trade unions as well as against the danger of fake company-union-employee shop committees.

2. Reopen idle plants

Thousands of plants, mines, and factories in the United States are closed or running at small fractions of capacity, thus depriving the workers of the jobs which are their right and products which the masses need. We therefore propose that all idle factories, plants, and mines shall be reopened and operated under the control of the workers within the given field of industry; the payment of all rent, interest, and profit, and provision of capital reserves shall be suspended during such operation; wages shall be paid with the trade union scale as a minimum; and any necessary financing shall be carried out through the provision of federal funds.

3. Expropriation of separate industries

Expropriation of the railroads and their operation under workers' control without the payment of rent, interest, or profit. Expropriation of separate gigantic monopolies in industry and public utilities (gas, electricity, communications) and their operation likewise under workers' control, without payment of rent, interest, or profit.

4. Public works

Both to provide jobs to all those unable to find work in ordinary industry and to supply the needs of the masses, we propose the immediate allotment of twenty billion dollars (one-half the cost to the U.S. of the last war) for a large-scale program of useful public works and for low-rental modern housing, such rental to be at a figure to cover the cost of upkeep alone, with all other costs covered by public funds; all work done on the public works program to be governed by union standards of hours and wages, not to be less than $30 per week.

5. Sliding scale of wages

Against increases in the cost of living, we propose to fight under the slogan of a sliding scale of wages. Wage agreements, under a strictly specified minimum, must provide for automatic increase of wages to correspond with increases in prices of consumer goods.

6. Sliding scale of hours
In the struggle against mounting unemployment, which has already plunged not less than fifteen million workers and their families into the abyss of pauperism, the Socialist Workers Party raises the demand for a *job and a decent living for every worker*. Along with the development of a program of public works and the reopening of closed factories, mines, and plants as a part of this program, we propose a *sliding scale of hours* in public and private industry—that is, the reduction of hours to the point which will permit the assimilation of all the unemployed into public or private industry; the equal division of working hours; and weekly wages for all at not less than the present fulltime union rates. Arguments that such a demand cannot be reconciled with the bookkeeping system of capitalist industry and the payment of interest, profit, and rent, have no validity whatever. What is at stake is the life or death of the million-masses of the workers, the only creative and progressive class in modern society. The "bookkeeping" must be reconciled with the life interests of the working class, come what may.

7. The farm problem
Nearly half of all working farmers in the United States have today the status of tenants or sharecroppers, subject to exorbitant rents and to eviction. To protect these farmers against the ravages of the depression and the insecurities of the crisis, we propose a moratorium on all rent payments of any type, the prohibition of evictions, cancellation, or tax indebtedness. We further propose

expropriation of all lands held by nonoperators and their transfer to tenants and sharecroppers. The small farmers or owner-operated farms are oppressed by heavy mortgages owned by the great banks and insurance companies. We therefore propose cancellation of all mortgage indebtedness on all such owner-operated farms.

B. Struggle against fascism
1. Workers' defense guard (workers' militia)

The experience of the class struggle the world over demonstrates that under conditions of the social crisis, the capitalist class increasingly resorts to naked and despotic violence of vigilantism and fascism. If the American working class is not to fall victim to the supine parliamentary cretinism and "constitutional" illusions that overwhelmed large sections of the European labor movement, it can no longer postpone with impunity the tasks of organizing its own militant workers' defense guards. Workers' defense groups are developments of the picket lines, "flying squads," etc., which spontaneously characterize strikes in this country. But the workers' defense guards must be permanent units, strongly disciplined, with duties extending beyond the strike situation, and progressively assuming the more pronounced political character of a workers' militia. Workers' defense groups are the first organized nuclei of the future workers' army.

Systematic organization of defense groups can and must begin with the party itself and especially the YPSL. But every effort should be made to draw in sympathetic nonmembers. The groups organized on party initiative would be for defense of party and YPSL public meetings, demonstrations, leaflet distribution, and other working-class meetings against fascist, vigilante, or Stalinist provocation. These groups are not a substitute for workers' defense guards having a broad mass labor support, but a nucleus, the organization of which the revolutionary party must assume as an immediate task.

C. Struggle against war preparations

The object of the present enormous military and naval budgets of the United States can only be to fight a war in defense and extension of the imperialist interest of American capitalism. We therefore propose: (a) the transfer of all war funds to the maintenance of the unemployed; (b) that the decision with reference to military or naval action against any other country shall rest with a popular referendum, with all those from the age of eighteen upward eligible to vote; (c) immediate withdrawal of all armed forces of the United States from the Far East; (d) immediate freedom for all colonies and possessions of the United States; (e) abolition of secret diplomacy; (f) nationalization under workers' control of the armament and munitions industry.

D. Workers' government[18]

The most general form of the campaign of agitation for the program of transitional demands is the propaganda for the slogan of the workers' government, a slogan dictated

---

18. The slogan of the workers' government was one on which the members of the Political Committee could not reach agreement. Shachtman and Burnham favored "workers' government," Cannon favored "workers' and farmers' government" (the formulation used by Trotsky in his draft of the Transitional Program), and two other members of the committee abstained. "Workers' government" was used in the PC resolution, but Cannon introduced an amendment calling for it to be changed to "workers' and farmers' government," and submitted it for discussion and vote in the membership referendum. For the outcome of the Cannon amendment, see page 441.

by the catastrophic character of the whole political development of our epoch. The aim of the transitional program is to break the masses away from support of the traditional parties of capitalism, to lead them to independent class politics and the conquest of power. The slogan of the workers' government summarizes the goal of the transitional program, the objective of independent class political action, and constitutes the answer to the Stalinist and Social Democratic politics of support of the New Deal, the Popular (or "Democratic") Front. We always stress our basic position of principle that only the power of a soviet government can abolish capitalism and institute planned socialist economy. We never fail to point to the calamitous failure of the labor, Social Democratic, and Popular Front governments as merely forms for the administration of the capitalist state. We raise the slogan of the workers' government, in the sense given it by the Bolsheviks in 1917, as an antibourgeois and anticapitalist slogan to assist the experience of the masses.

Our party alone fully comprehends the depth and scope of the crisis and its revolutionary implications. Our party alone proposes a revolutionary solution of the crisis by our generation. All other political parties either support capitalism or postpone its end to the distant future. Our party is fully aware that on the action of the American working class may rest the whole fate of world civilization.

The problem of the labor party[19]

by the SWP National Committee majority

The decline of American capitalism and the social crisis ensuing therefrom have already called forth the greatest trade union organizing campaign in American history, which brought with it a wave of strike struggles unprecedented in scope and revolutionary implications (the sit-down strikes). At the same time the experiences and results of these herculean efforts of the American proletariat have demonstrated the inadequacy of the purely economic struggle to solve even the most pressing immediate problems of the workers. The precipitous economic

---

19. Reprinted from *Internal Bulletin*, SWP, number 2 [June 1938], and *Socialist Appeal*, October 1, 1938. This draft, expanding Trotsky's April draft, was endorsed by the Political Committee in June, after agreement was reached that there really were no serious differences between the Cannon motion and the Burnham motion at the April plenum. But the vote was not unanimous (5 to 1), with Hal Draper opposing the resolution and announcing that he would submit his own resolution, opposing advocacy of a labor party, in the prereferendum discussion.

decline, as a result of the new crisis, adds new millions to the ranks of the unemployed, cancels out the gains of the strike victories, and even threatens the existence of the newly built trade unions. Instinctively sensing the inadequacy of trade unionism alone under these circumstances, the workers have begun to turn in million-masses toward political action. The further development of the crisis is certain to strengthen this tendency.

The organized participation of the workers in politics under the aegis of Labor's Non-Partisan League represents a profound departure from the old Gompers school of labor politics, although on the surface the two may appear to be identical. In the past the labor bureaucracy confined itself to "endorsing" this or that "friend of labor" on the capitalist party tickets. In the 1936 presidential elections, and in virtually all municipal and state elections since, we have seen for the first time a systematic and increasingly determined effort to organize and mobilize the political strength of the workers as a single unit. This new movement, represented by the LNPL, must be characterized as a stage in the development of the labor movement from complete subservience to the political parties of big capital to an independent party of the workers.

The fact that the movement as yet remains within the formal framework of the Democratic Party is in part due to the conscious restrictions placed upon it by the bureaucracy and in part to the as yet unclear aims of the masses. On the other hand, the increasing aggressiveness of this movement on the political field, and its mounting demands for more concessions and representation for labor—an attitude which has already impelled the workers in important local instances to put up independent or semi-independent tickets—testify to the profound impulse of the masses of the workers toward completely independent political action. This impulse is progressive and must consciously and deliberately be aided at every step by the Socialist Workers Party.

Parallel with the developing sentiment for an independent party of the workers, and in large measure interfused with it, there is a powerful trend in the direction of a new bourgeois liberal party designed to include and swallow up the incipient movement of the workers for independent labor political action. Under further pressure of the social crisis this trend can and most likely will also gain strength; the present Democratic Party may be split wide open and a new party of the democratic bourgeois front may emerge, with the labor bureaucracy occupying a prominent though politically subordinate place. Against such a development, as against the present attempts of the bureaucracy to subordinate the workers to the Democratic Party, we counterpose the slogan of independent labor political action through a labor party.

At the time of our national convention, we took insufficient account of the new developments in the labor movement, especially in their political aspects, and fell into the error of repeating abstract formulas on the question of the labor party which, in the light of great new developments, had become obsolete. It is necessary now to reconsider the question and to make a radical change in our tactics in regard to the developing labor party movement. Over a period of years we have discussed and debated this question with the opportunists only in the abstract. That could not be otherwise, because neither a labor party nor a formidable movement for its creation was anywhere to be seen. In these discussions we saw only two aspects of the question—a labor party which did not exist in reality, but which the opportunists sought to suck out of their fingers, or a possible fully developed labor party some time in the future.

We now have to gear our practical activity toward a third and hitherto insufficiently appreciated aspect of the question—namely, a powerful mass movement in the direction of the labor party which has not yet taken a clearly defined shape. We have always said that, confronted with a fully developed labor party, based on the trade unions, we would take a positive attitude toward it and most likely participate in it. We are now confronted with the necessity of concretizing this general point of view and of taking a direct part in the present developing *movement* for a labor party and of working with all our strength to push it on the road to independence.

The question of the attitude toward an existing labor party has never been a question of principle for revolutionary Marxists. No more should our attitude toward a genuine mass movement for a labor party be so considered. In our tactics we have always taken our point of departure from the concrete political situation and the tendencies of its development. Several years ago, before the crisis of 1929 and even later, until the appearance of the CIO, we could have hoped that the revolutionary, that is, the Bolshevik party would develop in the United States parallel to the radicalization of the working class and succeed in becoming the head of it. Under these conditions it would have been absurd to occupy oneself with abstract propaganda in favor of an unheralded "labor party."

The situation since that time, however, has radically changed and it would be inexcusable to close our eyes to it. The powerfully developing trade unions under the conditions of a deepening crisis of capitalism will project themselves all the more irresistibly upon the road of political struggle and upon the road of crystallization into a labor party.

If the official leaders of the trade unions, in spite of the imperious voice of the situation and the growing pressure of the masses, preserve a reserved position on the question of a labor party, it is precisely because the deep social crisis of bourgeois society now imparts to the question of the labor party a considerably greater sharpness than in all preceding periods.

Nevertheless we can with sufficient assurance predict that the resistance of the bureaucracy will be broken. The movement in favor of a labor party will continue to grow. A revolutionary organization occupying in relation to this progressive movement a negative or neutrally expectant position will doom itself to isolation and sectarian degeneration.

The Socialist Workers Party, section of the Fourth International, clearly realizes the fact that in virtue of unfavorable historical reasons its own development lagged behind the radicalization of wide layers of the American proletariat and precisely because of this the problem of creating a labor party is placed upon the order of the day through the whole course of development.

Consequently, the Socialist Workers Party gives positive and unambiguous support to the labor party movement in general and to all its local manifestations. It supports the affiliation of trade unions to Labor's Non-Partisan League as well as to local units of the movement having an independent or semi-independent form (Farmer-Labor Party of Minnesota, American Labor Party, etc.) and, in favorable circumstances, the National Committee authorizes its members to join branches of these bodies based on individual membership.

While the Social Democrats, Lovestoneites, etc., advocate a labor or farmer-labor party with a purely reformist program and more or less confine themselves to unprincipled top combinations under cover of this slogan, the Socialist Workers Party advances its program of transitional demands in order to fructify the mass movement in favor of a labor party and lead it in a revolutionary direction.

Preserving its own full organizational and political independence, the Socialist Workers Party carries on systematic and irreconcilable struggle against the trade union bureaucracy which resists the creation of a labor party, or attempts to convert it into an auxiliary weapon of one of the bourgeois parties. Explaining and propagandizing its program of transitional demands in the trade unions, at meetings, and so forth, the Socialist Workers Party indefatigably exposes on the basis of the living experience of the masses the reformist and pacifist illusions of the trade union bureaucracy and its Social Democratic and Stalinist allies.

When and how the labor party will be formed, what scope and mass base it will acquire in the period ahead and through what stages and splits it will pass, the future will disclose. Defending the labor party from the attack of the bourgeoisie, the Socialist Workers Party does not and will not, however, take upon itself any responsibility for this party. In relation to the labor party in all stages of its development, the Socialist Workers Party occupies a critical position, supports the progressive tendencies against the reactionary, and at the same time irreconcilably criticizes the half-way character of these progressive tendencies. For the Socialist Workers Party the labor party should on the one hand become the arena for recruiting revolutionary elements, on the other, a transmissive mechanism for influencing ever wider circles of workers. In its very essence the labor party can preserve progressive significance only during a comparatively short transitional period. The further sharpening of the revolutionary situation will inevitably break the shell of the labor party and permit the SWP to rally around the banner of the Fourth International the revolutionary vanguard of the American proletariat.

Minority resolution on the labor party[20]

by Hal Draper

(Following is the elaborated draft of the minority resolution, which is presented for the vote in the party referendum.)

1. The problem of the labor party is a problem of our strategy and tactics in the period of capitalist decline, and more specifically, in the present period of the death agony of international capitalism and the chronic social crisis of American capitalism. We must solve the series of questions that arise with regard to: (1) the objective significance of labor parties in this period; (2) the implementing of our transitional program so as to make it a real force in the upsurge of the American workers and in order to steer their development into revolutionary channels; and

---

20. Reprinted from *Internal Bulletin*, SWP, number 6, July 1938. Draper had submitted a hastily written resolution against advocacy of a labor party, which was printed in *Internal Bulletin*, number 2, along with the majority resolution. But when he had time he wrote this longer resolution as the document to be voted on in the referendum.

(3) the working out of positive tactics in reaching and influencing in our direction the sections of the working class which are breaking away from their old party ties and groping for independent class action.

The perspective of the labor party movement

2. The leadership of the LNPL movement is at present intent upon continuing its present course of tailing the old capitalist parties—i.e., the old policy of "rewarding friends and punishing enemies" in new, organized, form. It is not excluded that they will continue to remain within the bounds of this policy. The more probable outcome, and the one upon which the LNPL leaders themselves are banking, is that a realignment within the old party set-up will lead to a coalition between the LNPL forces and a split-off "left wing" of the Democratic Party (plus even Republican elements)—to form a characteristic third-party movement, a bourgeois democratic front. The mass basis of such a party would still be the trade unions affiliated to the LNPL, bestraddled by the generals without an army of the left Democrats, side by side with the LNPL leaders as the left face of the third-party leadership. The objective driving force of such a split would be precisely the sharpening of the social crisis, leading to differences in the ranks of the bourgeoisie on how to deal with it, the "left wing" seeking the shelter of the politically conservative labor forces.

3. But if such a Democratic split fails to mature rapidly enough, and if the movement for independent action among the workers threatens to go over the heads of the LNPL leaders, on the way to revolutionary action, then the stimulus will be present for the formation by the LNPL of their own independent party on a national scale, reluctantly pushed ahead by pressure from below to the formation of the famous "independent labor party." It is out of such

conditions that an "independent labor party" would arise.

4. This is why it is superficial and false to believe that the significance of an independent labor party would appear as a spur to the development of political class consciousness on the part of the workers. The relationship is the other way around: an independent LNPL party would be the *distorted reflection* of the workers' advancing consciousness, not its cause or stimulus. Nor is it true that it would in its turn stimulate further advance in political consciousness. On the contrary, its *raison d'etre* would be to utilize the new form in order to stem the flood and siphon it back into safe channels. It is the old trick of misleadership: running around in front of the masses in order to head them off.

5. It is important to distinguish the progressive and reactionary elements in such developments. On the one hand, there is the fact that a swing in sentiment by sections of the working class away from the old capitalist parties and toward independent political action manifests a *progressive subjective development* on their part. This we hail—this represents a stage in the development of the subjective preconditions of the revolution. But it is a fact that the same progressive *subjective* development is present when a worker breaks with the Democratic Party and joins the CP because he looks upon it as a working-class party; similar examples can be given. The fact that there is a progressive sentiment afoot does not ensure that it will not be corralled into a reactionary channel (any more than a sincere hatred of fascism ensures that it will not take the form of support of war against Germany). We must distinguish sharply between (1) the progressive character of the political action sentiment among the workers; and (2) the reactionary character of the labor party form into which it is crystallized. The former has an extremely important effect upon our tactical steps, as we shall show; the latter determines our basic strategical approach.

Our basic strategical approach

6. The basic question which must guide our policies is: Can a labor party play a progressive role? This question cannot be answered by the mechanical application of principles which apply any time, anywhere. It is determined by our analysis of the present era of capitalist development. When capitalism was expanding economically, the labor party could rally large masses of workers about the struggle for immediate demands, which the bourgeoisie was able to yield. In this postwar period of declining capitalism, however, this possibility no longer exists; the bourgeoisie must withdraw rather than grant further concessions. Even the successful struggle for immediate demands requires revolutionary orientation. With the intensification of the social crisis, whatever immediate gains or victories are registered are cancelled out by the development of the crisis itself. Where once a reformist political party acting within the framework of capitalism had an independent role to play in organizing the working class for immediate concessions, today the only working-class program which is actually independent of the capitalist class is the revolutionary program. Today a labor party, like every other political formation, is confronted with the harsh alternatives—defense of capitalism or the fight for socialism; the possibility of finding footing in a middle ground is no longer there.

7. The old type of program which, in a different period, provided this middle ground has now been taken over by the most enlightened section of the bourgeoisie itself—the "left," New Deal Democrats. It is precisely because the reformist labor leaders have no essential political independence from this program that there is no objective basis for their political independence from capitalist politics in general. Under such circumstances, "separating the workers from all capitalist

politics" is more and more equivalent to—leading them in a revolutionary direction. A labor party born under these auspices is marked from birth: to tie the workers to capitalist politics through new forms, dividing this labor with the left varieties of bourgeois politics (Rooseveltian demagogy, etc.).

8. To say however that a labor party can do nothing to solve even the most immediately pressing problems of the workers and that it cannot separate them from capitalist politics does not mean its role is merely one of futility. The vacuum from which the progressive significance of a labor party has fled is filled with a reactionary content. The establishment of such a political machine means a positive obstacle on the road of the development of the workers, a positive enemy of the revolutionary movement. Its positively reactionary character manifests itself on all the fields vital to the interests of the working class. With the threat of a new war overhanging, it cannot even allow itself the verbal denunciation of capitalist war which the Second International before the war could afford, but must appear openly as a social-patriotic recruiting machine and propagandist among the workers, partly even deliberately founded for the preparation of the national union. To teach the workers now to look upon such an organization as the center and rallying point for the political movement of the working class (i.e., to advocate the formation of a labor party where none exists) means to make it all the harder, in time of war, to break the workers away from their allegiance to it.

9. At a time when the old two-party system is breaking up, it is possible for a labor party to achieve an organizational, formal independence from the two old machines. But politically, it can only gravitate within the orbit of third-party politics. The PC majority agrees that if the LNPL forces formed a party in coalition with the left Democrats, it would mean a third party. But if the

LNPL is forced to form their party without these allies, what basic difference would there be between the two variants? In program? Support of capitalism? Methods? Mass basis? Why would one be progressive and not the other? It is true that significant differences would exist—for example, a party formed by the LNPL alone would be more sensitive to working-class pressure (just as the CP is more sensitive to this pressure than Roosevelt), etc.—but these do not determine the question of its progressive or reactionary character; and in action they would dictate a different tactical approach, not a different estimate of its objective significance.

The transitional program and the labor party

10. What conclusion must we draw with regard to the labor party from our estimate of the present social crisis and our advocacy of a transitional program? On the negative side, the present crisis *sharpens* the outlines of the preceding analysis. Where before the "abstract" analysis of the period of capitalist decline pointed to the reactionary character of a labor party formation, the present concrete circumstances reinforce the conclusion. Or—is a labor party reactionary when it is merely a question of capitalist decline, but becomes "progressive" when this decline takes over more intensified forms?

11. But it is the positive conclusions from the transitional program which point our road. The deepening social crisis in the United States dictates to the revolutionary party the need for a program for the masses that goes beyond the immediate demands elaborated heretofore, that goes outside the framework of capitalism. Convulsive upheavals in the coming period hold forth the possibility for the revolutionary party to advance in bold strides forward with great gains in influence and membership—*provided*

that we know how to (1) make this program a living force in the direct mass action of the workers; and (2) on the political field, on the basis of the experiences of the struggle, guide the political lessons which the workers draw toward the necessity of *revolutionary* organization, of revolutionary politics.

12. How will our program take hold in the workers' mass movement? The transitional program prepares the way for putting the question of power on the agenda. The *main* line which the party must follow in implementing the transitional program is to *teach the workers the necessity of depending on their own extraparliamentary strength and organization*—certainly not to teach them to depend upon, or hold to any present illusions in, the ability of a labor party to carry out this transitional program. What *organizational* forms must we strive for to carry out the transitional program? Under Section A of the National Action thesis (economic demands): "The organizations best fitted to cope with the problems of workers' control at the point of production are the *shop committees*. Every effort must be exerted to organize the shop committees, which may become organs of dual power in the factory and the nucleus of soviets, as the crisis takes on a revolutionary character in the future." Under Section B ("Struggle Against Fascism"): the organization of the workers' defense guard, the workers' militia. In Section C ("Struggle Against War Preparations"): the need for extraparliamentary organization, here most immediately counterposed to the perspective of a labor party, is most obvious. Section D (the slogan of a workers' government) means for us, as the form for which *we* strive, a workers' government based upon the councils of workers and farmers. Although the workers may have to pass through the experience of a labor party government, we must realize the danger of *ourselves* giving

this content to the slogan, in our own agitation. Carefully the party must lead the workers through the experiences of the shop committees, the workers' defense guard, etc., to the creation of councils of workers and farmers, and toward the national consolidation of these extraparliamentary organs of struggle as the crisis matures. That is the course which we must set in motion among the masses to counteract the People's Frontism and democratic front of the Stalinists and liberals. If this is the main line we put before the masses, our main line in political agitation is also to keep before their eyes the necessity for revolutionary organization. We cannot point both toward soviets and a reformist labor party as the means of carrying out our revolutionary transitional program.

13. The party ranks must understand this precisely as our *main* line. The great gap between the objective requirements of the situation and the subjective stage of development of the workers requires that we take the path of the transitional program in an effort to *hurdle* the course of reformist political development which the American working class has to go through. But the backwardness of the American workers imperatively demands that we supplement this strategy with a positive program of tactical steps *within* the labor party movement. Just as on the extraparliamentary field, we launch slogans which, starting from the elementary needs of the workers, are designed to bring them in struggle outside the framework of capitalism; so inside the labor party movement, we must conduct a struggle around demands which, starting from the desire for independent political class action, are designed to teach them through experience that the labor party cannot bring them a step forward, that our position is correct, that the way out lies in our direction.

Tactics in the labor party movement

14. Our labor party policy up to now is inadequate for our present needs for two reasons: first, because it was not linked with a program for bringing the masses into motion on a line alternative to that of the labor party movement, the transitional program which we have now developed; second, because it necessarily emphasized the negative aspect of blocking the formation of a labor party without taking sufficiently into account and paying serious attention to the necessity for tactical utilization of the progressive sentiment which has its distorted reflection in the labor party movement, through work inside, although our Declaration of Principles and previous resolutions already sketched the outlines of such a possible future course. This is the turn which the party must make on the labor party question.

15. It must be understood that such concrete tactics cannot be improvised; our considerations with regard to the period of capitalist decline do not automatically dictate our tactics for specific situations. These can be developed realistically only by a concrete knowledge of the situation, the relationship of forces, local differences, etc., and after full discussion. Our first step in making a turn toward concretizing our tactics must be a survey of the national and local scenes, and it is the task of the party leadership to carefully lay out a positive tactical approach to each. The PC majority solves the problem in short order by prescribing "complete and unambiguous support" in each and every instance. The sectarian is equally expeditious with the view that we should have nothing to do with this morass of reformism. The line of the party must be neither of these rule-of-thumb answers.

16. The important aspect of the labor party movement for us is the fact that there is *movement*. Where will this

movement lead to? Ahead of it lies either labor party action or revolutionary political action. We have stated that our basic approach demands that we seek to block the road toward the crystallization of this sentiment in the form of a labor party. Does this then mean turning it back in the direction from which it is coming, toward the capitalist parties? Obviously not; at the same time that we seek to block the road toward the labor party, we must push the politically awakening workers *forward*—which means, along the alternative road of revolutionary action. In proportion as our efforts have their effect, it is this *combined* action which will enable the advance guard of the workers to come most quickly to the revolutionary party. Blocking the reformist road—that is the sense of our strategical approach to the labor party question; pushing the workers forward from behind—that is the place of our tactics.

17. We can do neither effectively unless we are *in* the labor party movement. The nature of the movement itself provides the channels. The first is *through the trade unions*. In the last analysis our program can play a role in making the history of the American working class only if our roots are deep in the trade unions, if we are the best union militants, and under those conditions we cannot be isolated from the labor party movement. The second is through *serious fraction work in the labor party organizations, branches, etc*. If the labor party movement develops to much more far-reaching dimensions than it has so far, it may yet be necessary for us to throw a large portion of our forces into such activity. In cases where there is an established labor party and our party is not on the ballot, possible tactics may include such steps as registering in the labor party primaries. The question of whether such tactics are concretely permissible and to what extent they should be driven are not matters that can be settled outside of a specific examination of cases.

18. How do we work inside the labor party movement in order to push the workers forward, against their leadership, and over the heads of their leadership to us? We (i.e., our fractions in the trade unions and in the LP) raise slogans and demands adapted to the particular stage of development of the workers with whom we are dealing. Where the organization is endorsing capitalist party candidates, as in New York, Pennsylvania, etc., we can say: "Your leaders have ostensibly organized for independent political action and in order to solve your pressing problems; it is our opinion that they and the labor party can and will do neither. You don't agree with us? Then see for yourselves, try to get these things; we'll fight along with you without giving up our political convictions, but going through these experiences with you. Demand that your leaders put up independent candidates." In specific situations the fight for independent candidates can be an important lever in disillusioning the workers with what they can expect from the LP. But only if, in our own propaganda, we utilize such experiences in order to *foster* such disillusionment, to draw from them our general conclusions and lessons with regard to the labor party movement. It is this which is precisely the main emphasis in the press, for example. Furthermore, it is a matter of the simple truth to state that even if independent labor candidates are run, the problems of the workers will not be a step nearer solution. The demands which we put forward inside the LP as positive gains for the workers are the transitional demands. Where independent candidates are run, our attack shifts to center around the question of program, especially the transitional demands, and those demands again which will bring the workers in collision with the line of the party and its leadership. In the process of exposing the impotence and reactionary nature of the labor party or labor party movement, we must show that

there is an alternative path, which only the revolutionary party is following.

19. Where independent labor candidates are run, the tactic of critical support (with the emphasis on the *critical*) may be employed in order to avoid a head-on collision with the labor party sentiment of the workers where it would be difficult to explain our opposition in terms of the workers' own experiences, rather than in terms of our own revolutionary theory. But as in the preceding case, the value of such tactics depends completely upon employing them in the context of our general agitation around the LP question, utilizing these tactics in order to expose the LP in action.

20. The question of affiliation to a labor party is also a tactical question. It would become permissible only if it is no longer a question of attempting to block the formation of a labor party, but when we are faced with the fact of an established mass labor party—provided that complete organizational and programmatic independence of our own party can be maintained.

21. The question of supporting affiliation of trade unions to labor party movements is also a tactical question, depending on the question: Is there an established mass LP or is the question still open as to whether the working class will take this road or not? In Minneapolis, for example, where the FLP is precisely such an established mass party, our answer cannot be the same as in New Jersey, where the LNPL itself has not formed a LP because of the lack of mass support and interest among the workers. There we can still help to determine by our own activities whether the workers will be able to hurdle the LP stage or not. In each situation, local or national, we must decide: Are we going to accept as our starting point the fact that an established mass party exists and orient our first line of attack toward the question of program? There is no use blocking

the entrance to the LP road when the workers have already passed by. In this case, the question of advocating the formation of a LP becomes obsolete. But this is not the case at present on the national scene nor in almost all localities.

22. We believe it important to bring to the attention of the party membership some dangers in the present situation. The effects of social crisis do not remain completely outside our own organization. There is a tremendous pressure upon a party which insists upon maintaining intransigently a revolutionary line. A desperate attempt to escape from "isolation," the desire to find new shortcuts to mass influence, a dissatisfaction with results attained heretofore, which can lead to disorientation as well as to a healthy reaction—these represent the starting points. We raise this question because we believe that such tendencies have been manifested in new proportions in the reaction of sections of the party membership to the PC proposal. Pessimism and defeatism with regard to the future of the party shading into liquidationism, growing confusion in political ideas, openly opportunistic motivations and reasoning in approaching the labor party question—these are trends which it must be the task of the party leadership, majority and minority, to combat. In this sense also, the problem is the revolutionary party.

23. The road to the building of our party in the immediate period lies along the line of the struggle for the transitional program and the digging of our roots into the mass organizations of the working class. This means:

- Making every member a member of a trade union or other mass organization.
- Organization of fraction work inside the LNPL and LP movements.
- Bringing forward the transitional demands in the

trade unions and LP movements, and undertaking a campaign to popularize them in our press, popular pamphlets, etc.
- Emphasis on teaching the workers the necessity for reliance on their own extraparliamentary strength and organization.
- Building toward the organization of shop committees and local councils of workers and farmers, with a national perspective.
- Organization of opposition movement inside the LP movements around slogans designed to bring the workers into collision with their leadership.
- A national orientation toward throwing our forces into building the labor party movement can only divert us from this path. This is the positive line along which the party can be built.[21]

---

21. The Political Committee noted that the referendum vote was small, but it did not break down the voting by branches or say what proportion of the members had voted when it announced the results September 23, 1938:

	For	Against	Abstaining
International thesis ("Death Agony of Capitalism and the Tasks of the Fourth International")	399	29	5
Program of action	445	21	4
Majority labor party resolution	304	198	10
Minority labor party resolution	160	280	8

The PC entered these results into the minutes as the decision of the party and voted, "in view of the low number of votes cast on the various amendments submitted by NC members, by other individual party members, and by branches, which seems to indicate a confusion with respect to their status," to refer "the entire question of their disposition to the forthcoming plenum." See page 451 for what the November plenum did about the amendments.

Theses on the Jewish question[22]

Adopted by the SWP Political Committee

1. Our approach that of class struggle

Our approach to the Jewish question can be none other than that of the international class struggle. In its death agony the capitalist class maintains itself in power by resorting to unmitigated brutality and violence aimed at the working class, particularly at its vanguard. It utilizes every element of hatred and prejudice which it can fan into flame to bring about division among the masses and to establish a social basis for its fascist, gangster rule. The Jews, by virtue of the fact that everywhere they form only a small minority of the population, and because anti-Semitism has always been

---

22. Printed with permission of the Library of Social History. It was written by the SWP Commission on the Jewish Question, adopted by the Political Committee, and circulated to SWP branches and members for educational purposes and to stimulate practical activity. The first draft was prepared by Jack Weber.

fostered, sometimes openly, sometimes in masked form, constitute an easy scapegoat upon whom the big bourgeoisie can divert the pent-up, dangerous wrath of the backward elements among the masses, and particularly of the desperate middle classes. The fascist hirelings of the big bourgeoisie use the most vicious, lying propaganda to inflame to pogrom temperature the dormant antagonism to the Jews. Precisely because the fomenting of anti-Semitism has become an inseparable part of the technique of fascist reaction, the revolutionary party has a double duty to perform in combating it. It has the duty of exposing the real aims of the capitalists, hidden behind the smokescreen of anti-Semitism and thereby inoculating the masses against the poison; it has also the special task of mobilizing the real defense of the persecuted Jews, a defense of necessity based on the might of the organized working class. If these tasks are properly carried out, then we can at the same time hope to attract to our firm support the Jewish masses.

2. Democracy, assimilation, and the Jews

The speed of political and social democracy during the progressive period of capitalism in the advanced countries, seemed to hold out the hope that the Jews would in time become indistinguishable from the rest of the population—that, in short, they would be assimilated. This process went furthest in Germany and in the United States. The present decay of capitalism on a world scale and in each and every country, has, on the contrary, not merely arrested the movement towards assimilation but has brought its speedy reversal. To defend its hold on property and its exploitation of the toiling masses, national capitalism makes use of the ideology of national chauvinism. This is made the foundation of the totalitarian state. In the name of national chauvinism democratic rights are completely stripped from the working class. In exchange for these rights the masses are permitted the unrestricted play of anti-Semitism. The reactionary measures taken against the Jews in Germany and Austria, driving so many to suicide, are a yardstick by which to measure the strides taken by rotting capitalism back to the Middle Ages. At one stroke the Jews are deprived not only of their democratic rights as citizens, but of the elementary possibility of earning a livelihood. In this hideous fashion does capitalist democracy reach its end, not having lasted long enough to permit assimilation.

Many Jews—and not only Jews—delude themselves with the soothing thought that America is different, that these same phenomena cannot happen here. They continue to picture the United States as a great melting pot with a democracy far more securely founded than was European democracy. But the Jews and the entire working class must be forewarned—the same causes leading to decay are visibly at work here, and the same results are not merely possible but absolutely inevitable unless the working class learns, and learns quickly, to defend its hard-earned rights and to take the road to power. The second crisis piled on top of the first one leaves the capitalist ruling class in a serious predicament and in a quandary concerning the way out. That it is fearful of its continued domination and considers the advisability of strong measures—fascist measures—cannot be doubted. The symptoms of increased discrimination against the Jews, of anti-Semitism, are already present. We must immediately sound the alarm to put the working class on guard against all the reactionary conspiracies of the big bourgeoisie; more particularly we must awaken the Jewish masses to a sense of realization of the danger and above all we must propose the proper measures to be taken against the growing danger.

3. Bridge from Jewish nationalism to the class struggle

The blows dealt to the Jews in one country after the other have tended to give new vitality to the Zionist movement[23] the national solution proposed for the Jews by many. What is our attitude on Palestine as a homeland for the Jews? The Fourth International has inscribed on its banner the giving of aid by the proletariat to the struggle for the self-determination of oppressed nationalities. But the international dispersion of the Jews creates a special problem not present in this form for any other nationality. Palestine is a land already occupied by a hostile people, the Arabs. Palestine, considered as part of the capitalist world, can be nothing but the cat's-paw of imperialism, particularly of British imperialism at the present time. The history of Palestine in the generation since the war has been the self-same history of class exploitation as for all capitalist countries. The workers in Palestine have suffered all the ills of capitalism.

We do not yield at all to Jewish nationalism and hence we point out all these facts. But it must be our attempt to create a bridge between the oppressed Jewish masses who are inclined to Jewish nationalism and the proletariat, particularly the vanguard in the Fourth International. We must make clear to the Jewish nationalists that even to carry out their ideal, their solution, it is necessary first of all to rid the world of capitalism. The solution of the Jewish question and that of the working class is a common

---

23. The Zionist movement in this country was at this time a relatively small minority in the Jewish community and remained so until after the war.

one: the overthrow of capitalism. The Jews have reached an utter impasse because capitalism has reached an impasse. Only through the class struggle will the Jews find a road to the future. By building such a bridge we can achieve the goal of Lenin, whose acceptance of the formula of self-determination meant, among other things, one more means for mobilizing all the oppressed side by side with the workers against the capitalist system. National oppression is not the least of the forms of capitalist oppression.

4. The fight for unrestricted immigration

In view of the awful plight of the Jews, it must be made a special point in the program of the various sections of the Fourth International to fight against restrictions on immigration, particularly Jewish immigration. In the U.S. we must fight against the imposing of barriers such as the necessity to prove by showing money or through affidavits that the immigrant will not become a public charge. Part of our combating of anti-Semitism must take the form of a fight for unrestricted immigration for refugees, especially Jews.

5. The Jewish bourgeoisie

It is an elementary principle of Marxism that the class lines cut across the national lines. The Jewish bourgeoisie, fearful as they may be of the advent of fascism, remain first of all capitalist exploiters. It is their aim—as their assignment by their class for the preservation of the capitalist system—to seize hold of the Jewish movement so as to subordinate the Jewish masses to the capitalist class, so as to keep the Jews separate from the general masses and thus apart from the class struggle. That is why the Jewish big bourgeoisie will be the most ready to accept any kind of "Popular Front" (one thinks offhand of the millionaire Leon Blum). The American Jewish Congress represents the type of movement in which the Jewish bourgeoisie attempt arbitrarily to seize the reins of leadership for this purpose. In such a "congress" our aim can be only one of exposure and the counterposing of our program as the real solution. That a real sentiment exists against yielding leadership to these outright betrayers is shown by the almost universal repudiation of the idea of a plebiscite to make this fake congress the sole spokesman for the American Jews. Only by exposing the machinations of the Jewish bourgeoisie can we enlist the Jewish masses on the side of the workers in the class struggle.

6. Stalinism and the Jews

The Jewish workers have not yet absorbed the lessons inherent in the Birobidjan fiasco.[24] We must direct special propaganda concerning Birobidjan among the Jewish Stalinists and their sympathizers. We must press home this example of how Stalin has once more made of Russia the "prison of the nations," how once again Moscow has become the administrative center holding the oppressor's whip, in this case that of the bureaucracy, over the nationalities. We must press home the fact that under Stalin Russia also closes its doors to the Jewish refugees. Every aspect of the wave of anti-Semitism in Russia must be exposed to view so as to break away the Jewish masses from the CP, the party of Cain.

---

24. Birobidjan was a section of the Russian republic, on the border of China, set aside by the Soviet government for colonization by the Jews in 1928. It was made an autonomous region in 1934. It later came under attack by Stalin, who claimed it had become a haven for opposition elements.

Nor is our analysis to be confined to Russia alone. The Stalinists must be reminded of how Captain Scheringer boasted in Germany just before Hitler came to power that there was not a single Jew on the Central Committee of the CPG. They must be reminded how—just as they confused the Social Democratic workers with the socialist bureaucracy in the "third period"—they lumped together the Jewish masses in Palestine with the hireling assistants of British imperialism, which led them to approve the attacks by the Arabs, encouraged, if not directly engineered, by the British themselves. Our attitude towards these events in Palestine is to point out the role of British imperialism in setting Arab against Jew and vice versa, and to distinguish between the Jewish masses, the Arab masses, and their respective exploiters.

7. The Jews, other national minorities, and the workers

The Jews form a small minority of the American population—some 4.5 million out of 130 million. If the defense of the Jews depended on themselves alone, then their case would indeed be hopeless. But here again the Jewish masses must be shown the bridge to our movement, that of the Fourth International. For it is primarily upon the American workers that the Jews must lean for support in their struggle to maintain their joint rights. Our propaganda against anti-Semitism is directed not to Jews but first of all to the American working class. It draws at every point the lesson that the attack against the Jews is merely the spearhead of the attack against the American working class for the purpose of lowering their standards of living and rendering them powerless to resist this economic blow by depriving them of their democratic rights. The workers and the Jewish masses are natural allies in the antifascist struggle. Our propaganda among both is to convince them to defeat fascism the workers must establish socialism. Not only the general working class is the natural ally of the Jews, but all the other national minorities—Mexicans, Chinese, Japanese, Greeks, Poles, Russians—who are assigned a lower status by the American ruling class, can be enlisted in the struggle for the rights of national minorities including the Jews. Above all the Negroes must be linked up with the struggle against reaction, for the Negroes are the worst victims of capitalist exploitation. Their struggle for equal rights is of the utmost importance for the workers' cause.

National chauvinism is the cover for social patriotism. The struggle of the workers aided by the oppressed nationalities against chauvinism must inevitably take account of social patriotism and the propaganda for support of the capitalist class and its government in imperialist war. The fostering of social patriotism in the ranks of the working class means the weakening of the struggle against fascism. The Stalinists pursue precisely this course of betrayal, which plays into the hands of reaction and weakens the workers' movement.

8. Transition program and the Jews

The transition program includes the necessity for building workers' defense groups. This idea can find especially fertile soil for implanting and for growth into reality among the Jewish masses. It goes without saying that such defense groups constituted under our influence must not consist of Jews alone. Nevertheless, we must take full advantage of the great concentration of the Jews in New York City to enlist as many as possible in such defense organizations. In this respect the situation in Jersey City[25] and its implications for the Jews need hardly be emphasized. Jewish organizations must be encouraged to set up defense groups, of which groups should be offered for aid to the workers' organizations. Similarly we must exert our influence wherever possible to have workers' defense groups come to the aid of the Jews when necessary.

9. Jewish youth

The Jewish youth are the first to bear the brunt of anti-Semitic discrimination. They feel this immediately in seeking jobs, and in the schools and colleges. Thus an especially intensive campaign must be carried on among the youth, who can be rapidly won to our cause. The intellectual Jewish youth in particular are placed in a position which makes them receptive to revolutionary propaganda. Among the youth it is particularly necessary to combat the Stalinist poison of fatalism—that fascism is inevitable. Only the Fourth International can dispel this discouragement and can inspire the youth to fight for victory.

10. Program of action

    a. Concentration of propaganda on the Jewish question in the press.
    b. Public meetings throughout the city and the country on the Jewish question.
    c. Work in Jewish mass organizations. Assignments for joining them.
    d. Literature in Yiddish.

---

25. The Jersey City government's assaults on the CIO at this time represented an incipient fascist danger, according to the SWP, which tried to enlist not only unions but also the unemployed and oppressed minorities in campaigns against the Frank Hague regime and its extralegal bands.

e. Special efforts to influence Jewish Labor Committee.
f. Defense committee work. Aid to refugees. Refugees to speak on experiences abroad.
g. Reconstitution of Jewish fractions.
h. Campaign for a Yiddish press.

Picket line at German consulate, November 1938.

Open the doors to victims of Hitler's Nazi terror![26]

by the SWP National Committee

The entire world has been shocked to the depths by the outburst of a new campaign of brutal violence against the Jews in Germany.

The hideous terror of Hitlerism has never struck with such cruel and merciless force.

Throughout Germany, bands of Nazi gangsters organized and commanded by their leaders, have wrecked and looted stores owned by Jews. Jewish churches—synagogues—have been burned and destroyed by the instructed fascist mobs. The workers of Germany, who hate and despise Hitlerism with all their strength, were unable to come to the aid of the brutalized Jews because they are themselves still in the straitjacket of the Nazi terror.

The brown-shirted monsters do not even bother to

---

26. Reprinted from *Socialist Appeal*, November 19, 1938. This call for united action by the American labor and radical movements was made on the heels of a mass pogrom against Jews in Nazi Germany.

conceal their aim: the physical extermination of every Jew in Great Germany.

Already a "fine" has been levied against the Jews which means in effect the complete confiscation of all their property and its distribution among the Nazi sadists.

The regime of the ghetto is to be restored in Germany by the complete segregation of all Jews into marked-off slums. With this measure, Hitlerism shows again that it means barbarism, the destruction of all civilized progress, the return to the shame and depravity of the Middle Ages.

Why are the Hitlerites increasing their murderous attack upon the Jews?

For two reasons:

They hope to take the minds of the German workers and peasants off the misery from which they suffer, to make them think that the Jews—traditional scapegoats for reaction—are responsible for all their ills.

They hope to blackmail the international protest movement against fascism into cowardly silence.

If they accomplish these dastardly aims, they can continue without the slightest opposition their rule of blood and iron.

If they accomplish their aims, they will encourage the fascist reaction in every other country of the world to advance more boldly, more insolently, more successfully.

They must not be allowed to succeed!

The workers of the United States must take the initiative in a mighty and effective protest against the Hitlerite pogroms.

Our answer must be not the cowardly silence of beaten dogs, but the thunderous protest of courageous and militant fighters for freedom and international solidarity!

To let the fascist massacres go unanswered is only to prepare for our own defeat and enslavement at the hands of fascist reaction in this country.

The first step of solidarity with the German Jews and the German workers must be a vast outpouring of the workers from every shop and factory and office into a mighty protest demonstration at which labor will give voice to its resounding indignation. The Socialist Workers Party urges the workers, especially of the needle-trade unions of New York, to have their unions take the initiative in organizing a half-day stoppage of work so that they may parade in a huge demonstration to the largest halls in the city.

Let the persecuted, gagged, and chained toilers of Germany, the cruelly hounded Jews of Naziland, know that they have not been forgotten or abandoned by the working class throughout the world.

But it is necessary to do more than demonstrate and meet in imposing gatherings.

It is imperative to take action—concrete action—immediate action!

The Hitlerites are making the Jews a people without a country! They are driving them out of Germany. Poland is hounding and persecuting the Jews, too, and is also preparing to drive them out of the country.

No European country agrees to give refuge to the hounded and harassed Jewish people.

It is therefore up to us to act so that they may at least find a home to live in.

The United States calls itself a democratic country. The president of the United States frequently speaks about his respect for democratic liberties and his opposition to "dictatorships." The Congress of the United States considers itself the guardian of those democratic liberties.

One of the most serious and important democratic liberties is the right of asylum for all those who are persecuted, for all refugees from terroristic reaction.

WE THEREFORE DEMAND:

Throw open the doors of the United States to the victims of the Hitlerite pogrom regime!

We urge all workers and other labor organizations:

Demand that the American government use its emergency powers to open the doors to the horribly persecuted Jews of Germany!

The right of asylum is an old, a traditional, a respected right in this country.

Let us join in demanding that this right be extended now to those who are most urgently in need of it, to those for whom it makes the difference between life and death.

Workers!

Solidarity with those who suffer at the hands of fascism is one of the best ways of establishing, in this country, an unbreakable wall against the advance of American fascism.

Unite! Join hands!

Show the Hitlerite assassins and pogromists the real position of American labor by your protest meetings!

Show them that the American working class means it seriously when it says that it detests anti-Semitism and the anti-Semites like the plague!

Show the victims of the fascist terror that you mean it seriously, by stretching out to them the hand of fraternal solidarity, by demanding of the American government the free and unrestricted right of asylum for the Jewish scapegoats of fascist barbarism!

PART 5
Minutes, SWP National Committee plenum

Minutes, SWP National Committee plenum

New York, November 19–20, 1938[1]

FIRST SESSION, NOVEMBER 19, 1938

NC members present: Abern, Burnham, Cannon, Carter, Clarke, Cochran, Dunne, Goldman, Jay, Lewit, McKinney, Morrow, Skoglund, Spector, Swabeck, Widick, YPSL—Draper.
NC members absent: Dobbs, Dullea, Kerry, Rosenberg, Saunders, Shachtman, Trimble, Weber.
NC alternates present: Morgan, Erber, Sherman, Turner.
Fraternal delegates present: YPSL—Anne Russell; James; Lebrun; Glenner.
By invitation: Wasserman, Roberts, S. Stanley, Kluger.

---

1. This plenum was the first since the end of the SWP membership referendum discussion and vote and since the founding of the Fourth International, both in September 1938. Recent international events included the Munich crisis over Czechoslovakia, sometimes referred to here as "the September war crisis," and a mass pogrom against the Jews in Germany. These minutes were published in mimeographed form by the SWP national office for internal use only.

Chairman: Goldman.

Motion by Cannon: That since Comrade Shachtman is absent, because of illness, the first point on the agenda be made a report by Comrade Widick on the CIO convention, to be followed by report and discussion on the trade union resolution. Carried.

Motion: That two comrades who had attended the CIO convention and were now here be admitted to that session of the plenum dealing with trade union; that they supplement Comrade Widick's report. Carried.

Motion: To adopt the agenda proposed by the PC.[2] Carried.

Motion: To adopt the procedure regarding attendance recommended by the PC.[3] Carried.

---

2. The proposed agenda was: (1) International report—reporter: Shachtman; (2) Report on party referendum on National Program of Action and disposition of amendments—reporter: Burnham; (3) Twice-a-week *Appeal*—reporter: Cannon; (4) Trade union resolution—reporter: Widick; (5) Organization report and Program of Practical Action—reporter: Cannon; (6) Jewish question—reporter: Weber; (7) Defense—reporter: Novack; (8) YPSL—reporter: Abern.

3. The Political Committee had proposed that all sessions of the plenum be executive sessions, and that invitations to attend be extended to the following: two fraternal delegates from the YPSL, official visiting representatives of the British and Argentinian sections, the secretary of the All-America Pacific Bureau, fraternal delegates from the Canadian section, and all national functionaries. In addition to NC members and alternates, the plenum was attended by Frank Demby and Yetta Barsh for the YPSL, with Anne Russell as alternate; C.L.R. James, a member of the British section and of the International Executive Committee of the Fourth International; A. Lebrun, a member of the Brazilian (not Argentinian) section and of the IEC; and national functionaries Jac Wasserman, Harold Roberts, Sherman Stanley, Pearl Kluger, and George Novack. Delegates from the Canadian section evidently did not attend. The two members who had attended the CIO convention and gave supplementary reports at the plenum were John Poulos of Lynn, Massachusetts, who had represented Restaurant, Beverage and Allied Food Workers, Local Industrial Union No. 701, and Liam Don-

CIO convention
Report by Widick on the CIO convention.
General discussion.
Supplementary report by two comrades present.
Session adjourned.

SECOND SESSION, NOVEMBER 19, 1938

NC members present: Abern, Burnham, Cannon, Carter, Clarke, Cochran, Dunne, Goldman, Jay, Lewit, McKinney, Morrow, Skoglund, Swabeck, Weber, Widick, YPSL—Draper.
NC members absent: Dobbs, Dullea, Kerry, Rosenberg, Saunders, Shachtman, Spector, Trimble.
NC alternates present: Morgan, Stevens, Erber, Sherman, Milton, Turner.
Fraternal delegates: YPSL—Demby, Barsh; alternate—Russell; James; Lebrun; Glenner.
By invitation: Wasserman, Roberts, Kluger, Novack.
Chairman: Goldman.
Burnham on procedure: Several questions to come up before the plenum for which no provision has been made on the agenda. Question as to when they are to be taken up. Laid over.

Trade union resolution
Report by Widick on trade union resolution. (Resolution attached [page 443].)
General discussion.
Motion by Draper: That we lay over discussion of that

---

lon of Northampton, Massachusetts, who had represented Pulp and Paper Workers, Local Industrial Union No. 886.

sentence in the trade union resolution ("Above all, the sending of youth comrades into industry and a drastic revision of the present orientation of the YPSL with its preponderance of nonproletarian activity is imperative.") until the resolution on the YPSL is taken up. Carried.

Motion by Lewit: That we adopt the trade union resolution, with the above exception. Carried. Jay recorded as opposed.

Motion by Goldman: That the Political Committee be instructed to draw up either a short resolution, an editorial statement, or articles for the press, which would deal only with the question of trade union activity, taking into consideration the events of the past year. Carried.

Burnham on procedure: That the question of appeals from the Political Committee decisions (N.Y. elections, California pension plan)[4] be taken up at the end of point 2 on the agenda.

---

4. In September 1938, before Cannon and Shachtman had returned from Europe, the Political Committee, at Burnham's initiative, told the New York local that in the congressional elections that year the SWP should "give specific critical support to all independent candidates of the ALP, irrespective of whether such candidates have also received endorsement by any other parties or groups." This would have meant supporting ALP candidates endorsed by the Democrats or Republicans and running on their tickets. When Cannon and Shachtman were attending PC meetings again, this question was reopened, and a motion was passed to "support candidates who are running only on the ALP ticket and not on the tickets of the Republican, Democratic, or Fusion parties, that is, not on the tickets of any bourgeois parties." It was this decision that Burnham wanted the plenum to override. Also adopted by the PC in September was a proposal that the SWP in California support a $30-every-Thursday pension plan which was on the state ballot in November. Shortly before the plenum Cannon and Shachtman tried to get the PC to reconsider this support, but their motion was defeated. It was this PC decision that they wanted the plenum to override.

Amendment by Cannon: That the question of the California pension plan be taken up under point 5a on the agenda. Carried.

Carter on procedure: Comrades Burnham and Carter have a special point of view to present that should be discussed under the international report.

Ruling from the chair: That this point of view can come up under the international report.

Amendments

Report by Burnham.

Motion by Burnham: That his report as to the technical disposition of the amendments be adopted. Carried. (Report attached [page 451].)

Substitute motion by Jay: Because of the very small vote cast in the referendum, showing that the membership did not express its will, that the entire question of the referendum (international thesis, program of action, and labor party resolution) be tabled until our next convention where it will be taken up for consideration. Lost.

Appeals from decisions of Political Committee

New York City election policy: General discussion.

Motion by Burnham: The plenum upholds the original position of the Political Committee, in the problem of the New York elections, to give critical support to all ALP candidates irrespective of endorsement or lack of endorsement by other parties, while rejecting support of candidates of bourgeois parties endorsed by the ALP; and the plenum considers incorrect the reversal by the Political Committee to the position of giving support only to candidates appearing on the ALP and no other ticket. At the same time the plenum does not consider it possible to set up a universal rule on this problem. The tactic must be decided concretely, in the light of the general aim of deepening the movement for independent working-class political action. Lost: for 1, against 23.

Jay voting against with the following statement: Against the support of any ALP candidates on the grounds that the ALP is nothing more than a reformist party.

Motion by Goldman: In view of the specific circumstances prevailing at the time of the N.Y. election and in view of the necessity for our party to strengthen the movement for independent political action amongst the workers, the plenum endorses the action of the Political Committee in supporting critically only those candidates running on the ALP ticket and not on the tickets of any bourgeois parties. In doing so, the plenum does not set up a principle applicable at all times and under all conditions. Carried: for 22, against 2. Burnham recorded against. Jay recorded against with same statement as on the Burnham motion.

Session adjourned.

THIRD SESSION, NOVEMBER 19, 1938

NC members present: Abern, Burnham, Cannon, Carter, Clarke, Cochran, Dunne, Goldman, Jay, Lewit, McKinney, Morrow, Rosenberg, Skoglund, Spector, Swabeck, Weber, Widick.

NC members absent: Dobbs, Dullea, Kerry, Saunders, Shachtman, Trimble, YPSL—Draper.

NC alternates present: Morgan, Stevens, Erber, Sherman, Turner.

Fraternal delegates: YPSL—Demby, Barsh; James; Lebrun; Glenner.

By invitation: Wasserman, Roberts, Stanley, Kluger, Novack. Chairman: Goldman.

Sliding scale of wages
Widick-Burnham amendment to the slogan "sliding scale of wages":

The basic idea expressed in the thesis "The Death Agony of Capitalism and the Tasks of the Fourth International" on the question of wages indubitably is correct. It says: "The Fourth International declares uncompromising war on the politics of the capitalists which, to a considerable degree, like the politics of their agents, the reformists, aims to place the whole burden of militarism, the crises, the disorganization of the monetary system and all other scourges stemming from capitalism's death agony upon the backs of the toilers. The Fourth International demands *employment* and *decent living conditions* for all.

"Neither monetary inflation nor stabilization can serve as slogans for the proletariat because these are but two ends of the same stick. Against a bounding rise in prices, which with the approach of war will assume an ever more unbridled character, one can fight only under the slogan of *a sliding scale of wages*. This means that collective agreements should assure an automatic rise in wages in relation to the increase in price of consumer goods."

Closely connected with this question is the slogan of a sliding scale of hours about which the thesis states: "Against unemployment, 'structural' as well as 'conjunctural,' the time is ripe to advance, along with the slogan of public works, the slogan of *a sliding scale of working hours*. Trade unions and other mass organizations should bind the workers and the unemployed together in the solidarity of mutual responsibility. On this basis all the work on hand would then be divided among all existing workers in accordance with how the extent of the working week is defined. The average wage of each worker remains the same as it was under the old working week. Wages, under the strictly guaranteed *minimum*, would follow the movement of prices. It is impossible to accept any other program for the present catastrophic period."

The timeliness of these basic ideas has been amply demonstrated by the actions of the American workers in the recent period. Outstanding example of this is the series of auto strikes for a 32-hour week. Previously in the rubber industry, major plants reduced to 30 and, in some cases, to a 24-hour week in an effort to help solve the unemployment problem under union pressure. Yet these movements have had a very serious weakness. The question of keeping the old rate of weekly wages despite reduced hours was not treated by the trade unions. As a result, a strong tendency within the unions rejected the idea of a shorter workweek, of a sliding scale of hours. A reactionary sentiment against the unemployed worker is inevitable unless the question of wages is solved too. The answer is obvious. Reduce hours, but keep the present weekly wage rate. Only this can answer the problems confronting the auto, rubber, steel, and other industrial unions. Yet this idea, presented under the slogan of a sliding scale of wages, does not meet with response. Such has been the experience of Akron, and perhaps elsewhere. In our opinion, the present slogan gives a negative approach to the question. Workers take the idea of sliding scale of wages to mean perhaps the same thing. The term *sliding* has the connotation of "going down." It is necessary to give this basic idea a positive approach, one which fits the experience and understanding of the workers. And that approach can be obtained by using the slogan: "a rising scale of wages." The slogan, "sliding scale of wages" allows for the possibility of either a rise or fall in wages. We are interested only in raising wages always. A more aggressive and appealing tone is obtained in the slogan of a rising scale of wages. It takes the question of higher wages, in which the workers are keenly interested, and gives it a broader meaning, carrying with it revolutionary implications which can readily be explained and thus find acceptance among the masses of workers.

Furthermore, it must be understood that the basic content of the conception of "a sliding scale of wages and hours" is contained in a variety of slogans that are arising within the labor movement: e.g., "reduce hours with no reduction in wages"; "thirty-hour week with no wage reduction"; etc. Our support of the basic conception also comprises support of these specific slogans having the same content and direction; and we understand these as aspects of the Transitional Program to which we are committed.

Motion by Goldman: That the question of proper slogans to give effect to the idea of sliding scale of wages and hours be referred to the Political Committee for decision. Carried: 17 for.

Burnham and Widick not voting with the following statement: The motion in this form settles none of the issues which have been arising.

Amendment by Burnham: That in its consideration of the matter referred to it, the Political Committee is instructed to revise specifically the slogan "For a sliding scale of wages." Withdrawn.

Amendment by Burnham: That it is understood that the opinion of the National Committee is that the slogan "a sliding scale of wages" does not accomplish the purpose. Lost: for 6, against 12.[5]

Twice-a-week Appeal
Report by Cannon. (Resolution attached [page 455].)
Discussion.
Motion: To adjourn at 10:30 p.m., go to the YPSL dance in a body, and reconvene at 11 a.m. tomorrow. Carried.

FOURTH SESSION, NOVEMBER 20, 1938

NC members present: Abern, Burnham, Cannon, Carter, Clarke, Cochran, Dullea, Dunne, Goldman, Jay, Lewit, McKinney, Morrow, Rosenberg, Shachtman, Skoglund, Spector, Swabeck, Weber, Widick.
NC members absent: Dobbs, Kerry, Saunders, Trimble, YPSL—Draper.
NC alternates present: Morgan, Stevens, Erber, Sherman, Milton, Turner.
Fraternal delegates: YPSL—Barsh; James; Lebrun; Glenner.

---

5. When the Political Committee took up the plenum motion directing it to develop proper slogans to give effect to the idea of sliding scale of wages and hours, there was a general PC discussion in January 1939 which led Burnham to change his mind, at least partly. He then introduced a motion that was adopted by the PC: "We interpret the slogan of Sliding Scale of Wages and Hours as contained in the transition program as a general formula, summing up our conception of the problem therein referred to and the manner of meeting it. In the light of this conception we work out our concrete slogans on the basis (a) of slogans which communicate dramatically and easily to the masses our perspective; (b) more concrete slogans, in addition, to meet the specific problems of specific industries, branches of employment, or localities."

By invitation: Wasserman, Roberts, Stanley, Kluger, Novack.
Chairman: Goldman.

Twice-a-week Appeal
Discussion continued.
Motion: To adopt the resolution on the twice-a-week *Appeal*.
    Carried. Against: Stevens. Abstaining: Sherman, Burnham, Cochran.
Amendment by Burnham: (to point 1 of the resolution.) Instead of publishing the *Appeal* twice a week, we increase the present size of the *Appeal* to eight pages to be published once a week. Lost: for 5, against 17.
Proposal by Cannon: That we ask the PC members to come in with a recommendation regarding the balance of the agenda at the beginning of the next session. Accepted.
Session adjourned.

FIFTH SESSION, NOVEMBER 20, 1938

NC members present: Abern, Burnham, Cannon, Carter, Clarke, Cochran, Dullea, Dunne, Goldman, Jay, Lewit, McKinney, Morrow, Rosenberg, Shachtman, Skoglund, Spector, Swabeck, Weber, Widick.
NC members absent: Dobbs, Kerry, Saunders, Trimble, YPSL—Draper.
NC alternates present: Morgan, Stevens, Erber, Sherman, Milton, Turner.
Fraternal delegates: YPSL—Demby, Barsh; James; Lebrun; Glenner.
By invitation: Roberts, Kluger, Novack.
Chairman: Goldman.
Recommendation on procedure: That we finish the plenum tonight, at a late session; that we limit the reports to

fifteen minutes each, discussion speeches to five minutes.
Motion to adopt. Carried.

Organizational report and program of practical action
Report by Cannon. (Resolution attached [page 459].)
General discussion.
Resolution presented by Clarke:

> With the exception of the Newark local, the party failed to conduct any serious activity in the various state campaigns recently concluded. No SWP candidates appeared on the ballot—save for Newark where the party made a splendid showing—in any of the state, congressional, or local contests.
>
> Write-in campaigns have in all cases proved ineffective and roused little or no interest among the workers. In several states, it was possible to place at least one party candidate on the ballot, but these opportunities were uniformly missed.
>
> Responsibility for this failure rests with the Political Committee. Parliamentary activity is a vital part of our work and our program. Serious efforts must be made to correct the faults evidenced in the recent campaign.

Motion to adopt above resolution. Carried.
Motion by Demby: To establish a national educational department with a member of the National Committee in charge; that a national finance department be established.
Motion by Carter: That an organizational bulletin be issued for the use of the branches.
Motion by McKinney: That all these matters be referred to the Political Committee. Carried.
Comrade Cannon excused to fill a speaking engagement made before the postponement of the plenum.

International report
Report on international congress and resolution. (Attached [page 463].)
Supplementary reports by Comrades James and Lebrun.
Statement by Burnham and Carter on the section of the thesis, "The Death Agony of Capitalism," dealing with the regime in the Soviet Union:

The discussion on the problem of the nature of the regime in the Soviet Union is at present suspended in both our national section and in the international organization. We wish to express formally at this time our continuing adherence to our point of view on this issue previously put forward (namely, that the Soviet Union can no longer be regarded as a workers' state), a point of view which the events of the past year have served only to deepen and reinforce, and consequently our disagreement with this section of the thesis; and, further, our intention to present our point of view once more as soon as the opportunity for further discussion is at hand.

Amendment to the international resolution by Burnham:

The following paragraph appears in the thesis, "The Death Agony of Capitalism": "The bureaucracy replaced the soviets as class organs with the fiction of universal electoral rights—in the style of Hitler-Goebbels. It is necessary to return to the soviets not only their free democratic form but also their class content. As once the bourgeoisie and kulaks were not permitted to enter the soviets, so now *it is necessary to drive the bureaucracy and the new aristocracy out of the soviets*. In the soviets there is room only for the representatives of the workers, rank-and-file collective farmers, peasants, and Red Army personnel."

The specific position put forward in this paragraph has never been discussed in either our national section or in the international organization. While accepting the thesis as a whole as the officially adopted resolution of the international congress, and therefore the position of our party, the plenum, in the name of the SWP specifically suspends any declaration of agreement or disagreement with this paragraph, and submits it for educational discussion and clarification to the membership.

Lost: for 3, against 18. Sherman abstaining.
Reported by Shachtman, and in supplementary discussion by Comrades James and Lebrun, that the international congress had voted down the recommendation of the American delegation, as instructed by motion of the PC, to withhold decision on this particular paragraph.[6]
Amendment by Shachtman to international resolution:

The following paragraph appears in the thesis, "The Death Agony of Capitalism": "The bureaucracy replaced

---

6. On July 21, the Political Committee rejected a motion by Carter that it adopt his amendment to eliminate from the Transitional Program the two sentences about driving the bureaucracy and new aristocracy out of the soviets. On August 4 the PC tabled two motions on the same subject by Burnham, who supported the Carter amendment, and then adopted a substitute motion by Shachtman: "Since the policy and slogan in these two sentences of the international thesis have never been discussed either by the national or international organization, action on them for the time being is suspended. Our delegates to the international conference are instructed to advocate postponement of definitive action on them, together with provisions for subsequent decision by the international organization. Discussion on the position in question shall be opened in our own organization, and decision on the disposal of the matter shall be referred to the next plenum of the National Committee." Trotsky's attitude toward the position held by Carter is expressed in *The Transitional Program for Socialist Revolution*.

the soviets as class organs with the fiction of universal electoral rights—in the style of Hitler-Goebbels. It is necessary to return to the soviets not only their free democratic form but also their class content. As once the bourgeoisie and kulaks were not permitted to enter the soviets, so now *it is necessary to drive the bureaucracy and the new aristocracy out of the soviets*. In the soviets there is room only for the representatives of the workers, rank-and-file collective farmers, peasants, and Red Army personnel."

Since the international conference provided for an international discussion of this paragraph, the plenum of the SWP instructs the PC to provide for an educational discussion of the question.

Carter: Question on procedure: If Comrade Burnham's amendment is defeated, I want to introduce an amendment to Comrade Shachtman's major motion.
Ruling by the chair: That Comrade Carter's motion will be in order.
Motion by Carter: The plenum expresses its disagreement with the following section of the thesis: (See section quoted above).
Clarke: Point of order: This is out of order.
Abern: Motion to table.
Burnham: Point of order: Comrade Carter has the floor to speak on his motion.
Cochran: Point of order: Motion has been made to lay on the table, nobody has the floor.
Ruling by the chair: If Comrade Carter insists on his right to speak, it has to be granted to him.
Carter: Propose supper recess and return to discuss the question. Ruled out of order.
Burnham: Point of personal privilege: I want to suggest,

by agreement, a recess which is needed now in any case, to see if we can't dispose of this question in a more dignified manner.

Shachtman: Motion to grant. Carried.

Session adjourned for 30 minutes.

SIXTH SESSION, NOVEMBER 20, 1938

NC members present: Abern, Burnham, Cannon, Carter, Clarke, Cochran, Dullea, Dunne, Goldman, Lewit, McKinney, Morrow, Rosenberg, Shachtman, Skoglund, Spector, Swabeck, Weber, Widick.

NC members absent: Dobbs, Jay, Kerry, Saunders, Trimble, YPSL—Draper.

Fraternal delegates: YPSL—Demby, Barsh; Lebrun; Glenner.

By invitation: Kluger, Novack.

Chairman: Goldman

International (continued)

Statement by Burnham and Carter (endorsed by Spector):

The question of the character of the new soviets in Russia involves intimately and directly the whole problem of socialist democracy. This question came before the plenum through the wording of the international resolution, the events of the party referendum, and the specific actions of the international conference as related by the reporter.

The procedure proposed in our amendment to the international resolution was the only serious, responsible, and democratic approach to the disposition and handling of this question as it stands at present, an approach which at the same time guaranteed the integrity of individual and collective political views, and the discipline and authority of the international and national organizations.

The rejection of the amendment by the plenum was both irresponsible and a gross violation of the genuine content of party democracy.

Both because of the time limitations and more particularly of the attitude of the committee members, it is impossible to initiate a serious discussion of this problem at this time.

Because of our basic disagreement with the positions given in the paragraph under dispute, we are unable to vote for the international resolution.

Motion by Burnham: In light of the above statement, move to table Carter's motion. Carried.

Motion: To adopt the international resolution. Carried: for 13, not voting 3—Burnham, Carter, and Spector with above statement.

Shachtman: Reserves the right to make a statement in connection with his vote.[7]

Motion by Lebrun: Recognizing the absolute necessity of maintaining regular international connections, and the prime importance for the development of the Fourth International of a revolutionary leadership capable of ensuring regular and politically authoritative

---

7. After the plenum, at a PC meeting December 12, 1938, Shachtman made a motion: "On the paragraph in the international program on the Russian question which was in dispute at the Plenum, the next circular to the branches shall contain the information that the pages of the *New International* and the discussion bulletin are open for a free discussion of the question." This motion was adopted, but neither the magazine nor the bulletin printed any articles on the subject, probably because none were submitted.

work, the plenum approves the designation by the congress of Comrade Trent for the IS and asks the Political Committee to take steps necessary for the sending of Comrade Trent to Europe. Carried.[8]

Motion: To elect the third member to the International Executive board from the American section. Carried. Anderson nominated.[9] (Further action tabled.)

Resolution on YPSL
Report by Abern (Resolution attached [page 467].)

International
Motion by Goldman: That the Political Committee be instructed to issue a manifesto in connection with the Pan-American Conference to be held at Lima, calling upon all the Latin American peoples and the workers of North and South America to join in a struggle against United States imperialism. Carried.[10]

YPSL
Report by Carter on his resolution. (Attached [page 477].)

---

8. The founding conference of the Fourth International assigned Shachtman (using the pseudonym Trent) to membership on the International Secretariat in Europe. The PC agreed to release Shachtman for this work, but the transfer was never completed.

9. Two leaders of the SWP were elected to the 15-member International Executive Committee at the founding conference of the Fourth International (Cannon and Shachtman) and the delegates instructed the SWP leadership to elect a third member of the IEC after the conference. This decision reflected not only the prestige of the SWP in the International but also the belief that war was imminent and that the International center might soon have to be moved from Paris to the United States, where a strong nucleus of the IEC would have added responsibilities. Anderson, who was elected to the open IEC post by this plenum, was Carl Skoglund of Minneapolis.

10. For the manifesto on Lima, see page 451.

Motion by Erber: That the national office of the party secure and mail to all NC members the resolutions and documents of the YPSL convention, together with the report of the party delegation. Carried.

Motion by Demby: To reaffirm the previous decisions of the Political Committee on the YPSL, and the plenum binds the delegation to the YPSL convention to carry out these decisions. Carried.

Motion: To adopt the resolution on the YPSL presented by the Political Committee, eliminating the one word (Boston). Carried: for 23, against 1.

Motion: To adopt the resolution submitted by Carter. Lost: for 2, against 22.

Motion by Cannon: To approve the greetings to the YPSL convention sent by the national secretary in the name of the plenum. Carried.

International

Election of third member to International Executive Committee. Anderson elected unanimously.

Trade union resolution

Motion by Lewit: To eliminate the sentence: "Above all, the sending of youth comrades into industry and a drastic revision of the present orientation of the YPSL with its preponderance of nonproletarian activity is imperative." Carried.

International

Statement by Shachtman, Sherman, Widick: Our votes to endorse and approve the theses and resolutions of the world conference do not imply agreement, or for that matter, disagreement, with the formulations contained in the paragraph on the Russian question at issue.

Motion on procedure by Cannon: That we refer the following points on the agenda: Jewish, defense, and unemployment, to the Political Committee; that the question of the California pension plan be submitted to the plenum members for a referendum by mail, with arguments on both sides, and the decision of the referendum be regarded as the decision of the plenum. Carried.[11]

Slogan—'workers' and farmers' government'
Motion on procedure by Lewit: That we have two speakers on each side, 15 minutes each. Carried.
Shachtman: Speaking for the slogan: "workers' government."
Weber: Speaking for the slogan: "workers' and farmers' government."
Motion: That we submit the question for further arguments on both sides by mail, and a mail vote be taken.
Motion by Morrow: That an immediate vote be taken.
Substitute motion by Goldman: That we instruct the

---

11. The "Jewish Question" point referred to the PC was not taken up until March 1939, when it adopted a motion by Lewit to dissolve the Jewish subcommittee and replace it with a Jewish bureau that would "undertake national Jewish work" and seek to establish a monthly publication in the Yiddish language. But the personnel of the approved bureau was not selected that day, and no further reference to it could be found in the minutes. The "Defense" point came up at a PC meeting in December 1938 which adopted the resolution on page 481 of this book. The "Unemployment" point came up at a meeting in December where the PC adopted the resolution on page 483. In a referendum by mail, held in February 1939, the NC voted not to give critical support to the California pension plan; the exact vote was never reported to the NC, PC, or branches. The issue was reopened when the plan was again put on the California ballot later in 1939. This time the new NC, which had been elected in July 1939, voting in another mail referendum in August 1939, approved a motion by Burnham to give critical support to the plan. The vote was 12 to 5, with 1 abstention.

Political Committee to gather all the material and the opinions of the members of the NC; that this material be sent to the members of the NC; that a time limit be set after which a mail vote be taken.

Motion by Cannon: That we conduct a referendum in the NC on this question; all comrades who want to submit arguments must do so within three weeks; that the vote must be completed two weeks after this period expires; the decision of the NC becomes the position of the party. Carried.[12]

Motion by Goldman on procedure: In order to make the work of future plenums more efficient and more

---

12. The NC held a referendum on workers' government versus workers' and farmers' government at the same time as its referendum on the California pension plan in February 1939. Before the voting the NC put out a special internal bulletin for NC members with arguments pro and con on both these disputes; this bulletin appeared in January. The results of this referendum were never reported to the PC, NC, or branches, nor does anything in the SWP minutes or other papers indicate how the vote went. An examination of the resolutions submitted for the second convention (July 1939) and the third convention (April 1940) did not turn up the use of either governmental slogan. An examination of all the editorials in the *Socialist Appeal* and the New International and of all SWP pamphlets put out by Pioneer Publishers, from February 1939 until October 1940, showed that governmental slogans were not used often and that when they were used the formulation was workers' government one half the time and workers' and farmers' government the other half. In October 1940, six months after Shachtman and Burnham, the chief proponents of workers' government, had split from the SWP, the PC adopted a series of slogans to be printed regularly in the *Socialist Appeal* as a popular summary of the SWP program. The last of this series was "For a workers' and farmers' government," which was the formulation used in SWP convention resolutions, election platforms, pamphlets, and articles during the next twenty-seven years. In 1967 an SWP convention voted to change it to "For a workers' government." In 1982 the SWP National Committee voted to change the slogan back to "For a workers' and farmers' government."

fruitful, the PC is instructed to present the agenda of and resolutions to be submitted to any plenum to all members and alternates of the National Committee at least one week prior to the holding of the plenum. Carried.

Plenum adjourned.

DOCUMENTS

Trade union resolution[13]

1. A marked trend towards unity has been an outstanding feature of the developments in the American labor movement in the recent period. It was expressed clearly in the events of the AFL convention, where the progressive revolt of a large section of the membership, especially the Teamsters union, against the reactionary policies of the "diehard" clique in the executive council was revealed. The action of international unions of the CIO, of state CIO councils, and local unions, calling for unity with the AFL was another manifestation of this trend. Roosevelt administration pressure for unity, as part of his strategy of achieving national unity in wartime, has increased tremendously following the September war crisis. The swing to the right in the off-year elections has further

---

13. Reprinted from *Socialist Appeal*, November 26, 1938. The reporter and principal author of this resolution was B.J. Widick, SWP labor secretary. It was adopted by the plenum with only one vote against.

443

served to strengthen sentiment for the unification of the CIO and the AFL; both organizations feel themselves to be in greater jeopardy from reactionary forces consolidated in Congress to foist union-smashing legislation on the divided labor movement. The hegemony of the industrial workers in the American labor movement, as reflected in the increase in industrial unions within the AFL, the growth of power of the large truckdrivers' international union with its pro-unity sympathies, and the permanence of the CIO, has served to aid the shift in the direction of unity, because of the vital needs of this decisive force in the labor movement.

In light of these developments, we strongly reiterate our unequivocal support of unity in the labor movement, and reiterate the following considerations from our convention trade union resolution: "Although it is impossible for us at the present time to influence decisively the course of events, or to determine the pace and method of trade union unity, we are nevertheless bound to concentrate our propaganda and agitational activity among the workers in favor of the most desirable basis for unity, that is, democratic organization and a wide measure of autonomy for the affiliated unions, especially such a measure as would facilitate the organization of the basic industries into industrial unions and preserve the integrity of those already in existence. Every attempt to carve up the industrial unions into craft formations must be stubbornly resisted as thoroughly reactionary."

2. Basing itself on the numerically greater dues-paying AFL membership in comparison to the CIO, and the increase of Stalinist influence in alliance with John L. Lewis, there has arisen a certain tendency within our own ranks which can best be described as "pro-AFLism." It has appeared in some of the trade union publications influenced

by our comrades and in some policy proposals in certain instances. This attitude is false. In spite of specific tactics in separate union situations, dictated by exceptional circumstances, and though avoiding any "organizational fetishism," we have been, and remain, *pro-CIO*. The key to a thorough understanding of and support for the CIO lies in recognizing that it is primarily a social movement reflecting the needs, desires, and aspirations (even if often in distorted form) of the most decisive sections of the industrial proletariat. Historically, it remains a progressive break from the conservative and antiquated traditions of the AFL. The future of the American labor movement depends on the success of this mass movement of industrial unionism in the economic field, and its development on the political field as the leading force in an independent working-class political party.

3. While our propaganda and agitation for the creation of a labor party is a very important task of the party primarily in the trade unions, it must be accompanied by the equally important struggle for the popularization of our program of transitional demands as a vital part of our strategy of rallying the workers against the blows of the social crisis on the economic and political fields. The inescapable contradictions of the present policies of the trade union movement in seeking to alleviate the miseries inherent in a decaying capitalist society within the framework of that reactionary society, open the way for fruitful activity of our party centering around the slogans of (1) Sliding scale of hours and wages; (2) Open the idle factories; (3) Workers' defense guards, and other demands contained in the Transitional Program.

4. One of the gravest dangers to the labor movement has been the deadly alliance of John L. Lewis and other CIO bureaucrats with the reactionary Stalinist machine.

Despite protests of an ever increasing section of the CIO movement, the criminal and irresponsible policies of the Stalinists were forced down the throats of important unions with the aid of John L. Lewis. The ruinous practices of Harry Bridges, West Coast CIO director, brought a spontaneous revolt of progressive unionists which was temporarily defeated only by drastic intervention of John Brophy, Stalinist CIO director.[14] The autonomy of the auto workers' union has been seriously jeopardized and all progressive tendencies within that union badly crippled by the infamous bloc of Lewis and the Stalinists. Everywhere within the CIO and other unions, the Stalinists hound and seek to destroy genuine progressive and revolutionary workers who resist their "rule or ruin" policy with its warmongering, dictated by the needs of the Soviet bureaucracy, and who seek to tie the American labor movement to the Roosevelt war machine in return for a Stalin-Roosevelt bloc. Ruthless disregard of vital union democracy, slandering and framing of progressives, creation of a dictatorial-bureaucratic structure for the CIO: these are the methods of the Stalinist agents within the labor movement.

5. Blocs with non-Stalinist workers, and even with conservative elements genuinely interested in saving the union movement from destruction at Stalinist hands are not only permissible but at times necessary. While always expanding our own program independently and maintaining our right of criticism, our party, in a certain sense, supports the "lesser evil" within the trade unions. Stalinists are the main enemy in the present instance

---

14. CIO director John Brophy was not a Stalinist although, like Lewis and some of the other CIO officials, he cooperated with them closely at this time.

because of the deadly role of this cancerous force within the unions. In order to save the unions from destruction, we unite with all serious elements to exclude the agents of Stalinism from control of unions. It must be emphasized that our tactic of a "lesser evil" within the unions has nothing in common with its reactionary namesake on the parliamentary field. We are interested in preserving the unions from destruction and that is the basis for the "lesser evil" tactic in the unions. Even union conservatives have a common interest in this aim, at least to the extent of wishing to preserve the unions, which are their own sole basis, from actual destruction, and a united front with them on this basis is correct. But in the political field, we have no interest in preserving capitalism and its state. Quite the contrary, we seek to destroy it through revolutionary action.

Our action, for example, in supporting the Martin administration, as against the Stalinists, in the auto workers' union was based on these considerations. It was correct to seek to preserve that union from the Stalinist disrupters. In our failure to give sufficiently clear criticism of certain reactionary maneuvers of the Martin forces, we did not, however, draw a sharp enough line between our program and the limited program of Martin and his allies. Our role in the auto struggle was tactically sound but incomplete as a result.[15]

---

15. Homer Martin was president of the UAW from 1936 to 1939. At the 1937 UAW convention, the Trotskyists gave critical support to a CP-led caucus against Martin. In early 1938, however, the political lineup in the union changed. In response to a Stalinist bid for power, Martin adopted a militant program to win support from the ranks. SWP members supported this development. After the Stalinists had been defeated, however, Martin began to move rapidly to the right. By the end of 1938, the SWP was sharply criticizing Martin and when he led

6. Nevertheless, in combating Stalinism in blocs with other tendencies, we must resist the swing of the workers, disillusioned by their experiences of Stalinism, toward syndicalist conceptions and against "politics" and political parties in general. These reactionary tendencies, which only disarm the workers in the struggle against capitalism, must be fought by the Marxist party.

7. While the most important and largest field of our trade union activity remains at present in the Minneapolis area, there have been other labor centers where modest but definite progress has been recorded. In Lynn, Massachusetts, in the CIO movement. In steel in New Jersey and elsewhere; the painters and maritime workers in New York City; the development of a cadre in auto; the activity in Akron—these are a few of the places where our work is integrating the movement with the trade unions and building the party.

8. Experience has shown the need for greater *concentration* of our work in those unions and centers where roots already have been established or concrete prospects are opened up. Intensification of our party work around these areas rather than a diffusion of our limited forces over the whole field must be the guiding system of organizing our trade union work in the future. Colonization of comrades into these places should be an integral part of this program of action, wherever possible.[16]

---

a pro-AFL split in early 1939, the SWP auto fraction resolutely opposed it. This latter event precipitated what became known in SWP history as the "auto crisis." For more information, see "The Truth About the Auto Crisis" by George Clarke in *Background to "The Struggle for a Proletarian Party"* (Pathfinder, 1979).

16. For reasons not stated in the minutes, the plenum deleted the following sentence from the resolution at this point: "Above all, the

9. There has been an improved coordination of national trade union work in the past period despite the big obstacle presented by lack of finances for the trade union department, which made it impossible for the labor secretary to function for four months during the summer in NYC. A national steel fraction, covering New Jersey, Ohio, East Chicago, and Connecticut has begun to function. Maritime work has been improved somewhat on a national scale. Exchange of information, advice, and policy has been given in the field, to a greater or lesser degree. However, any really satisfactory trade union work on a national scale must be based on adequate support of this department. Means must be found to place the party labor secretary on a full-time basis.

10. Our advances in trade union work are reflected in the party press. The increasing news and attention given to labor events in the *Socialist Appeal* are one manifestation of the progress made in the direction of a trade union orientation. Even greater attention of the party must be devoted to this question. Activizing the non–trade union comrades around this work; giving the party a much stronger proletarian character; recruiting in the unions through the good work of the fractions: these are the problems which the party must solve in the coming period.

---

sending of youth comrades into industry and a drastic revision of the present orientation of the YPSL with its preponderance of nonproletarian activity is imperative."

Report on amendments to resolutions acted upon by party referendum[17]

The spring session of the NC made no explicit provisions for amendments to the resolutions which were to be offered for vote in the party referendum. Nevertheless, amendments were in fact presented, by members of the NC, party branches, and individual party members.

There were four amendments to the international thesis, one to the Program of Action, and three to the resolution on the labor party. With the exception of the Goldman amendment to the labor party resolution, the total ballots—including "for," "against," and "abstained"—cast were less than one-half of the ballots cast in the case of the

---

17. From plenum material supplied to the members when they arrived. The reporter and author was James Burnham. There was general dissatisfaction in the party with the referendum as a way of settling important political questions and with the relatively low vote on the resolutions as well as the amendments, but the Burnham report was adopted after a substitute motion to table all results of the referendum to the next convention received only one vote.

resolutions to which they were proposed as amendments.

Postponing consideration of the Goldman amendment, this voting is sufficient indication that either the permitting of amendments in referendum votes is unworkable or that at the very least in these specific cases the amendments were not comprehensible to the membership and the membership was consequently unable to express its will with respect to them.

The amendments in question are: the Carter amendment to the international thesis (contained in bulletin no. 6); the resolution of the South Side branch, Chicago, on the international thesis (bulletin no. 7); a brief amendment to the international resolution submitted by the Upper West Side branch, New York; an amendment to the international resolution submitted by Comrade Burch of the Lower East Side branch, New York (bulletin no. 7); the Cannon amendment to the Program of Action (bulletin no. 2); the Louisville resolution on the labor party (bulletin no. 7); an amendment to the labor party resolution submitted by Comrade Sanders of the North Side branch, Chicago.

On the grounds given above, I propose that all of these be ruled out of order by the plenum of the NC.

The total ballots cast on the Goldman amendment to the labor party resolution exceeded half of the total on the resolution proper. I propose that this vote be ruled in order, and that in accordance with the vote the Goldman amendment be declared *lost*.

In spite of the technical ruling, however, the subject matter of three of the amendments should properly come before this meeting of the NC for disposition in some manner or another. (The remainder are either of secondary rhetorical importance, or contrary to the main sense of the resolutions carried in the referendum.) These three are the Burch amendment dealing with the slogan of "the sliding scale of wages"; the Cannon amendment, proposing the slogan "a workers' and farmers' government"; and the Carter amendment dealing with the slogan of "drive the bureaucracy out of the soviets." It is my understanding that proposals will be made to the NC on each of these subjects.

Resolution on twice-weekly 'Socialist Appeal'[18]

For some time the party has been considering the problem of expanding our press to meet the requirements of intensified political work projected in our Transitional Program. The heavy tasks imposed upon us by the general situation necessitate, and the resources of our growing movement make possible, a decisive strengthening of our most important weapon—the *Socialist Appeal*. The time has come for a bold step forward.

Therefore, after due consideration of the matter, and after consultation with the party branches, the plenum

---

18. From plenum material supplied to the members. The reporter and author was James P. Cannon. The plenum adopted this resolution with one vote opposed and three abstentions. As a result the *Socialist Appeal*, which had been the official weekly paper of the SWP since its founding, was published twice a week from February 1939 through November 1939, after World War II had begun. In February 1941 its name was changed to *The Militant*, which had been the name of the Left Opposition paper from 1928 to 1934.

of the National Committee decides:

1. To publish the *Socialist Appeal*, in its present size, twice a week!

2. To raise a twice-a-week *Appeal* fund of $2,500 to meet the doubled publication costs and provide a reserve fund to guarantee its maintenance during the first months. Proportionate quotas are to be assigned to all party units and the campaign for this fund is to begin at once and be completed within sixty days. The first number of the twice-weekly *Appeal* is to appear about February 1, or sooner if the fund is on hand before that time.

Resolution on organization of party work[19]

In the period between the present plenum of the National Committee and the national convention in the spring we must bring about a decisive improvement in our methods of work. Determined efforts must be made to replace scattered and desultory activity in organization as well as in propaganda and agitation—characteristic of Social Democratic organizations and propaganda circles—by systematic planned work and activity organized on the Bolshevik campaign principle. The membership must be activized on the basis of universal and individual responsibility for an organized series of separate actions flowing from our own general political positions and Leninist organization concepts. It is the responsibility of the party leadership to

---

19. Reprinted from *Socialist Appeal*, November 26, 1938. The reporter and author was James P. Cannon. This resolution, adopted without opposition, was an attempt to find organizational answers to explain

plan and direct these actions and to concentrate all party energy on them for a given period of time in each case. Special "weeks" or longer periods must be dedicated to specific tasks and the striking power of the entire membership brought to bear upon them.

Particular attention in the next period should be concentrated on the following specific tasks:

1. The popularization of our program of transitional demands as a whole, and each item separately. Internal educational work along this line must be coordinated with editorial exposition, agitation, leaflet distribution, etc., in one comprehensive plan.

2. A special campaign against perfidious Stalinism, the greatest plague of the labor movement, directed especially to the Stalinist youth and trade unionists. The role of the Stalinists as undisguised agents of imperialism must be exposed and denounced far more vigorously than before by concrete illustrations, especially on questions of social patriotism, trade unionism, and betrayal of the Latin American people (Cuba!).[20]

3. The party must strive to increase and strengthen its professional staff. The intensified work of a revolutionary political party is incompatible with amateurism and the sluggish routine that always goes with it. More and more qualified comrades, ready for sacrifice, must be encouraged

---

and solve the problems that kept the SWP from making significant progress under difficult political conditions.

20. On the eve of the plenum the Cuban dictator Fulgencio Batista was wined and dined at the White House by Roosevelt, and his visit was hailed by the *Daily Worker*. In August the Central Committee of the Cuban CP decided to "take a more positive stand towards Colonel Batista since he has ceased to be the center of reaction and now professes democracy." In return, the brutal dictator legalized the Cuban CP.

to devote their full time to party work. A party functionaries wage fund, provided by special contributions from better-paid party members and sympathizers, must be established to assure professional party workers a reliable minimum of support in their work. The party must come to its next convention with an increase in the number of full-time party workers in general, and at least one full-time party organizer in each district.

4. The party work in the trade unions, which has recorded a modest improvement since the party convention, must be organized more systematically. The work on a national scale must be directed and coordinated by a full-time labor secretary. A part of the *Appeal* staff should specialize in trade union matters. In general the convention orientation toward concentration on trade union work must be reinforced by the necessary organizational and literary measures.

5. Since the convention big strides have been made toward the financial stabilization of the party press, the prerequisite for its further expansion. The crux of this problem is the prompt payment of bundle-order accounts by the branches. Carelessness and negligence in this respect, still prevailing in sections of the party, are the chief factors undermining the foundation of the *Appeal* and the *New International* and, at times, threatening their existence. These intolerable practices must be ended, by drastic measures if necessary.

A workers' party, operating without subsidy, can publish papers only if they are paid for. Those who take a light-hearted attitude toward this question act as disorganizers of the party press. Particularly now, with the party steering toward a twice-a-week publication of the *Appeal*, with its consequent doubled expense of production, the party must insist on a strict and responsible payment for bundle orders. The plenum endorses the previous decision of the Political Committee instructing the business managers of the party publications to cut off the bundle orders of branches violating this rule, regardless of which branch may be affected or what excuses are offered. The party is determined to stabilize the financial structure of its press and to permit no disruption of it.

At least two national tours of prominent party speakers are to be organized before the spring convention.

Resolution on world conference of Fourth International[21]

The plenary session of the National Committee of the Socialist Workers Party, having heard the report of its delegation to the world conference of the Fourth International, declares its endorsement and approval of the theses and resolutions adopted by the conference.

The National Committee considers the decision adopted by the conference to found and organize the Fourth International (World Party of the Socialist Revolution) as an indispensable step of the highest political and historic significance for the revolutionary and labor movements of the world.

The National Committee further reaffirms its adherence to the Fourth International and to the Executive Committee and Secretariat elected at the conference, and

---

21. Reprinted from *Socialist Appeal*, November 26, 1938. The reporter and author was Max Shachtman. For reasons stated in the minutes, three NC members did not vote when this resolution was adopted.

Socialist Appeal

In Two Sections — Section 1

Official Weekly Organ of the Socialist Workers Party Section of the Fourth International

See Section 2 for Documents of World Congress

VOL. II—No. 46 — Saturday, October 22, 1938 — Five Cents per Copy

WORLD CONGRESS FOUNDS FOURTH INTERNATIONAL

Congress Climaxes 15 Years' Struggle

Fourth International Emerges From Fight Against Degeneration in the Third International

By MAX SHACHTMAN

Thirty Delegates From Eleven Countries Raise New Banner

New International Created in Midst of European War Crisis Gives Voice to Revolutionary Opposition to Imperialist War

YOUTH INTERNATIONAL FORMED

The Fourth International has been founded. Meeting in the midst of the threatening war crisis in Europe, 30 delegates from eleven countries proclaimed the new World Party of the Socialist Revolution. A Youth International was simultaneously created.

The delegates represented organizations of the United States, France, Great Britain, Germany, the Soviet Union, Italy, Latin America, Poland, Belgium, Holland, and Greece.

NINE COUNTRIES REPRESENTED AT YOUTH CONGRESS

Delegates Gather Despite Many Obstacles

By NATHAN GOULD

Ten Years of the Fight To Build A Revolutionary Party in the US

By JAMES P. CANNON

The Pioneer Contingent

Trotsky Will Speak

by electrical transcription to our GRAND CELEBRATION MASS MEETING, heralding the foundation of the Fourth International and the Tenth Anniversary of our struggle for a revolutionary workers party in this country. Hear JAMES P. CANNON, MAX SHACHTMAN, JAMES BURNHAM, ANTOINETTE KONIKOW, and others, at the Center Hotel, 108 West 43rd Street, New York City, Friday, October 28, 1938, at 8 P. M.

declares formally that the Socialist Workers Party is the United States section of the Fourth International (World Party of the Socialist Revolution).

The National Committee declares, finally, in favor of the continuation of the maximum amount of support—financial, political, and moral—and the closest collaboration in the regular work of the Executive Committee and Secretariat of the Fourth International, and instructs the Political Committee to take all the necessary steps to realize this support and collaboration.

Resolution on the youth[22]

The social crisis of American capitalism leaves but a few decisive years during which it will be determined whether America will be swept into the fascist abyss or will be the starting point of the world revolution. In the revolutionary struggle against capitalism and fascism, the ability of the Socialist Workers Party to attract the youth is of paramount importance.

While capitalist technology in general has largely removed economic distinctions between adult and young workers, it has not removed social and other distinctions

---

22. From plenum material supplied to the members. The reporter and author was Martin Abern, who had been national secretary of the first communist youth organization in this country, the Young Workers League, and CLA representative to the Spartacus Youth League in the early days of the American Left Opposition. This resolution was adopted by a vote of 23 to 1. Discussion of the youth had been deferred by both the founding convention and the April 1938 plenum, so this marked the real start of the SWP's discussion of that question.

between the adults and youth in general. On the contrary, the social crisis has intensified these differences, which manifest themselves in a new state of declassed youth, demoralized, despairing, desperately seeking a way out of their dilemma. Capitalism seeks to solve this problem in part by regimentation and thus creates the social factors for the development of fascist ideology in the youth. To illustrate from another side: pacifist views at one time had their attraction among working youth and particularly among the students. In the latter-day imperialist epoch and especially since the advent of fascism, sharpened antagonisms between the imperialist nations and with the Soviet Union have enormously increased militarist preparations and militarist outlooks. The youth is literally born into militarism and war; pacifist *ideology* is largely alien to this period and the needs of youth, the first victims of warfare. In the conditions described, if the revolutionary party and youth organizations are unable to attract the mass of the youth, they will become both the victims and adherents of fascist ideology and organization. Here alone is a major task for the youth organization and party to solve.

The declassed youth are attracted by an organization of combat, cemented by the conflict with its enemies. Such an organization develops an internal cohesiveness, a spirit of comradeship, a brotherhood of arms; that gives it a power of attraction that can never be equaled by opponent organizations that rely mainly on greater material resources. The fascist organizations can attract the youth only in the absence of a fighting, socialist youth organization which offers the youth a program which meets their needs—something which the fascists in any event cannot really solve.

The creation of a special youth organization is made

necessary by recognition of the following:

1. The problems of life and manner of living of the youth create an outlook and psychology that differ from those of the adult.

2. Capitalism has created special social problems for the youth.

3. The fact that youth form the bulk of the armed forces of the state gives the youth organization a special role in antimilitarist work.

An organization of socialist youth, approaching the problems and activities of the youth with a socialist, revolutionary understanding, *could* attract *masses* of youth, whereas the party could, through a direct political appeal, only win the few class-conscious and intellectually advanced youth.

From this it follows that the youth organization must be an auxiliary of the party, created for a special purpose. It must be politically subordinated to the party, but must retain organizational autonomy within its sphere of work. Since it is the task of the youth organization to *educate* and through diverse activities prepare the youth for later service in the party, its requirements for membership should be interest in and sympathy with the aims of the organization, and not a requirement of full political understanding of its program. In other words, the youth organization is a *broad* organization, so functioning as to be able to attract the *inexperienced, but ready to learn* youth; although it remains narrow in the sense that the youth organization will in no circumstances admit youth consciously opposed to its program. The youth organization must be broad and flexible with the new, untutored, or unlearned youth, but it must not thereby be merely a social and debating society. Education and class-struggle activities to the greatest degree possible are the necessary tasks of the kind of mass youth organization sought for. The discipline in the youth organization should not be merely a discipline imposed from above by the organization, not the more rigid discipline expected of politically matured party members, but must flow especially from the internal spirit of the membership and their common fight for an ideal and goal.

During the past year, however, there has been evidence that in the political struggle against the reformist Socialist Party, in which the youth participated, there developed habits and methods which in varying degree run counter to the Bolshevik views of the youth movement and its relations with the party. In quite large part these views were permitted to persist because of insufficient unity and decisiveness on the part of the youth leadership in dealing with them. As an instance, aggravated by a lull in party activities, especially in the summer period, concepts arose in the youth which might be described as budding youth "vanguardism," and which naturally gave rise to friction between the party and the youth. These concepts developed also in other localities, with greater or lesser degree. Where the party representatives to the youth committees were either inexperienced in youth problems or failed to function on youth committees, the youth's antagonism toward the party was not mollified. The debate on the labor party question—a legitimate dispute on a tactical question—gave rise on occasions, in New York and also elsewhere, to antagonisms which were inimical to an organization which ought always to aim for intelligent discussion and decision in debates on party and youth problems. Such an atmosphere gave encouragement to and created in measure artificial hostility in relation to the party and partially vanguardistic conceptions of a youth organization. Either false or not properly understood concepts on the role of a youth organization arose more naturally where there also existed a low morale or isolation from the mass of youth in general. Improvement is definitely to be noted in these respects in the recent period.

The party itself shares some of the responsibility for that situation, as a result of which in a measure the party (New York)[23] lost prestige with the youth. Here, too, mutual discussions between the respective party and youth committees have contributed to a better understanding and improvement as to youth relations, but there must yet be much more improvement.

Although it is necessary to establish that the youth organization must participate as actively as possible in the political life of the party, but under the direction of the party, the concept of political subordination of the youth to the party defines and limits these rights. Participation in the political life of the party is an important factor in the education of the youth, but does not imply the assignment to the members of the youth organization who are not also members of the party of the right to make decisions for the party or to participate in making these decisions with equal rights.

While such party-youth conflicts and misunderstanding as have existed resulted in part from false ideas developed during the faction struggle against the Socialist Party leadership, this does not give the whole answer. There existed, and to some extent still exist, notions among the youth to regard the normal role of the youth organization as that of a political party *for young workers* standing on an equal basis with the SWP, as the party of the adult

---

23. The parenthetical phrase in the original resolution said "(New York, Boston)" but Boston was deleted when the resolution was adopted, for reasons not explained in the minutes.

workers. Where such ideas may still remain in the youth, they must be overcome if party-youth relations are to exist properly and correctly.

Historically, this concept of a "youth party" was the result of decades of experience during which Social Democratic ideology prevented the youth from carrying out its real role—that of a fighting, mass youth movement. Any concept today among the youth which still envisages the role of the YPSL to be that of a "youth party" in the face of an existing revolutionary party—wherein the youth organization emulates the SWP, except that the latter functions among adult workers and the former among young workers and students—must be entirely eliminated.

While the YPSL has made some gains in certain localities, it has, on the whole, only managed to hold its own nationally. But lack of substantial progress in this period of world-shaking events actually means relative stagnation and retrogression. Much evidence of this condition is to be seen. The lack of great progress has had its effect on the morale of the YPSL ranks. The almost entirely political character of the activities and purely theoretical education (the latter, however, lacking in important instances) undertaken by or given to the members has led too much to mere assimilation of book knowledge without *the building of a revolutionary character and morality. This finds its result in evidence of cynicism, pseudointellectualism, and a blasé, smug, smart-aleck attitude. Such an atmosphere, suitable perhaps for bohemians, is alien to a revolutionary youth movement. It retards the willingness and necessity for the organization of its ranks to sacrifice, both in personal effort and financially, in the interests of the organization, and it lays heavy hands upon discipline and organizational efficiency.*

It is necessary for the YPSL immediately to make a sharp break with its past bad concepts and habits and methods of work. Sweeping changes both in the character and orientation of the league are required at once. It is necessary to proceed swiftly to transform the YPSL *into a fighting mass organization of revolutionary youth.*

The adoption by the youth of the program of transitional demands makes it even more imperative that these changes be made. Unless the YPSL transforms itself into a *fighting political movement*, a *youth movement*, and a *mass movement*, it will not be able to rally the working youth to its program.

The fact that the YPSL is a fighting organization, infused with a willingness to struggle and a determination to conquer, must find its expression in all aspects of the movement. First of all, they must be organizationally geared for combat. The YPSL must in effect become a genuine fighting organization.

The colorful appearance of the youth organization must be the outward expression of its fighting spirit. To "dress up" the present organization, without a simultaneous regeneration of idealism, would be incongruous. Uniforms, salutes, banners, emblems, etc., come more naturally to a fighting organization. The resolution of the YPSL National Committee on the role and tasks of the youth points out correctly, however, that it is not necessary to wait until the spirit of the movement changes before changing its appearance. The spirit and the appearance react one upon the other. These external changes should be made at once. The appearance of the YPSL membership in uniform, with banners, with marching, and songs, at the party and youth anniversary celebration of the Fourth Internationalist movement in the United States, at the New York meeting at the Center Hotel,[24] had a noticeable effect on

---

24. This refers to a meeting celebrating the tenth anniversary of the American Left Opposition and the founding of the Fourth International,

the morale and spirit of the entire audience present, and is a case in point.

Since it is the primary task of the youth organization to train young people for a lifetime of revolutionary service to the party and movement, its major function becomes an educational one. But not, however, only in the sense of book learning. It must be educational in the broad sense of building and training young people in knowledge, character, and revolutionary morality. Devotion and the spirit of self-sacrifice, as the expression of idealism and the seriousness and determination of our movement, must be instilled in the youth from the moment he enters the organization. This must result from the patient efforts of the more mature youth comrades and members of the party, who should make themselves the companions and unofficial teachers and guides of the youth.

Since the bulk of the youth members are learning, preparatory to being admitted into the party, only the necessary core of leading members of the youth organization should be permitted to maintain dual membership. Twenty-one years should become the upper age of the youth movement. Application to the party for admittance is mandatory at this age. Dual membership may be maintained for a transitional period not to exceed six months. Leading members of the youth movement may maintain dual membership only with permission of the party in agreement with the youth organization. But members of the youth movement may join the party at the age of eighteen years upward after consultation between the representative party and youth committees.

Admission of members of the youth organization into

---

in New York City on October 28, 1938. Trotsky's recorded message to this meeting is in *Writings of Leon Trotsky (1938–39)* (Pathfinder, 1974).

the party must become an important and formal event. Admittance should be in groups at regular intervals. Party membership, symbolized by the presentation of party cards, should be bestowed upon the "graduates" at membership meetings of the youth organization attended by selected representatives of the party.

The SWP looks with high hopes to the future of the youth organization. We believe it is necessary for the youth to make these changes at its forthcoming convention in Chicago.[25] The YPSL can become a mass organization, sensitive to the problems and needs of the youth, by projecting itself into their struggles; by organizing, leading, and guiding them. In this manner the YPSL can give later to the party its most devoted, capable, and thoroughly trained professional revolutionists.

On our part, we realize well that neither the national party nor the local branches have in the past given the YPSL the attention, guidance, and aid that the youth warrants. But it pledges to remedy its own deficiencies and laxness on its part. It will endeavor to improve understanding and relations with the youth from top to bottom, by exchange of representatives on the respective committees and by greater participation in its work in the form of better and more political guidance and directives and by greater material aid (organizational, finances, etc.) than in the past.

---

25. The Tenth National Convention of the YPSL was held in Chicago November 25–27, 1938, a few days after the SWP plenum. The convention adopted a transitional program for young people and ambitious plans to turn the YPSL into a fighting mass youth movement.

Resolution on the SWP and the youth[26]

by Joseph Carter

The progress of the YPSL in the past year has been in keeping with the slow development of the SWP. The highly political character of the league as it issued out of the struggle in the Socialist Party was, as its activities show, fully maintained. The fact that, for example, the league in New York and Chicago was (and is) numerically as strong or stronger than the party, has displayed greater vitality and activity, and consists of more mature youth strengthened this character.

In these conditions, the YPSL, though its leaders and members accepted the principle of the political leadership of the party over the youth league, in practice functioned as a "youth party"; the young comrades assumed

---

26. From plenum material supplied to the members. The author was Joseph Carter, who had been one of the leaders of the Spartacus Youth League in the early 1930s. His minority resolution was defeated by a vote of 2 to 22.

the role—in their external activities and within the movement as a whole—of mature revolutionary socialists, i.e., party members. Numerous frictions developed out of this situation.

A radical change in the character of the YPSL is imperative if these difficulties are not to be repeated and if we are to develop the league from a "youth party" into a broad, colorful, youthful movement which will train young people for the SWP. The prerequisite for such a transformation is a realistic approach to the problems of the youth and, on the basis of the experiences of the revolutionary youth movement, a clear definition of the fields of activity and methods of work of the youth league.

The basis of our youth work should be a recognition of the divergent interests, needs, and habits of adolescents and of youth eighteen years of age and older. Every attempt to embrace these groups in one organization has failed. The revolutionary youth leagues under such conditions have in practice worked primarily among the more mature youth and necessarily became "youth parties," that is, highly political organizations conducting activities suitable for a revolutionary party. In given circumstances—such as in the struggle against the SP leaders—such a role is highly progressive. However, once a revolutionary party exists the role of the youth league must be changed.

Its proper sphere of activity should be among youth between the ages of fourteen and eighteen. Its general tasks remain the same: the winning of the youth for socialism, their cultural and political training for effective participation in the class struggle and for membership in the SWP. However, the political training of the youth will assume more indirect forms, suitable to adolescents and dependent upon local conditions and inclinations; along varied cultural and educational lines as well as through their direct participation in the class struggle (for example, various forms of aid to strikers and refugees; in defense of the economic interests of high school students and adolescents and, in particular cases, cooperation with the party in work among the NYA and CCC boys). Along these lines—which should be elaborated by a joint party-Yipsel committee—the YPSL can be converted into a socialist cultural center for youth.

The party itself, then, will assume the more advanced tasks previously set for the YPSL: opponents work, "youth" industrial and unemployed activity, antimilitarist and antifascist work, activity in the settlement houses, etc. In a word, the party will seek to win the more mature youth through its own organization. In practice, this will mean the early infusion of much needed trained youth into the party from the ranks of the YPSL; and engender activities which will give the party a greater attractiveness for both youth and adult workers.

The need for this transformation is particularly pertinent in view of the social crisis in the United States. Since all social, economic, and political questions are now being posed more sharply than ever before, the YPSL, if it continues to operate among the more mature youth, will in fact increase rather than decrease its highly political, that is, vanguardist, character. It will be unable to cope with the problems of these youth and simultaneously attract and educate the adolescent, immature youth.

On the other hand, the growing maturity of the young workers and unemployed youth under the lash of the social crisis and in face of the danger of war and fascism creates an exceptionally fertile field for direct party work. Even the meager experiences we have had indicate that these youth will more readily join the party than the youth league—particularly if the latter includes adolescents; and that they can be won in far greater numbers if the party makes special efforts in that direction.

We therefore propose to the Yipsel convention the above general position on the character of the YPSL and its relation to the party. More specifically, we propose:

1. That the YPSL convention establish the upper age limit for *new members* at eighteen. That members of the YPSL over twenty-one should join the party and drop out of the YPSL within three months. That those between eighteen and twenty-one should join the party and drop out of the YPSL within six months. Exceptions to this rule—which will be necessary for leading comrades for at least a year—are to be made by joint agreement between the Political Committee of the party and the National Bureau of the YPSL (on recommendation by the respective party and league bodies).

2. Each party body is to elect a youth committee to be responsible for work among young people over eighteen years of age. In special cases, youth branches may be formed with the consent of the Political Committee.

3. The present system of exchange of representatives in corresponding committees of the party and the league is to be reinforced by regular quarterly reports on party-Yipsel relations by party branches and local committees.

Resolution on defense work[27]

Faced with the terrible intensification of world reaction, resulting in unprecedented numbers of political prisoners and refugees within the revolutionary ranks, and with the sharpening of class conflicts in the United States, the party needs a reliable organization to aid and defend victims of reactionary persecution here and abroad.

The American Fund for Political Prisoners and Refugees has already laid the foundations for future work along these lines. Now it is necessary to broaden the base and scope of this committee and transform it into a mass organization with a life of its own as the director of the defense and relief movement supported by the party.

In adopting this policy and perspective, the plenum

---

27. From plenum material supplied to the members. George Novack was designated as reporter on this resolution, which the plenum referred to the Political Committee without discussion. The PC adopted it in December.

proposes: (1) That the American Fund be immediately converted into a national mass membership body with local branches; (2) That the American Fund hereafter handle all the labor defense cases of the party; (3) That the national fraction be instructed to draft a program of action for defense work; (4) That, in accordance with the resolution of the world congress, the international relief work of the American Fund should be closely coordinated with the work of the Secours International at Paris and our other international colleagues.

Unemployed resolution[28]

Of the 15 million unemployed suffering from the miserable conditions brought by the social crisis of American capitalism, only a small segment has been united into organizations to fight against the oppressive standards foisted upon them. Of these, less than 100,000 pay dues into the bankrupt Stalinist-controlled Workers Alliance. For the first time in its history, the AFL convention took note of its unemployed members, numbering 1.4 million. The CIO likewise has at least that many. While both labor organizations have taken some measures to aid the unemployed, the fact remains that the huge bulk of this vast reservoir of men has not yet found a means of uniting to struggle against its class enemies.

---

28. From plenum material supplied to the members. After hearing reports by Widick and New York local organizer, E.R. McKinney, the PC approved this resolution in December. It reflected tactical changes dictated by a growing number of local splits from the Workers Alliance

The recent national convention of the Workers Alliance consummated the final rites over this once large organization, and turned it into another Stalinist stooge outfit, subject to the whims of the Soviet bureaucracy and its needs. The deal between the Workers Alliance leadership and the Roosevelt administration, reflected in the complete dependence of this organization to the WPA set-up, has changed the alliance from an independent unemployed organization to a glorified company union, incapable of struggling seriously or successfully for the needs and demands of the unemployed. Its dependence on government "handouts" and its belly-crawling servility has alienated every progressive tendency, and combined with the dictatorial methods of the Stalinist leadership, forced a split of militant sections of the alliance from it. In New York City, in Harrisburg, in Harlem, and elsewhere, splits have occurred and a new organization created.

Our party has and should identify itself with these progressive tendencies and assist the unemployed in organizing into bodies which will fight militantly for their demands. Wherever possible, and where a sufficient base for such actions exists, our comrades should aid in forming unemployed organizations independent of the WAA, cooperating on a national scale with such new unemployed unions as have been formed in New York. The time is not yet ripe for the unification of these local movements in a national organization, but the general orientation should be in that direction.

The most successful—in obtaining concessions for the

---

of America following the WAA's national convention in Cleveland in September, where the Stalinists had pushed through an amendment prohibiting oppositional tendencies inside the organization without the permission of the leadership.

unemployed—organizations have been those allied directly to the union movement, as for example, the Federal Workers Section of Local 544, in Minneapolis. It has been followed somewhat in steel and by the auto workers' international union, and other CIO unions with considerable success. Union affiliation of the unemployed gives them more backing and prestige in fighting against present relief and WPA conditions. It unites more closely the unemployed and the employed. It makes the unemployment question a direct responsibility of the union movement and serves as a radicalizing force against the tendency of conservatism of the employed unionists. While it can hardly be expected that the "ideal" organization, a national unemployed movement chartered and affiliated to the union movement, is forthcoming in the next period, our party must concentrate its efforts in bringing closer the alliance of the employed and unemployed. Fraternal delegations to union councils, formation of unemployed divisions of unions, as done in Akron, in auto, and elsewhere, demands for local union charters for the unemployed organizations from either the CIO or the AFL, depending on which body locally represents the militant and decisive section of the union movement; these are the lines along which our unemployed activity must center.

To facilitate and assist in this work, a special effort must be made to have all eligible youth and party comrades join an unemployed organization.

Yankee imperialism at Lima[29]

Manifesto of the Socialist Workers Party

Hitler's Munich triumph[30] has impelled American imperialism to launch a gigantic counteroffensive for the conquest of the world. The slogans abandoned by Anglo-French imperialism at Munich—"democratic antifascist front," "common action against the aggressor," "collective security"—have now become the weapons of Wall Street. Under these slogans Roosevelt called the Latin American

---

29. Reprinted from *Socialist Appeal*, January 7, 1939. The first draft of this document was written by A. Lebrun, a member of the Pan-American Committee and of the International Executive Committee, and was adopted by the Political Committee in December 1938. The U.S.-initiated conference in Lima, Peru, began on December 9. The "Declaration of Lima" called for joint action by U.S. and Latin American governments in the face of "foreign threats" in the Western Hemisphere.

30. At Munich in September 1938, Hitler achieved political and psychological triumphs, as well as important territorial gains, when the British and French governments accepted his demands for the possession of the German-speaking part of Czechoslovakia.

countries to Lima, and they inspired the "Declaration of Lima."

The first fruit garnered by American imperialism following Munich is the capitulation of Great Britain to America's trade demands. The Munich crash gives the United States what Hull could not obtain in three years of tenacious striving: a month after Munich the Anglo-American commercial accord is signed, and it is followed by the American-Canadian accord; Great Britain opens the door of its empire to the Yankee rival. Meanwhile Stalin, terrified, looks toward Roosevelt as a savior.

The United States takes over the front line in the battle against Nazi and Japanese imperialism, declares open war against German barter trade, places German products on the blacklist, incites world opinion against German barbarism, and ostentatiously breaks the neutrality law in favor of China. The United States bars the road to further conciliation between England and Germany—through the Anglo-American and American-Canadian accords, which cover nearly two-thirds of world commerce—obliging England to declare economic war against Germany.

Lima is the stage on which the American imperialists have played the first act of their worldwide counteroffensive against Germany and Japan. The United States delegation sought to consolidate Yankee hegemony in Latin America, to eradicate all European influence, to expel Germany and her allies from Latin America's markets, and, in short, to destroy all positions hitherto conquered by rival imperialisms. As the United States comes to the front of the stage, the world conflict assumes a new form. Now it is not simply the old conflict between the starved imperialisms, impelled to the offensive by their desperate condition, against the satiated imperialisms who benefited from Versailles[31] and are constantly on the defensive, having as their only aim the preservation of their booty. Now a new partition of the world is being pressed most determinedly by the United States.

Elsewhere, Wall Street still develops its counteroffensive, under purely economic forms (war against controlled commerce, restoration of complete liberty of commerce, lowering of tariffs, loans, etc.). In the Western Hemisphere, however, that counteroffensive assumes definite political forms, ranging from collective declarations against aggressors and proposals for defensive alliances to ever more precise plans for military strategy.

American imperialism aims at more than monopolizing the markets and the sources of raw materials of the entire Western Hemisphere. It also aims at making the Americas, from Cape Horn to Patagonia, the physical, economic, and strategic base required for the coming decisive struggles for the possession of the world. This is why Roosevelt bellicosely proclaims, alongside of the evangelical preaching of Hull, that the United States will defend tooth and nail all the countries in the hemisphere. The "good neighbor," Wall Street, in reality aims to transform its neighbors into American-controlled Manchukuos[32] and Czechoslovakias.

Authoritative military circles do not conceal what they understand by defense of our hemisphere: the military unification of the Americas under the direct control of Washington.

---

31. The Versailles treaty of 1919 that marked the end of World War I benefited the military victors in that war, especially American, British, and French imperialism.

32. The Japanese imperialists invaded Manchuria in 1931 and after consolidating their hold set up the so-called independent state of Manchukuo, which was nothing but a puppet of the Japanese government.

The U.S. War Department considers military control of Latin America and the possession of its sources of raw materials as vital to the development of the defensive and offensive power of the American war machine. Among materials which the United States must secure abroad, the War Department has classified twenty-one as "strategic" and a few others as "critical," that is, materials which are not sufficiently produced at home to provide for the necessities of a war. Most of these materials are to be found in the rest of the Western Hemisphere. Among these raw materials are Canadian nickel, Bolivian tin, rubber, manganese, Brazilian and Colombian coffee, Argentine wool, Chilean nitrate, Mexican silver, petroleum from Venezuela, Colombia, Mexico, etc.

Latin America contains another raw material of primary importance which American military experts greedily eye: man, cannon fodder. The potential manpower reserves of Latin America equal those of the United States. Today, in fact, its immediately available trained manpower is superior to that of the Yankee metropolis! Washington estimates that Latin America can immediately put into the field more than a million men with military training. This means that, as soon as war breaks out, the very first shots will initiate payment to Uncle Sam of blood tribute by the oppressed peoples of Latin America!

American totalitarianism

The political and military objectives of Wall Street in Latin America are totalitarian, embellished though they are by Rooseveltian democracy. Washington seeks a monopoly in everything: in raw materials and markets, in ideology and politics, in foreign relations, in military missions, war supplies, naval and air lines and bases, in military preparations. Washington wants no other powers—not even "democratic" France!—to maintain military missions in Latin America. Washington obliges the Latin American countries, one after another, to dispense with long-established European military, naval, or aviation missions and to establish new, exclusively American ones. It even leases war vessels to Brazil. The old plan for a second canal, in Nicaragua, is taken from the archives. Military aides are sent to all the Latin American capitals with the objective of molding their military mechanisms into the strategic plans elaborated in Washington. American military, naval, or aviation missions are already operating in Brazil, Argentina, Peru, Haiti, Guatemala, Colombia, and they are coming in other countries; they do not instruct, nor will they instruct, the forces of these countries in the special problems of their own defense, but aim to create strategic bases for the war plans of American imperialism. Cuba already is nothing more than an outpost of the American naval system, as much so as Puerto Rico. All this is geared into Roosevelt's gigantic armament program, for which we are being called upon to provide astronomical sums.

The pretext for building this tremendous apparatus is a threat by a foreign totalitarian power. Under world conditions today, however, who can believe that threat is imminent, when we see Japan entirely absorbed in China, Germany geared to the Herculean task of devouring Eastern Europe, and Italy preoccupied in the Mediterranean? This pretext was unmasked for their own purposes by the representatives of "democratic" English imperialism at Lima, the Argentine delegates.

No, these sensational preparations are not for defensive purposes. That pretext merely serves to delude American workers and to frighten the peoples and governments of Latin America into seeking shelter under the wings of the

Yankee eagle. If these arms, apart from their use in the coming interimperialist war, are employed in Latin America, they will be used there, when the necessity arises, to crush revolutionary mass movements for national independence in the semicolonial countries! The Yankee imperialists cannot be defenders of those peoples of whom they are the principal exploiters and oppressors. Woe to any people which listens to the mermaid song of Washington! That song is as deceiving as the tunes emanating from Berlin, London, Tokyo, Paris, or Rome.

The enslaved peoples of Latin America cannot but feel a sarcastic note in the call for common defense of democracy issued by Roosevelt-Hull to the Latin American governments. What sort of democracy can these governments defend, the satrapies of Getulio Vargas, Benavides, Somoza, Trujillo, Batista, and Company? Today, they are the devoted lackeys of Wall Street, but tomorrow they will unhesitatingly sell themselves to Hitler or to the Mikado, if the switch would serve to continue them in power.

What they mean by democracy

The defense of "democratic" institutions means concretely to Washington two things: the eradication of German-Nipponese competition and the preservation of the concessions and privileges of the big American trusts against the bourgeois-nationalist independence movements exemplified by Toro in Bolivia and Cárdenas in Mexico.

Behind Roosevelt's sonorous phrases is the determination to assure the monopoly of Latin America's markets. The constant turmoil and the growing political and economic restrictions in the European and Asiatic markets make the Latin American markets ever more important to Wall Street. Latin America now takes 20 percent of all American exports. Despite its supremacy in commercial relations with the twenty southern republics since 1918, the United States feels itself threatened by competitors and, as a matter of fact, during the last two years did lose first place in five of the principal countries of Latin America (Mexico, Brazil, etc.). The American share of South American importing markets was 44 percent in 1920, but that figure decreased to 30 percent in 1928; last year it rose again to 34.4 percent for the whole of Latin America—more than the combined imports from Great Britain, Germany, Japan, and Italy. But Germany—practically eliminated in 1920 as a consequence of the war—has meanwhile pushed into second place ahead of England and has become, thanks to its methods of control, subsidies, etc., the most serious competitor of the United States, seeking to open a breach in the zone of Yankee monopoly.

To defend itself against its competitors, Wall Street raises the liberal slogan of return to free commerce; in actual content, however, that slogan gives Latin America the same status as was held by the American colonies when they did not have the right to trade except with the British crown. As for the "defense of international law," it means simply that in spite of the fictitious sovereignty of the dependent nations of the New World, the Yankees reserve for themselves the right to intervene in the internal life of these states to restore, if necessary by force, the privileges and monopolies that they enjoy there, or to impose new ones.

The right to be squeezed

In essence, Secretary Hull calls upon the Latin American states to concede the right of Wall Street to repeat its past infamous exploits in Mexico, Cuba, Haiti, Nicaragua, etc.—the right to collect, with machine guns and cannons when required—the dividends, interest, and superprofits on the five billion dollars (40 percent of America's total investments abroad) invested in the mines, petroleum, public services, electricity, meat packing, territorial concessions, and plantations which constitute the key positions in the economic life of Latin America.

The gentlemen of Wall Street are terrified by the danger that the Mexican example[33] will prove contagious. They move to block the road to more audacious expropriations. They grant the degree of "democrats" and "antifascists" to dictators like Vargas and Benavides, while they insinuate through the kept press that Cárdenas favors fascism.

In squeezing the Latin American lemon, Wall Street piles contradiction upon contradiction. It obliges the tributary countries to buy only in the American markets, but at the same time drains into its own coffers the gold of these countries, demands prompt payments for old debts, the end of exchange control by the Latin American governments, and the immediate handing over of Wall Street credits now frozen in Latin American banks for lack of exchange. As if this were not enough, Wall Street tries to deprive these countries of their traditional markets for products which America also produces (wheat, cotton, sugar, etc.). The catalog is not complete without referring to the reprisals and boycotts organized by Wall Street against any country which, like Mexico, dares to expropriate imperialist concessions. Wall Street cannot but strangle the goose that lays its golden eggs.

The fight is against imperialism

We are confident that the Latin American masses will not allow themselves to be duped into abandoning the

---

33. The Mexican government's example in 1938 was to nationalize the foreign oil companies.

anti-imperialist struggle, which will continue despite the efforts of dollar diplomacy to stifle it.

It must be stressed that the principal enemy of the Latin American peoples is not fascism in general but imperialism. Fascism in Latin America is only one of the uniforms used by one of the imperialist cliques.

In the advanced democratic countries, not to struggle above all against your own national capitalist class and its "democratic" governments, means not to defend democracy but to prepare the way for fascism. If the examples of Italy, Germany, Austria, and Spain did not suffice, we now have the fresh examples of Czechoslovakia and France. Czech democracy quietly and automatically transformed itself into fascism. In France the much-acclaimed chief of the People's Front Daladier, decided almost overnight, with the complete support of his party, to begin the reactionary offensive and consciously prepare for the transition to fascism.[34] The same process of democratic degeneration will inevitably take place in this country unless the American workers succeed in overthrowing the capitalists and establishing a workers' government. In the dependent and semicolonial countries of Latin America the fight against fascism is first of all a struggle against finance capital—i.e., American finance capital, which holds the lion's share and is the chief imperialism oppressing the two continents—and its native agents. The Latin American capitalists, far from being able to lead a struggle for the independence of their countries, simply

---

34. After Munich the French People's Front government decided that the way to prepare for the coming war was to launch a savage attack on the rights, wages, and conditions of the French workers and take back the gains they had won since the great strike of 1936. Symptomatic of the new atmosphere was an unsuccessful general strike on November 30, 1938, whose defeat led millions of workers to quit the unions.

become agents of Yankee imperialism. The liberation of Latin America is a task that falls to the workers and peasants in struggle against the imperialists and against their own immediate exploiters.

The reactionary dictatorships that rule most of Latin America are maintained by the support they get from Washington or London, the imperialist capitals. The danger of a Nazi, Italian, or Japanese invasion of Peru, Argentina, or Nicaragua does not lie in a spectacular armed invasion by the armies and navies of the totalitarian powers. The rivalries among the imperialist bandits serve to protect Latin America from such an invasion. In order to make a landing on the coast of Brazil, Germany would first have to destroy the American fleet, and probably the British as well. But their chances of doing that are still remote.

The fascist danger is at home

The immediate danger of fascist domination in Latin America is internal. It rears its head in each and every country. It is nourished by the patronage of American imperialism and by the fact that the Latin American countries are transformed into economic vassals of the northern colossus.

When petty-bourgeois nationalists like Haya de la Torre or Grau San Martín, or "socialist" leaders like Grove, abandon the traditional struggle against U.S. imperialism in order to unite with it for a "common" struggle against fascism, the Nazi agents in Latin America are quite content. The capitulation of these leaders makes it easier to reach the masses with fascist demagogy. It also makes it easier for the fascists to make connections with those national capitalists (mainly the local industrialists) who aspire to economic independence. The agents of Hitler or Mussolini can thus mask themselves as nationalists. They can make use of the masses' hatred of the great foreign monopolies—mostly American or British—to make them believe that the anti-imperialist fighters and the revolutionary militants are nothing but agents of Wall Street and London. This method is the principal one used by all the native fascists in Latin America backed directly or indirectly by Hitler or Mussolini: the Integralistas of Brazil, the Gold Shirts of Mexico, the Nacistas of Chile, the Brown Shirts of Argentina, etc.

Thus, to suspend the struggle against Yankee or British imperialism, even for a single moment, is to hand the masses over to the mercies of the fascists, to make it easier for the fascist enemy to conquer from the inside.

Rulers cannot fight fascism

The reactionary dictatorships in the majority of Latin American countries cannot serve as instruments of struggle against international fascism but rather as channels for its penetration. The mock constitution granted (by divine right?) to Brazil by President Vargas on November 10, 1937, was directly modelled on totalitarian lines. His coup d'etat was planned and carried out with the active participation of the Integralistas and other Nazi agents. If Vargas did not at that time transform himself into a Brazilian Henlein, it was only because he feared popular opposition and civil war and could not count on sufficient direct aid from Hitler. He chose, therefore, to return to the fold of his old Yankee masters. Meanwhile his "democratic" constitution cloaks a regime of terror, concentration camps, deportations to plague-infested islands, torture, and murder. Trade unions are organs of the state and political parties are prohibited. This is the kind of "democracy" Roosevelt asks the Latin American people to defend against the advance of the fascists from across the Atlantic!

These regimes, by their very nature, favor the penetration not only of fascist ideas, but of fascist economic and political influence. Thus the German consul in Salvador assumes the post of director of the country's agricultural and credit bank. In Peru, more than half the country's banking activity is controlled by the Bank of Italy. In Brazil, Vargas divides the Amazon region between the Mikado and Henry Ford. In Santo Domingo, Trujillo opens a land concession to 40,000 Nazified Germans. In these countries farm hands and European immigrants, suffering under the general economic backwardness, and contemptuous of the cultural inferiority of their new lands, are easily attracted by the racial myths and respond to the perfected demagogic technique of the German and Italian propaganda machines.

The conclusion from all this is clear: semicolonial Latin America, an oppressed continent, cannot escape fascism without struggling against imperialist oppression. But this struggle means national independence. It means an agrarian revolution to bring about the distribution of the land to the tillers. It means expropriation of the foreign monopolies. It means the granting of unrestricted democratic liberties to the people and the elevation of the living standards of the masses. This is the only program that can liberate the millions of Latin American slaves from the chains of imperialist oppression, of fascism, and creole dictatorships!

'Antifascist' illusions

Unfortunately, this program is rejected not only by imperialist hirelings but by nationalist petty-bourgeois leaders who are impressed by the advance of the fascist powers and by noisy Stalinist demagogy. Haya de la Torre, for example, believes in the "sincerity" of Roosevelt. Why? Because Roosevelt has not yet used troops and cannons like some of his predecessors and teachers (Wilson!). Haya de la Torre simply does not understand that Wall Street is not yet reduced to methods of last resort and desperation. Hitler cannot wait; but Roosevelt can.

In essence, however, Roosevelt's foreign policy is that of his predecessors and of his Republican rivals. Landon's place in the American delegation at Lima demonstrates that fact. There are no differences on imperialist policies within the ruling class of the United States.

Roosevelt's demagogy is ably served by Stalin and his minions in deluding the Haya de la Torres. On April 17 of this year Stalin's personal organ, *Pravda*, urged the United States to have "a more active foreign policy" and to enter into "common action with all the democratic elements of Latin America, as the only possible way of resisting the destructive forces of fascism." Thus, while Roosevelt drags the dictators and *fuehrers* of Latin America into the "democratic antifascist front," the Stalinists attempt to entice into it the popular anti-imperialist leaders. Stalin's supreme hope lies in Wall Street and he demonstrates to it his usefulness. The Popular Front of Chile is the most finished expression of that policy.

If Browder, *fuehrer* of American Stalinism, could not find a place in the American delegation as a lackey of Hull-Landon, his superiors in the hierarchy of labor lieutenants of Wall Street did appear. John L. Lewis's daughter (CIO) and Tracy (AFL) were there to provide a "working-class" sanction for America's predatory policy. The Latin American peoples were presented with the spectacle of a sacred union extending from Landon to Browder.

Lackeys do not speak for us

The labor lieutenants of Wall Street, lackeys of the imperialist exploiters of the Western Hemisphere, by their presence at Lima attempted to convey to the Latin American peoples and their most popular leaders (the Haya de la Torres, Grau San Martíns, Groves, etc.) the idea that the American working class solidarizes itself with the imperialists of their own country. This is false! These lackeys of imperialism represent only the labor aristocracy which lives off the crumbs cast to them by the imperialists from their feasts at the expense of the Latin American peoples.

But the vast majority of the American proletarians do not have anything in common with these aristocrats and lackeys. Though miserably deceived by the labor lieutenants and the Stalinist hirelings, the millions of American proletarians have true class instincts. They feel in their depths that the enemy who exploits them in this country is the same oppressor who keeps under an even more terrible yoke the semislave masses of peasants and workers south of the Río Grande. Speak out to your brothers in the north, workers and peasants of Latin America, and they will learn to answer you in a common tongue, in unison against the common oppressor!

The Socialist Workers Party of the United States, section of the Fourth International, revolutionary vanguard of the American workers, before the brother peoples of Latin America denounces the grim comedy of Lima. We warn our brothers in Latin America against the maneuvers of the American delegation, which spoke there for Wall Street. We appeal to the semicolonial peoples of the south to unite with us against the common enemy: imperialism, and that includes the American brand. We pledge our unremitting aid in rallying the working class of this country in effective solidarity with the Latin American peoples in their struggles for national freedom.

The liberation of Latin America from the imperialist yoke, the destruction of the threat of fascist intervention at its very roots, can be achieved only by common action of the American working class with the worker and peasant masses of Central and South America.

To this great historic task, the Bolshevik-Leninists of the United States summon all the revolutionary, anti-imperialist, and national-democratic forces of Latin America.

Your national independence will be a gigantic step in speeding the socialist revolution in the United States. Likewise the victory of the proletarian revolution in this country will guarantee the complete liberation of the peoples of Latin America. Our fate is indissolubly linked with yours.

In the coming struggle for freedom, the historic task of the revolutionary vanguard of the United States and of Latin America, organized under the banner of the Fourth International, will be to place itself in the forefront of that battle and lead it to a triumphant conclusion.

For the national independence of the Latin American countries!

For the agrarian revolution and the national and social liberation of the semicolonial peoples!

For the proletarian, socialist revolution in the United States!

For the Federation of Socialist Soviet Republics of all the Americas!

PART 6
Minutes, Second National Convention of the Socialist Workers Party

Minutes, Second National Convention of the Socialist Workers Party

New York, July 1–5, 1939[1]

FIRST SESSION, SATURDAY, JULY 1, 1939

Convention opened by Comrade Cannon, 12:05 p.m. Retzkin and Barsh elected as secretaries.

---

1. In the SWP literature of the period, this convention was referred to by many names: the antiwar convention, the New York convention, the July convention, the 1939 convention, the second convention. But none of these names convey the two things that, retrospectively, it should be remembered for: (1) It largely completed the process of laying the programmatic foundations of the party, which was begun with the preparation of the first convention and continued through the April and November plenums. In this year and a half or two the leaders of the SWP, aided and stimulated by Trotsky, put down in writing, in some cases for the first time and in others more comprehensively than ever before, the main things they had learned over the years about revolutionary program and practice. In the decades that followed this outburst of sustained creativity, the programmatic foundations of the SWP were expanded or altered here or there, but not essentially. (2) The same convention that completed that process also served as the arena for a preliminary alignment of the delegates into two tendencies that developed, only a few weeks after the convention, into a fateful factional fight that convulsed the SWP for many months and turned out

505

 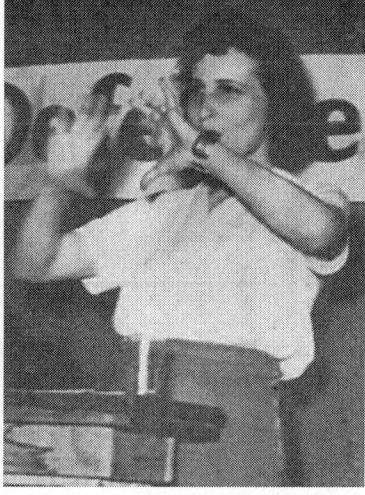

Above, June 30, 1939, New York rally of 1,000 greeting second SWP convention. **Below**, speakers at rally: Reuben Plaskett, Genora Johnson.

Presiding Committee elected: Shachtman, Dunne, Abern, Cannon, Burnham, Trimble, Gould.

Convention procedure
Agenda[2]
Motion by Weber: To add the Jewish question.
Motion by Gould: To refer to Presiding Committee for recommendation to next session. Carried.
Agenda adopted as read.

---

to be, at bottom, a struggle over the programmatic foundations that the whole leadership had helped to set. These minutes, prepared by Alex Retzkin and Yetta Barsh, the convention secretaries, were published in mimeographed form by the SWP national office. One part of the proceedings (about the nomination and election of National Committee members and alternates) was deleted for security reasons. No earlier draft of the minutes containing that information could be located for this book, but information supplementing the minutes on this point is provided in our footnotes or can be found in James P. Cannon's *The Struggle for a Proletarian Party*.

2. The agenda recommended by the National Committee was: (1) United States Political Perspectives in the Light of the War Crisis and the Corresponding Tasks of the Party—reporter: Burnham; (2) The Preparations of the Party for War—reporter: Cannon; (3) The Struggle Against Fascism and the Workers' Defense Guard—reporter: Smith [see below]; (4) Organizational report—reporter: Cannon; (5) Party press—reporter: Abern; (6) The War Crisis and the Work in Trade Unions—reporter: Widick; (7) Unemployed organization—reporter: McKinney; (8) Negro question—reporter: Johnson [see below]; (9) The War and the Fourth International—reporter: Shachtman; (10) Youth report—reporter: Gould; (11) Antiwar manifesto—report by committee; (12) Committee reports: (a) Resolutions Committee; (b) Constitution Committee; (c) Other committees; (13) Election of National Committee.

Smith was Farrell Dobbs, who did not attend the convention despite this assignment and his election to a convention committee. Two days before the convention began, the National Committee directed him to stay away until he had completed his work in a strike in Dallas. J.R. Johnson was the name used by C.L.R. James, a noncitizen, after he decided to remain in the United States instead of returning to Britain.

Rules:

Motion carried that Robert's Rules of Order govern with the exception that motions require no seconds and subject to other modifications that the convention may adopt.

Time schedule for agenda adopted.

The following convention committees were proposed by the National Committee: Credentials—5; Conflicts and Grievances—5; Resolutions—5; Conventions and Arrangements (appointed by NC); Constitution—5; Trade Union—7; Unemployed—7; Antifascist Workers' Guard—7; Organization—7; Negro—7; Declaration of Principles—5; Nominations—15.

Motion by Sparrow: To increase Organization Committee to 12. Carried.

Nominations Committee—To be selected, not from the floor, but by the delegations, meeting separately as follows: New York—2; Ohio, Michigan—2; Minnesota—2; California—2; New England, New Jersey, Chicago, Missouri, youth—1 each; Remaining delegates—2. This committee to bring in a slate for the NC.

Motion by Findley: That New York have 4 on the committee. Defeated.

Motion by Retzkin: That this question be deferred until Credentials Committee reports. Defeated.

NC proposal carried.

Election of committees:
Credentials: Gates, Retzkin, Thurman, Carli, and Coover.
Conflicts and Grievances: Dunne, Geldman, Ferguson, Querio, Selander.

Status of alternates:
Motion: Alternates have rights only as substitutes for

regular delegates.

Motion by Zola: The alternates seated at the beginning of the session remain seated for the remainder of the session.

Motion by Thurman: That alternates may speak if the regular delegate does not speak at the same time.

Discussion: Shachtman opposed to Zola motion. Burnham opposed to Thurman motion.

Vote: Original motion carried. Motions by Zola and Thurman defeated.

Election of committees continued:

Resolutions: Shachtman, Preis, Weber, Lear, and Hill.

Constitution: Abern, Cannon, Trimble, Retzkin, and Bern.

Trade Union: Widick, Reid, Trimble, Ontell, B. Stevens, Lewit, Clarke, Kwalik, Dostal, Cochran nominated.

Motion by Trimble: That there be a committee of 11 and that nominations be reopened. Defeated.

Motion by Wright: That pending report of Credentials Committee, vote be by show of cards. Carried.

Vote: Widick 65, Clarke 60, Trimble 57, Reid 50, Cochran 47, Ontell 37, Lewit 36, Dostal 36.

Motion by Retzkin: That since there is a tie for seventh place, the committee of 8 stand. Carried.

Unemployed: McKinney, Selander, Geldman, Breitman, G. Johnson, and Dale.

Motion: That committee of 6 stand. Carried.

Alternates seated as regular delegates: Breitman (Newark), Dale and Glover (Los Angeles), Swanson and Williams (Minnesota), Wolfe (New Haven).

Election of committees continued:

Antifascist Workers' Guard: Burnham, Smith, Hughes, Hansen, Ontell, Williams, Erber, and Milton.

Motion: That committee of 8 stand. Carried.

Organization: Abern, Cannon, Sparrow, Weiss, D. Stevens,

Gould, Roberts, Weber, Bleeker, Carter, Ferguson, Coover, Fraser, Manret, Cochran, H. Smith nominated.

Vote: Abern 61, Cannon 61, Carter 55, Gould 53, Sparrow 53, Weiss 49, Coover 49, Fraser 49, Ferguson 45, Weber 44, Cochran 42, Smith 31.

Negro: McKinney, Kerry, Johnson, Saunders, Gates, D. Stevens, McGee, Weiss, Wright, Paine, Birchman, Plaskett nominated. Motion: That the committee of 12 stand. Carried.

Declaration of Principles: Burnham, Shachtman, Mont, Lear. Motion: That committee of 4 stand. Carried.

Time of sessions: 10 a.m. to 2 p.m. and 3 p.m. to 7 p.m.

Credentials Committee report by Gates:
Recommends that three delegates be seated from Downtown branch, New York, on the basis of convention assessment payments.

Motion by Lands: That four delegates be seated.

Discussion: Retzkin for Lands's motion. Cannon against.

Motion by Ferguson: That the Credentials Committee go into the matter of assessment payments more closely and that the seating of delegates be deferred until then. Carried.

Recommendation: That Wills act as delegate for Houston until the regular delegate arrives.

Motion by Cannon: That this matter be referred back to committee pending further information. Carried.

Recommendation: That delegate from Astoria branch, New York, be seated even though he does not have a regular credential in view of the fact that the city organizer has certified him. Carried.

Fraternal delegates: Motion that the following be fraternal delegates: regular NC members, delegates from foreign sections with credentials, one delegate from the Pan-American Bureau, all members of executive bodies of the Fourth International. Carried.

A delegate raised the point that someone was giving out a leaflet calling for a break with the SWP. Presiding Committee recommended that the individual be barred from the convention hall until his case was disposed of by the branch to which he belongs. Carried.

Adjournment: 2:15 p.m.

SECOND SESSION, SATURDAY, JULY 1, 1939

Convened 3:20 p.m.

Chairman: Dunne.

Chairman announced that the following had been selected by the respective delegations to constitute the Nominations Committee: New York delegation—Demby and Retzkin; Minnesota delegation—Geldman and Dunne; California delegation—Stevens and Sparrow; Ohio-Michigan delegation—Reid and Clarke; Massachusetts and New England delegation—Thompson; Illinois delegation—Gates; New Jersey delegation—Roberts; Missouri delegation—Washburn; youth—Gould; Miscellaneous delegations—Farrow and Fraser.

Abern assumed chairmanship.

Greetings from the Fourth International were read, as follows:

From the Executive Committee of the Fourth International to the Socialist Workers Party of the U.S.

Dear Comrades:

The Executive Committee of the Fourth International sends you its warmest greetings on the occasion of the convention of the American section of the Fourth International. Your party is today the most important section of the Fourth International, not only by virtue of its numerical forces but also because of the political weight of its leadership and the quality of its cadres.

Our comrades all over the world are proud of their fighting brothers in the United States and they applaud your successes, particularly the high political level of the *New International,* the semiweekly appearance of the *Socialist Appeal,* your serious trade union activity, the public actions like the anti-Nazi demonstration in New York. It is hardly necessary to dwell upon the preponderant role that your section has played in the political guidance of the Fourth International, or to emphasize the very exceptional sacrifices that the militants of the SWP have made toward furthering the solidarity and political work of the Fourth International. For that proves that for the sections of the Fourth International internationalism is a living reality, and your example is a new and singularly convincing proof of the existence of the Fourth International as the world vanguard, steeped in the best traditions of Bolshevik internationalism.

At the same time, dear comrades, we do not gloss over the fact that much still remains to be done before you become the great revolutionary party of the working class of the United States. We hope that you will indefatigably continue and intensify your activity along the road of Bolshevism, toward a continual strengthening of your trade union work, toward a tireless agitation among the most exploited sections of the population (the youth, unemployed, women), toward an increasingly active and vigilant internationalism.

Today we point, as an example for the other sections of the Fourth International, to your methods of work, which have shown that you know how to combine unwavering firmness and the greatest flexibility, in the spirit of Bolshevism. Our International has succeeded in enunciating correct principles and in hammering out the only Marxist program corresponding to the character of our epoch; now it must learn how to work. It must definitively rid itself of all remnants of a sectarian and propaganda-circle existence, and in all countries acquire the methods of Bolshevik work. Then, through their own development and inspired by your example, the comrades of the other sections will be able to help you in their turn and to collaborate in your development.

Long live the Socialist Workers Party of the U.S.!
Long live the Fourth International!

*Executive Committee of the
Fourth International*

Johnson presented greetings from foreign sections of the Fourth International.

Political report by Comrade Burnham: "United States Political Perspectives in the Light of the War Crisis and the Corresponding Tasks of the Party."

Discussion: Stevens (Los Angeles), Wright (New York), Burch (New York), Weiss (California).

Trimble (California) presented the following amendment to the resolution as presented by the NC:

Substitute amendment to Sections 22 & 23 of Political Resolution by Glen Trimble

We have said, and we repeat, that our opponents within the labor movement—the social reformists, the

Stalinists, and the labor bureaucracy—are separated from us now by no mere ideological divergences, but by their having become part of the war machine. They have joined the camp of the class enemy. Ours is the only party that can or will fight uncompromisingly against the imperialist war confronting us on today's world agenda.

It is plainly impermissible for the American section of the Fourth International to *advocate* the creation or building of national or local labor parties in this situation and this period. It is no part of our task to advocate the creation of a political instrument which, if it genuinely included the mass organizations, would inevitably reflect the current mass leadership—the social reformists, the Stalinists, and the labor bureaucracy—precisely those elements who *are already* aligned in the camp of the class enemy!

In the face of the war, we must concentrate our main energies upon our essential task—the building of our party, the only party that can or will fight uncompromisingly against the war, that can or will achieve the socialist revolution. This task is paramount. In its accomplishment, fraction work in existing labor parties is permissible. In some cases in the brief period before the irreconcilable wall between revolutionary socialism and reformism is drawn by the inexorable logic of the war situation, critical support of certain labor candidates will be permissible under the careful supervision and check of the National Committee.

In all these relations we must keep uppermost a thorough understanding that our party, and ours alone, stands opposed to the military camp of the class enemy.

MINUTES / 515

Discussion: Greenberg (New York), Findley (New York), Erber (youth), Hill (Missouri), Geldman (Minneapolis), Thompson (Worcester, Massachusetts), Kerry (San Francisco), Clarke (Detroit).

Summary by Burnham.

Motion by Saunders (Washington): That the new NC set up a subcommittee to study the agricultural problem and to bring in a program within three months that party members can present to the farmers, sharecroppers, and agricultural proletarians. Carried.

Motion by Washington local: To strike out the section dealing with the labor party from the resolution and to substitute in its stead a section to the effect that the SWP does not advocate the formation of a labor party but where a labor party exists and runs independent candidates, and where the SWP is not strong enough to run independent candidates, the SWP should give critical support to the LP candidates. Defeated.

Trimble amendment defeated, 12 voting for it. No count of those opposed.[3]

Resolution of the National Committee as amended[4] unanimously carried [Text on p. 553].

Report of Comrade Burnham approved and adopted.

---

3. The Trimble amendment was intended primarily to register opposition to the SWP's new position on the labor party. What it registered, in the first convention action on the question, was a lower proportion against the new position (around 16 percent) than in the previous year's referendum vote (almost 40 percent).

4. The amendments referred to were submitted by the National Committee some weeks after the first draft was published in the *Socialist Appeal* and the internal bulletin. On motions by Cannon, paragraphs 8A and 8B were added to include suggestions by Trotsky and paragraphs 27, 28, and 29, were added to incorporate ideas Burnham had expressed in a memorandum on internal problems.

FIRST SESSION, SUNDAY, JULY 2, 1939

Convened 10:30 a.m.
Chairman: Abern

Supplementary report of Credentials Committee presented by Gates:
Texas—Convention received an official communication from branch designating Denning as delegate. Wills presented her own credential and asked to be seated as his alternate until he arrived. Credentials Committee decided that it could not determine delegates. Hence no delegates without bona fide credentials should be seated. Motion: That Wills will not be seated as an alternate until an official communication from branch is received. Carried.
Puerto Rico—No credential or communication from branch was presented by Comrade Slavin. Motion: That Comrade Slavin not be seated as a fraternal delegate from Puerto Rico until an official communication is received. Carried.
Lexington, Kentucky—Comrade Kwalik, member at large, asks convention to seat him as a fraternal delegate. Motion: That we do not seat members at large as delegates. Carried.
Rochester—Comrade Speyer requested he be seated as an alternate delegate in place of regularly elected alternate who is not present. Regular delegate is present. Motion: That he not be seated as an alternate delegate. Carried.
West Coast—Made no payment of assessment money. California organization authorized by NC to use assessment for expenses. Motion: That assessment be waived in this instance. Carried. Motion: That Edith Mann

be seated as alternate only for Steve Roberts. Carried.

Credentials Committee went through books on dues and assessment payments for delegate elections. By and large the same representations at the convention would have been elected if delegates were elected on a dues-paying basis or on assessment-paying basis. Several branches would either lose or gain one or more delegates depending on which representation basis is accepted by the convention.

Motion by majority of Credentials Committee: To adhere to decision of NC that basis for delegate elections be assessment payments.

Motion by minority of Credentials Committee (presented by Retzkin): That in view of the fact that the discrepancy between the NC ruling on convention representation and the constitution has resulted in branches following different procedures in electing delegates, that we grant the representation which the branches claim on the basis of dues-paying members.

Motion by Credentials Committee: In order that such confusion shall not recur in the future, the convention directs the Constitution Committee to bring in a proposal for a specific and definite basis for representation at conventions.

Discussion: Lewit (New York), McGee (Minneapolis), Findley (New York), Kerry (San Francisco), Geldman (Minneapolis), Burch (New York), Ferguson (Akron), Weber (New Jersey), Cannon, Thompson (Massachusetts), Gould, Mills (Indiana Harbor).

Motion by Mills (Indiana Harbor): That branches be seated according to dues-paying membership, but be held responsible for assessment within next thirty days.

Discussion by Trimble.

Retzkin accepts Mills's amendment.
Mills's amendment carried.
Motion by Credentials Committee on referring representation basis question to Constitution Committee carried.
Fitchburg, Massachusetts—Four comrades are members at large, not a branch, request fraternal representation. Motion to grant. Carried.

Report by Comrade Cannon: "The Preparation of the Party for War."
Discussion: Lands (New York), Revyuk (Illinois), Abern, Retzkin (New York), Gould.
Session adjourned at 2:00 p.m.

SECOND SESSION, SUNDAY, JULY 2, 1939

Convened 4:10 p.m.
Chairman: Shachtman.
Roll call taken.
Discussion continued: Widick, Milton, Erber, Clarke (Detroit), Demby (New York), Gates (Illinois), Burnham, Craine (Illinois), G. Johnson (Flint), Lear (Akron), Stevens, Johnson, Preis (Cleveland), Ferguson (Akron), Dale (California), Phillips (New York).
Summary by Comrade Cannon.
Motion: To adopt the report of Comrade Cannon. Carried unanimously.

Further Credentials Committee report (Gates):
Delegations represent 911 members. Assessments: 494 members paid for. Delegates present so far, 74. Alternates present so far, 35. Fraternal delegates present so far, 12. Regular women delegates, 6; alternate women, 9.
Motion: To accept report. Carried.

Report by Comrade Burnham: "The Struggle Against Fascism and the Workers' Defense Guard."
Supplementary report made by Comrade R. Stiler on Antifascist Labor Guards.
Supplementary report made by Comrade Dunne on Minneapolis experience with defense guards.
Greetings from Leninist Party of Brazil read by Comrade Shachtman as follows:

> To the second annual congress of the Socialist Workers Party, United States section of the Fourth International:
> The Central Committee of the Leninist Workers Party sends its fraternal greetings, expressing its hope and its certainty that our American brother section will emerge from its convention stronger and better armed for the struggle against the threatening imperialist war.
> The Socialist Workers Party, which is today the standard-bearer of the Fourth International, will become in the antiwar struggle the standard-bearer of the workers of the entire American continent in the struggle against Yankee imperialism, the most powerful of the imperialisms and the greatest oppressor of the colonial and semicolonial peoples of Latin America. In our sector of the struggle we shall wage, along with you, the revolutionary struggle until victory is won.
> Long live the Fourth International!

Comrade Dunne requested a point of special privilege, which was granted to him.
Comrade Dunne requested that Comrade Roberts of California be granted 10 minutes on his point of view since he was inadvertently removed from speakers' list yesterday by Comrade Dunne.
Motion: That Comrade Roberts be granted the floor on

this point whenever he feels it is appropriate. Carried.
Session adjourned at 8:10 p.m.

FIRST SESSION, MONDAY, JULY 3, 1939

Convened 10:45 a.m.

Discussion on workers' defense guard:
K. Johnson (Flint).
Amendment by Milton: "That in order that the workers' defense guards have a trade union base it is the task of our comrades in the first place to incorporate the slogan of the workers' defense guard in their program for progressive groups in all trade union and unemployed organizations where such progressive groups exist, and to raise it individually where such groups do not exist. Naturally, this slogan of workers' defense guard should not be presented in a mechanical manner, but as a concrete need, and in the present situation of the developing fascist movement, this need is apparent and should be followed by concrete proposals for the formation of the workers' defense guard."
Bleeker (New York).
Amendment by C. Williams (Minneapolis): "However, the antifascist labor guard must be considered primarily as a political agitational group whose function will be to create genuine interest in the ranks of militants in the unions. The antifascist labor guard cannot be considered as a substitute for the workers' defense guards of the unions. Only a workers' defense guard based upon the mass movement can be an effective army against fascism." (Add to Section 7.)
Amendment by Retzkin (New York): Strike out next to last

sentence in resolution which reads: "In addition, it has proved and will prove to be an incomparably effective means of opposition to Stalinism and of creating rifts in the Stalinist ranks."
Reid (Youngstown), Hughes (New York), Cochran, Bern (youth).
Summary by Comrade Burnham.
Amendment by Milton. Carried.
Amendment by Williams. Lost.
Amendment by Retzkin. Carried.
The following statement by E. Rhodes read, with recommendation from Resolutions Committee of nonconcurrence. Recommendation of Resolutions Committee carried.

Submitted by E. Rhodes, Downtown branch, New York.

I would like to introduce as a point for discussion, the question of uniforms for the labor guard.

I agree with the majority of the members of our party that at present the labor guard is the greatest source for recruiting members into the party.

Also that we should fight the fascists with their own weapons, such as drills and drums and even guns when they begin to use guns, but not uniforms, especially since at present the uniform consists of a blue shirt. As soon as we become known at all, we will most likely be known as the Blue Shirts. There is also the possibility of being mistaken for the cops during a riot because it will be rather difficult during a fight to look for a tiny label on the pocket of a shirt. When the guard becomes an organization large enough to fight it will be impossible for the guards to know every member.

We must consider the psychological effect of a uniform. Most people who would join a labor guard, would not be likely to join an army. A uniform, because of its association with armies, immediately places a barrier to some people. When we have a demonstration and we shout our slogan, "Antifascists join our ranks!," there are many who do join us and if instead of a uniform we had as our symbol, an armband with the words "Labor Guard" printed on it, we could at the correct psychological moment distribute these armbands to anyone who joined us and they would immediately become a part of the labor guard. (The drilling and education could come later.) This would constitute a real guard, since it is our aim to draw the masses into it. As for the shirts, the more varied in style and color the better because it would then resemble what it is meant to be, a representation of the masses.

Report adopted as amended [Text of resolution on page 569]. Session adjourned at 12:55 p.m.

SECOND SESSION, MONDAY, JULY 3, 1939

Convened 3:13 p.m.
Proposed by Presidium:
1. Night sessions Monday and Tuesday. Carried.
2. Reorganization of agenda: a) Negro; b) Press; c) Unemployed. Carried.

Question of Jewish work: Weber assigned to draw up document on Jewish work, no action necessary. Incoming NC to communicate with Comrade Crux by cablegram, but in a more extended form. Carried.

Negro Committee report: Presidium recommends 15 minutes each for McKinney and Wright for presentation of minority reports, to be taken out of discussion time. Carried.

Report on Negro work by Johnson.

**Program of Action
for Negro department of the SWP**

The committee on Negro work of the convention recommends to the convention that a part of the $10,000 fund to be raised for party activities be devoted to the establishment of a national Negro department with full-time functionaries; one in the national office and one in the field. The Negro department shall direct the Negro work of the party and the following are recommendations for its activities; and those of the party:

1. Regular column in each issue of the *Socialist Appeal* dealing with news items pertaining to social, economic, and political conditions of the Negro—housing, etc.; the activities of Negro organizations and news of the activities of Negro organizations, etc., in the colonies.

2. Special Negro number of the *New International*.

3. Pamphlet of a popular character on the Negro, giving historical background, present conditions, etc., pointing out that socialism is the only road for the Negro to follow for his emancipation.

4. Organization tour by Comrade Johnson for the purpose of organizing the work on a national scale and in the localities.

5. Pamphlet on the Negro and the CP dealing with the attitude of the Communist International in both the United States and in the colonial countries.

6. Theoretical study as outlined in the note at the

bottom of page 23 of Bulletin No. 9.[5]

7. Work out adaptation of the Transitional Program for the work among Negroes, with emphasis on the demand for equality.

8. Organization of committee on Negro work by all party locals, to study the local situation, methods of organization, etc.

9. Extensive circulation by the party locals of the publication of the International African Service Bureau and of *Spark* to aid in laying the basis for the building of the Negro organization and in recruiting for the party.

10. Study by the defense department of the party of legal discriminations against the Negroes, and help in defense of Negroes involved in cases of discrimination and activities in the class struggle.

Recommendations of Negro Committee majority:
1. Title of resolution "Self-Determination and the American Negro" to read: "The Right of Self-Determination and the Negro in the United States of North America."
2. Amendments to the resolution on self-determination:
   a) Page 1, par. 1, line 3, insert words: "war and" before the words "postwar emigration." [page 577, line 3]
   b) Page 3, par. 2, line 4, insert word: "reactionary"

---

5. *Internal Bulletin*, SWP, number 9, June 1939, contained the transcripts of discussions with Trotsky in Mexico about the Black struggle in the United States, held in April 1939. In one of these, James said: "The party should produce a theoretical study of the permanent revolution and the Negro peoples. This should be very different in style from the pamphlet previously suggested. It should not be a controversy with the CP, but a positive economic and political analysis showing that socialism is the only way out and definitely treating the theory on a high level." These Mexican transcripts are in *Leon Trotsky on Black Nationalism and Self-Determination* (Pathfinder, 1978).

after word "fantastic," so that phrase reads: "concealed behind its fantastic and reactionary slogan of 'Back to Africa.'" [page 580, line 7]
c) Page 3, par. 2, line 5, after word "desire": insert parenthetically: "(revolutionary in its essence)." [page 580, line 8]
d) Page 3, par. 2, at end of paragraph add: "This desire may very well fall into the hands of reactionary leaders. But only the most energetic defense of the right of self-determination of the Negro masses can lead their movement into revolutionary channels." [page 580, line 27]
e) Page 4, last line, insert words: "the right of" before word "self-determination." [page 580, line 12]
f) Page 3, line before last, insert words: "masses of" before word, "Negroes." [page 582, line 30]
g) Page 5, line 3, after "U.S.A.," add: "The advocacy of the *right* of self-determination does not mean the advancing of the *slogan* of self-determination." [page 582, line 4]
h) Page 5, line 4, the two sentences beginning with: "Furthermore," and ending with: "Within itself," to be reworded to read: "Furthermore, a party predominantly white in membership which in present-day America advocates such a slogan prejudices it in the minds of Negroes, who see it as a form of segregation." [page 582, line 7]
i) Page 5, line 13, after words "finally come to," add: "as to the necessity of a Negro state." [page 582, line 15]
3. Amendments to resolution "The SWP and Negro Work":
a) Page 1, par. 2, line 6, insert word: "politically" before words "more advanced." [page 584, line 14]

b) Page 1, par. 2, line 7, reword to read: "and through the work of the party among the Negroes and in wider fields influencing," etc. [page 584, line 16]
c) Page 1, par. 2, line 10, insert words: "masses of," before word "Negroes." [page 584, line 20]
d) Page 2, par. 2, line 2, strike out word "boasted" before word "benefits." [page 585, line 4]
e) Page 2, par. 3, line 2, insert word "politically" before words "more advanced"; line 8, strike out words "in Moscow"; line 10, substitute word "its" for "the" "latest turn," etc.; line 13, substitute word "racial" for word "contradictory"; line 17, substitute word "departure" for "exodus"; line 19, add word "Negro" before "members"; in last line, substitute word "undermining" for "destroy." [page 585, par. 2]
f) Page 3, par. 2, sentence beginning with "Such a desire" to be reworded to read: "Such a desire is legitimate and must be vigorously supported even when it takes the form of a rather aggressive chauvinism." [page 586, line 6]
g) Page 3, par. 2, line 9, after words "for equality" insert words: "and is essentially progressive." [page 586, line 17]
h) Page 3, par. 2, line 15, substitute words "gravely undermined" for words "practically destroyed." [page 586, line 25]
i) Page 4, line 9, strike out word "critical." [page 587, line 18]
j) Page 4, line before last, strike out words "and activity." [page 587, line 35]

Minority report by Wright.
Amendments proposed: "On Self-Determination":
1. To add to the opening section a section dealing with

the relation of Negro proletarians to the Negroes as a whole. Should the decisive mass of Negro workers be won to the Fourth International, that would have a decisive bearing on the question.
2. On page 3, line 14, add section dealing with possible effects of the development of "counterrevolutionary crisis" on the Negroes. Suggested formulation: "It is by no means excluded that in a counterrevolutionary crisis the desire for a Negro state may assume a more reactionary character than did the Garvey movement." [page 580, line 11, after "Palestine"]

Minority report by McKinney.
Amendments proposed: Page 3, eliminate second paragraph. [page 580, par. 1] Page 5, eliminate three sentences beginning with "But the SWP . . . decline." [page 582, line 11]
Greetings from Revolutionary Socialist League of Great Britain:

> Dear Comrades:
> Revolutionary greetings and best wishes for the success of your national convention.
>
> Yours fraternally,
> *(Signed) C.P. Stanton*
> Secretary, RSL
> British Section,
> Fourth International

Speakers in discussion: Birchman, Stevens, Saunders, Gates, Plaskett.
Recommendations of Plaskett:
1. That the party in every issue of its press (*Appeal,* etc.) carry an article pertinent to the Negro problem. (This is not to be interpreted to mean theoretical articles.)
2. In centers where Negroes comprise a large part of the

population (Harlem, Third Ward of Newark, etc.) an investigation of their everyday problems should be undertaken by the party to further the work in these centers and for utilization in the party press.
3. That the legal section of the party help in the work among Negroes by a study of legal discrimination in courts, etc., and that the legal section suggest means of combating this discrimination.
4. That special interest be taken concerning the housing problem in relation to the Negro.

Further discussion: Weber, Burnham, McGee.

Summary by Johnson.

Motion by McKinney: The convention recommends to the incoming National Committee that a general political resolution on the Negro in the U.S. be prepared, one section to deal with the question of self-determination. Resolution to be adopted by party referendum within a period of sixty days after presentation to the party.

Motion by Wright: Resolution on self-determination be adopted as the basis of a final draft. All amendments to be referred to NC. Carried [Text on page 577].

Resolution on "SWP and Negro Work" carried [Text on page 577].

Motion by Johnson to refer Program of Action to incoming NC carried.

Recommendation of Burnham (Wherever the phrase "advocacy of the right of self-determination" appears, it be replaced by "recognition and defense of the right of self-determination") referred to NC.

Recommendations of Plaskett (above) referred to NC.

Motion by Negro committee:

The committee on Negro work recommends to the national convention that it instruct the incoming NC to prepare as soon as possible a general resolution on the Negro problem in America. This resolution should deal with the question as a whole, in all its aspects and from the broadest point of view, and is to serve as the basic document of the party on the question. Such a resolution alone will throw into correct perspective and reduce to its proper proportions the single aspect of the problem represented by the right of self-determination.

The convention should recommend further to the incoming NC, that upon completion of this general resolution, it is to take immediate steps to institute discussion on it in the party to the end that the party adopt such a basic document as speedily as possible.

Motion carried.[6]
Greetings read from Socialist Workers League of Canada:

TORONTO, JULY 2, 1939

Socialist Workers Party
National Convention, New York City
Dear Comrades:
The Socialist Workers League of Canada extends its warmest fraternal greetings to its sister section in the United States on the occasion of its second national convention.

---

6. Before the newly elected leadership could implement this motion, World War II began and the SWP was plunged into a factional crisis that threatened its very existence. All of the party's practical work suffered until the crisis was resolved by a split in April 1940 and the withdrawal of many of the party's leaders, including C.L.R. James, who had been put in charge of the SWP's National Negro Department after the July convention. Despite the lack of the general resolution urged in the convention motion, the SWP played an important part in the Black struggle during the war. See *Fighting Racism in World War II* by C.L.R. James, George Breitman, Edgar Keemer, and others (Monad, 1980).

The Canadian movement records its appreciation of the great contribution which the American movement has made, both of an inspirational and material nature, to the Fourth International. The growth of the influence and prestige of the American movement has been a tower of strength to every other national section, particularly for Canada.

The SWL plans to hold its first national convention later in the year, when the intensive campaign now being conducted across the Dominion with five field organizers, will have been completed. It extends a cordial invitation to the American movement to participate in this conference, so that side by side we shall march forward to the Socialist United States of America.

With fraternal greetings,
Socialist Workers League of Canada
H. Kennedy, National Secretary

Comrade Wright announces that he will submit further amendments on the Negro question at the close of (or immediately after) the convention.

Greetings read from International Communist League of Mexico:

Dear Comrades:

The Mexican Section of the Fourth International sends you its most sincere revolutionary greetings on the occasion of your annual congress; desiring for it the greatest success in the fight against imperialism, which exploits the workers of the metropolis as well as the semicolonies of Latin America.

The lackeys of imperialism in Mexico, with the Stalinists—with Lombardo at their head—are attempting to shackle the masses of the workers to the defense of imperialist interests and because of that we believe that one of the tasks of your congress shall be the fight against the agents of imperialism within the working class. The workers of the entire continent shall have on the order of the day: the transformation of the imperialist war into a civil war against our exploiter and for a socialist revolution.

Long live the Fourth International!

> Central Committee
> International Communist League
> (Mexican Section of the Fourth International)
> *Felix Ibarra, Secretary*

Collection taken for comrades in mishap en route to the convention.

Motion of thanks in the name of the Presidium and of the convention to the comrades in charge of the food. Carried by acclaim.

Motion to reconvene at 7:45 p.m. Carried.

THIRD SESSION, MONDAY, JULY 3, 1939

Convened 8:30 p.m.
Chairman: Trimble.

Report by Comrade Abern on party press.
Greetings read from Plentywood, Montana:
Socialist Workers Party
116 University Place
New York City
   Convention greetings STOP Hope for an inspirational

program to clear minds of those befuddled by Roosevelt and his prowar and prostarvation supporters.
> John Boulds
> A.N. Wankel
> Pete Gallagher
> Wayne LaGrange
> Fred Brinkman

Discussion on press report: Lear (Akron), Faben (Illinois), Clarke (Detroit), Erber (youth). Special permission granted Roberts to discuss, Lands (New York), Donahue (Rochester), Turner (Boston), Craine (Illinois), Morrow, Dostal (St. Paul), Lewit, Walsh (Columbus), Bern (youth), Shachtman, Thompson (Worcester), Burnham, Phillips (New York), Cochran, Mills (Indiana Harbor).

Motion by Abern: Convention approves the campaign for a $5,000 press fund which is provided for in the organization resolution and leaves to the discretion of the incoming NC the frequency of the *Socialist Appeal*. Carried.

Report of Comrade Abern adopted unanimously.

Further Credentials Committee report (Gates):
Trade union representation: 45 out of 78 regular delegates, 23 out of 38 alternates. Average age: Delegates 28 ½, alternates 30.

FIRST SESSION, TUESDAY, JULY 4, 1939

Convened 11:45 a.m.
Chairman: Gould.
Recommendations from Unemployed Committee: To have each reporter present his respective resolution,

then to have discussion until reporter on organization arrives. These resolutions not to be voted on but referred to incoming NC. Accepted.

Report by McKinney on resolution [Text on page 589].

Report by Preis and presentation of his resolution on unemployed [Text on page 593].

Discussion: Greenberg (New York).

Motion to close discussion on unemployed report. Carried.

Motion by McKinney: To refer both resolutions to incoming NC and request NC to insert section on youth and unemployed. Carried.

Report by Comrade Shachtman: "The War and the Fourth International."

Resolution on Fourth International read by chairman.

Resolution on the Fourth International

The Second National Convention of the Socialist Workers Party greets the founding of the Fourth International (World Party of the Social Revolution) as the basis for rallying and centralizing the revolutionary forces in all countries who stand uncompromisingly for the principles of Marx and Lenin.

The convention endorses the theses and resolutions of the founding conference of the Fourth International, especially the program of revolutionary transitional demands.

The convention instructs the National Committee to continue maintaining the closest political and economic relations with the International and extending material support to sister sections whenever the occasion requires it.

The convention, noting the pitiful collapse of the Brandlerite "International" and the London Bureau, and the attempts being made by the last survivors of these bankruptcies to reconstitute a new edition of the centrist International, instructs the National Committee to exercise the influence of the SWP in exposing the centrists and in winning the genuinely revolutionary elements now under their sway.

Discussion: Johnson.
Motion by Findley (New York): That a regular bulletin of information concerning our sister parties in other countries be sent out by the national office. Carried.
Carter: Both Carter and Burnham agree with resolution but still disagree on party position on Russian question. However, will not raise discussion at this time.
Summary by Comrade Shachtman.
Resolution adopted as presented.
Report accepted.
Adjourned at 1:40 p.m.

SECOND SESSION, TUESDAY, JULY 4, 1939

Convened 2:45 p.m.

Organization report by Comrade Cannon.[7]

---

7. This report, and especially the differences over the counterposed formulations in sections 2(b) and 2(c) of the organization resolution, produced a long and sharp debate, whose heated character was unexpected by most of the delegates and is not conveyed by the minutes. Two weeks before the convention Burnham had noted, in a memorandum to the Political Committee, "This convention is unprecedented in that we approach it without any major conflict on any basic political issue." The National Committee was unanimously in favor of the political resolution, and the convention adopted it unanimously. In spite of that, the imminence of war and uncertainty about what

Organization Resolution (Program of Expansion)

A party of the Leninist type, such as we aspire to build, is distinguished from reformist organizations and propaganda sects in its organization methods as well as in its political principles.

The Leninist party is a combat organization that aims at the conquest of power. It conducts its activity on the campaign principle. It is democratic in its internal life and centralized in action. It coordinates organization work with the work of literary propaganda and agitation and implements political decisions by organizational measures. It constructs a strong apparatus, and it relies on the leadership of a staff of professional revolutionists in the center and in the field.

Proceeding from this Leninist concept of organization, and aiming at an expansion of our activities by a forced march in the next period, as projected in the political resolution, the convention sets before the

---

it would do to the SWP and its members were stimulating moods of impatience, edginess, and volatility among those circles in the party that were most vulnerable to bourgeois and petty-bourgeois pressures. The form that this took before and at the convention was expressed in the Burnham memorandum as follows: "Why are we not growing faster?" This was certainly a legitimate question, but of no help when it was coupled with simplistic, purely organizational conclusions. At the convention some of the delegates tried to consider the proposal for a new national organization department directed by a full-time organization secretary on its abstract merits, but many of the delegates saw it as a move to reduce the role of the party's chief executive officer, the national secretary (Cannon). The division of the delegates over this issue was not identical with the factional alignments that took place over the Russian question a few months later, after Stalin signed his pact with Hitler and World War II began, but it was similar. Cannon's book, *The Struggle for a Proletarian Party,* contains the assessments of this convention episode written by Cannon and his opponents after the faction fight began in the autumn of 1939.

party the following program of expansion:

1. *Press:*

(a) The transformation of the *Socialist Appeal* into a three-times-a-week publication.

(b) Pamphlets: The publication of at least six cheap, popular pamphlets on the following topics:

1. Let the People Vote on War (already prepared).
2. Build Workers Defense Guards.
3. A Job for Every Worker.
4. Thirty-thirty.
5. Expropriate the Sixty Families.
6. Labor and the 1940 Elections.

(c) Leaflets: Periodic issuing of four-page leaflets on key slogans for mass distribution nationally.

2. *Staff:*

(a) Increase the staff by the assignment of twenty more full-time organizers for field work and in the center.

(b) Formulation of majority of organization committee: Establish a national organization department directed by a full-time organization secretary.

(c) Formulation of Cannon: The object of extending the departmentalization of national work, under full-time direction as the NC finds feasible.

(d) Full-time functionary for the direction of national trade union work.

3. *Conferences:* Active workers conferences in Far West, Middle West, Ohio-Michigan, East.

4. *Tours:* National and regional tours at intervals of not more than two months.

5. A systematically organized and centrally directed recruiting campaign.

6. *Finances:* Raise an organization press fund of $10,000 within three months to be equally divided between the organization work and the *Socialist Appeal*.

One-third of the $10,000 fund is to be raised by the national office. Two-thirds to be raised by quotas accepted by the convention delegates.

Comrade Carter presented opinion of majority of Organization Committee on establishment of organization department and organization secretary.
Motion by Weber: That the matter of the organization department be referred to the incoming NC.
Discussion on question of reference: Shachtman, McKinney, Cannon, Weber.
Roll call vote: Motion of reference defeated, 65–11.[8]
Discussion on organization report: Cochran, Burnham, Clarke, Saunders, Fraser, Turner, Milton, Dunne, Abern, Gates.
Amendment by Weiss (to majority formulation on organization department): "Establish, if feasible, a national organization department directed by a full-time organization secretary."
Shachtman.
Motion by Dunne: To adjourn for one-half hour to give Presiding Committee a chance to consider and to make a report on procedure and discussion continuance. Carried.
Adjourned at 8:45 p.m.

THIRD SESSION, TUESDAY, JULY 4, 1939

Convened 9:30 p.m.
Recommendation of Presiding Committee: Convention

---

8. This was the only roll call vote of the convention but the minutes omit the delegates' names and votes, unlike the minutes of the founding convention.

decide to eliminate now all further discussion and to proceed forthwith with summaries by reporters. Carried.

Request by Weber for point of special privilege granted. Points out that discussion hinged on formulation of organization department and not on rest of resolution. Hence mistake made in not referring.

Summary by Carter.

Summary by Cannon.

Formulation of Cannon on organization department—Section 2(c) of Program of Expansion. Carried, 45–25; 2 abstentions.

Weiss amendment. Defeated.

Majority formulation—Section 2(b). Defeated 29–33; 1 abstention.

Resolution on organization work adopted unanimously.

Motion by Presiding Committee: Work in the trade union resolution be read and referred to incoming NC.

Amendment: That resolution be referred without reading.

Motion as amended carried [Text on page 597].

Motion of Presiding Committee: That report on youth be written and sent to branches. Carried.

Motion of Presiding Committee: That antiwar manifesto be referred to the incoming NC to be issued later. Carried.[9]

Motion of Greenberg (New York): That every question that has been excluded from discussion at this convention on which there are two or more points of view be referred to the branches of the party and the NC to act on the decisions of the branches of the party on these questions. Defeated.

Session adjourned at 11:35 p.m.

---

9. The youth report, if written, was not sent to the branches, and the antiwar manifesto was not published by the National Committee.

FOURTH SESSION, TUESDAY, JULY 4, 1939

Reconvened midnight.

Report of Constitution Committee.

Amendment of Retzkin to Article IX, Section 3: "Charges against any member shall be made in writing and the accused member shall be furnished with a copy in advance of the trial. Charges shall be filed and heard in the branch to which the member belongs. In cases where it may not be feasible to hear charges in the branch, the latter may waive this right in favor of a direct hearing by the proper local or national body. Charges against members of higher bodies shall be heard in those bodies. Charges filed before the branch, etc. (as at present)." Defeated.

Amendments submitted by Constitution Committee:
1. Persons who have been expelled from the party or who have resigned may not be readmitted to the party without the approval of the National Committee. Carried.
2. Questions decided by the party convention may be subjects of new discussions only when such discussion is formally authorized by the National Committee, or in the established preconvention discussion period. Carried.
3. Political collaboration with nonmembers of the party must be formally authorized by the party committee having jurisdiction. Carried.
4. Amend Article IX, Section 3, to read as follows: "Charges against any member shall be made in writing and the accused member shall be furnished with a copy in advance of the trial. Charges shall be filed and heard in the branch to which the member belongs,

or in a higher body which may decide to act directly in the case. Charges filed before the branch shall be considered by the branch executive committee (or a subcommittee elected by it) at a meeting to which the accused member is summoned. The branch executive committee shall submit a recommendation to be acted upon by the membership of the branch. Charges considered by higher bodies of the party shall, however, be acted upon by said bodies." Carried.
5. Amend Article XI, Section 1, to read: "National conventions of the party shall be held at least every two years. Special conventions may be called by the National Committee or on the demand of branches representing one-third of the membership." Carried.
6. Amend Article XI, Section 3, to read as follows: "The National Committee shall appoint an auditing committee to make periodic audits of the financial accounts of the national office and national departments and institutions, and report on same to the National Committee. Branch, local, and district committees shall appoint auditing committees to make periodic audits of the financial accounts of the corresponding party units and of party departments and institutions responsible to said units." Carried.

Amendment to Article VI, Section 1: Strike out "The International Bureau for" and substitute "The party is affiliated to the Fourth International." Carried.

Amendment to Article VIII, Section 1: Strike out words "charter members." Insert instead "members in good standing of the YPSL." Carried.

Amendment to Article XI, Section 3: "Representation at the convention shall be proportionately based upon dues-paying membership at the time of the branch election of delegates to the convention. The National Committee shall levy a compulsory assessment to finance the national convention, from which totally unemployed members shall be exempted." Carried.

Amendment to Article XI, Section 4: "Regular members of the National Committee, if not regular delegates, shall be fraternal delegates to the convention." Carried.

Amendment to Article XI, Section 5: "The YPSLs shall be represented at the party convention by three regular delegates elected by the National Committee of the YPSL." Carried.

Amendment (Trimble)—Add to Section VI, Article 4: "New members of established branches shall serve a minimum of three months." Defeated.

Resolutions Committee report.

Two resolutions on a party emblem were presented as follows:

> The adoption of an emblem or symbol for the SWP is desirable at this time for agitational and propaganda purposes. However minor a place such an emblem may appear to take now in the work of the party, no one can deny its potential use or significance in the coming days. The emblem should be, and would be, the incarnation in the mind of the workers of all that the party stands and fights for, in the same way that the hammer and sickle once stood for Bolshevism, and that the swastika represents today, in an international language, fascism. The party needs such an emblem on its flag and

banners, on its publications and papers, on placards, posters, street corner platforms, stickers, and such ballots as we may have.

Be it therefore resolved that this convention instruct the incoming National Committee: (1) to appoint a resident committee of three to create such an emblem for the party; (2) to set a time limit of one month for the completion of this work; and (3) to take appropriate steps, if necessary a national referendum, to secure the most rapid acceptance of this emblem.

> Submitted by Dale Edwards
> and Lyman Paine,
> Delegates from Upper West
> Side, New York

Resolved: That the SWP adopt an emblem to be used on the masthead of the *Appeal,* and for other decorative purposes; that a committee be formed to consider this.

> Submitted by G. Donoghue,
> Rochester Local.

Resolutions Committee recommends that resolution of Rochester comrades be adopted by convention. Carried.

Resolutions of Downtown Branch of New York

1. *RESOLVED* that delegates to the national convention, 1939, are elected on the basis of members in good standing and that if the number of delegates is contested by the Credentials Committee, our delegates demand to be seated by virtue of Section 3 of

Article XI of the party constitution of the SWP, even if it is necessary to bring the question to the vote of the seated delegates.

*Presented by Sterling,
amended by McCormack*

2. *RESOLVED* that the party enter into an intensive national educational campaign among the membership on what the membership is to do upon the outbreak of war.

Presented by Nomen

3. *RESOLVED* that Comrade Rhodes's document be read at the convention and presented for discussion by the delegates from the Downtown branch.

Presented by Rhodes

4. The Downtown branch wishes to register its disapproval of the incompetent manner in which the National Committee handled the convention discussion: in particular, the lack of material published on crucial matters for convention discussion and the tardiness in distribution of such discussion bulletins to the branches. (Two of the three bulletins published were actually received by the membership at so late a date that no discussion on the basis of these bulletins could possibly be held in the branches.)

Presented by E. Konikow

The following action was taken on the above resolutions:
1. Recommend this be filed because decided. Carried.
2. Recommended this be filed because decided. Carried.
3. This resolution was disposed of at a previous meeting.
4. Requires no action.

Election of National Committee: 24 members and 10 alternates elected to the National Committee. 74 ballots cast.[10]

Convention adjourned at 7:45 a.m., July 5.

---

10. We were able to insert in the mimeographed minutes of the first SWP convention the names of the people nominated for National Committee and alternates, the number of votes they received, etc., but we lacked similar information to insert in the minutes of the second convention. A nominations committee was chosen the first day of the convention, to draw up a National Committee slate to be presented to the convention, but apparently its slate was not presented. Instead, Shachtman arose and nominated a slate, after which V.R. Dunne arose and nominated another. The two slates overlapped partly. No record of the nominations made or the vote they received was available for this book. The names of the 24 regular members elected can be pieced together by examining minutes of later plenums, but the names of only nine of the ten alternates elected can be deduced this way. Elected to the National Committee were: Abern, Breitman, Burnham, Cannon, Carter, Clarke, Cochran, Dobbs, Dunne, Erber, Goldman, Gordon, Gould, Kerry, Lewit, McKinney, Morrow, Selander, Shachtman, Skoglund, Swabeck, Weber, Murry Weiss, Widick. Nine alternates (listed here alphabetically, instead of in the order of precedence, which is not known): William Farrell (Morgan), Jules Geller, Albert Glotzer (Gates), Blake Lear, Esther Lieberman (Stevens), Les Reid, Larry Trainor (Turner), Manuel Trbovich (Mills), John G. Wright. Accounts of the election by both of the postconvention factions will be found in Cannon's *The Struggle for a Proletarian Party* (pp. 75-77, 282). Nine months later, 8 of the 24 regular members and 2 of the 9 known alternates withdrew from the SWP in the April 1940 split.

Delegates at second convention: **above**, Joseph Hansen, Grace Carlson; **below**, Howard Stump, Ernest Erber.

Above, Vincent R. Dunne, Ernest Rice McKinney; **below**, C.L.R. James, Albert Goldman.

ATTACHMENTS

Information about the delegates[11]

Number of regular delegates: 72
Average age: 28½
Length of time in SWP:
 63 charter members
 5 members for 1 year
 2 members for 10 months
 1 member for 8 months
 1 member for 6 months

---

11. By permission of the Library of Social History. This information was tabulated by the Credentials Committee from the registration forms filled out by the regular delegates. It therefore does not include data about SWP leaders who attended the convention as fraternal delegates. Some of the regular delegates obviously had more than one previous political affiliation. One year and a half after the founding convention the number of regular delegates who had been "native" SP or YPSL members (38) was almost as large as the number who had belonged to the WPUS and SYL (47).

Previous political affiliation:
   Socialist Party 37
   American Workers Party 25
   Communist League of America 19
   Communist Party 11
   Young Communist League 9
   Spartacus Youth League 3
   Fieldites 2
   Young People's Socialist League 1
   Industrial Workers of the World 1
   Revolutionary Workers League
   (Oehlerites) 1
   Lovestoneites 1
   POI (France) 1
   POUM (Spain) 1
Occupations:
   White collar 21
   Workers 21
   Business 1
   Teachers 8
   Unemployed 6
   Students 1
   Party functionaries 5
   YPSL functionaries 3
   Trade union functionaries 3
Trade unionists: 46

A PARTIAL LIST OF DELEGATES' NAMES[12]

Martin Abern (N.Y.)
Milton Alvin (N.Y.)
Yetta Barsh (N.Y.)
Irving Bern (youth)
Robert L. Birchman (Ind.)
Sylvia Bleeker (N.Y.)
George Breitman (N.J.)
Arthur Burch (N.Y.)
James Burnham (N.Y.)
James P. Cannon (N.Y.)
Carli
Joseph Carter (N.Y.)
George Clarke (Mich.)
Bert Cochran (N.Y.)
Oscar Coover (Minn.)
Reva Craine (Ill.)
Jack Dale (Calif.)
Frank Demby (N.Y.)
G. Donoghue (or Donahue) (N.Y.)
Ted Dostal (Minn.)
Vincent R. Dunne (Minn.)
Dale Edwards (N.Y.)
Ernest Erber (youth)
Farrow
Richard Ferguson (Ohio)
Paul Fielding (Ohio)
Al Findley (N.Y.)
Richard Fraser (Wash.)
Albert Gates (Ill.) [Albert Glotzer]
Max Geldman (Minn.)
Glover (Calif.)
Nathan Gould (youth)
Greenberg (N.Y.)
Joseph Hansen (N.Y.)
Pete Hesser (Calif.)
Sam Hill (Mo.)
Hughes (N.Y.)
Genora Johnson (Mich.)
J.R. Johnson (N.Y.) [C.L.R. James]
Kermit Johnson (Mich.)
Tom Kerry (Calif.)
Dave Lands (N.Y.)
Blake Lear (Ohio)
Dan Leeds

---

12. From the Credentials Committee's reports to the convention, it is clear that there were at least 128 delegates—78 regular, 38 alternate, 12 fraternal. Unfortunately, the committee's list did not survive. This partial list of 89 has been compiled from references in the minutes and in *Socialist Appeal* articles about the convention. Thirty-seven of the 89 on the partial list had also been delegates to the founding convention. In some of the cases where pseudonyms were used in the convention and the minutes we have added the real name in brackets.

Rose Faben (Ill.)
McGee (Minn.) [Grace Carlson]
Ernest R. McKinney (N.Y.)
Edith Mann (Calif.)
Daisy Manret (N.Y.)
Charles Martell (Ohio)
M. Mills (Ind.) [Manuel Trbovich]
Harry Milton (N.Y.)
Felix Morrow (N.Y.)
Robert Ontell (Calif.)
Lyman Paine (N.Y.)
Larry Phillips (N.Y.)
Reuben Plaskett (N.J.)
Art Preis (Ohio)
Ruth Querio (Pa.)
Les Reid (Ohio)
Alex Retzkin (N.Y.)
Emil Revyuk (Ill.)
L. Roberts (N.J.)
Steve Roberts (Calif.)
Saunders (Wash.)
Marie Schimmel (Calif.)
Ted Selander (Ohio)
Max Shachtman (N.Y.)

Morris Lewit (N.Y.)
Hildegarde Smith (Kans.)
Ray Sparrow (Calif.)
Bertha Stevens (Calif.)
David Stevens (Calif.)
[David Weiss]
Robert Stiler (Ohio)
Howard Stump (Pa.)
Harold Swanson (Minn.)
Pauline Thompson (Mass.)
Henry Thurman (Ohio)
Glen Trimble (Calif.)
Larry Turner (Mass.)
[Larry Trainor]
Walsh (Ohio)
Everett Washburn (Mo.)
Jack Weber (N.J.)
Murry Weiss (Calif.)
B.J. Widick (N.Y.)
C. Williams (Minn.)
[Charles Scheer]
John G. Wright (N.Y.)
Bernard Wolfe (Conn.)
George Zola (N.Y.)

PART 7
New York convention resolutions

Political resolution[1]

The perspective of United States imperialism

1. In common with every other great power, the course of United States imperialism is set directly toward the second world war. The entire life of the nation is being grooved into the war channel. Every political, economic, and social issue is being more and more subordinated to the war preparations.

---

1. After the Munich conference of September 1938, which allegedly was going to preserve "peace in our time," signs of the imminence of war multiplied. In January 1939 Barcelona fell to the fascists and in March the People's Front government surrendered, freeing the German and Italian troops in Spain for service elsewhere. In March Germany occupied Czechoslovakia, in April Italy invaded Albania. In March, at a congress of the Communist Party of the Soviet Union, Stalin began to put out signals of his willingness to make a deal with Hitler. Roosevelt's response to these developments was to accelerate U.S. preparations for the coming war. This meant pulling back from his New Deal reforms, opening an offensive against the gains and rights of the newly unionized workers, firing hundreds of thousands of WPA workers, slashing

2. After six years, the New Deal, as a primarily internal program of huge governmental expenditures and subsidies, liberal demagogy, and social concessions to the farmers and workers has ended in definitive collapse. The intolerable economic crisis continues. The business cycle refuses to turn upward for more than fitful and unsatisfying periods. The impossibility of a solution on the New Deal basis, and the fatuousness of any proposed solution on the basis of old-fashioned, chamber-of-commerce Republicanism, have become apparent. Internal measures having failed and offering no hope, the United States bourgeoisie turns to external measures, to the war. It plans to solve its problems through acquiring a greater share in the world market, in particular by gaining monopoly control over Latin America and a major position in the Far East. Indeed, it aims at nothing short of world hegemony. In the present stage of the war preparations, Roosevelt has taken aggressive leadership. His New Deal has ended, and will not be revived, except occasionally in his holiday words or in those of his agents. *The New Deal has been transformed into the War Deal.*

3. Because of the needs both of the war and of tottering U.S. industry, the War Deal is also a deal of social reaction. The months since Munich and the November elections have witnessed a growing reactionary wave. This has been

---

welfare standards, and vastly increasing military appropriations. The resolution analyzing these trends in the spring of 1939 was drafted by the Political Committee and submitted as part of the SWP preconvention discussion; it was published in the *Socialist Appeal*, May 23, 1939, and *Internal Bulletin*, SWP, number 8, May 1939. The National Committee amended the resolution by adding paragraphs 8A, 8B, 27, 28, and 29. The amended resolution, unanimously adopted by the convention, was published in the *Socialist Appeal*, August 4, 1939, and is reprinted here. James Burnham was the principal author.

marked above all by the sharpest and most brutal attack since 1929 on the unemployed and by the sustained drive against the democratic rights of labor. In the period ahead, this attack and this drive will continue, and it is planned to climax them by the imposition of totalitarian military dictatorship on the day that war begins.

The struggle against war

4. The character of the present period dictates unequivocally the main task of the party: *the struggle against the war.* Just as the bourgeoisie subordinates every other question to preparation *for* the war, so must the party subordinate every question to the struggle *against* the war. What is required is not a temporary or episodic campaign, but a sustained, deliberate, and enduring policy. The SWP must aim to be and to become known to the masses as the *antiwar party.*

5. In accordance with our analysis of the nature of capitalist war as an integral phase of capitalism, the struggle against the war cannot be conceived as a "special" campaign, but must, rather, infuse all of our activities: trade union work no less than our press; youth and defense and unemployed work no less than our occasional manifestos.

6. We must recognize that our opponents within the labor movement—the social reformists, Stalinists, and the labor bureaucracy—are separated from us now not by mere ideological divergences but by their having become *part of the war machine.* They have joined the camp of the class enemy. Our attack against them must correspondingly increase in sharpness and intransigence. We must reveal them to the workers in their full and true light.

7. Our press and platforms must be constantly used to make clear the character of the coming war. We must continue to support the popular referendum on war declaration, as a means for reinforcing antiwar sentiment

among the masses, for putting forward our own program, and for exposing the antidemocratic nature of the warmakers. Similarly, with the demand for "No secret diplomacy" and with exposures of the secret maneuvers of the State Department we must show the war as a conspiracy against the people. Our unqualified opposition to all imperialist armaments, to all varieties of "national defense," must be modified in no way whatever in the face of prejudices seeking some patriotic loophole. With our slogan of "All war funds to the unemployed" we sum up both our analysis of bourgeois armaments and their relation to the reactionary drive against the masses.

8. The first aim of U.S. imperialism in the war is monopoly control over Latin America, and the U.S. plans also to use Latin America as a strategic base and a source of raw materials and personnel in the conduct of the war. Our struggle against the war cannot be divorced from the firmest and widest support of the Latin American masses in their own struggle against U.S. imperialism. During the past year, the Fourth International, which is the sole organization supporting on a world scale the anti-imperialist movements of the colonial and semicolonial peoples, has made notable progress in a number of Latin American countries. The SWP must in the next year vastly increase its concentration upon Latin American work, and must link this with what has been almost entirely lacking in the past: political activity among the Latin Americans resident within the United States.

8a. The outbreak of the war is certain to be followed within a comparatively short period, far shorter than in the case of the last world war, by tremendous social convulsions within all of the warring countries. The war itself will have smashed the illusions of Popular Frontism, New Dealism, reformism, and Stalinism. The subsequent social convulsions will provide every premise for the revolutionary advance, at an entirely unprecedented speed and with unparalleled scope, of the masses toward the overthrow of the world system of imperialism and the conquest of workers' power.

8b. A realistic appraisal of the present world crisis can lead to no other conclusion than that the outbreak of the war cannot be long delayed. However unlikely, it is not however absolutely excluded that the present rulers of the imperialist powers, seeing in the war their own certain downfall, may find some means of postponing general hostilities for a few years. But in this case there is sure to result the most terrible economic crisis, aggravated unbearably by the weight of the colossal armament expenditures. A postwar situation—inflation, high cost of living, scarcity of food, vast unemployment—with its attendant social convulsions would come about without a war. Just as in the case of the results of the war itself, this would bring about and constitute a *prerevolutionary situation*. Within the nonfascist powers, the fascists could grow rapidly. But in this instance also New Dealism, Popular Frontism, reformism, Stalinism would go to pieces both in fact and in their hold on the minds of the masses. As in the case of Italy and Germany, the crisis and the growth of fascism would be accompanied by the wide and rapid radicalization of the exploited masses. Under such circumstances, as in the other variant, the prospects and perspectives for the revolutionary party and the social revolution would be in the highest degree promising.

Democratic rights

9. During the past eight months there has taken place a growing attack upon the democratic rights of labor, an attack required by the bourgeoisie equally as part of the war preparations and in order to aid the suffering business

cycle. The illegality of sit-downs has been made explicit by the courts.[2] The courts, state legislatures, Congress, and the police are engaged in a nationwide drive to limit or smash the rights of picketing, boycotts, closed shop, strikes, and demonstrations, and through a variety of other means they strive to hamstring labor organization. This attack will not diminish but on the contrary will increase in intensity during the next period.

10. These democratic rights are indispensable to the very existence of organized labor, both in the struggle against the war and in the fight for jobs and food. The end term of the present series of attacks, from the point of view of the bourgeoisie, is the total wiping out of labor's rights through a wartime military dictatorship or through outright fascism. We understand and explain the present attacks in this sense.

11. The party must, consequently, bring to the forefront during the coming period the question of defense of democratic rights of labor. The struggle against war and reaction is intimately and acutely bound up with this question. In the defense of democratic rights, broad united fronts are both possible and desirable. In localities where it is feasible, the party should take the initiative in forming committees for the defense of democratic rights of labor. As the tactic for defending democratic rights, the party should advocate the wide use of militant methods of mass action—strikes, demonstrations, marches, etc.—in place of the hopeless confinement of tactics to parliamentary and legalistic maneuvers.

The fight for jobs

12. The continuance of the unparalleled economic crisis, the persistence of the army of unemployed at a level of

---

2. The U.S. Supreme Court outlawed sit-down strikes in April 1939.

twelve or more millions, and the drive of reaction against the unemployed, place the fight for jobs squarely and enduringly in the front rank of the problems of the working class and of the party. Short of the actual outbreak of war itself, which would temporarily absorb (under a dictatorial regime) a considerable percentage of the unemployed in either the war industries or the army, there is not the slightest prospect of a major economic upturn. Even the vast armament outlays of the prewar Roosevelt program have a comparatively minor effect on U.S. economy as a whole. Chronic and staggering crisis for the masses of the people has become the normal condition of U.S. capitalism.

13. The older program of "immediate demands" and restrained and legalistic methods of fighting for them are no longer adequate to rouse the masses to struggle or to make any headway against the onslaught of social and economic reaction. We must be bold, open, and resolute in advancing the broad and positive slogans of our Transitional Program: a job and a decent living for every worker; the opening of idle factories under workers' control; the thirty-hour week and $30 minimum weekly wage; $20 billion public works program; expropriation of the Sixty Families; etc.

14. We must take care not to permit the Transitional Program to become a mere literary exercise. It is not intended as a finished document valid as a whole and just as it stands for all times and occasions. In the first place, it must be lifted out of the pages of our press and thrust into the midst of the unions and other mass organizations. In the second place, it must be understood as a *method* for linking the party with the actual struggles of the masses. The conception of the Transitional Program must be used to give depth and extension to issues which arise naturally out of the living experience of the masses. The popular

movement for a referendum on war is a prominent example of such an issue. Another, extremely important at present, is the drive for a thirty-hour week begun by the electrical workers and the plumbers and, in a somewhat different form, by the auto workers. This thirty-hour-week is a concretization of the transitional demand for a "sliding scale of hours," and should receive the full and active support of the party.

The Communist Party

15. The Communist Party must occupy a central place in the propaganda and general activities of the party in the coming period. The total of all other opponent organizations—Social Democratic Federation, Socialist Party, Lovestoneites, etc.—does not add up to a small fraction of the importance of the Communist Party. Insufficient attention to the Communist Party, almost equal attention to other opponent groups, has been one of the most serious weaknesses in the work of the party during the past year. The Communist Party is far and away the greatest obstacle in this country to the building of the revolutionary movement.

16. It is necessary to dispel certain illusions, shared to one or another extent by our own membership, with respect to the Communist Party. It is false that the Communist Party consists only of bureaucrats and hopeless petty bourgeois. In its ranks and especially in its sympathizing circles it includes many genuine and militant workers, as its influence in the trade unions proves. It is deceptive to consider that the CP is characterized through and through and in *every* respect by an iron monolithism. The framework of the party is wholly monolithic. But in the heart of that monolithic framework there have grown in the present period profound conflicts and paradoxes, springing

from the conflicting and paradoxical social and political situation of international Stalinism. These internal conflicts are the compelling sources of splits and defections from the Stalinist movement. It is even false to believe that splits have not taken place in the Stalinist movement. Especially in recent times, after the third Moscow trial, after Munich, after the fall of Barcelona, what might be described as slow and passive—but very extensive—splits have occurred. But these splits have led the dissident Stalinists, with a few exceptions, only to complete retirement from political activity or to bourgeois politics.

17. The basis for influencing the Communist Party, for recruiting its members and sympathizers, and for hastening its dissolution as an obstacle to the growth of the revolutionary movement, is present. What is required for success is a conscious, deliberate, and sustained policy on our part. We must root out all traces of a defeatist or passive attitude toward Stalinism, and orient boldly on the perspective of major and fruitful work in that arena.

The struggle against fascism

18. In the months since Munich and especially since the fall of Barcelona, and with the failure of the 1938 upturn in business to extend into 1939—thus signaling the definitive collapse of the New Deal's policies, the fascist and semifascist movements in this country have been growing rapidly in numbers and boldness. The nationwide notoriety achieved by Hague through his use of fascist and semifascist methods symbolizes this development. The nationwide series of meetings and mobilizations by the Nazi Bund provided a kind of dress rehearsal for native movements. The Silver Shirts have been especially active in small towns and villages. It is reported that there are now more than 800 fascist and near-fascist organizations

in the United States. At the present time the most successful and advancing of these is the Coughlin movement, which, since Coughlin's reappearance on the scene after two years of quiet, has taken on a more and more openly fascist character. Though it is doubtful that a movement led by a Catholic priest can be the authentic fascist movement in this country, Coughlin's followers are being prepared in ideology and methods for fusion into the definitive fascist movement of the not-too-distant future.

19. It is absolutely inadmissible to neglect or minimize the importance of the current growth of U.S. fascism. Fascism in this country is capable of spreading like wildfire, of strangling the labor movement before it is aware what is happening. The great army of disillusioned unemployed and the disinherited youth are particularly and immediately vulnerable. Europe has taught that in order to defeat fascism the labor movement must never let fascism get a step in advance, that it must anticipate and prepare for the fascist developments *before* they take place.

20. It is the immediate duty of the party to prepare educational and propaganda material in its press and in cheap pamphlets dealing with the native fascist and near-fascist movements. This material should be put in the most popular and simple form, directed especially toward the youth and the unemployed, and must aim at mass circulation to combat the fascist ideas directly on the ground where they chiefly germinate.

21. The struggle against fascism at home, however, cannot even now be confined to propaganda and agitation. It is necessary to fight the fascist movements in action from the very beginning. Our slogan "For workers' defense guards against fascism" cannot any longer be confined to agitation, but must be put into concrete effect. A beginning has been made in a few localities. But the

party must now attempt in every section of the country where it has branches to begin the actual organization of at least skeleton defense units, which will work indefatigably to broaden their base, especially through union support. Ideally these should be based on and built through the unions, as in Minneapolis. But where this is not possible, the party must nevertheless lead the way and itself take the initiative in forming, together with sympathizers and nonparty workers now ready to participate, initiating nuclei of the antifascist defense guard, functioning as independent, organized, disciplined, and active institutions.

The labor party

22. During the past year, the sentiment among the workers for a labor party has remained inert, held back by Roosevelt, the labor bureaucrats, and the Stalinists. Any extended general campaign on our part around the labor party slogan would have been on the whole academic, and our agitation on this issue has been largely, and correctly, confined to specific and local situations where it was relevant. Nevertheless, the organized intervention of labor in politics has continued and in some respects increased during this same year. The collapse of the New Deal and its transformation into the War Deal, the wave of social reaction, the more openly reactionary character of the Roosevelt administration, the approach of the 1940 elections, are all raising or beginning to raise once more in the minds of the workers questions about political action. So untenable is worn-out New Dealism becoming that even Lewis and the Stalinists have in the recent weeks been compelled to make certain criticisms of Roosevelt. It is hardly conceivable that the disillusionment of the workers with Roosevelt can in the main take the form of a swing back to Republicanism; and in any

case it would be disastrous if this were permitted to happen. The slogan for a labor party, properly developed in connection with the other aspects of our program, can play a significant role in directing the disillusionment with Roosevelt and the dead New Deal into the sole progressive direction—toward independent political activity by the working class. We must be ready to utilize every concrete situation as it arises for propaganda and action in this direction.

23. The slogan for the labor party, as we conceive it, is in no way incompatible with direct entry of the party, under its own name, in elections. On the contrary, experience has amply proved the great value of the party name and party candidates appearing on the ballot, with the wide opportunities for revolutionary education which this opens up. In all localities where this is practically feasible, and where it will not conflict with the development of genuine independent working-class political action on a broader scale, the party must in the next period try to enter elections directly.

The prospects for the party

24. The defeats of the working class on an international scale, the lack of organized resistance to the approach of the war, and the apparent passivity of the working class in this as in other countries, above all since the fall of Barcelona, have not been without adverse effect in some quarters of the radical labor movement. In some cases this takes the form of the entirely erroneous opinion that our perspective for the next period must be one merely of consolidating a tight and firm cadre and of excluding the possibility of important numerical growth.

25. While the factors that have led to this feeling cannot be denied, the inference drawn is by no means necessarily

correct, and other equally important national and international conditions point to a contrary conclusion. The war is approaching, but the masses, in the United States as in most other nations, are *not* in favor of the war, and have not succumbed to a blatant war chauvinism. They are on the whole against the war, however incompletely they understand the implications of their opposition. As the only party which fights the war, there is every objective foundation for the growth, even the rapid growth, of the party as the organization concretely embodying the antiwar sentiments of the masses. Again, there is no revolutionary opposition to the party, hardly the pretense of any; and consequently every serious feeling or thought directed against the present order of war and tyranny and starvation can find genuine outlet only in the ranks and actions of our party. Again, the masses want to fight fascism and its growth at home; and only our party has proposed or attempted to carry out a serious fight against fascism. Finally, the end of the New Deal once again poses sharply before the workers the problems of political action; and here also our party alone gives an answer.

26. It is entirely possible that the coming period will be one of rapid growth for the party. It is certain that if we do not have this as our perspective, if we decide in advance that growth is impossible, then stagnation is assured. But our problem and aim is not to retreat, but to advance and to gain. The party has never taken *recruiting* seriously; it has always allowed new members to drop like ripe fruit into the ranks of the party, after suitable and lengthy fertilizing by our ideas and theories. To assure the success of the party in the next months we must radically alter this attitude: we must become crusaders and recruiting agents, not at all satisfied with a formally correct program, but resolved that this program will become

the program of masses of workers. Habit and routine dictate caution and reserve. The future of the party and the needs of the American revolution demand audacity and a bold offensive.

A campaign party

27. The serious advance of the party in the mass movement depends upon its adoption of the campaign principle in its activity. As in the case of a military campaign, a political campaign means the concentration and coordination of all available forces in advancing toward and achieving a concrete and definite objective or set of objectives. For the party, it means gearing in the entire national organization and every aspect of its activities—press, pamphlets, leaflets, meetings, tours, demonstrations, petitions, fund-raising, motions in unions and other mass organizations, street meetings—as a single unit revolving around the specific axis of the campaign. Campaigns cannot be properly conducted loosely or haphazardly, nor for vague or "general" programmatic aims. They require systematic organization, and by their very nature have simplified and limited aims.

28. For the next immediate period, the party will concentrate its activities on the following three campaigns: (1) Against the war; (2) Jobs; (3) Antifascist, in particular anti-Coughlin. These campaigns, in turn, shall be still further limited and concretized around the following slogans:

(1) Against the war:
Let the people vote on war!
All war funds to the unemployed!
(2) Jobs:
Thirty-thirty!
Expropriate the Sixty Families!

Open the idle factories, and operate them under workers' control!

(3) Antifascist:

Build workers' defense guards!

29. It shall be the task of the incoming National Committee to organize the entire work of the party for the coming period around these campaigns, with the aim of penetrating with these central slogans deeper into the mass movement than ever before in our history, of becoming known to the workers as precisely the party of these slogans, and of extending all of our activities, especially recruitment, through these campaigns.

Resolution on workers' defense guard[3]

1. The collapse of the New Deal, and the insuperable, ever-mounting internal conflicts of United States capitalism are beginning to pose more and more directly to the U.S. bourgeoisie the necessity for abandoning parliamentary democracy and resorting to fascism as the sole means for preserving its power and privilege; and these same factors simultaneously open the minds of large numbers among the unemployed, farmers, middle classes, and demoralized proletarians to fascist demagogy and organization.

---

3. Starting with the 1938 discussion of the Transitional Program, the SWP and its press paid increasing attention to the American fascist movement and how to combat it through the formation of workers' defense guards. In September 1938, following threats from the fascist Silver Shirts, a strong workers' defense guard was set up in Minneapolis with the support and participation of SWP members. (For details, see *Teamster Politics* by Farrell Dobbs (Pathfinder Press, 2015).) Discussion of this question took place in many unions and in some cases evoked sympathy or support, but the Minneapolis guard remained the only

2. Recent months have witnessed a profound transformation in the character of the fascist movement in the United States. Before this, it had been confined largely to individual cranks, eccentrics, and dilettante intellectuals, and "foreign" groups such as the various Italian fascist societies and the Nazi Bund. Now, for the first time, it is becoming a serious, native mass movement. In the first stage of this transformation, the Coughlinites in the big cities, and to a lesser extent the Silver Shirts in the farming areas and smaller towns, are playing a major role. Whatever may be the eventual fate of these two particular groups, and whatever may be the episodic rises and declines of the fascist movement as a whole, it is certain to grow in extent and depth until its sources have been

---

one that was officially based on the unions. In February 1939 the fascist German-American Bund called a mass rally at Madison Square Garden in New York. The attendance of 18,000 was exceeded by 50,000 who came out in a counterdemonstration called by the SWP outside the Garden and who fought the cops protecting the fascists. The SWP's success in this episode, which proved that many thousands were willing to fight the fascists even when their unions and other organizations refused to join in the antifascist struggle, persuaded the SWP leadership that it should experiment with the creation of antifascist groupings even if the leaders of the labor movement defaulted in this field. These were set up in New York, Newark, and a few other places, and they were called antifascist labor guards to distinguish them from union-based workers' defense guards. The SWP convention in July was the first to consider and evaluate the question in its various aspects. Farrell Dobbs, who had played a key role in the organizing of the Minneapolis guard, was supposed to be the convention reporter and he prepared notes that were used in the writing of the convention resolution. When he became involved in an important strike at the time of the convention and the National Committee directed him to follow through on that even if it meant missing the convention, James Burnham was designated as substitute reporter at the convention. The resolution adopted there was published in the *Socialist Appeal*, July 7, 1939, and is reprinted here.

rooted out. This can be accomplished by nothing short of the social revolution.

3. The transformation of the fascist movement dictates the transformation of the methods of defense against it. Theoretical analysis and abstract propaganda, to which specifically antifascist activities had to be more or less confined so long as fascism in this country remained primarily a threat for the future, become altogether inadequate when fascism has become a reality of the present.

4. The long-term defense against fascism can be only the achievement of the social revolution. Meanwhile, however, there is the immediate and direct problem of the physical defense of the organization, lives, and liberties of the workers, which the fascists aim first to weaken and then to destroy, from the physical assaults of the fascist gangs. The experience of all countries, including the United States, proves beyond any doubt whatever that the agencies of the bourgeois-democratic state will not and cannot carry out this defense; but that on the contrary, reliance upon these agencies guarantees the smashing of the workers and the victory of the fascists. Only the workers themselves, relying on their own means and strength, can defend their own organizations and life and liberties. The only possible form of defense against the fascists is the *workers' defense guard*. Whereas formerly the workers' defense guard has been primarily a slogan for agitation, the point has now been reached, and more than reached when the concrete task of the actual building of the workers' defense guard must begin in action.

5. The workers' defense guard is, from one point of view, an outgrowth and development of the picket squads used by virtually all unions in strikes. From the beginning, however, the defense guard differs in key respects from the picket squad. The guard is permanent, whereas the

picket squads are usually created only for the duration of the strike. The duties of the guard are not merely picketing, defense against scabs, etc., but at all times the defense of the headquarters and rights of the union and its members. Moreover, the tasks of the guard must be conceived, from the start, not in narrow terms of the given single union which may be first involved, but of the labor movement as a whole, and indeed of all groups, individuals, organizations, racial minorities, etc. threatened or attacked by the fascists, vigilantes, or other reactionaries. The duty of the guard is to defend all who need defense from the assaults of the fascists. To carry out this duty, the guard must be trained and disciplined, and function democratically as an autonomous body. From a second point of view, the workers' defense guard is the preparation for the far broader organization of the masses, with far greater tasks, which will in the future have the task of defending the masses against the counterrevolution.

6. From the nature of the workers' defense guard and its tasks, it follows that the guard should take form wherever possible through the established unions. Revolutionists within the unions must attempt to win the union members as a whole to a realization of the necessity of the guard and must aim to have the unions initiate the actual building of the guard. Where a union forms units of the guard, the aim must be from the beginning to extend the scope and base of the guard beyond the normal confines of union organization and activity: by drawing into the guard unemployed, youth, and others who are not members of the union (and in many cases are not in a position to be members of any union), by linking up with other unions in the building of the guard, by establishing relations with the guard in other cities, and by amplifying the types of activities undertaken by the guard.

Above, Max Shachtman speaking at February 20, 1939, anti-Nazi rally of 50,000 in New York called by SWP. **Below**, Minneapolis Teamster Local 544 Union Defense Guard.

7. In localities where it is at present impossible to enlist the established unions in the task of building the guard, it is now necessary, in addition to constant agitation for union initiative, to take concrete steps in the formation of the guard with what forces are available. Where such forces are meager it would be an error to regard the group that can be formed as a workers' defense guard in the full sense; rather, since the genuine guard can be built only by enlisting the masses, are such groups skeletons or embryos of the guard. They cannot substitute their actions for that of the masses, but must aim to win the masses especially in the trade unions to the task of building the guard, by adding, on however a modest scale, the lesson of action and example to that of agitation. In New York City, Newark, and elsewhere, first steps have been taken along these lines by the formation of the antifascist labor guard.

8. The struggle against fascism makes possible, and demands, the broadest possible united front. The essential requirements for membership in the defense guard must be formulated simply as a willingness to fight the fascists, to defend labor and other organizations and groups from fascist and vigilante attacks, and to accept the democratic discipline of the guard. While taking every precaution to make sure of the integrity of every applicant and to preserve the guard from provocateurs, stool pigeons, and irresponsible or light-minded elements, the effort must be made to enlist membership and support as broadly and widely as possible on this basis.

9. The significance of our party's advocacy and support of the guard is in no way limited to the specific and all-important tasks which the guard can and must fulfill. Advocacy and support of the guard is an integral and decisive part of the political program of our party, and a political weapon of the utmost importance. Experience has

already shown, and will more fully confirm in the future, that the slogan of building the guard meets with an immediate response from the best sections of the workers and the youth, and concretizes the whole meaning of our conception of the struggle against fascism in a manner accomplished by no other part of our program.[4]

Supplementary motion: The convention instructs the incoming National Committee to appoint a special commission to be in charge of carrying out and coordinating on a national scale the work of the party in connection with the building of the workers' defense guard.

---

4. The convention voted to delete the next to last sentence: "In addition, it has proved and will prove to be an incomparably effective means of opposition to Stalinism and of creating rifts in the Stalinist ranks." Whoever deleted that also deleted the following sentence: "Indeed, the perspective of the workers' defense guard is a condensation of the perspective of the social revolution."

The right of self-determination and the Negro in the United States of North America[5]

In 1930 Negroes in America constituted nearly twelve million, or 10 percent of the American population. Of these, two-thirds were still in the South, despite the war and postwar emigration to the North. In the cities of the North and East, the Negroes form only a small minority of the population, generally less than 10 percent. In the cities of the South, the proportion is much higher, but in only one large city, Birmingham, Alabama, do the Negroes constitute as much as one-half of the white population. Similarly in the state areas of the South, they are outnumbered by the whites. In only one state of America, Mississippi, are the Negroes in a majority, and that of only 2 percent, though there are large county areas inhabited by a majority of Negroes.

---

5. The author of this resolution was C.L.R. James (J.R. Johnson). It was adopted by the convention as "the basis for a final draft" presumably by the National Committee, and all amendments introduced at

Cut off for centuries from all contact with the continent and customs of his origin, the Negro is today an American citizen. In his daily work, language, religion, and general culture, he differs not at all from his fellow workers in factory and field, except in the intensity of his exploitation and attendant brutal discrimination. These discriminations are imposed by capitalism in the pretended name of the Negro's racial characteristics, but in reality to increase profit by cheapening labor and to weaken the workers and farmers by fostering racial rivalries.

The minority status of the Negro in the political divisions of capitalist America, even in the South, and the absence of a national Negro language and literature and of a differentiated political history, as in prewar Poland or Catalonia and the Ukraine of today, have caused in the past a too facile acceptance of the Negroes as merely a more than usually oppressed section of the American workers and farmers. This in turn has led to a neglect of the Negro's political past and a lack of historical imagination in envisaging his future political development.

The American Negroes were among the earliest colonists of America, and for three centuries their history has been one of continual economic exploitation, social discrimination, and political expropriation by all classes of whites. Up to 1935, organized labor, as represented by

---

the convention were referred to the National Committee. The text printed here includes the amendments reported by the majority of the convention Committee on Negro Work, but does not include the amendments offered by John G. Wright and Ernest R. McKinney (see the minutes). The National Committee elected at the New York convention never got around to writing the final draft, but in its absence the present text was accepted as the party's position. It was the first resolution on the American Black struggle adopted by the SWP or its predecessors going back to 1928.

the AFL, discriminated against the Negro as sharply as the capitalist class; today the poor whites of the South are the most savage of lynchers and the most rabid upholders of the theory of white superiority. The world economic crisis and consequent organization of the CIO including hundreds of thousands of Negroes, the organization of the Southern Tenant Farmers Union comprising both white and black, have shown that this division between the black and white workers is beginning to close under economic pressure. But not even a socialist revolution can immediately destroy the accumulated memories, mistrust, and suspicions of centuries; and today, in this period of capitalistic decline in America, the racial prejudices are more than ever based on economic privileges, possessed by one group of workers at the obvious and immediate expense of the other. Negroes today are being pushed out of jobs which, before the depression, whites disdained. Three centuries of property and privilege have used their wealth and power to make the Negroes feel that they are and must continue to be outcasts from all sections of American society, rich and poor; and the political backwardness of the American working-class movement has made it an easy victim to this propaganda, fortified by tangible if slight economic advantages. It is not improbable, therefore, that the bulk of the Negroes have absorbed their lesson far more profoundly than is superficially apparent and that on their first political awakening to the necessity of revolutionary activity they may demand the right of self-determination, i.e., the formation of a Negro state in the South. Thus, in their view, they would be free from that exploitation, discrimination, and arrogance, inseparable in their experience from any association with numerically superior whites. The desire to wipe out the humiliating political subservience and social degradation of centuries might find expression in an overpowering demand for the establishment and administration of a Negro state.

The past political history of the Negroes gives not insignificant indications that their political development may very well follow this course. The Garvey movement, one of the most powerful political mass movements ever seen in the U.S.A., concealed behind its fantastic and reactionary slogan of "Back to Africa"—the desire (revolutionary in its essence) for a Negro state. The Negroes no more desired to go to Africa of their own free will than German Jews before Hitler wanted to go to Palestine. The masses of Negroes, particularly in the South, dominated by the heritage of slavery and the apparently irresistible numbers and state power of the whites, did not dare to raise the slogan of a black state in America. But in a revolutionary crisis, as they begin to shake off the state coercion and ideological domination of American bourgeois society, their first step may well be to demand the control, both actual and symbolical, of their own future destiny. The question of whether the Negroes in America are a national minority to which the slogan of self-determination applies will be solved in practice. The raising or support of the slogan by the masses of Negroes will be the best and only proof required. It is inconceivable that propaganda by any American revolutionary party can instill this idea into their minds if they did not themselves consciously or unconsciously desire it. This desire may very well fall into the hands of reactionary leaders. But only the most energetic defense of the right of self-determination of the Negro masses can lead their movement into revolutionary channels.

Should the masses of Negroes raise this slogan, the SWP, in accordance with the Leninist doctrine on the question of self-determination and the imperative circumstances of the particular situation, will welcome this awakening and pledge itself to support the demand to the fullest extent of its power. The boundaries of such a state will be a matter of comradely arrangement between different sections of a revolution victorious over American capitalism and intent only on creating the best possible milieu for the building of the socialist commonwealth. The Fourth International aims at the abolition of the old and not at the creation of new national boundaries, but the historical circumstances and the stages of development of different sections of society will at given moments be decisive in the road to be followed at a particular historic moment. The demand for a Negro state in America, its revolutionary achievement with the enthusiastic encouragement and assistance of the whites, will generate such creative energy in every section of the Negro workers and farmers in America as to constitute a great step forward to the ultimate integration of the American Negroes into the United Socialist States of North America. The SWP is also confident that after a few years of independent existence the victories of the new regime in both states will lead inevitably to a unity, with the Negroes as anxious and willing partners, their justifiable suspicions and doubts weakened by the concrete manifestation of the desire for collaboration by the whites and the contrast between the capitalist and the socialist state. Such a development in America will have immediate and powerful repercussions not only among the millions of African Negroes but also among oppressed nationalities, particularly of color, everywhere, and will be a powerful step toward the dissolution of those national and racial antagonisms with which capitalism, particularly in this period of its desperate crisis, is poisoning and corrupting human society.

The SWP, while proclaiming its willingness to support

the right of self-determination to the fullest degree, will not in itself, in the present stage, advocate the slogan of a Negro state in the manner of the Communist Party of the U.S.A. The advocacy of the *right* of self-determination does not mean advancing the *slogan* of self-determination. Self-determination for Negroes means that the Negroes themselves must determine their own future. Furthermore, a party predominantly white in membership which, in present-day America, vigorously advocates such a slogan, prejudices it in the minds of Negroes, who see it as a form of segregation. But the SWP will watch carefully the political development of the masses of the Negroes, will emphasize their right to make this important decision themselves and the obligation of all revolutionaries to support whatever decision the Negroes may finally come to as to the necessity of a Negro state. The SWP recognizes that the Negroes have not yet expressed themselves on this important question. The opposition to a Negro state comes mainly from the articulate and vocal but small and weak class of Negro intellectuals, concerned with little else besides gaining a place for themselves in American capitalist society, and fanatically blind to its rapid decline. Negro members of the Fourth International, however, have every right to participate in the formation of the ideology of their own race, with such slogans and propaganda as correspond to the political development and revolutionary awakening of the great masses of the Negro people; and, while conscious of the ultimate aims of socialism, must recognize the progressive and revolutionary character of any demand unfolding among great masses of Negroes for a Negro state, and if necessary vigorously advocate it.

The SWP and Negro work[6]

The American Negroes, for centuries the most oppressed section of American society and the most discriminated against, are potentially the most revolutionary elements of the population. They are designated by their whole historical past to be, under adequate leadership, the very vanguard of the proletarian revolution.[7] The neglect of Negro work and of the Negro question by the party is therefore a very disquieting sign. The SWP must recognize that its attitude to the Negro question is crucial for

---

6. The author of this resolution was C.L.R. James. The Committee on Negro Work's amendments—the only ones introduced at the convention—were included in the text adopted by the convention.

7. C.L.R. James wrote a column about this sentence in the *Socialist Appeal*, August 22, 1939, under the pen name J.R. Johnson. "There is, in the sentence quoted, an overstatement, in my opinion," he said. "It would be more correct to say, 'in the very vanguard.'" No one else in the Committee on Negro Work or in the SWP leadership expressed any differences with James's opinion.

its future development. Hitherto the party has been based mainly on privileged workers and groups of isolated intellectuals. Unless it can find its way to the great masses of the underprivileged, of whom the Negroes constitute so important a section, the broad perspectives of the permanent revolution will remain only a fiction and the party is bound to degenerate.[8]

The SWP proposes therefore to constitute a national Negro department which will initiate and coordinate a plan of work among the Negroes and calls upon its members to cooperate strenuously in the difficult task of approaching this work in the most suitable manner. Our obvious tasks for the coming period are (a) the education of the party; (b) winning the politically more advanced Negroes for the Fourth International; and (c) through the work of the party among the Negroes and in wider fields, influencing the Negro masses to recognize in the SWP the only party which is genuinely working for their complete emancipation from the heavy burdens they have borne so long. The winning of masses of Negroes to our movement on a revolutionary basis is, however, no easy task. The Negroes, suffering acutely from the general difficulties of all workers under capitalism, and in addition, from special problems of their own, are naturally hesitant to take the step of allying themselves with a small and heavily persecuted party. But Negro work is complicated by other, more profound, causes. For reasons which can be easily understood, the American Negro is profoundly suspicious of all whites, and recent events

---

8. For more information on Trotsky's theory of permanent revolution, see *The Permanent Revolution and Results and Prospects* (Pathfinder, 1969). From at least 1933, Trotsky held that the Black struggle was an expression of the permanent revolution.

have deepened that suspicion.

In the past, the Negro masses have had disastrous experiences with the Republican and Democratic parties. The benefits that the Negroes as a whole are supposed to have received from the New Deal and the Democratic Party can easily be seen for the fraud that they are when it is recognized that it is the Democratic Party of Franklin Roosevelt which by force and trickery prevents the Negroes from exercising their votes over large areas in the South.

The CP of the U.S.A. from 1928 to 1935 did win a number of Negroes to membership and awakened a sympathetic interest among the politically more advanced Negro workers and intellectuals. But the bureaucratic creation of Negro "leaders," their subservience to the twists and turns of the party line, their slavish dependence on the manipulations and combinations of the CP leadership, were seen by interested Negroes not as a transference of the methods and practices of the Kremlin bureaucracy to America, but merely as another example of the use of Negroes by whites for political purposes unconnected with Negro struggles. With its latest turn beginning in 1935, the CP has become openly a party of American bourgeois democracy. Not only to expand, but merely to exist in this milieu demanded that it imbibe and practice the racial discriminations inherent in that society. The Negroes, very sensitive to all such practices, have quickly recognized the new face of the CP beneath the mask of demagogy with which it seeks to disguise the predicament in which it finds itself, and the result has been a mass departure from the party (80 percent of the New York State Negro membership) and a bitter hostility to the CP, which reached a climax when well-known former Negro members of the CP testified against it before the Dies [House Un-American Activities] committee. Once more the Third International has struck a deadly blow at the American working class, this time by undermining the confidence that was being slowly forged between the politically advanced sections of the black and white workers.

Furthermore, the awakening political consciousness of the Negro not unnaturally takes the form of a desire for independent action uncontrolled by whites. The Negroes have long felt and more than ever feel today the urge to create their own organizations under their own leaders and thus assert, not only in theory but in action, their claim to complete equality with other American citizens. Such a desire is legitimate and must be vigorously supported even when it takes the form of a rather aggressive chauvinism. Black chauvinism in America today is merely the natural excess of the desire for equality and is essentially progressive while white American chauvinism, the expression of racial domination, is essentially reactionary. Under any circumstances, it would have been a task of profound difficulty, perhaps impossible, for a revolutionary party composed mainly of whites to win the confidence of the American Negro masses, except in the actual crises of revolutionary struggles. Such possibilities as existed, however, have been gravely undermined by the CP. Today the politically minded Negroes are turning away from the CP, and Negro organizations devoted to struggle for Negro rights are springing up all over the North and East, particularly in Harlem. The nationalist tendencies of the Negroes have been fortified, and in addition to the poisoning of racial relations by capitalism, the SWP has now to contend with the heritage left by the CP and the pernicious course it is still actively pursuing.

The SWP therefore proposes that its Negro members, aided and supported by the party, take the initiative and collaborate with other militant Negroes in the formation of a Negro mass organization devoted to the struggle for Negro rights. *This organization will NOT be either openly or secretly a periphery organization of the Fourth International.* It will be an organization in which the masses of Negroes will be invited to participate on a working-class program corresponding to the day-to-day struggles of the masses of Negro workers and farmers. Its program will be elaborated by the Negro organization, in which Negro members of the Fourth International will participate with neither greater nor lesser rights than other members. But the SWP is confident that the position of the Negroes in American society, the logic of the class struggle in the present period, the superior grasp of politics and the morale of members of the Fourth International, must inevitably result in its members exercising a powerful influence in such an organization. The support of such an organization by the SWP does not in any way limit the party's drive among Negroes for membership, neither does it invalidate the necessary struggle for the unity of both black and white workers. But that road is not likely to be a broad highway. Such an organization as is proposed is the most likely means of bringing the masses of Negroes into political action, which, though programmatically devoted to their own interests, must inevitably merge with the broader struggles of the American working-class movement taken as a whole. The SWP, therefore, while recognizing the limitations and pitfalls of a mass organization without a clearly defined political program, and while retaining its full liberty of action and criticism, welcomes and supports any attempt by Negroes themselves to organize for militant action against our common oppressors, instructs its Negro members to work actively toward the formation of such an organization, and recommends to the party members to follow closely all such manifestations of Negro militancy.[9]

---

9. Whatever the possibilities of an independent Black organization were in July 1939, the SWP was unable to explore or utilize them until after the split of April 1940, when James left the SWP. That the possibilities were real became manifest early in 1941 when a new national organization, the Negro March on Washington Movement, led by A. Philip Randolph, appeared on the scene and quickly became a pole of attraction for many thousands of Black militants throughout World War II. Prepared for its appearance by the SWP's 1939 resolutions, members of the SWP played an active role in its work from the very beginning, despite their political differences with the Randolph leadership.

Resolution on organization of the unemployed[10]

by E.R. McKinney

The degeneration of the unemployed organization movement nationally, under the People's Front, prowar, antimilitant, pro-Roosevelt leadership of the Stalinist party, throws a direct and immediate responsibility on the Socialist Workers Party to modify its position and orientation on the question of a new national organization of the home relief and project workers.

This stifling of the militancy of the unemployed workers by the warmongering Stalinist bureaucracy reaches its worst right at the time when the need for militant and aggressive mass actions by the unemployed is most urgent.

The big employers and the banks intensify their drive to lower even more the present relief standards. The first

---

10. From material supplied to the delegates at the convention. The position in this resolution was held by only a minority of the Unemployed Committee (McKinney, Breitman). It was referred to the incoming National Committee.

phase of this offensive by big business and finance closes with the vote of their deputies in Congress to reduce the number of WPA projects, to establish a "bipartisan" WPA board, to "separate" from the WPA for sixty days the unemployed who have been on WPA for eighteen months or more and to "accept" Roosevelt's request for an appropriation so low that hundreds of thousands of WPA workers will be thrown into the streets.

Roosevelt, the New Deal president and idol of the Stalinist WAA and the liberals, is the head and front of this conspiracy to starve and increase the misery of the home relief and WPA workers. He has compromised on relief appropriations with the business interests and connived with their lackeys in the capitol at Washington to get his war budget passed. His WPA "request" was reduced to $1.477 billion for next year, one third less than for the present year. Roosevelt has no belief that business will improve and absorb the unemployed but rather it is his plan to solve the unemployment problem by conscripting the unemployed into the army and hurling them into the war. He is interested in the New Deal today only insofar as it can be useful in regimenting the workers for war and integrating them into the huge New Deal war machine.

There is no national organization of the unemployed today to combat the Roosevelt–economy bloc offensive against relief standards, or to resist the Roosevelt–New Deal conspiracy to lead the workers into the coming war.

The Workers Alliance has gone over to the government and the employers. Its president, David Lasser, testified before a congressional investigating committee that he is putting in his time, not leading the unemployed in a militant struggle for higher relief, but "trying to make capitalism work."

Organizations such as the UPWU in New York City, under

Above, April 1, 1939, unemployed picket line in New York.
Below, Minneapolis–St. Paul cavalcade against WPA cuts.

the domination of the most backward SP right wing, are moving in the same direction as the Stalinist-controlled WAA, becoming more bureaucratized and less and less militant. Scattered independent organizations are weak and due to their isolation cannot make any effective protest.

The organized trade union movement, including the CIO, has made only very weak and sporadic attempts to organize the unemployed and tie them up with the employed workers. There is little reason to believe that this situation will be appreciably changed in the near future.

This total situation: the economic plight of the unemployed, the danger of their falling by thousands into the fascist trap, and the imminence of war, dictates the course that our party should take: organized and sustained agitation among home relief and WPA workers for a new national organization of the unemployed. The party and the party forces in the unemployed field must take the lead in this. This is the most fruitful field of activity of our party on a national scale in the coming period. It is the most important field in which the party can operate as an antiwar, antifascist party. Therefore the party must take the initiative in this urgent political and organizational task.

Recommendations

1. Subcommittee of NC and non-NC comrades on unemployed work.

2. National functionary in direct charge.

3. Newark unemployed paper[11] to become sort of national "organizer."

4. Two-cent pamphlet: "Why Starve? Organize and Fight."

---

11. *The Hunger Fighter* was the monthly paper of the Workers Relief and WPA Union of Essex County, New Jersey, whose members had left the Workers Alliance in February 1939. Its editor was George Breitman.

Resolution on unemployed work[12]

by Art Preis

1. Mass unemployment is a permanent feature of American capitalism in decline. In the U.S., this phenomenon has assumed greater relative scope than anywhere in the world. This flows from the nature of American capitalism as the most highly developed in the world.

2. The end of the New Deal reform program, now transformed into a drive toward war and reaction, is expressed

---

12. This resolution was printed in the mimeographed minutes of the convention, but in the interests of consistency we have transferred it from there to here, where it logically follows the resolution by McKinney, to which it refers. Art Preis was not a member of the convention's Unemployed Committee, but his document was endorsed by a majority of the committee (their names are at the end of the document) and on their behalf he presented it to the convention. (The minutes report that G. Johnson was elected to this committee, but either that was an erroneous report or she later was replaced, without mention in the minutes, by Kermit Johnson, one of the cosigners of the Preis resolution.) Like the McKinney resolution, this was referred to the incoming National Committee.

in the tremendous increase in war appropriations and the sharp reduction in federal funds for jobs and relief.

3. During the period of intensified blows upon the unemployed, no organized resistance of a widespread and militant character has thus far developed. Only sporadically and where the organized unemployed have had revolutionary leadership, has militant mass action accompanied the acceleration of the drive against the unemployed. The unemployed organizations have become atomized due to the degenerating influence of Stalinism in the only existing national independent unemployed organization, the Workers Alliance, and due to the failure of the trade union movement as yet to take genuine responsibility for the organization and defense of the unemployed.

4. The sense of immediacy and desperation which grips the 12–15 million unemployed, unaccompanied by any progressive organizational outlet of a unified and national character, poses more sharply than ever the potential menace to the organized labor movement of the jobless millions. As an indirect drag upon wage and hour standards, and as an agency for direct and overt attack upon the trade unions, which are regarded as job monopolies by increasing numbers of the unemployed, the jobless are the most fertile soil for the growth of a mass fascist movement in the U.S.

5. In the fight against fascism, no greater task confronts the SWP than the imperative necessity of organizing and leading in mass actions the unemployed millions. The history of the past ten years of unemployed organizations has likewise demonstrated that only revolutionists are willing and capable of organizing and leading the unemployed, for even in its most immediate aspects, all militant unemployed actions tend to be aimed directly toward the state.

6. But paralleling the necessity for defending the

immediate physical standards of the unemployed themselves, is the equally important need, from the long-term perspective, of tying the organized unemployed together with the organized employed workers. The tendency of present social developments and forces is to drive a wedge between the permanently jobless and the employed workers, in which the jobless are being psychologized into regarding themselves as a group whose interests and status are not merely different, but directly opposed to those of the employed workers, particularly the most secure section, which is in the labor unions.

7. From the standpoint of the most desirable form which the unemployed might take, the organization of the unemployed and WPA workers directly linked with the trade union movement is unquestionably the long-term perspective, dictated both from the objective position of the unemployed in relation to the labor movement and the primacy of the trade union problem in the whole orientation of the SWP.

8. However, even if this is the most desirable form of organization, the immediate needs of the unemployed dictate a course of expediency in which the party must attempt to organize the unemployed by whatever means and in whatever form is possible and feasible. This means that in certain communities, as in the Ohio-Michigan area and Minneapolis, the unemployed movement will be directly attached to the trade unions or a section of them. Elsewhere, we may work within existing independent organizations with some mass base, but led by opponent political groups—that is, the WAA (CP), Workers' Security League (SP), United Unemployed and WPA Workers of America (Lovestoneites). Elsewhere, we may be compelled to work in local independent organizations or actually initiate and organize new independent organizations in the localities and regions.

9. While it is not directly excluded that our inability

in the future to link the unemployed movement with the organized labor movement may compel us as a matter of expediency to put forward as an agitational slogan the need for a new national independent organization, the present basis for such an organization is so meager and the forces and resources of our party are so inadequate at the present time that it would be unrealistic and adventuristic for our party to commit itself to the definite perspective of initiating and organizing such an independent national organization.

10. Rather, the party should attempt to establish mass bases of unemployed organizations of whatever form possible in the immediate future, and particularly utilize every possibility of linking these movements directly to the trade unions or establishing fraternal relations with them. In particular, we must take special consideration towards organizing that strata of the unemployed which will make the most stable, homogeneous, and militant organization, that is, the least demoralized and most proletarian group of the unemployed, the two million WPA laborers.

Organizational recommendations

Insofar as the practical immediate work in the unemployed field is concerned we endorse the recommendations embodied in the resolution presented by Comrade McKinney. In addition, we recommend the following points:
1. Uniform program in all local and regional organizations.
2. National fraction with a bulletin.
3. Special attention to the trade union possibilities.
4. All unemployed comrades into some organization.
(Signed by following members of the convention committee: Max Geldman, Ted Selander, Kermit Johnson, Jack Dale)

Resolution on work in trade unions[13]

1. The most important task of the party in the coming period in the trade unions remains the penetration by revolutionists of the mass industrial unions connected with basic industry. A substantial upturn in industrial production arising from war program will give rise to new activities of organization. Strike struggles will be the inevitable counterpart of increased organization activity. Rise in cost of living and other factors. New opportunities will be opened for extending party influence in the trade union movement and possibilities for active participation and intervention with a clear-cut progressive program militantly advocated.

2. The party members must seriously avail themselves

---

13. This obviously unfinished resolution was printed in the mimeographed minutes, but since it was referred to the incoming National Committee without even being read to the convention, we thought this was a more appropriate place to print it than in the minutes.

of these opportunities to extend the influence of the party in order to become organizers in new fields and outstanding militants in the strike struggles. Concentration of party forces from national scale should be made in a few basic industries. Local surveys to determine points of concentration and activity should be followed by a determined effort to penetrate the factories and plants. In the course of this activity the composition of the party will be altered in favor of worker-militants with roots in industry and unions.

3. Despite increased industrial production, intensified rationalization makes the problem of unemployment a permanent and decisive problem facing the unions. Discontent of workers arising from this insecurity presses this problem to the fore even in the old-line craft unions. It is significant that the most vigorous struggle for the shortening of the workweek as a solution to this problem has occurred in several building-trades unions in New York. This demand for a shortening of the workweek is now penetrating the mass-production unions such as auto, etc. The foremost task of party members in the unions is to become the most aggressive and vigorous proponents of the struggle for the thirty-hour week. The concrete application of this slogan will vary according to specific conditions in the industries and communities. The slogan of the thirty-hour week is being transformed increasingly from a propaganda program to a slogan of action.

4. Effective execution of the slogan for the thirty-hour week is intimately connected with a drive to organize unemployed industrial workers into sections or auxiliaries of their unions, thus maintaining unity between employed and unemployed. Party members in unions must be the most active sponsors of the needs of the unemployed within the unions. Demands of the Transitional Program should be advanced as warranted by the specific conditions.

Glossary of people, groups, and periodicals*

†*Abern, Martin* **(1898–1949)** – Member, CLA's first NC, 1929. Business manager of *New International*, 1938–39. Member, SWP NC and PC, 1938 and 1939. Left SWP in 1940.

Altman, Jack (d. 1959) – Alternate member, SP National Executive Committee, 1937. Right-wing SP city secretary, Local New York, 1937.

Amalgamated Clothing Workers – Founded 1914. Affiliated to CIO from 1935 on. Dominated by Hillman bureaucracy, then allied with John L. Lewis machine.

American Federation of Labor (AFL) – Founded as federation of skilled-craft unions, 1881. Resisted industrial union organizing in mid-1930s, but gained from labor upsurge and became largest union federation.

American Fund for Political Prisoners and Refugees – Founded by SWP and collaborators, 1938. Widened its functions

---

* Focus here is on role or function in 1938–39 rather than on full lives of people, organizations, and journals listed

† All entries in italics identify members of SWP in 1938–39. Names of almost 200 members at SWP's first and second conventions are listed on pages 133–38 and 547–49, but here we give data only about National Committee members and alternates elected at these two conventions plus a few other members mentioned in minutes. These entries indicate members' political routes to SWP from 1929 on; roles they played or posts they held in 1938–39; and year they quit or were expelled from SWP if it was because of political differences. NC members with date "1938" were elected at first SWP convention, their term extending to mid-1939; NC members with date "1939" were elected at second convention, their term extending to third convention, in April 1940. "Left SWP in 1940" category is most pertinent to this book because serious split of April 1940 began to take shape soon after second SWP convention in July 1939.

599

and became a general defense organization. Changed name to American Labor Aid in 1939. Dissolved during World War II.

American Jewish Congress – Founded 1916. A middle-class civil rights group. Not yet Zionist in 1938–39.

American Labor Party of New York (ALP) – Founded 1936 as a channel to get labor votes for Roosevelt. Split in 1944, when Liberal Party was formed. Supported Progressive Party, 1948. Dissolved 1956.

American Workers Party (AWP) – Founded 1933 as successor to Conference for Progressive Labor Action. Called "Musteites" after its leader, A.J. Muste. Fused with CLA in 1934 to form Workers Party of the United States (WPUS).

Anarcho-syndicalists – Opponents of working-class political parties, political action, and central government, who expect trade unions to direct transition to classless society.

Antifascist labor guards – Experimental formations organized in a few cities by SWP and supporters to fight fascist attacks in absence of union–based workers' defense guards, 1939.

Appeal Association (or Appeal caucus or group) – Name taken by left wing in American SP, 1936–37, after its monthly journal *Socialist Appeal*. Its national conference (Chicago, February 1937) was called Appeal Institute.

Aragon, Paula **(1915–1982)** – Member, YPSL national committee, 1937–38. Jailed one month in California for organizing activity in garment workers' strike. Left SWP in 1940.

Bardacke, Gregory **(1912–1992)** – Member of both Appeal and Clarity groups in SP. Member, SWP NC, 1938. Left SWP in 1939.

Batista, Fulgencio **(1901–1973)** – Cuban dictator 1933–44, 1952–58. Fled to U.S. to escape revolution led by Fidel Castro.

GLOSSARY / 601

Becket, Charles – Oehlerite agent operating inside of Appeal group in Chicago SP, 1937. Demonstratively quit during first SWP convention.

Benavides, Oscar (1876–1945) – Right-wing president of Peru, 1933–39.

Blum, Leon (1872–1950) – Leader of French SP between two world wars and premier of first People's Front government in 1936.

Bolshevik-Leninists – Name Trotsky and his supporters preferred to call themselves in 1930s.

Bolsheviks – Members of majority faction at 1903 congress of Russian Social Democratic Labor Party. Led by Lenin. Became separate party in 1912. Organized October 1917 revolution that established first workers' state. Changed name to Communist Party, 1918. SWP also used this name in general sense to signify serious revolutionary activity, for example, when it referred to need for "Bolshevik work" in U.S.

Bonapartists – Authoritarian rulers ostensibly having popular mandate but usually resting on military, police, and state bureaucracies. Modeled on Napoleon I and Napoleon III, who reestablished monarchical regimes in France. In 1920s Trotskyists warned Stalin was preparing way for Bonapartist restoration of capitalism; after purges in late 1930s they concluded Stalin himself was Bonapartist.

Brandlerites – Members of Right Opposition in Communist movement, which generally supported positions of Bukharin in USSR in late 1920s. After leader of Right Opposition group in Germany, Heinrich Brandler (1881–1967).

Breitman, George (1916–1986) – Joined WPUS, 1935. Active in unemployed movement. District organizer, North Jersey SWP, 1938–39. Member, SWP NC, 1939.

Bridges, Harry (1900–1990) – President of International Longshoremen's and Warehousemen's Union and regional director of CIO in California. Closely followed CP line in 1930s.

Brophy, John (1886–1963) – Opponent of Lewis in UMWA in 1920s who was reconciled when CIO was organized and he was offered post of director.

Browder, Earl (1891–1973) – Became general secretary of American CP on Stalin's directive in 1930, after expulsion of Trotskyists and Lovestoneites. Deposed by Stalin, 1945, and expelled, 1946.

Bukharin, Nikolai (1888–1938) – Stalin's ally in CPSU leadership after Lenin's death, 1924–28. Head of Comintern, 1926–29. Formed Right Opposition against Stalin's policies but quickly recanted, 1928–29. Convicted in third Moscow trial frame-up and executed.

Burnham, James **(1905–1987)** – Member, AWP National Committee, 1933. Co-editor of *New International*, 1938–39. Member, SWP NC and PC, 1938 and 1939. Left SWP in 1940.

Caballero, Francisco Largo – see Largo Caballero, Francisco.

Cannon, James P. **(1890–1974)** – Member, CLA's first NC, 1929. Member, SWP NC and PC, 1938 and 1939. National secretary, 1938–39. Delegate to founding conference of FI, 1938. Member, IEC of FI, 1938–39.

Cárdenas, Lázaro (1895–1970) – President of Mexico, 1934–39. Granted asylum to Trotsky, 1937. Carried through expropriation of foreign-owned oil properties, 1938.

Carter, Joseph **(1910–1970)** – Founding member of CLA, 1929. First national educational director of SWP, 1938. Member, SWP NC, 1938 and 1939. Left SWP in 1940.

Chautemps, Camille (1885–1963) – A leader of Radical Party and premier of France, 1930, 1933–34, 1937–38.

Chiang Kai-shek (1887–1975) – Military dictator of China from 1927 until revolution drove him out of country in 1949.

Civilian Conservation Corps (CCC) – A New Deal work program for single unemployed men, 1933–42. Had over 500,000 members in 2,600 camps in 1935.

Clarity group in SP – Centrist group, which claimed to control SP National Executive Committee in 1937. Joined with right wingers to expel left wing.

Clarke, George (1913–1964) – Founding member of CLA, 1929. Detroit SWP organizer, 1938–39. Member, SWP NC, 1938 and 1939. Left SWP in 1953.

CNT (National Confederation of Labor, Spain) – Largest labor federation in country during civil war, 1936–39. Led by anarchists and anarcho-syndicalists. Supported People's Front government.

Cochran, Bert (1916–1984) – Joined CLA, 1934. Active in auto union, Cleveland. Member, SWP NC, 1938 and 1939. Left SWP in 1953.

Comintern – see Communist International.

Communist International (Comintern, Third International) – Founded under Lenin's leadership as revolutionary successor to Second International, 1919. Embraced social patriotism and class collaboration at seventh congress, 1935. Dissolved by Stalin as gesture to wartime imperialist allies, 1943.

Communist League of America (CLA) – Founded at national conference in Chicago in 1929, seven months after its leaders were expelled from CP for "Trotskyism." Published *The Militant,* 1928–34. Became American section of International Left Opposition, 1930. Joined in calling for new International, 1933. Fused with AWP to form WPUS, 1934.

Communist Party (CP) – Founded as American section of Comintern, 1919. Obedient instrument of Stalin by 1929, after expulsion of Cannon and Lovestone factions. Rabidly anti-Roosevelt, 1932–35. Rabidly pro-Roosevelt, 1935–39. Hailed Moscow trials, 1936–38. Opposed both a labor party and a referendum on war, 1938–39.

Communist Party of Soviet Union (CPSU) – Changed name from Bolshevik Party, 1918. Leninist until 1924, Stalinist thereafter.

Congress of Industrial Organizations (CIO) – Founded as a committee inside AFL, 1935. Became separate labor federation after expulsion from AFL, 1938. Established strong industrial unions in several previously unorganized mass industries. After two years was as strong as AFL, but thereafter lagged behind AFL although both grew during war. Fused with AFL as AFL-CIO, 1955.

Coughlinites – Followers of profascist priest, Charles Coughlin (1891–1979), who were organized in such groups as the Christian Front and the National Union for Social Justice at end of 1930s.

CPSU – see Communist Party of Soviet Union.

Crux – A pseudonym of Leon Trotsky.

Curtiss, Charles (1908–1993) – A founding member of CLA, 1929. Representative of Fourth International in Mexico, 1938–39. Alternate member, SWP NC, 1938 and 1939. Left SWP in 1951.

Daily Worker (New York) – Founded in 1924 as official paper of CP. Forerunner of *Daily World*.

Daladier, Edouard (1884–1970) – A leader of Radical Party and premier of France, 1933–34, 1938–40. While head of People's Front government, signed Munich accord with Hitler and broke general strike, 1938.

Debs, Eugene V. (1855–1926) – Leader of Pullman strike, 1894. A founder of SP, 1901, and its presidential candidate in four elections. Most popular socialist figure in country's history.

Degrelle, Leon (1906–1994) – Chief candidate for fascist dictator of Belgium before World War II.

DeLeon, Daniel (1852–1914) – Joined Socialist Labor Party, 1890. Became its principal leader until his death.

Delson, Max (1903–1985) – Member, SP National Executive Committee, 1937. A leader of Clarity group in SP, 1937.

Dies committee – A witch-hunting body of the U.S. House of Representatives headed by Rep. Martin Dies (D., Texas), set up in 1938. Better known later as House Un-American Activities Committee.

Dobbs, Farrell **(1907–1983)** – Joined CLA, 1934. Active in Minneapolis and Midwest teamsters' struggles. Member, SWP NC, 1938 and 1939, and PC, 1938.

Draper, Hal **(1914–1990)** – Joined YPSL, 1933. Elected national secretary at YPSL convention that adhered to Fourth Internationalist movement, 1937. YPSL representative to SWP PC, 1938–39. Left SWP in 1940.

Dullea, Robert D. **(1901–1996)** – Joined SP, 1931. Active in CIO textile organizing committee in Ohio and Michigan. Member, SWP NC, 1938. Left SWP in 1953.

Dunne, Vincent R. **(1890–1970)** – Alternate member, CLA's first NC, 1929. Active in Minneapolis union struggles. Member, SWP NC, 1938 and 1939.

Durruti, Buenaventura (1896–1936) – Leader of left wing of Spanish anarchists and an organizer of workers' militias at start of civil war. Directed defense of Madrid against fascists and died in that battle.

Eden, Anthony (1897–1977) – British Tory politician and diplomat in 1930s. Later foreign minister, 1935–38, and prime minister, 1955–57.

Engels, Frederick (1820–1895) – Karl Marx's closest collaborator and co-founder of Marxist movement.

Erber, Ernest **(1913–2010)** – Joined YPSL, 1931. Elected national chairman, 1935; reelected at 1937 convention. Alternate member, SWP NC, 1938. Member, SWP NC, 1939. Left SWP in 1940.

Esquerra (Catalan for "Left") – Middle-class party of Catalonia, leading party in the Generalitat.

Fabian Society – British middle-class group founded in 1884 dedicated to infiltrating government and institutions in order to spread principles of socialism very gradually.

Farmer-Laborites – Members of Farmer-Labor Party of Minnesota or, in general, advocates of such a party nationally or in other states.

Farrell, William (1910–1984) – Joined WPUS, 1934. Columnist in *Socialist Appeal*, 1938–39. Alternate member, SWP NC, 1938 and 1939.

Federal Workers Section, Minneapolis – Founded in 1935 as auxiliary of Teamsters Local 574 to organize unemployed and WPA workers under the local's sponsorship, 1935. For its history, see Farrell Dobbs's *Teamster Politics* (Monad, 1975).

Fieldites (League for Revolutionary Workers Party) – Centrist sect specializing in anti-Trotskyism after B.J. Field was expelled from CLA for violating discipline during a strike in 1934.

Ford, Henry (1863–1947) – Founder of auto empire, noted for antilabor and anti-Semitic views. Forced to recognize United Auto Workers, CIO, 1941.

Foster, William Z. (1881–1961) – CP presidential candidate three times and CP national chairman, 1945–57.

Fourth International (FI) (World Party of Socialist Revolution) – Founded under Trotsky's leadership as revolutionary successor to Third International, 1938.

Franco, Francisco (1892–1975) – Leader of fascist forces in Spanish civil war, 1936–39. Fascist dictator from 1939 to his death.

Frey, John P. (1871–1957) – President of Metal Trades Department of AFL, 1934–50.

Friends of Durruti – Dissident tendency among Spanish anarchists, 1936–38.

Fusion Party – A municipal "good government" reform party in New York, formed in 1933 to help elect Fiorello LaGuardia mayor.

Garvey movement (Universal Negro Improvement Association) – Founded in U.S., 1916, by Marcus Garvey (1887–1940). Became mass "back to Africa" movement in 1920s, before Garvey was arrested and deported.

Geller, Jules (1913–1990) – Joined Workers Party, 1935. First SWP candidate on ballot (for mayor, St. Paul, 1938). Alternate member, SWP NC, 1939. Left SWP in 1953.

German-American Bund – Founded in U.S. by Fritz Kuhn, 1936. Supported Hitler and opposed communism, labor unions, and Jews. Active until World War II.

Glee, Martin – Joined CLA early 1930s. Opposed defense of Soviet Union and criticism of Spanish POUM as New York minority delegate to first convention. Left SWP in 1938 or 1939.

Glotzer, Albert (1908–1999) – Member, CLA's first NC, 1929. Alternate member, SWP NC, 1938 and 1939. Left SWP in 1940.

Goebbels, Joseph (1897–1945) – German Nazi leader and minister of propaganda, 1933–45.

Goldman, Albert (1897–1960) – Joined CLA, 1933. Left CLA to join SP, 1934. Founded *Socialist Appeal*, 1935. Became part of left wing in SP when WPUS members joined. Trotsky's attorney in U.S. Member, SWP NC, 1938 and 1939. Delegate for FI to France, 1939. Left SWP in 1946.

Gompers, Samuel (1850–1924) – President of AFL, 1886–1924.

Gordon, Sam (1910–1982) – Joined CLA, 1930. Columnist for *Socialist Appeal*, 1939. Member, SWP NC, 1939.

Gould, Nathan (1913–1997) – Joined CLA, 1931. National secretary, SYL, before its members joined YPSL. Delegate to founding conference of FI, 1938. YPSL representative to SWP PC, 1938. Member, SWP NC, 1939. Left SWP in 1940.

GPU – Soviet secret police. Also known at different times as Cheka, NKVD, KGB, etc.

Grau San Martín, Ramón (1887–1969) – President of Cuba, 1933–34, 1944–48.

Green, William (1873–1952) – Conservative president of conservative AFL, 1924–52.

Grove, Marmaduke (1878–1961) – Chilean colonel who held power for ten days in 1932, proclaiming "socialist republic." Ousted by right-wing coup.

Hague, Frank P. (1876–1956) – Democratic mayor of Jersey City 1917–47 and Democratic national vice chairman. Used legal and extralegal violence to try to block organizing by CIO.

Haya de la Torre, Victor Raúl (1895–1979) – Organizer of APRA (American Revolutionary Popular Alliance) in Peru, 1924. A populist movement that took some anti-imperialist positions, APRA later degenerated into a liberal anticommunist party.

Haywood, William D. ("Big Bill") (1869–1928) – Leader of Western Federation of Miners. An organizer of IWW, 1905. Arrested for opposing World War I in 1917. Joined CP shortly after it was founded. Went into exile in USSR, 1921.

***Heisler, Francis* (1896–1994)** – Joined WPUS, 1935. Author of *The First Two Moscow Trials,* book published by SP in 1937. Delegate to first convention from Chicago. Left SWP in 1940.

Henlein, Konrad (1898–1945) – Nazi leader in the Sudentenland.

Hillman, Sidney (1887–1946) – President of Amalgamated Clothing Workers, 1915–46. Vice-president of CIO, 1935–40. A founder of ALP in New York.

Hindenburg, Paul von (1847–1934) – German chief of staff in World War I. Conservative president of Germany, 1925–34. Appointed Hitler chancellor, 1933.

Hitler, Adolf (1889–1945) – Head of German National Socialist Workers Party (Nazis), 1921–45, and of German government, 1933–45.

Hoan, Daniel (1881–1961) – SP right-winger. Mayor of Milwaukee, 1916–40.

Hoover, Herbert (1874–1964) – Republican president of U.S., 1929–33. An "isolationist" before World War II.

Hull, Cordell (1871–1955) – Southern Democrat and poll-taxer. Roosevelt's secretary of state, 1933–44.

Independent Labor League – see Lovestoneites.

Independent Labour Party (ILP) – British centrist group, adhering to London Bureau, 1932–39.

Industrial Workers of the World (IWW, the Wobblies) – Founded as revolutionary industrial union, 1905. Rejected political action or work in AFL. Went into decline after formation of CP in 1919.

International African Service Bureau – Small radical propaganda group in Britain mobilizing support for colonial independence and labor struggles, 1938–39. Leaders included C.L.R. James and George Padmore. Published *International African Opinion*.

International Executive Committee (IEC) of Fourth International – Highest body between congresses, established at founding conference in September 1938.

International Ladies Garment Workers Union (ILGWU) – Founded 1900. Affiliated in 1937 to CIO until 1940, then to AFL.

International Left Opposition – see Left Opposition.

International Secretariat (IS) of International Left Opposition, Movement for Fourth International, Fourth International – Administrative agency, located in Europe, 1930–39.

International Typographical Union (ITU) – Founded 1852. Sympathetic to CIO but remained in AFL until 1939. Reaffiliated to AFL in 1944.

"ISP" (for "International Socialist Party") – Temporary initials used in resolutions prepared for first convention of SWP before convention selected its name.

James, C.L.R. (1901–1989) – Born in Trinidad. Joined Trotskyists in Britain, 1935. Elected to IEC of Fourth International, 1938. Moved to U.S., 1938. Left SWP in 1940. Returned to SWP, 1947. Left for good, 1951.

Jewish Daily Forward (New York) – Founded in 1897. Defended positions of the SP Old Guard.

Jewish Labor Committee – Founded 1933 but not pro-Zionist until later.

Joerger, Meldon – Leader of small New York group in SP left wing that was opposed to giving material support to the Spanish government during the civil war. Left SWP in 1939.

Johnson, J.R. – A pseudonym of C.L.R. James.

Kerensky, Alexander (1881–1970) – Member of a faction of Russian Social Revolutionary Party. Prime minister of bourgeois Provisional Government in 1917 before it was overthrown by Bolshevik-led uprising in October.

Kerry, Tom **(1901–1983)** – Active in maritime unions and a leader of the SWP's maritime fraction in 1930s and 1940s. Member, SWP NC, 1938 and 1939.

Kuomintang – Chinese bourgeois nationalist party, founded by Sun Yat-sen, 1912. Became ruling party of China under Chiang Kai-shek in 1920s. Overthrown in civil war led by Chinese CP, 1949.

Labor's Non-Partisan League (NPL) – Founded as political arm of CIO unions, with minor AFL participation, 1936, as a way of winning labor votes for Roosevelt and Democrats. It declined in influence after CIO leaders split over 1940 elections, ending up as lobbying arm of United Mine Workers.

La Follette, Robert M., Jr. (1895–1953) – U.S. senator, 1906–25. Member of Progressive Republican dynasty in Wisconsin and son of Progressive presidential candidate in 1924.

LaGuardia, Fiorello H. (1882–1947) – Liberal Republican. Mayor of New York, 1934–45. Was endorsed at different times by Republicans, Democrats, ALP, Stalinists, Social Democrats, and fascists.

Landon, Alfred (1887–1987) – Republican governor of Kansas, 1933–37; Republican candidate for president against Roosevelt, 1936.

Largo Caballero, Francisco (1869–1946) – Leader of the left wing of the Spanish SP. Premier from September 1936 until May 1937.

Lash, Joseph P. (1909–1987) – National secretary, American Student Union, 1936–39.

Lasser, David (1902–1996) – Right-wing member of SP and president of Workers Alliance; aided anti-Trotskyists in both organizations. Resigned from Workers Alliance to take WPA job in 1940.

League for Industrial Democracy (LID) – Founded 1905 by SP leaders and sympathizers.

League for Revolutionary Workers Party – see Fieldites.

League of Nations – Predecessor of United Nations. Founded by imperialist victors of World War I, 1919. Preached peace but failed to block Japanese invasion of China, Italian invasion of Ethiopia, Hitler's takeover of Austria and Czechoslovakia. Gave up ghost in World War II.

***Lear, Blake* (1910–1995)** – Joined CLA, 1934. Active in teachers union, Akron. Alternate member, SWP NC, 1939. Left SWP in 1940.

Lee, Algernon (1873–1954) – A leader of right-wing split from SP that created Social Democratic Federation, 1936.

Left Opposition – Originally, a tendency in Russian CP advocating proletarian democracy and Leninist internationalism, 1923. Its members were expelled and outlawed in USSR, 1927, and then in whole Comintern. International Left Opposition (ILO) was organized at a meeting in France, 1930. This was international nucleus of future FI.

Left Wing Correspondence (Chicago) – Bulletin published by small group that claimed to be left wing of Appeal Association in SP, 1937. Principal editor was Melos Most.

Lehman, Herbert H. (1878–1963) – New Deal Democrat and banker. Governor of New York, 1933–43. U.S. senator, 1949–57.

Lenin, V.I. (1870–1924) – Founder of Bolshevik Party, first workers' state, and Communist International. Prepared fight against bureaucratization of CPSU and Soviet state but died before he could carry it out.

Lewis, Alfred Baker (1897–1980) – Alternate member, SP National Executive Committee, 1937. Right-wing leader of SP in Massachusetts, 1937.

Lewis, John L. (1880–1969) – President, UMW, 1920–69. Chief founder and leader of CIO, 1935–40. Withdrew UMW from CIO, 1942.

Lewis, Kathryn (1911–1962) – Daughter of John L. Lewis and an official in CIO.

***Lewit, Morris* (1903–1998)** – Active in plumbers' union, New York. Member, SWP NC, 1938 and 1939.

Lieberman, Esther – Leader of SWP fraction in teachers' union, New York. Alternate member, WPUS NC, 1936; SWP NC, 1938 and 1939.

Lombardo Toledano, Vicente (1893–1969) – Stalinist head of Mexican Confederation of Workers, largest union federation in country. Led slander campaign designed to prepare Mexican public opinion for Trotsky's assassination.

London Bureau – Loose federation of centrist parties opposed to Second and Third Internationals but equally opposed to founding of Fourth International, 1932–39.

Lovestoneites – Followers of Jay Lovestone (1897–1990), expelled from CP as Right Oppositionists, 1929. Known as Communist Party (Opposition) in 1929, as Independent Labor League in 1938–39. Disbanded to support U.S. war effort, 1941.

Loyalists – Name given to Spanish republican government during civil war, 1936–39, and to its defenders.

Ludlow, Louis L. (1873–1950) – Democratic congressman from Indiana, 1929–49. Introduced amendment to U.S. Constitution to require national referendum before declaration of war, 1935.

Marine Firemen, Oilers, Watertenders and Wipers Association – Founded 1883. Affiliated to Maritime Federation of Pacific in 1935–37. 5,000 members in 1936. Affiliated to Seafarers' International Union in 1957.

Martin, Homer (1902–1968) – President of UAW, 1936–39. Led small split to AFL, 1939. Left labor movement, became employers' representative.

Marx, Karl (1818–1883) – German founder of modern socialist movement, Communist League, First International.

Marxian Labor College – A Chicago educational group in which Appeal group members participated.

McCormack, Paul – Joined left wing in SP, 1937. Alternate member, SWP NC, 1938.

McKinney, Ernest Rice (1886–1984) – Joined AWP, 1933. SWP organizer in New York and Newark, 1938–39. Member, SWP NC and PC, 1938 and 1939. Left SWP in 1940.

Mensheviks – Members of minority faction at 1903 congress of Russian Social Democratic Labor Party. Became separate party after 1912. Supported Provisional Government and opposed Bolshevik seizure of power in 1917. Remained part of Second International.

Mikado (i.e., Hirohito) (1901–1989) – Title of Hirohito (1901–1989), emperor of Japan.

Militant (New York) – Weekly newspaper of American Left Opposition and CLA, 1928–34. Renamed *New Militant* when published by WPUS, 1934–36. Replaced by *Socialist Appeal*, paper of SP left wing and of SWP, 1937–41. Renamed *Militant*, 1941.

Militant faction in SP – Loose grouping opposed to right-wing control of SP, 1934–36.

Milton, Harry (1907–1984) – Joined CLA, 1931. Active in ILGWU,

New York. Fought in Spain with POUM militias, 1937. Alternate member, SWP NC, 1939. Left SWP in 1940.

Mooney, Tom (1883–1942) – Socialist and union militant convicted of murder in 1916 antilabor frame-up, San Francisco. Served 23 years in prison before being pardoned in 1939.

***Morrow, Felix* (1906–1988)** – Joined CLA, 1933. Active in defense cases. Associate editor, *Militant*, 1939. Member, SWP NC, 1938 and 1939. Left SWP in 1946.

Moscow trials – Three spectacles staged by Stalin where his opponents "confessed" proimperialist conspiracies (August 1936, January 1937, March 1938).

Most, Melos – Joined Appeal Association in SP, 1936. Led small sectarian group in Appeal Association. Left SWP in 1938.

Movement for Fourth International (MFI) – Name used by predecessor of FI, 1936–38.

Murray, Philip (1886–1952) – Vice-president, UMW, 1920–42. Vice-president, CIO, 1936–40. President, CIO, 1940–52. President, United Steel Workers, 1942–52.

Muste, A.J. (1885–1967) – Founded Conference for Progressive Labor Action, 1929, which organized AWP, 1933. National secretary of WPUS, 1934–36. U.S. delegate to international conference of MFI, 1936. Broke with Marxism and returned to church, 1936.

National Action Committee (NAC) of Appeal Association in SP – Elected at Appeal Institute, Chicago, February 1937; 19 members and 8 alternates. Served as national leadership of Appeal group until SWP's founding convention.

National Executive Committee (NEC) – Name used by some delegates and in some documents at SWP's first convention to designate highest party body between conventions. But actual name it was given in SWP constitution was National Committee (NC).

National Youth Administration (NYA) – New Deal jobs and training agency for youth of families on relief, 1935–43.

GLOSSARY / 615

Nazi Bund – see German-American Bund.
Nazis – German fascists, in power 1933–45.
Negrín López, Juan (1889–1956) – Right-wing leader of Spanish SP who displaced Largo Caballero as premier in May 1937. Resigned in exile in France after end of civil war.
New Deal – Roosevelt's election slogan, 1932. Name given to social legislation enacted while he was in office, most of it before World War II.
New International (New York) – Theoretical magazine of CLA, WPUS, and SWP, 1934–40 (except from summer 1936 to end of 1937). Edited by Shachtman, Burnham, Spector, 1938–39. Changed name to *Fourth International,* 1940, and *International Socialist Review,* 1956.
Nin, Andrés (1892–1937) – A founder of Spanish CP. Secretary of Red International of Labor Unions in mid-twenties. For supporting Left Opposition, was expelled from CPSU, 1927, and deported from USSR, 1930. Leader of Spanish Left Opposition, 1930–35. Cofounder of POUM, 1935, which signed People's Front pact, 1936. Arrested by GPU and assassinated.
Novack, George **(1905–1992)** – Joined CLA, 1933. National secretary, American Fund for Political Prisoners and Refugees, 1938–39.
Nyon Conference – September 1937 conference at Nyon, Switzerland, between Great Britain, France, the Soviet Union, and the Mediterranean nations to discuss "sea piracy." Also sought compromise in Spanish civil war and a delay in the outbreak of world war. Generally seen as a victory for British imperialism.
Oehlerites (Revolutionary Workers League) – Small sectarian group headed by Hugo Oehler (1903–1983) after its members were expelled from WPUS for violating discipline in 1935.
Old Guard – Name applied to right wing of SP before it split away to support Roosevelt and formed SDF, 1936.

Oneal, James (1875–1962) – Member of SP right wing and a founder of SDF.

Parker, Edward (1917–1942) – Joined SYL before WPUS was founded. Organizer for Illinois Workers Alliance. Moved to San Francisco and was active in Seafarers' International Union. Killed during Second World War.

Paris Commune – First example of a workers' government, March–May 1871. Drowned in blood by counterrevolution.

Pioneer Publishers – Published SWP's books and pamphlets in 1930s. A predecessor of Pathfinder Press.

POI (International Workers Party, France) – French section of MFI and FI, 1936–39.

Political Committee (PC) of SWP, 1938–39 – Elected by NC in January 1938: Dobbs, Cannon, Burnham, Abern, Shachtman, McKinney, with Widick as first candidate (alternate) and Goldman as second candidate. Since Dobbs was unable to move to New York until end of 1939, Widick served on PC throughout its entire 18-month term. A seventh member, named by YPSL, was Gould, replaced by Draper in June 1938. In the 1939–40 faction fight Cannon noted his opponents had had a 6–1 majority on the 1938–39 PC.

Porter, Paul (1907–2002) – Right-wing leader of Wisconsin SP, which published his pro-Stalinist pamphlet *Which Way for the Socialist Party?* shortly before national SP convention where right-wingers hoped to expel left wing, March 1937.

POUM (Workers Party of Marxist Unification, Spain) – Founded by fusion of Left Opposition with right-centrist Workers and Peasants Bloc, 1935. Affiliated with London Bureau. Signed People's Front pact, 1936. Persecuted and outlawed by People's Front government, 1937.

Pravda (Moscow) – Daily paper of CPSU.

Preis, Art (1911–1964) – Joined AWP, 1933. A leader of Toledo Auto-Lite strike, 1934. Author of resolutions on unemployment at first and second SWP conventions.

Prieto y Tuero, Indalecio (1883–1962) – Right-wing leader in Spanish SP. War minister in Largo Caballero and Negrín cabinets, 1936–38, ousted at CP's demand.

Progressive Party – Refers to Wisconsin Progressive Republicans, who hoped in late 1930s they could expand into a national party (not to Progressive Party that ran presidential ticket in 1924).

Provisional Government – Russia. Bourgeois government that held office in 1917 between overthrow of tsarism and uprising that transferred power to soviets.

Reid, Les – Active in steelworkers union, Youngstown. Alternate member, SWP NC, 1939.

Reiss, Ignace (1899–1937) – Polish-born officer of GPU. Murdered by GPU after he denounced Moscow trials and expressed solidarity with FI.

Right Opposition – Name of right wing of CPSU, led by Bukharin, Rykov, and Tomsky, that briefly challenged Stalin's "third period" policies, 1928–29.

Rodríguez Salas, Eusebio – Commissioner of public order in Barcelona and member of Stalinist party. Led police in attack on Barcelona telephone exchange, May 1937.

Roosevelt, Franklin D. (1882–1945) – Democratic president of U.S. 1933–45, elected to four terms. His "New Deal" reforms were unable to restore economy to pre-depression levels, not reached until World War II, but they enabled him, with help of union bureaucrats, Stalinists, and Social Democrats, to contain radicalization of workers and their allies and keep it from reaching an independent political form.

Rosenberg, Irving **(1905–1989)** – Joined AWP, 1933. Active in CIO clerks' union, Newark. Member, SWP NC, 1938. Resigned at PC request, 1939, because his commercial activities tended to discredit SWP.

SAP (Socialist Workers Party, Germany) – Centrist group founded after expulsion of left-wingers in German Social Democratic Party, 1931. Affiliated to London Bureau. Briefly endorsed idea of Fourth International, 1933, but then fought pro-FI groups bitterly until its demise at start of World War II.

Saunders, Robert S. (1893–1971) – Joined SP, 1932. Active in carpenters' union, St. Louis. Member, SWP NC, 1938.

Scheringer, Richard (1904–1986) – Former Reichswehr officer who defected from Nazis to German CP, 1930, and became CP propagandist.

Schmidt, Peter J. (1896–1952) – President of RSAP (Revolutionary Socialist Workers Party), Dutch section of Fourth Internationalist movement, and member of its Amsterdam secretariat, 1935–36. Split from RSAP and FI after first Moscow trial, 1936.

Second International – Founded as a loose association of Social Democratic and labor parties, 1889. Included revolutionists and reformists. Collapsed when most sections supported own capitalist governments in World War I. Revived as reformist opponent of Third International, 1919.

Sedov, Leon (1906–1938) – Son of Natalia Sedova and Trotsky. Went into exile with parents, 1929. Became a leader of movement and member of IS in his own right. Murdered by GPU in Paris.

Selander, Ted (1903–1996) – Joined AWP, 1933. A leader of Toledo Auto-Lite strike, 1934, and unemployed movement, Ohio. Alternate member, SWP NC, 1938. Member, SWP NC, 1939.

Shachtman, Max (1903–1972) – Member, CLA's first NC, 1929. Editor, *Socialist Appeal* and *New International*, 1938–39. Member, SWP NC and PC, 1938 and 1939. Delegate to founding conference of FI, 1938. Member, IEC of FI, 1938–39. Left SWP in 1940.

Sherman, Bill (1896–196?) – Joined CLA before fusion with AWP in 1934. Active in unemployed movement. Alternate member, SWP NC, 1938. Left SWP in 1940.

Silver Shirts of America – Fascist organization founded by William Dudley Pelley, 1932. Active enemy of radical and union movements throughout 1930s.

Sixty Families – A term for U.S. ruling class popularized by Ferdinand Lundberg's 1937 book, *America's Sixty Families*. Book documented existence of economic oligarchy headed by sixty immensely wealthy families, including Rockefellers, DuPonts, etc.

Skoglund, Carl (1884–1960) – Member, CLA's first NC, 1929. Active in Minneapolis strikes, 1934. President, Teamsters Local 544, 1938–40. Member, SWP NC, 1938 and 1939. Member, IEC of FI, 1938–39.

Smith – see Farrell Dobbs.

Social Democrats – A term synonymous with revolutionary socialism or revolutionary Marxism until World War I, when most parties with that name betrayed struggle for socialism. Thereafter it was used to designate reformists who only claimed to be for socialism.

Social Democratic Federation (SDF) – Right-wing split off from American SP, 1936. Reunited with SP, 1957.

Social fascist – Epithet used by CP and Comintern to smear working-class and socialist opponents, 1928–34.

Socialist Appeal (Chicago, New York) – Mimeographed journal in SP, Chicago, founded by Albert Goldman and Ernest Erber, 1935. Printed magazine of SP left wing, 1935–37. Weekly or twice-weekly newspaper of SWP, 1938–41. Name changed to *Militant,* 1941.

Socialist Party (SP) – Founded 1901. Became mass movement before World War I. Left-wing majority, supporting Russian revolution of 1917, was expelled and formed CP, 1919. Experienced some growth in 1930s. WPUS members joined SP in 1936. They and other left-wingers, expelled in 1937, founded SWP. SP declined to small sect by start of World War II.

Social Revolutionary Party (SRs), Russia – Populist party, founded 1900. Became most influential party among peasants before 1917 revolution. Opposed Bolshevik-led insurrection against Provisional Government.

Somoza García, Anastasio (1896–1956) – Dictator of Nicaragua from 1936 until his assassination.

Southern Tenant Farmers Union – A predecessor of United Farm Workers, founded in 1934 by H.L. Mitchell, SP member. Affiliated CIO United Cannery, Agricultural and Allied Workers in 1937 and disaffiliated in 1939. Claimed 35,000 members in 200 locals in five southern states in 1939.

Soviets (Russian for "Councils") – Workers', peasants', and soldiers' bodies that first emerged in unsuccessful Russian revolution of 1905. Reappeared in 1917 and became base for new workers' state.

Spark (Cape Town) – Journal of Workers Party of South Africa, a Trotskyist group in 1930s.

Spartacus Youth League (SYL) – Youth section of CLA, 1931–34, and of WPUS, 1934–36. Published *Young Spartacus*, 1931–35. Dissolved into YPSL, 1936, which adhered to FI, 1937.

Spector, Maurice **(1898–1968)** – Member, CLA's first NC, 1929. Co-editor, *New International,* 1938–39. Member, SWP NC, 1938. Left SWP in 1939.

Stakhanovites – Soviet workers rewarded with special privileges for setting norms of intense speedup on the job, starting 1935. Named after coal miner Alexi Stakhanov (1906–1977), who reportedly exceeded his quota sixteen-fold by sheer effort.

Stalin, Joseph (1879–1953) – General secretary, CPSU, 1922–53. Lenin asked for his removal because he was using this post to bureaucratize party and state apparatuses.

After Lenin's death in 1924, gradually eliminated all his opponents, starting with Trotsky. Virtual dictator thereafter.

Stevens, E. – see Lieberman, Esther.

Swabeck, Arne (1890–1986) – Member, CLA's first NC, 1929. CLA national secretary, 1931–34. Member, SWP NC, 1938 and 1939. Left SWP in 1967.

Sweet, Thaddeus C. (1872–1928) – Speaker of New York State Assembly, 1914–20.

Thermidorians – A reactionary wing of Great French Revolution at end of eighteenth century that overthrew revolutionary Jacobins led by Robespierre and thus opened the road for Bonaparte but did not go back so far as to restore old feudal regime. In late 1930s Trotsky and his supporters used same term for Stalinists, who had liquidated Leninism and wiped out leaders of 1917 revolution but still based themselves on new property relations established by that revolution.

Third International – see Communist International.

Thomas, Norman (1884–1968) – National chairman and member, SP National Executive Committee, 1937. SP presidential candidate six times. Supported expulsion of left wing in 1937.

Toledano – see Lombardo Toledano.

Toro, David (1898–1977) – Military ruler of Bolivia, 1936–37.

Tracy, Daniel (1886–1955) – President, International Brotherhood of Electrical Workers, AFL, 1933–40.

Trade Union Educational League (TUEL) – Founded as syndicalist group, anti-political and pro-AFL, in 1920 by William Z. Foster before he joined CP. When he was recruited to CP in 1921, TUEL became a CP auxiliary organization, affiliated to Red International of Labor Unions. Its name was changed to Trade Union Unity League in 1929 and, following Moscow's "third period" tactics, became thoroughly isolated. TUUL was dissolved in 1935.

Trade Union Unity League (TUUL) – see TUEL.

Trainor, Larry (1905–1975) – Joined CLA, 1933. Active in printers' union, Boston. Alternate member, SWP NC, 1938 and 1939.

Trbovich, Emanuel – Active in steelworkers' union. Alternate member, SWP NC, 1939. Left SWP in 1950.

Trimble, Glen – Joined SP in 1930s. A leader of left wing in California SP. Member, SWP NC, 1938. Left SWP in 1940.

Trotsky, Leon (1879–1940) – A leader of Russian revolution in 1917. Head of Red Army in civil war, 1918–1920. Organizer of Left Opposition in CPSU to defend Leninism against Stalinist bureaucracy, 1923. Deported, 1929. Founder of FI, 1938. Lived in Mexican exile from 1937 to his assassination by Stalinist agent.

Trujillo, Rafael (1891–1961) – Dictator of Dominican Republic from 1930 until his assassination.

Tyler, Gus (1911–2011) – Alternate member, SP National Executive Committee, 1937. A leader of Clarity group and supporter of left wing's expulsion.

UGT (General Workers Union, Spain) – Second largest labor federation in 1930s. Dominated by Spanish SP.

United Auto Workers (UAW) – Chartered as AFL union, 1935. Affiliated to CIO, 1936. Defeated move by its president, Homer Martin, to return to AFL, 1939.

United Mine Workers (UMW) – Founded as industrial union, 1890. A founder of CIO, 1935, and principal bulwark of CIO until 1940, when its president, John L. Lewis, resigned as CIO president.

Van Zeeland, Paul (1893–1973) – Leader of Catholic Party and premier of Belgium, 1935–37.

Vargas Dornelles, Getulio (1883–1954) – President of Brazil, 1930–45, 1951–54.

Waldman, Louis (1892–1982) – Right-wing SP leader and co-founder of Social Democratic Federation, 1936.

Weber, Jack (b.1896) – Joined CLA, 1930. Author of Jewish theses, 1938. Member, SWP NC, 1938 and 1939. Left SWP in 1944.

Weiss, Murry (1915–1981) – Joined CLA, 1932. Member, SWP NC, 1939. Left SWP in mid-1960s.

Widick, B.J. (1910–2008) – Joined CLA, 1934. Active in American Newspaper Guild and United Rubber Workers in Akron. SWP national labor secretary, 1938–39. Member, SWP NC and PC, 1938 and 1939. Left SWP in 1940.

Wilson, Woodrow (1856–1924) – Democratic president of U.S., 1913–21.

Workers Alliance of America (WAA) – National unemployed organization founded by SP, 1935. Fused with CP-led Unemployed Councils and WPUS-led National Unemployed Leagues, 1936. Thereafter dominated by CP. Dissolved, 1941.

Workers Party (WP) – Name of group that split from SWP in April 1940. Called "Shachtmanites" after their leader, Max Shachtman. Changed name to Independent Socialist League, 1949. Dissolved into SP, 1958.

Workers Party of United States (WPUS) – Revolutionary party created through fusion of CLA and AWP in December 1934. Voted to dissolve and join SP, March 1936.

WPA (Works Progress Administration, later Works Projects Administration) – New Deal public works agency to provide federal jobs for unemployed, 1935–43. At peak had 3.5 million on its payroll.

Wright, John G. (1902–1956) – Joined CLA, 1933. Translator of articles and books by Trotsky. Alternate member, SWP NC, 1939.

Young People's Socialist League (YPSL, or Yipsels) – Founded as youth section of SP, 1911. Majority adhered to FI movement at Ninth National Convention in September 1937. A later majority broke with SWP in 1940 and adhered to WP.

Zam, Herbert – Former Lovestoneite and a leader of Clarity group in SP in 1937.

Zinoviev, Gregory (1883–1936) – Close co-worker of Lenin before Russian revolution of 1917. President of Comintern, 1919–1926. Collaborated with Stalin against Trotsky, 1923–25, and with Trotsky against Stalin, 1926–27. Convicted in first Moscow trial frame-up and executed.

Index

Abern, Martin, 27–29, 41–42, 48, 93–96, 107, 114, 118–21, 125–26, 136–37, 345–46, 349, 353, 355, 359–62, 435–36, 438, 467n, 518, 531–32, 537, 549, 599g
Active workers conferences, 536
Adler, Al, 136
Adventurism, 202
Agitation, 374, 395–96, 459–60
Agrarian reform, 498, 501
Allen, Cecil, 111, 134
"All-inclusiveness," 263, 272
Altman, Jack, 58, 61–62, 599g
Alvin, Milton, 549
Amalgamated Clothing Workers, 185, 599g
American exceptionalism, 369–70, 370n
American Federation of Labor (AFL), 182–87, 322, 599g
  bureaucracy in, 192–93
  and unemployed, 483
  and unity with CIO, 186–90, 443–44
American Fund for Political Prisoners and Refugees, 481–82, 599–600g
American Jewish Congress, 407–8, 600g
American Labor Party (ALP), 168, 317–18, 357, 385, 424n, 425–26, 600g

American Workers Party (AWP), 31–32, 600g
Anarchists, 212, 241, 244–45, 247–49, 254
Anarcho-syndicalists, 244–45, 600g
Antifascist labor guards, 600g
  See also Workers' defense guards
Antifascist struggle, 332–34, 378–79, 409–11, 495–99, 561–63, 566–67, 569–75
Anti-imperialism, 494–96, 498–99, 500–501
Antilabor legislation, 444, 558
Antilabor offensive, 554–55
Anti-Semitism, 403–6, 409–10, 415–16, 418
Antiwar work, 49, 100, 281–82, 327–29, 367–68, 379, 469, 555–56, 566–67
Appeal Association, 32–35, 57, 62, 70n, 600g
Aragon, Paula, 130, 600g
Argentina, 491
Assimilation, 404–5
Asylum, 417–18
Austria, 56n
Auto industry, 428

Bardacke, Gregory (Jay), 346, 353, 355, 357, 359–64, 423–26, 600g
Barsh, Yetta, 422n, 549

625

Batista, Fulgencio, 460n, 492, 600g
Becket, Charles, 85, 96–97, 101–4, 123, 601g
Belgian Trotskyists, 334n
Benavides, Oscar, 492, 494, 601g
Berger, Victor, 58
Bern, Irving, 532, 549
Bernstein, Hilliard, 64
Bernstein, M.J., 238
Besch, Howard H., 137
Bienstock, A., 238
Birchman, Robert L., 111, 119–20, 134, 527, 549
Birney, Earle (Robertson), 354, 361
Birobidjan, 408
Bitner, J., 238
Black, George, 114, 137
Blacks, 297, 325, 410, 522–29, 577–88
 and CP, 582, 585–86
 independent organization of, 587–88
 and labor, 578–79
 and SWP, 18–19, 49–50, 523–24, 528–29, 577–88
Bleeker, Sylvia, 520, 549
Blum, Leon, 408, 601g
Bolivia, 492
Bolshevik-Leninists (Spain), 246–47, 255
Bolshevik Party, 29n, 45n, 214, 218, 230, 271–73, 380, 601g
Bonapartism, 218, 224, 601g
Boulds, John, 112, 135
Bourgeoisie, 292–94, 297
Bourgeois nationalists, 492, 498

Brandlerites, 311, 533, 601g
Brazil, 490–91, 497–98
Breitman, George, 25–27, 112, 135, 549, 601g
Bridges, Harry, 446, 601g
Brooks, G., 107, 113, 136
Brophy, John, 446, 602g
Browder, Earl, 499, 602g
Brown, Tom, 104, 114, 137
Browne, Robert, 113, 116, 118, 136
Browner, Fred, 104, 113, 121, 136
Brown Shirts, 497
Bukharin, Nikolai, 37, 601–2g
Burbank, David, 135
Burch, Arthur, 513, 517, 549
Bureaucratism, 271–73
Burnham, James, 41–43, 106–8, 110, 114, 124, 137, 345–46, 349–50, 352–53, 355, 357–59, 361, 369–70n, 379n, 423–31, 433–37, 509, 513, 515, 518–19, 528, 532, 534–35, 537, 549, 602g
Butterworth, Bill, 354, 361

California pension plan, 424–25, 440–41n
Campaign principle, 459–60, 535, 566
Cannon, James P., 27–29, 32, 40–44, 46, 48, 50n, 51, 91, 100, 103–5, 110, 114, 119–22, 125–26, 137, 151–53, 341–42n, 344–46, 351–53, 355–56, 359–66, 379n, 421–22, 424–25, 430–32, 439–41, 509–10, 517–18, 534–38, 549, 602g

Capitalism, 238, 291–96,
302–4
crisis of, 157–58, 160, 163–
64, 213–14, 275, 292–96,
369–71, 392–93, 554–55
Cárdenas, Lázaro, 492, 494,
602g
Carli, 549
Carlo, J., 238
Carlson, Grace (McGee), 112,
135, 517, 528, 550
Carson, Dan, 111, 117–18,
124, 134
Carter, Joseph, 42–43, 107,
110, 114, 125, 137, 344–46,
353, 355, 360–61, 363–64,
425, 432–33, 435–38, 534,
537–38, 549, 602g
Casano, Rose, 111, 134
Centrism, 31n, 311–12
Chautemps, Camille, 257,
602g
Chauvinism, 166, 325–26,
404–5, 410, 565, 586
Chiang Kai-shek, 45n, 602g
Chile, 499
China, 45, 232, 276–79
See also Sino-Japanese war
Civilian Conservation Corps
(CCC), 479, 602–3g
Clarity group, 58, 60–64,
603g
Clarke, George, 96, 101, 111,
134, 344–46, 349, 353, 355,
360–61, 431–32, 435–36,
515, 518, 532, 537, 549,
603g
Class collaboration, 146,
166–67, 192–96, 307
Class struggle, 165–66, 205–6

Class-struggle left wing, 205–6,
323
CNT (Spain), 247, 254, 603g
Coalitionism, 307, 331
Cochran, Bert, 83, 104, 113,
115–17, 136, 344, 346, 349,
351–53, 355–56, 359–61,
430–31, 435–36, 532, 537,
549, 603g
Cohen, W., 238
Collectivization, 301–2
Colombia, 491
Colonial revolution, 275–77,
329–30, 498
Commission on the Jewish
Question, 366, 440n
Communism, 302–3
Communist International
(Comintern), 27, 257, 272n,
308–11, 334–36, 603g
degeneration of, 30–31, 174,
309–10
and Hitler's rise to power,
31, 309–10, 409
under Lenin, 129n, 305,
308–9
Communist League of
America (CLA), 27–32, 53n,
603g
Communist League of China,
282
Communist Party (Soviet
Union), 223–24, 604g
Communist Party (U.S.), 26–28,
76, 195–96, 315–17, 603g
and Blacks, 582, 585–86
bureaucratic structure of,
175–76, 263
and capitalist parties, 33n,
167, 315, 357

Communist Party (U.S.)
(*continued*)
and Jews, 408–10
and Moscow trials, 315–16, 561
and People's Frontism, 33, 195–96, 315–16
strength of, 37, 171–72, 315–16, 560
SWP efforts toward, 172, 350–51n, 460, 521, 560–61
and unemployed, 144–45, 589, 594
and unions, 193–97, 316, 445–47
and U.S. imperialism, 172, 279–80, 315, 446, 514, 555
and World War II, 49
Congress of Industrial Organizations (CIO), 444–46, 604g
and Blacks, 579
bureaucracy in, 186, 192–94, 446
growth of, 36, 182–86, 322
and unemployed, 143–45, 483
and unity with AFL, 186–90, 443–44
Consumers' boycott, 280–81
Coover, Oscar, 112, 134, 549
Coughlin, Charles, 562, 570, 604g
Craine, Reva, 518, 532, 549
Cuba, 329, 460, 491
Curtiss, Charles, 96, 111, 130, 133, 604g
Cyons, S., 238
Czechoslovakia, 487, 495

Daily Worker, 460n, 604g
Daladier, Edouard, 495, 604g
Dale, Jack, 518, 549, 596
Debs, Eugene V., 26–28, 604g
Defeatism (revolutionary), 45n, 98, 165–66, 251, 276, 280, 328–29
Defeatism (Soviet), 41–44, 84, 273
Defense work, 481–82
Degrelle, Leon, 333–34, 604g
DeLeon, Daniel, 26, 604g
Delson, Max, 58, 605g
Demby, Frank, 432, 439, 518, 549
Democracy, 331–33, 492
"Democratic antifascist front," 487, 499
Democratic centralism, 29, 34–35, 75, 99, 123–25, 153, 175–76, 260–61, 305–6, 535
"Democratic" imperialism, 159, 210, 225, 308, 310
Democratic Party, 167–68, 382–83, 390, 585
Democratic rights, 294, 300–301, 331–33, 405, 555–58
Deren, E., 238
Dictatorship, 297–99, 332
Dictatorship of the proletariat, 214, 217–18, 234, 298–99
Dies committee, 586, 605g
Dilettantism, 262
Discrimination, 325
See also Racism
Dobbs, Farrell, 40, 106–7, 112, 119–20, 131, 134, 139–41, 507n, 569–70n, 605n
Dominican Republic, 498

Donlon, Liam, 422–23n
Donoghue, G., 532, 542, 549
Dostal, Theodore, 112, 135, 532, 549
Drake, Freddie, 114, 136–37
Draper, Hal, 43, 107, 114, 137, 423, 605g
Dual power, 239–41, 245, 375, 395
Dullea, Robert, 114, 116, 136–37, 351–53, 355, 361, 605g
Dunne, V.R., 28, 40, 51, 101, 112, 119–20, 134, 342n, 345, 353, 355, 359, 361, 519, 537, 544n, 549, 605g

Eastman, D., 238
Eden, Anthony, 257, 605g
Edwards, Dale, 542, 549
El Salvador, 498
Enestvedt, J., 112
Engels, Frederick, 75, 305, 605g
Erber, Ernest, 114, 137, 354, 356, 359–62, 439, 515, 518, 532, 549, 605g
Esquerra, 243, 605g
Ethiopia, 158–59
Ettlinger, Dick, 96–97, 104, 108, 113, 116, 120, 124, 136
Extraparliamentary action, 396, 402

Faben, Rose, 532, 550
Fabian Society, 56–57, 605–6g
Farmer-Labor Party (Minnesota), 385, 400, 606g

Farmers, 297, 324, 377–78
Farrell, Bill (Morgan), 101, 113, 136, 345, 353, 356, 361, 364, 606g
Farrow, 549
Fascism, 294–95, 325, 332–34, 403–4, 496–97, 557–58
  in Spain, 250–52, 334–35
  in U.S., 168, 296, 372, 374, 405, 418, 467–68, 558, 561–63, 569–72
  See also Antifascist struggle
Federal Workers Section Local 544, 146, 485, 606g
Ferguson, Richard, 136, 510, 517–18, 549
Feudalism, 238
Fielding, Paul, 549
Fieldites, 130, 606g
Findley, Al, 508, 515, 517, 534, 549
Fishler, Harry, 111, 133
Five-Year Plan, 231
Ford, Carl, 135
Ford, Henry, 498, 606g
Forsen, Clem, 112, 134
Fourth International, 69–70, 226–27, 256–57, 312–13, 463–65, 511–14, 556, 606g
Fractions, trade union, 127–28n, 139–41, 205, 449
France, 158–61, 491, 495
Franco, Francisco, 248, 606g
Franco-Soviet Pact, 231
Frankel, Jan (John Glenner), 343n, 366n
Fraser, Richard, 537, 549
French turn, 32–34
Frey, John P., 187, 606g
Friedman, Sam, 113, 136

Friends of Durruti, 246–47, 606g
Furth, Al, 104, 111, 133
Fusion Party, 62, 606g

Garrett, Manny, 114, 137, 354, 361–62
Garvey movement, 580, 607g
Geldman, Max, 112, 135, 515, 517, 549, 596
Geller, Jules, 135, 607g
German-American Bund, 561, 570, 607g
Germany
 and Britain, 159–61, 488
 economy of, 158–59
 Jews in, 404–5, 415–18
 and Latin America, 491–93, 496–98
 1919 revolution in, 307–8
 See also Fascism; Hitler, Adolf
Gilbert, S., 238
Giordano, Felix, 107, 112, 117, 135
Glee, Martin, 42, 45, 48, 100, 106–8, 112–13, 117–18, 121–22, 126, 128–29, 136, 238, 270, 607g
Glenner, John. See Frankel, Jan
Glotzer, Albert (Gates), 96, 100, 107, 114, 137, 349, 353, 356, 361–62, 510, 516, 518, 527, 537, 549, 607g
Glover, 549
Goddard, M., 238
Goebbels, Joseph, 433–35, 607g

Goldman, Albert, 45, 92–96, 107, 114–16, 118, 124, 137, 345–46, 349–50, 352–55, 359–61, 363–64, 423–24, 426–27, 429–31, 438, 440–42, 607g
Gold Shirts, 497
Gompers, Samuel, 382, 607g
Gordon, Sam, 113, 116, 136, 607g
Gould, Nathan, 114, 137, 345–46, 349–53, 356, 361, 507, 517, 549, 607g
Gourin, H., 238
GPU, 249, 310, 607g
Grau San Martín, Ramón, 496, 500, 608g
Graves, Frank, 114, 125, 137, 342n
Great Britain, 158–61, 487–89, 491–93
Great Depression, 31, 157–58, 295–96, 371
 1937 downturn in, 36, 163–64, 188, 369–70, 381–82
Green, William, 168, 187, 189, 608g
Greenberg, 515, 533, 538, 549
Grote, R., 238
Grove, Marmaduke, 496, 500, 608g
Guatemala, 491

Hague, Frank, 411n, 561, 608g
Haiti, 491
Hamilton, L., 134
Hansen, Joseph, 549
Hansen, R.M., 112, 135

Hargis, Al, 112, 135
Harrison, N., 238
Hartman, Carl, 113, 136
Hawaii, 329
Haya de la Torre, Victor Raúl, 496, 498–500, 608g
Hayes, 134
Haywood, William, 26, 608g
Heisler, Francis, 97, 100, 104, 106–8, 110–11, 116–18, 121, 134, 608g
Henlein, Konrad, 497, 608g
Herman, Paul, 111, 134
Hesser, Pete, 549
Hill, Sam, 112, 125, 135, 515, 549
Hillman, Sidney, 194, 608g
Hindenburg, Paul von, 333, 608g
History of American Trotskyism, The (Cannon), 28n, 30
Hitler, Adolf, 30–31, 333, 487, 496–97, 499, 608g
Hoan, Daniel, 58, 609g
Hoffman, Eugene, 135
Hoover, Herbert, 167, 609g
Hopkins, Arthur, 112, 135
Houchin, Wilbert, 134
Housing problem, 528
Hudson, Carlos, 112, 135
Hughes, 521, 549
Huhn, Walter, 113, 136
Hull, Cordell, 162, 489, 493, 609g
Hungarian revolution (1919), 109
Hunger Fighter, The, 592n

Ibarra, Felix, 531
Ideological struggle, 268–70

Immediate demands, 374, 392, 559
Immigration restrictions, 407, 417–18
Imperialism, 303, 307
  See also United States imperialism
Imperialist war, 275–76, 293, 303, 327–29, 554–56
Independent labor candidates, 400
Independent Labor League.
  See Lovestoneites
Independent Labour Party (ILP) (Great Britain), 311, 609g
Independent political action, 357–58, 382–84, 426
  See also Labor party
Industrial unionism, 182–85, 188–89, 191–92, 207, 321, 444–45
Industrial Workers of the World (IWW), 198, 609g
Inflation, 427
Integralistas, 497
Interimperialist rivalry, 158–61, 164–66, 275, 293, 487–90
International African Service Bureau, 524, 609g
International Communist League (Mexico), 530–31
Internationalism, 81, 512
International Ladies Garment Workers Union (ILGWU), 197–98, 206, 609g
International party, 306
International solidarity
  with China, 276, 280–82
  with colonial revolution, 329–30

International solidarity (cont'd)
  with Jews, 415–18
  with Latin America, 438,
    500–501, 556
  with Spanish workers,
    252–57
International Typographical
  Union, 203, 609g
Isaacs, Harold (Harold
  Roberts), 342n, 422n
Isolationism, 36, 157, 162
Italy, 158, 491–93, 553n

James, C.L.R. (J.R. Johnson),
  44, 433–34, 513, 518,
  523–24, 528, 529n, 534,
  549, 609–10g
Japan, 158–59, 275–82, 491
  See also Sino-Japanese war
Jewish Daily Forward, 57, 610g
Jewish Labor Committee, 412,
  610g
Jewish question, 403–12
Jim Crowism, 325
  See also Racism
Joerger, Meldon, 269–70,
  610g
Johnson, Genora, 518, 549
Johnson, J.R. See James, C.L.R.
Johnson, Kermit, 520, 549,
  596

Kahn, C., 134
Karsner, Rose, 51, 342n
Katz, Dorothea, 112, 135
Kennedy, H., 530
Kerensky, Alexander, 212,
  610g
Kerry, Tom, 40, 515, 517, 549,
  610g

Kirschbaum, M., 238
Kluger, Pearl, 342n, 422n
Knisley, John, 136
Kohler, Lester, 110, 114, 137
Konikow, E., 543
Kuehn, Karl S., 135
Kujac, Paul, 106, 113, 120,
  136
Kuomintang, 275, 324n, 610g
Kwalik, 516

Labor party, 317–19, 381–
  87, 389–402, 445, 514–15,
  563–64
  movement for, 185, 356–59,
    382–86, 396–98, 563–64
  SWP opposition to, 56,
    168–69, 317–19, 359
  SWP shift of position on, 20,
    52–53, 349, 356–59, 362,
    383–87
  tactics inside of, 168–69,
    319, 396–400
Labor's Non-Partisan League,
  372, 382–83, 385, 390–91,
  400, 610g
La Follette, Robert, 368, 372,
  610g
LaGuardia, Fiorello, 33, 61,
  168, 315, 610g
Laidler, Harry W., 61
Landon, Alfred, 499, 611g
Lands, Dave, 510, 518, 532,
  549
Largo Caballero, Francisco,
  242n, 243–44, 247–49, 254,
  611g
Larsen, Ronald, 135
Lash, Joseph P., 64, 611g
Lasser, David, 590, 611g

INDEX / 633

Latin America, 329–30, 487–501, 556
Latinos, 556
League for a Revolutionary Workers Party. *See* Fieldites
League for Industrial Democracy, 58, 611g
League of Nations, 231, 331, 611g
Lear, Blake, 96, 103, 113, 136, 518, 532, 549, 611g
Lebrun, A., 433–34, 437–38
Lee, Algernon, 57, 611g
Leeds, Dan, 549
Left Opposition, 27, 29–31, 611g
 in USSR, 41n, 216–17, 230
 See also Fourth International
Left Wing Correspondence, 118, 123–24, 152, 611g
Lehman, Herbert H., 168, 612g
Lenin, V.I., 45n, 169, 305, 612g
Leninist party, 67–69, 259–61, 459–60, 535–36
Leninist Party of Brazil, 519
"Lesser-evilism" in unions, 446–47
Lewis, Alfred Baker, 58, 612g
Lewis, John L., 168, 193–94, 444–46, 612g
Lewis, Kathryn, 499, 612g
Lewit, Morris, 114, 137, 345–46, 351–53, 355, 359–61, 423–24, 439–40, 517, 532, 550, 612g
Liberals, 357–58, 383
Liberia, 329

Lieberman, Esther (Stevens), 345, 349, 353, 356, 359–62, 430–31, 612g
Lima conference, 487–88
Little Steel strike, 187–88, 193
Loewy, J., 137
Lombardo Toledano, Vicente, 530, 612g
London Bureau, 311, 533, 612g
Lovestoneites, 37–38, 76, 80, 170–71, 197–98, 311, 385, 560, 595, 612g
Ludlow, Louis L., 368, 613g
Ludlow amendment, 52, 555, 566
 SWP shift of position on, 19–20, 52, 363–64, 367–68

Marxism, 173–74
McCormack, Paul, 96, 100–101, 103, 106–7, 111, 117–18, 120–21, 133, 543, 613g
McKinney, Ernest R., 103, 106, 114–16, 118–20, 137, 344, 349–53, 355, 359–63, 365–66, 432, 527–28, 533, 537, 550, 613g
Manchukuo, 489
Mann, Edith, 516–17, 550
Manret, Daisy, 550
Margolin, E., 238
Marine Firemen, Oilers, Watertenders and Wipers Association, 82, 613g
Maritime unions, 198
Martell, Charles, 550
Martin, Herbert, 125, 134
Martin, Homer, 447–48, 613g
Marx, Karl, 305, 613g

Marxian Labor College, 95, 613g
Mendelson, Saul, 97, 107, 114, 120, 138
Mensheviks, 212, 214, 613g
Mexico, 492–94
Middle classes, 297, 302, 320, 323–25, 372–73, 404
Militant, The, 49, 613g
Militant faction (SP), 314, 613g
Militarism, 468–69
Miller, Abe, 113, 117, 120, 136
Miller, M., 238
Milton, G., 238
Milton, Harry, 114, 138, 349–50, 354, 356, 361–64, 518, 520–21, 537, 550, 613–14g
Minneapolis teamsters, 32, 40
Minneapolis trial (1941), 336–37n
Mooney, Tom, 130, 614g
Morgenstern, Bernard, 113, 116, 120, 136
Moriarty, M., 238
Morocco, 244
Morrow, Felix, 346–49, 353, 355, 359, 361, 440, 532, 550, 614g
Moscow trials, 38–39, 561, 614g
Most, Melos, 85, 96, 98–100, 103–5, 111, 115–16, 118–21, 123–26, 130–31, 134, 151–52, 614g
Movement for the Fourth International, 39
Munich conference, 487–88, 553n, 561
Murray, Philip, 193–94, 614g

Mussolini, Benito, 496–97
Muste, A.J., 31, 39, 614g

Nacistas, 497
Nationalization, 215, 301, 376, 379
National minorities, 409, 580
National oppression, 329–30, 406–10, 578–80
National Youth Administration (NYA), 479, 614g
Nazis, 415–17, 615g
Negrín, Juan, 243, 248–50, 254, 615g
Negroes. *See* Blacks
New Deal, 163, 371, 554, 561, 569, 593–94, 615g
New International, 461, 512, 523, 615g
Nicaragua, 491
Nin, Andrés, 249, 310n, 615g
Nomen, 543
Novack, George, 342n, 349, 365, 366n, 422n, 615g
Noyes, Daniel, 112, 135
Nyon conference, 250, 615g

O'Brien, Vaughan T., 113, 137
Oehlerites, 101, 171, 615g
Old Bolsheviks, 209
Oneal, James, 57, 616g
Ontell, Robert, 550
"Open door" policy to China, 162
Open the books, 375
Organizers, 461, 536
Orgon, Roy, 112, 135

Pacifism, 327–28, 367–68, 468
Paine, Harry, 134

INDEX / 635

Paine, Lyman, 113, 136, 542, 550
Palestine, 406, 409
Pamphlets, 141, 402, 523, 536, 592
Pan-American conference, 366
Paris Commune, 109, 616g
Parker, Edward, 130, 616g
Parliamentary cretinism, 378
Party democracy, 73–75, 85, 103, 174, 259, 264, 271, 273–74, 289–90, 305–6, 436–37
Party loyalty, 102, 262–63, 270, 273–74
Pauperization, 373
Pease, A., 134
Pemble, Carl, 103, 114, 116, 138, 151
People's Frontism, 33, 62, 310, 323, 334–35
  in Chile, 499
  in France, 335
  in Spain, 241n, 242, 251, 253–54, 257, 308, 335
  in U.S., 167–68, 195, 380
Permanent revolution, 584
Peru, 491, 498
Pessimism, 401, 564
Petty-bourgeois pressures, 534–35n
Philippines, 329
Phillips, Larry, 518, 532, 550
Pioneer Publishers, 342n, 616g
Plaskett, Reuben, 135, 527–28, 550
POI (France), 32, 34, 616g
Poland, 158

Political revolution, 41, 218, 224–27
Popular Frontism. *See* People's Frontism
Porter, Paul, 58, 616g
Poulos, John, 101, 111, 134, 422n
POUM (Spain), 243–47, 249, 254, 311, 616g
Pravda, 499, 616g
Preis, Art, 106, 113, 116, 120–21, 124, 136, 143–49, 518, 533, 550, 616–17g
Prerevolutionary situation, 557
Prieto y Tuero, Indalecio, 243, 617g
"Pro-AFLism," 444–45
Professionals, 323–25
Progressive Party, 372, 617g
Proletarian orientation, 81–82, 177–79, 181, 199–200, 266–68, 461
Provisional Government (Russia), 241n, 617g
Public works program, 376, 559
Puerto Rico, 329, 491

Querio, Ruth, 550

Racism, 295, 325, 578–79, 581–83
Radicalization, 167, 299, 557
  "Debsian," 27
  of 1930s, 31, 36, 39
Rakoczy, Harold, 133
Randolph, A. Philip, 588n
Rasmussen, Hugo, 114, 138
Rasmussen, Paul, 106, 134

Rate of profit, 292–93
Recruitment, 174, 178, 201, 267–68, 386, 449, 536, 564–67, 584
"Red unions," 322
Reformism, 211–12, 513–14
Regroupment, 100
Reid, Les, 113, 136, 521, 550, 617g
Reiss, Ignace, 310n, 617g
Republican Party, 167–68
Retzkin, Alex, 107, 113, 116–17, 120, 128, 135, 508–10, 517–18, 520–21, 539, 550
Revolutionary party, 304–6
  See also Leninist party
Revolutionary Socialist League (Great Britain), 527
Revyuk, Emil, 124, 134, 153, 518, 550
Reynolds, Lillian, 129
Rhodes, 543
Ricco, Frank, 104, 111, 133
Right Opposition, 37–38, 617g
Right to strike, 204, 294–95
Roberts, J., 110, 114
Roberts, L., 550
Roberts, Steve, 517, 532, 550
Robins, Harold, 134
Rodríguez Salas, Eusebio, 242, 617g
Roosevelt, Franklin D., 36–37, 52n, 162–63, 167–68, 188, 193, 279, 443, 460n, 489, 498–99, 590, 617g
Rosenberg, Irving, 353, 355, 359–61, 617g
Rosenberg, J., 238
Ross, H., 238

Rubber industry, 428
Russell, Anne, 422n
Russian revolution, 209–10, 213–18, 229–30, 308

Salisbury, Rodney, 112, 130, 135
Sallume, David, 96
SAP (Germany), 311, 618g
Satir, Norman, 103, 134
Saunders, 515, 527, 537, 550
Saunders, Robert S., 112, 125, 135, 618g
Scheer, Charles (C. Williams), 520, 550
Scheringer, Richard, 409, 618g
Schimmel, Marie, 550
Schmidt, Peter J., 39, 618g
Second International, 174, 211, 257, 306–8, 618g
Secours International, 482
Sectarianism, 43–46, 76, 177, 266, 268–70, 281, 513
Sects, 170–71
Sedov, Leon, 310n, 618g
Selander, Ted, 93, 106, 115, 138, 550, 596, 618g
Self-determination, 215, 244, 303, 329–30, 379, 406–7, 523–29, 579–82
Shachtman, Max, 27–28, 32, 41–42, 47–51, 96–98, 100, 107–8, 110, 113, 121–26, 128, 136, 151–53, 342n, 345, 347–48, 352–55, 359–61, 363, 365–66, 434–40, 509, 519, 532–34, 537, 544n, 618g
Shade, Julius, 112, 134

INDEX / 637

Sherman, Bill, 48, 106, 115, 118, 126, 136, 138, 354, 356, 361, 364, 430–31, 434, 439, 619g
Shoemaker, L., 113, 137
Shoeworkers' union, 198
Shop committees, 204, 206, 375, 395–96, 402
Shultz, Dorothy, 135
Silver Shirts, 561, 569n, 570, 619g
Sino-Japanese war, 45, 159, 275–82
  SWP support for China in, 276, 281–82
Sit-down strike, 185, 201–3, 207, 372–73, 381, 558
Sixty Families, 559, 566, 619g
Skoglund, Carl, 28, 40, 95, 112, 120, 135, 342n, 438n, 619g
Sliding scale of wages and hours, 376–77, 427–30, 445, 560, 566, 598
Smith, Hildegarde, 110–11, 133–34, 550
Social Democracy, 211–13, 216, 619g
  See also Second International
Social Democratic Federation, 314, 560, 619g
Social Democratic Party (Germany), 333–34n
"Social fascism," 205n, 619g
Socialism, 222–23, 296–97, 301–4, 312, 328–29
Socialism in one country, 217, 309, 312

Socialist Appeal, 619g
  coverage of Black struggle in, 523, 527
  coverage of class struggle in, 199, 358, 449, 461
  frequency of, 430–31, 455–56, 512, 536
  fund drive for, 456, 536–37
  as journal in SP, 32–33, 57
Socialist democracy, 436
Socialist Party (SP), 28, 313–15, 560, 619–20g
  bureaucratic structure of, 176, 263
  disintegration of, 37, 62–65, 68–71, 76, 170, 314–15
  expulsion of left wing in, 34–35, 55, 62–63, 314–15
  gag law in, 61–62, 70–71
  growth of left wing in, 55–58, 60–61, 314
  Old Guard in, 56–58, 64, 314, 615g
  and trade unions, 197, 313, 385–86
  Trotskyist entry in, 32–35, 57, 146
  and unemployed movement, 145, 592, 595
Socialist Workers League (Canada), 529–30
Socialist Workers Party (SWP)
  composition of
    minorities and women, 49–50, 518
    working class, 80–81, 178–79, 266, 548
  discipline of, 43–44, 46, 85–86, 96–97, 101–4, 122–23, 127, 260, 263–64, 270–74, 288–89, 539–40

Socialist Workers Party (SWP)
(*continued*)
election campaigns of,
320–21, 432, 564
emblem of, 541–42
finances of, 461–62, 523,
536–37
and Fourth International,
54, 81, 283–84, 363, 365,
437–38n, 463–65, 511–13,
533–34
inefficient administration
of, 266, 269
internal education in, 460,
543, 584
leadership of, 72, 82–83,
85–87, 260–62, 284–86
membership, 28, 37, 69,
133–38, 266, 518, 547–49n
rights and responsibilities
of, 262–63, 284–85,
287–88
National Committee of,
85–87, 119–20, 137–38,
285–86, 544n
national spread of, 80, 266
1940 split in, 42, 48, 505–7n,
529n, 534–35n, 544n
organizational principles of,
43, 119, 122–23, 459–60,
535
Political Committee of,
342n, 363–64, 367–68,
369–70n, 424n, 425–26,
430n, 616g
professional staff of, 460–61,
536
proletarianization of, 49–50,
71–73, 176–79, 199–200,
204–5, 266–68, 597–98

Socialist Workers Party (SWP)
(*continued*)
referendum on labor party
in, 53, 402n, 425, 451–52
revolutionary continuity of,
26–30
trade union activity of, 40–
41, 71–73, 82–83, 105–6,
168–70, 190–92, 199–201,
321–23, 597–98
in agriculture, 141
in auto, 140, 447–48
and blocs with other
tendencies, 196–98,
446–48
and colonization, 141,
448
and concentration of
forces, 140, 448, 598
guidelines for, 200–204
in maritime, 40, 82,
140–41, 448–49
in Minneapolis, 40, 448
in steel, 140, 448
trade union department of,
139–40, 207, 449
See also Antifascist struggle;
Antiwar work; Fractions,
trade union; Party
democracy; Proletarian
orientation; Recruitment
Social patriotism, 196, 279,
307–8, 328, 334, 393, 410
Social Revolutionaries
(Russia), 212, 214, 620g
Somoza, Anastasio, 492, 620g
Southern Tenant Farmers
Union, 579, 620g
Soviet constitution, 217, 224,
231–32, 310

INDEX / 639

Soviets, 217–18, 224, 230–32, 299, 395–96, 620g
Soviet Union
  bureaucracy in, 108–10, 209–10, 217–24, 230–33, 309–12, 433–35
  civil war in, 214
  class nature of, 41–42, 108–10, 218–20, 222–24, 237–38, 330–31
  defense of, 41–42, 75–76, 129, 166, 218–19, 222, 225–27, 234–35, 328–29, 330–31
  economy of, 230–35
  foreign policy of, 160–61, 210, 225, 231–32
  and imperialist war threat, 159–62
  and Jews, 408–9
  purges in, 221, 232, 310
  threat of capitalist restoration in, 220–25, 235
  as transitional society, 222–24
Spanish civil war, 38, 60–61, 239–57, 553n, 561
  and Barcelona events (May 1937), 239–46
  and Barcelona government, 242, 245
  and Catalan government, 241, 244
  defense of Loyalists in, 45, 117–18, 251–54, 334
  and interimperialist rivalry, 250–51
  lack of revolutionary leadership in, 241–42, 246–47, 257

Spanish civil war (*continued*)
  left-wing Socialists in, 243–44, 247
  right-wing Socialists in, 243
  and Stalinism, 210, 232, 241–44, 257
  and struggle for democratic rights, 251
  tasks of Marxists in, 251–53, 255
  and Valencia government, 242–43, 245
  See also Fascism; People's Frontism
Spark, 524, 620g
Sparrow, Ray, 508, 550
Spartacus Youth League, 57, 467n, 620g
Speaking tours, 462, 536
Spector, Maurice, 39, 115, 120–21, 138, 345–47, 352–53, 355–56, 359–61, 363–64, 369–70n, 436–37, 620g
Speyer, 516
Stakhanovism, 223, 620g
Stalin, Joseph, 37–38, 242, 408, 488, 499, 620–21g
Stalinism, 173, 209–13, 217–22, 312, 321–22, 330–31
  See also Communist Party (Soviet Union); Communist Party (U.S.); Soviet Union
Standard of living, 370
Stanley, Sherman (Stanley Plastrik), 98, 113, 116–17, 136, 342n, 422n
Stanton, C.P., 527
State, 144, 297–99, 302–3

State capitalism, 44
Steele, Joseph, 134
Sterling, Max, 113, 136, 543
Stern, Herman, 108, 113, 120, 129–30, 136
Stern, I., 238
Stevens, Bertha, 550
Stiler, Robert, 136, 354, 361, 519, 550
Stirling, J., 107, 111, 134
Students, 468
Stump, Howard, 113, 136, 550
Swabeck, Arne, 98, 115–16, 138, 621g
Swanson, Howard, 550
Sweet, Thaddeus C., 62, 621g
Syndicalism, 198, 448

Taber, John, 111, 138
Tactics, 374
Tannem, C. Claston, 106–7
Teamsters, 443–44
Technology, 467–68
Thermidor, 209–10, 621g
Third-party movements, 390, 393–94
"Third period," 30, 205n, 322, 409
Thomas, Norman, 33, 58, 61, 65, 621g
Thompson, Pauline, 515, 517, 532, 550
Thurman, Henry, 508–9, 550
Tibbets, R., 112, 134
Toro, David, 492, 621g
Tracy, Daniel, 499, 621g
Trade union democracy, 191–92, 194, 206, 321, 444, 446

Trade union dues, 207
Trade Union Educational League (TUEL), 205n, 621g
Trade unions
  bureaucracy in, 143–44, 184–85, 192–96, 382, 385–86, 514, 555
  caucuses in, 205–6
  under fascism, 294–95
  and government, 188, 206–7
  growth of, 40, 182–86, 199–200, 381
  and political action, 357–58, 382–85, 392–93
  threat of Stalinism to, 195–97, 445–48
  and unemployed, 207, 321, 427–28
  See also American Federation of Labor; Class-struggle left wing; Congress of Industrial Organizations; Industrial unionism; Socialist Workers Party, trade union activity of; individual unions
Trade union unity, 186–92, 321–22, 443–44
Trainor, Larry (Turner), 349–50, 354, 359–61, 532, 537, 550, 622g
Transitional demands, 346–48, 354–55, 375, 386, 399, 445, 460
Transitional Program, 358, 373–75, 379–80, 389, 394–97, 410–11, 427, 524, 559–60

INDEX / 641

Transitional Program (*cont'd*)
   discussions on, 50–52, 343n
   SWP adoption of, 19–20,
     53–54, 345–48, 354–56
Trbovich, Manuel (Mills),
   110–11, 134, 517–18, 532,
   550, 622g
Trimble, Glen, 47–48, 100–101,
   105–7, 111, 126, 130, 133,
   513–15, 517, 541, 550, 622g
Trotsky, Leon, 129, 305, 622g
   and Moscow trials, 38
   and SWP, 53–54, 379n
   and Transitional Program,
     19–20, 50–53, 341–42n
Trujillo, Rafael, 492, 498,
   622g
"Two-class party," 323–24
Tyler, Gus, 58, 65, 622g

UGT (Spain), 247, 254, 622g
Ultraleftism, 30, 46, 212–13,
   269–70, 281
Unemployed movement,
   47, 143–47, 326, 483–85,
   489–96
   SWP work in, 47, 146–
     49, 484–85, 566–67, 592,
     594–96
   and unions, 143–44, 146–49,
     326, 483–85, 592, 594–95,
     598
Unemployment, 36, 47,
   292–94, 326, 370, 483,
   558–59, 593, 598
   and fascism, 326, 592, 594
United Auto Workers (UAW),
   82–83, 198, 446–47
United front, 252–53, 306,
   335–36, 558, 574

"United front from below,"
   335–36
United Mine Workers (UMW),
   185, 194
United States imperialism,
   159, 161–66, 188, 278–80,
   295–96, 328–30, 487–501,
   553–54n
United Unemployed and WPA
   Workers of America, 595

Van Zeeland, Paul, 333, 622g
Vargas, Getulio, 492–94,
   497–98, 622g
Versailles treaty, 489
Von Romer, Harry, 135

Waldman, Louis, 57, 622g
Walsh, 532, 550
War budget, 379, 556, 566
War drive, 36–37, 158–67,
   279, 293, 374, 553–56, 590,
   593–94
Warner, Robert, 135
Wars of national liberation,
   276
Washburn, Everett, 135, 550
Wasserman, Jac, 96, 115,
   118–19, 129, 138, 342n,
   422n
Weber, Jack, 112, 135, 346,
   349–50, 353, 356, 360–61,
   366, 440, 507, 517, 522,
   528, 537–38, 550, 623g
Weisbord, Albert, 171
Weiss, David (Stevens), 513,
   527, 537
Weiss, Murry, 513, 537–38,
   550, 623g
Whiteside, George, 111, 134

Widick, B.J., 100, 113, 120–21, 136, 344–46, 349, 353, 356, 359–61, 363–64, 422–23, 426–29, 439, 518, 550, 623g
Wildcat strikes, 203–4
Wills, 510
Wilson, Woodrow, 499, 623g
Wolf, Erwin, 310n
Wolfe, Bernard, 550
Woll, Matthew, 187, 189
Worker-farmer alliance, 320
Workers Alliance of America (WAA), 47, 143–47, 483–84, 590–92, 594, 623g
  SWP work in, 146–49, 595
Workers' and farmers' government, 379n, 440–41
Workers' control, 202–3, 375–76, 559, 567
  and Soviet Union, 217–18, 237–38
  and Spain, 249
Workers' councils, 299–300, 395–96, 402
Workers' defense guards, 378–79, 395–96, 445, 520–22, 562–63, 567, 569–75
  SWP initiatives for, 378–79, 410–11, 520–22, 562–63, 569–70n, 571–75
  and trade unions, 571–75
Workers' democracy, 123, 175–76, 214–18, 230, 238
Workers' government, 280, 283, 379–80, 440–41
Workers' militia, 301
Workers Party (Shachtmanites), 48–49n, 623g

Workers Party of the U.S. (WPUS), 32, 48, 69, 314, 623g
Workers Security League, 595
Workers' state, 41, 298–302
  Soviet Union as, 214–15, 234–35, 237–38
Working class, 296–97, 304
Works Progress Administration (WPA), 484–85, 553n, 590, 595–96, 623g
Workweek, 427–29, 598
World War I, 164, 213, 293, 295, 307
Wright, John G., 107, 113, 120, 136, 513, 526, 530, 550, 623g
Wyle, Flo, 111, 133

Yiddish, literature in, 411–12, 440n
Young People's Socialist League (YPSL), 467–80, 623g
  bohemianism in, 472
  lack of proletarian base in, 178, 424, 439, 448–49n
  low morale in, 471
  need to transform character of, 471–73
  as SP youth group, 32, 57
  support for Fourth International by, 63
  and SWP, 126–27n, 286–87, 439, 470–72, 474–75, 477–80, 540–41
  SWP members in, 474, 480
  youth vanguardism in, 470–72, 477–78
Young workers, 207

Young Workers League, 467n
Youth, 326–27, 467–70
Youth organization, 327, 467–71
See also Young People's Socialist League

Zam, Herbert, 58, 624g
Zimmerman, P., 100, 111, 116, 124, 153
Zinoviev, Gregory, 272, 624g
Zionism, 406–7
Zola, George, 509, 550

ALSO BY JAMES P. CANNON

Socialism on Trial
Testimony at Minneapolis Sedition Trial

The revolutionary program of the working class, presented in response to frame-up charges of "seditious conspiracy" in 1941, on the eve of US entry into World War II. The defendants were leaders of the Minneapolis labor movement and the Socialist Workers Party. $15. Also in Spanish, French, and Farsi.

The History of American Trotskyism, 1928–38
Report of a Participant

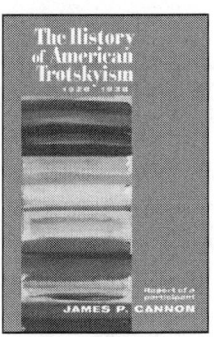

"Trotskyism is not a new movement, a new doctrine," Cannon says, "but the restoration, the revival of genuine Marxism as it was expounded and practiced in the Russian Revolution and in the early days of the Communist International." Talks by a founding leader of American communism on building a proletarian party in the United States. $17. Also in Spanish and French.

Notebook of an Agitator
From the Wobblies to the Fight against the Korean War and McCarthyism

Spans four decades of working-class battles—defending IWW frame-up victims and Sacco and Vanzetti; battles on the San Francisco waterfront; labor's fight against the McCarthyite witch-hunt. Includes the 1934 strike call and seven articles from *The Organizer*, daily bulletin of the Minneapolis Teamster strike. $20

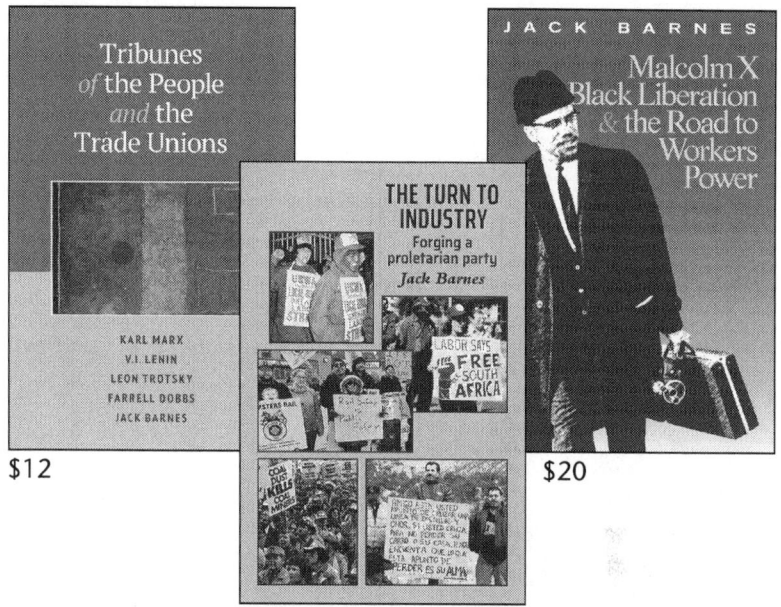

$12 $20

$15

Three books to be read as one ...

... **about building the only kind of party worthy of the name "revolutionary" in the imperialist epoch.**

- A party that's working class in program, composition, and action.
- A party that recognizes, in word and deed, the most revolutionary fact of our time:

    That working people—those the bosses and privileged layers fear as "deplorables" and "criminals"—have the power to create a different world as we organize to defend our own interests, not those of the exploiting class. That along that revolutionary course, we'll transform ourselves and awaken to our capacities—to our own worth.

Three books about building such a party. Also in Spanish and French.

Special Offer!
All three $30

The Turn to Industry and *Tribunes of the People and the Trade Unions* $20

Either book plus *Malcolm X, Black Liberation, and the Road to Workers Power* $25

WWW.PATHFINDERPRESS.COM

ALSO FROM PATHFINDER

Cuba and the Coming American Revolution
JACK BARNES

This is a book about the struggles of working people in the imperialist heartland, the youth attracted to them, and the example set by the Cuban people that revolution is not only necessary—it can be made. It is about the class struggle in the US, where the revolutionary capacities of workers and farmers are today as utterly discounted by the ruling powers as were those of the Cuban toilers. And just as wrongly. $10. Also in Spanish, French, and Farsi.

Red Zone
Cuba and the Battle against Ebola in West Africa
ENRIQUE UBIETA GÓMEZ

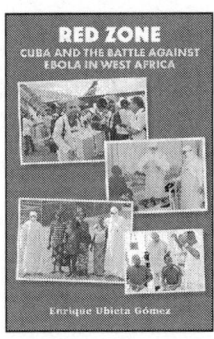

When three African countries were hit in 2014–15 by the largest Ebola epidemic on record, Cuba's revolutionary government responded to an international call and sent what no other country even pretended to provide: more than 250 volunteer doctors, nurses, and other medical workers. This firsthand account of their actions shows the kind of men and women only a socialist revolution can produce. $17. Also in Spanish and French.

Malcolm X Speaks

"Being here in America doesn't make you an American. No, I'm not an American. I'm one of the 22 million Black people who are the victims of Americanism. One of the 22 million Black people who are the victims of democracy, nothing but disguised hypocrisy." $15. Also in Spanish.

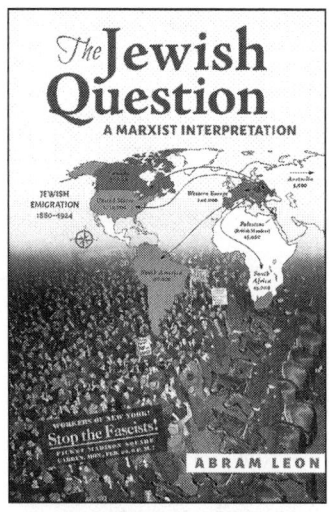

The Jewish Question
A Marxist Interpretation
ABRAM LEON

Why is Jew-hatred still raising its ugly head? What are its class roots—from antiquity through feudalism, to capitalism's rise and current crises? Why is there no solution under capitalism without revolutionary struggles that transform working people as we fight to transform our world? The author, Abram Leon, was killed in the Nazi gas chambers. This 2020 edition has an improved translation, new introduction, and 40 pages of illustrations and maps. $17. Also in Spanish and French.

Are They Rich Because They're Smart?
Class, Privilege, and Learning under Capitalism
JACK BARNES

Exposes growing class inequalities in the US and the self-serving rationalizations of well-paid professionals who think their "brilliance" equips them to "regulate" working people, who don't know what's in our own best interest. $10. Also in Spanish, French, Farsi, and Arabic.

Teamster Rebellion
FARRELL DOBBS

The 1934 strikes that won union recognition for truckers and warehouse workers in Minneapolis and helped pave the way for the working-class social movement that built the industrial unions. The first of four volumes by a central leader of these battles. $16. Also in Spanish, French, Farsi, and Greek.

WWW.PATHFINDERPRESS.COM

'THE HISTORY OF EXISTING SOCIETY IS THE HISTORY OF CLASS STRUGGLES'

Labor, Nature, and the Evolution of Humanity
The Long View of History

FREDERICK ENGELS, KARL MARX, GEORGE NOVACK, MARY-ALICE WATERS

Why is it important to know that social labor, transforming nature, has been the motor force of humanity's evolution for millions of years? Because without that knowledge, working people are unable to see beyond the capitalist epoch, beyond the class exploitation that warps all human relations, ideas, and values. The dictatorship of capital had a beginning ... and it will have an end. But only the revolutionary conquest of state power by the working class can open the door to a world free of capitalism's dog-eat-dog social reality. A world built on human solidarity. A socialist world. $12. Also in Spanish and French.

The Communist Manifesto
KARL MARX AND FREDERICK ENGELS

Communism, say the founding leaders of the revolutionary workers movement, is not a set of ideas or preconceived "principles" but workers' line of march to power, springing from a "movement going on under our very eyes." $5. Also in Spanish, French, Farsi, and Arabic.

Understanding History
Marxist Essays
GEORGE NOVACK

How did capitalism arise? Why and when did this exploitative system exhaust its once revolutionary role? Why is revolutionary change fundamental to human progress? $15

The Origin of the Family, Private Property, and the State
FREDERICK ENGELS

The emergence of class-divided society gave rise to repressive state bodies and the oppression of women to enable the ruling classes to pass along wealth and privilege. Engels discusses the consequences for working people of these class institutions—from their ancient forms to their modern versions. $15. Also in Farsi.

Sexism and Science
EVELYN REED

Are human beings innately aggressive? Does biology condemn women to remain the "second sex"? Taking up such biases cloaked as the findings of science, Reed explains that the disciplines closest to human life—anthropology, biology, and sociology—are permeated with rationalizations for the oppression of women and the maintenance of the established capitalist order. $15. Also in Farsi and Arabic.

The Origins of Materialism
GEORGE NOVACK

The rise of a scientific world outlook in ancient Greece, and the development of agriculture, manufacturing, and trade that prepared the way for it. $15

Woman's Evolution
From Matriarchal Clan to Patriarchal Family
EVELYN REED

$25. Also in Farsi and Indonesian.

WWW.PATHFINDERPRESS.COM

New International
A MAGAZINE OF MARXIST POLITICS AND THEORY

NEW INTERNATIONAL NO. 14
Revolution, Internationalism, and Socialism:
The Last Year of Malcolm X
JACK BARNES

"To understand Malcolm's last year is to see how, in the imperialist epoch, revolutionary leadership of the highest political capacity, courage, and integrity converges with communism. That truth has even greater weight today as billions around the world, in cities and the countryside, from China to Brazil, are being hurled into the modern class struggle by the violent expansion of world capitalism." —Jack Barnes. $14. Also in Spanish and French.

NEW INTERNATIONAL NO. 12
Capitalism's Long Hot Winter Has Begun
JACK BARNES

Today's global capitalist crisis is but the opening stage of decades of economic, financial, and social convulsions and class battles. Class-conscious workers confront this historic turning point for imperialism with confidence, Jack Barnes writes, drawing satisfaction from being "in their face" as we chart a revolutionary course to take power. $14. Also in Spanish, French, Farsi, Arabic, and Greek.

NEW INTERNATIONAL NO. 13
Our Politics Start with the World
JACK BARNES

The huge economic and cultural inequalities between imperialist and semicolonial countries, and among classes within them, are accentuated by the workings of capitalism. To build parties able to lead a successful revolutionary struggle for power in our own countries, vanguard workers must be guided by a strategy to close this gap. $14. Also in Spanish, French, Farsi, and Greek.

NEW INTERNATIONAL NO. 10
Imperialism's March toward Fascism and War
JACK BARNES

"There will be new Hitlers, new Mussolinis. That is inevitable. What is not inevitable is that they will triumph. The working-class vanguard will organize our class to fight back against the devastating toll we are made to pay for the capitalist crisis. The future of humanity will be decided in the contest between these contending class forces." $14. Also in Spanish, French, Farsi, and Greek.

NEW INTERNATIONAL NO. 11
U.S. Imperialism Has Lost the Cold War
JACK BARNES

The collapse of regimes across Eastern Europe and the USSR claiming to be communist did not mean workers and farmers there had been crushed. In today's sharpening capitalist conflicts and wars, these toilers are joining working people the world over in the class struggle against exploitation. $14. Also in Spanish, French, Farsi, and Greek.

NEW INTERNATIONAL NO. 7
Opening Guns of World War III: Washington's Assault on Iraq
JACK BARNES

Washington's murderous 1991 war on Iraq heralded conflicts among imperialist powers, growing capitalist crisis, and spreading wars. Working people in the region—from the Kurds, to Palestine and Israel, to Iran, Iraq, and Syria—are fighting for space to defend national rights and class interests. $14. Also in Spanish, French, and Farsi.

WWW.PATHFINDERPRESS.COM

THE BOLSHEVIKS AND THE FIGHT AGAINST NATIONAL OPPRESSION

Lenin's Final Fight
Speeches and Writings, 1922–23
V.I. LENIN

In 1922 and 1923, V.I. Lenin, central leader of the world's first socialist revolution, waged what was to be his last political battle—one that was lost following his death. At stake was whether that revolution, and the international communist movement it led, would remain on the revolutionary proletarian course that brought workers and peasants to power in October 1917. $17. Also in Spanish, Farsi, and Greek.

Workers of the World and Oppressed Peoples, Unite!
Proceedings and Documents of the Second Congress, 1920

The debate among delegates from 37 countries takes up key questions of working-class strategy and program and offers a vivid portrait of social struggles in the era of the October revolution. 2 vol. set. $45

Questions of National Policy and Proletarian Internationalism
V.I. LENIN

Why the fight of oppressed nations for self-determination is decisive in the worldwide proletarian struggle to take and hold power. Why workers and farmers in imperialist countries have a deep class interest in championing this right. $16

To See the Dawn

Baku, 1920—First Congress of the Peoples of the East

How can peasants and workers in the colonial world achieve freedom from imperialist exploitation? By what means can working people overcome divisions incited by their national ruling classes and act together for their common class interests? These questions were addressed by 2,000 delegates to the 1920 Congress of the Peoples of the East. $17

The Revolution Betrayed

What Is the Soviet Union and Where Is It Going?
LEON TROTSKY

In 1917 workers and peasants of Russia were the motor force for one of the deepest revolutions in history. Yet within ten years a political counterrevolution by a privileged social layer, whose chief spokesperson was Joseph Stalin, was being consolidated. The classic study of the Soviet workers state and its degeneration. $17. Also in Spanish, Farsi, and Greek.

The First Ten Years of American Communism

Report of a Participant
JAMES P. CANNON

A founding leader of the communist movement in the US tells the story of the early years of the effort to build a proletarian party emulating the Bolshevik leadership of the October 1917 revolution in Russia. Among other things, Cannon writes, "Everything new and progressive on the Negro question came from Moscow, after the Bolshevik revolution and as a result of it." $17

WWW.PATHFINDERPRESS.COM

CUBA'S SOCIALIST REVOLUTION

Playa Girón/Bay of Pigs
Washington's First Military Defeat in the Americas

FIDEL CASTRO,
JOSÉ RAMÓN FERNÁNDEZ

In fewer than 72 hours of combat in April 1961, Cuba's revolutionary armed forces defeated a US-organized invasion by 1,500 mercenaries. In the process, the Cuban people set an example for workers, farmers, and youth the world over that with political consciousness, class solidarity, courage, and revolutionary leadership, we can stand up to enormous might and seemingly insurmountable odds—and win. $17. Also in Spanish.

Women in Cuba: The Making of a Revolution Within the Revolution
VILMA ESPÍN, ASELA DE LOS SANTOS, YOLANDA FERRER

The integration of women into the ranks and leadership of the Cuban Revolution was inseparable from its working-class course from the start. This is the story of that revolution and how it transformed the women and men who made it. $17. Also in Spanish, Farsi, and Greek.

The First and Second Declarations of Havana

Nowhere are the questions of revolutionary strategy that today confront men and women on the front lines of struggles in the Americas addressed with greater truthfulness and clarity than in these uncompromising indictments of imperialist plunder and "the exploitation of man by man." Adopted by million-strong assemblies of the Cuban people in 1960 and 1962. $10. Also in Spanish, French, Farsi, Arabic, and Greek.

Cuba and Angola: The War for Freedom
HARRY VILLEGAS ("POMBO")

Cuba and Angola
Fighting for Africa's Freedom and Our Own

FIDEL CASTRO, RAÚL CASTRO, NELSON MANDELA

Two books that tell the story of Cuba's unparalleled contribution to the fight to free Africa from the scourge of apartheid. And how, in the doing, Cuba's socialist revolution was also strengthened. $10 and $12. Also in Spanish. *Cuba and Angola: The War for Freedom* is also available in Farsi and Greek.

Our History Is Still Being Written
The Story of Three Chinese Cuban Generals in the Cuban Revolution

ARMANDO CHOY, GUSTAVO CHUI, MOISÉS SÍO WONG, MARY-ALICE WATERS

"What was the key measure to uproot discrimination against Chinese and blacks in Cuba? It was the socialist revolution itself." New edition sheds light on Chinese Cubans' involvement in Cuba's internationalist course, including in Africa and Latin America. $15. Also in Spanish, French, Farsi, Greek, and Chinese.

How Far We Slaves Have Come!
South Africa and Cuba in Today's World

NELSON MANDELA, FIDEL CASTRO

Speaking together in Cuba in 1991, Mandela and Castro discuss the role of Cuba in the history of Africa and Angola's victory over the invading US-backed South African army. That victory accelerated the fight to bring down the racist apartheid system. $7. Also in Spanish and Farsi.

WWW.PATHFINDERPRESS.COM

PATHFINDER AROUND THE WORLD

UNITED STATES
(and Caribbean, Latin America, and East Asia)
Pathfinder Books, 306 W. 37th St., 13th Floor
New York, NY 10018

CANADA
Pathfinder Books, 7107 St. Denis, Suite 204
Montreal, QC H2S 2S5

UNITED KINGDOM
(and Europe, Africa, Middle East, and South Asia)
Pathfinder Books, 5 Norman Rd.
Seven Sisters, London N15 4ND

AUSTRALIA
(and Southeast Asia and the Pacific)
Pathfinder Books, Suite 103, 124-128 Beamish St.
Campsie, Sydney
Postal address: P.O. Box 73, Campsie, NSW 2194

NEW ZEALAND
Pathfinder Books, 188a Onehunga Mall Rd.
Onehunga, Auckland 1061
Postal address: P.O. Box 13857, Auckland 1643

JOIN THE PATHFINDER READERS CLUB
BUILD YOUR LIBRARY!

$10 / YEAR
25% DISCOUNT ON ALL PATHFINDER TITLES
30% OFF BOOKS OF THE MONTH

Valid at pathfinderpress.com and local Pathfinder book centers

Go to: www.pathfinderpress.com/products/pathfinder-readers-club